PUBLIC MANAGEMENT

Barry Bozeman

Editor

PUBLIC MANAGEMENT

The State of the Art

Jossey-Bass Publishers
San Francisco

Substantial discounts on bulk quantities of Jossey-Bass books are available to corporations, professional associations, and other organizations. For details and discount information, contact the special sales department at Jossey-Bass Inc., Publishers. (415) 433-1740; Fax (415) 433-0499.

For sales outside the United States, contact Maxwell Macmillan International Publishing Group, 866 Third Avenue, New York, New York 10022.

Manufactured in the United States of America

The ink in this book is either soy- or vegetable-based and during the printing process emits fewer than half the volatile organic compounds (VOCs) emitted by petroleum-based ink.

Library of Congress Cataloging-in-Publication Data

Public management : the state of the art / Barry Bozeman, editor.
    p.   cm. — (Jossey-Bass public administration series)
    Based on papers presented at the National Public Management Research Conference held at Syracuse University on Sept. 20–21, 1991.
    Includes bibliographical references and index.
    ISBN 1-55542-546-1
    1. Public administration — Congresses. 2. Public administration — United States — Congresses. I. Bozeman, Barry. II. Series.
JF1351.P835 1993
350 — dc20   93–4025
                                                 CIP

FIRST EDITION
HB Printing   10 9 8 7 6 5 4 3 2 1   *Code 9349*

*The Jossey-Bass
Public Administration Series*

*Consulting Editor
Public Management and Administration*

*James L. Perry
Indiana University*

CONTENTS

PREFACE

During the past fifteen years or so, the term *public management* has been offered as a rival to, a substitute for, or a synonym of *public administration.* But certain identifiable themes have emerged, and a number of articles and books have told us what is new and different about public management. Here is yet another view, one not taken from the formal literature:

> Public management research entails a focus on strategy (rather than on managerial processes), on interorganizational relations (rather than intraorganizational relations), and on the intersection of public policy and management.

The National Public Management Research Conference

The view of public management just given was provided in the conference call for the National Public Management Research Conference. On September 20 and 21, 1991, seventy-three public management researchers and theorists convened at Syracuse University and presented ideas about the content, meaning, and prospects of public management.

One of the motives for the Syracuse conference was to bring together disciples of various public management theories and approaches. In that sense, if in no other, the conference was a huge success. The mix of management scientists, Freudian theorists, phenomenologists, administrative historians, political economists, and epistemological nihilists (to name a few of the types of thinkers who attended) was a thing to behold. In many cases, the attendees talked past one another. But in a surprising number of instances there was genuine and mutually gratifying dialogue. Public management theory, whatever it is, is not dull.

Public Management does not fully capture the dialogue from the Syracuse conference or its paper presentations, discussions, and informal exchanges. But the book was inspired by the conference, and the contributions are versions of papers presented there. Perhaps this puts us at risk for "just another conference volume" odium. Since this was not "just another conference," however, that risk is diminished.

The state of public management research and theory was well reflected in the Syracuse conference, perhaps even more than in this book. The announced purposes of the conference were (1) to assess the state of the art in public management research, (2) to present the best and most current public management research, (3) to encourage the development of public management research by identifying gaps in theory, research, and methodology, and (4) to facilitate communication among public management researchers.

If unsolicited testimonials from good friends can be believed, the conference was quite successful in meeting these objectives. (A more impressive effectiveness indicator is the fact that a second National Public Management Research Conference in Madison, Wisconsin, was scheduled for 1993.) More to the point, however, these seem to be good objectives, and so they can serve for this book as well. The chapters in *Public Management* are quite diverse, but they meet the objectives with state-of-the-art reviews (for example, the Bozeman and Behn contributions), excellent new directions in research and theory (Maynard-Moody and Kelly; Frost-Kumpf and associates; Lynn), critical assessments (Golembiewski), and prescriptions for change (Emmert and associates). Let us suspend judgment for now on the meeting of the fourth objective, which depends chiefly on the public management research community's interest in this book.

Organization of the Book

It seems no mark of failure to note that the chapters contained in this book do not fall into nice, tight categories. If an objective is to reflect the best work in a field, and if that field happens to be fragmented and in the throes of intellectual ferment, then a representative volume will be likewise fragmented and reflective of the field's dissonance.

Part One includes a number of succinct statements about the nature of public management—what it is, what it might be, what it should be. These brief statements were prepared specifically for this book. The chapters in Part Two include critical statements about the prerequisites of theory and the state of current public management theory. Part Three includes chapters propounding theories, demonstrating theoretical links, and synthesizing theoretical streams in public management. Part Four presents studies concerned with the effectiveness and strategic dimensions of public management. The intersection of management and politics is the theme of the chapters in Part Five. Part Six includes two contributions that pertain to management information systems and have broader implications for empirical approaches to public management research. Finally, Part Seven focuses on the interaction of management and policy design issues and includes three chapters with implications for prescriptive theory.

Acknowledgments

Without the National Public Management Research Conference, this book would never have been developed. Those who contributed to the conference contributed to this book. From the very beginning, Dean John Palmer of Syracuse University's Maxwell School gave encouragement for the idea of the conference. He, along with Ben Ware, Syracuse University's vice president for research, provided generous funding.

The organizing committee for the conference worked hard and later served as the "editorial board" for this book. All the submissions for this book were reviewed by at least two members of the conference's organizing committee. The review work was a particularly difficult task, since many excellent papers presented at the conference were not included here, because of space limits. (An available proceedings volume includes twenty or so first-rate conference papers not contained in this book.) The organizing committee included Stuart Bretschneider, H. Brinton Milward, Hal G. Rainey, Patrick Scott, and Jack Stevens.

Special thanks are owed to James L. Perry, the consulting editor for Jossey-Bass, who supported the publication of this book and provided many very useful suggestions. Similarly, Alan Shrader, Jossey-Bass editor of the Public Administration Series, is a delight to work with and is a good friend of the public management community.

The faculty, staff, and students of the Maxwell School's Center for Technology and Information Policy (TIP) hosted the conference and did most of the detail work in supporting both the conference and the book. Patricia Simone was the unanimous MVP. She was the primary coordinator for every step and helped organize a disorganized editor (not to mention a few disorganized contributors). Among the other TIP associates who helped with the conference or the book, Scott Dinstell, Monica Gaughan, Gordon Kingsley, Julia Melkers, and Patrick Scott were particularly energetic.

Finally, and perhaps most important, there is a special debt to the contributing authors of *Public Management*. The papers presented at the conference really were the best of contemporary public management research, by many of the best researchers and theorists. One's first impulse is to publish one's work in the premier journals in the field; the journal route is, after all, the shortest route to tenure, promotion, and, often, academic accolades. Many of the conference papers not accepted for this book had already been accepted by the leading journals, but not a single contribution accepted for this book was withdrawn for submission to a journal. It is gratifying that the participants had enough faith in *Public Management* to invest their best effort and ideas.

Syracuse, New York   Barry Bozeman
May 1993

THE EDITOR

BARRY BOZEMAN is professor of public administration and affiliate professor of engineering at Syracuse University, where he is also founding director of the Center for Technology and Information Policy, a joint program of the Maxwell School of Citizenship and Public Affairs and the L. C. Smith College of Engineering. He received his Ph.D. degree (1973) from Ohio State University in political science. Bozeman's research interests include research and development policy, public management, and organization theory. His most recent research examines the creation, evolution, and impacts of organizational red tape. Bozeman's recent books include *All Organizations Are Public: Bridging Public and Private Organizational Theories* (1987), *Public Management Strategies: Guidelines for Managerial Effectiveness* (1990 with J. D. Straussman), and *Investments in Technology* (1983, with A. Link). His articles on public management and organization theory have appeared in a variety of academic journals, including the *Journal of Public Administration Research and Theory, Public Administration Review, American Journal of Political Science, Managerial and Decision Economics,* and the *Journal of Policy Analysis and Management.* Bozeman has served as an officer in a number of professional associations, including the Academy of Management, the American Society for Public Administration, and the Association for Public Policy Analysis and Management and is on the editorial boards of eight academic journals, including the *Journal of Public Administration Research and Theory, Administration and Society,* and *Public Productivity and Management Review.* He has served as a consultant to a number of government agencies, including the Office of Personnel Management, the Department of Energy and its national laboratories, the National Science Foundation, the U.S. General Accounting Office, the Internal Revenue Service, and the United Nations.

THE CONTRIBUTORS

Robert W. Backoff is professor of public policy and management, political science, and management and human resources at the Ohio State University. He received his Ph.D. degree (1974) from Indiana University in political science. Backoff was the 1992 recipient of the Elmer B. Staats Public Service Award of the National Association of Schools of Public Affairs and Administration and is coauthor of *Strategic Management of Public and Third-Sector Organizations* (1992, with P. C. Nutt).

Robert D. Behn is professor of public policy at Duke University, where he is director of the Governors Center. Behn is also an adjunct scholar with the Council for Excellence in Government in Washington, D.C. He received his Ph.D. degree (1969) from Harvard University in engineering. Behn's most recent book is *Management Counts: Lessons for Public Managers* (1992).

Stuart Bretschneider is associate professor of public administration at the Maxwell School of Public Affairs, Syracuse University. He received his Ph.D. degree (1980) from the Ohio State University in public administration. He is president-elect of the International Institute of Forecasting, associate editor of the *International Journal of Forecasting,* and managing editor of the *Journal of Public Administration Research and Theory.* His articles have been published in *Management Science, Decision Sciences, Public Administration Review, International Journal of Forecasting,* and *Evaluation Review.*

John M. Bryson is professor of planning and public affairs at the Hubert H. Humphrey Institute of Public Affairs, University of Minnesota. He received his Ph.D. degree (1978) from the University of Wisconsin, Madison, in urban and regional planning. He is coauthor of *Leadership for the Common Good* (1992, with B. C. Crosby).

Daniel T. Bugler is a senior research associate in the Center for Technology and Information Policy, Maxwell School of Public Affairs, Syracuse University, where he is a doctoral candidate in public administration. He received his M.P.A. degree (1989) from the Maxwell School.

Barbara C. Crosby is an associate of the Reflective Leadership Center at the Hubert H. Humphrey Institute of Public Affairs, University of Minnesota, where she is also coordinator of the Hubert H. Humphrey Fellowship Program. She received her M.A. degree (1980) from the University of Wisconsin, Madison, in journalism and mass communication. She is a doctoral student in leadership studies at the Union Institute.

Michael Crow is vice provost for research and professor of science and technology policy at the School of International and Public Affairs, Columbia University. He received his Ph.D. degree (1985) from Syracuse University in public policy. His articles have been published in *Science and Public Policy, Technovation, Revue d'Économie Française,* and the *Journal of Technology Transfer.*

Jameson W. Doig is professor of politics and political affairs in the Woodrow Wilson School and the Department of Politics, Princeton University. He received his Ph.D. degree (1961) from Princeton University in political science. His publications include *Criminal Corrections: Ideals and Realities,* (1983, with C. McCoy and others), *Leadership and Innovation,* (1987, with E. C. Hargrove and others), and *Combating Corruption/Encouraging Ethics,* (1990, with W. L. Richter, F. Burke, and others).

Debora E. Dunkle is a research specialist and assistant director of the Center for Research on Information Technology and Organizations, University of California, Irvine. She received her Ph.D. degree (1974) from the State University of New York, Buffalo, in political science. She is coauthor of *Managing Information Systems* (1989, with K. L. Kraemer, J. L. King, and J. P. Lane).

Barbara A. Else is a program analyst and management intern at the Agency for Health Care Policy and Research, U.S. Public Health Service. She received her M.A. degree (1991) from the University of Arizona in public administration.

Mark A. Emmert is provost and vice president for academic affairs at Montana State University, where he is also professor of political science. He received his Ph.D. degree (1983) from the Maxwell School at Syracuse University in public administration. He has also received fellowships from the American Council on Education and the Fulbright Commission.

Lee Frost-Kumpf is assistant professor in the Graduate School of Public Policy and Administration, Pennsylvania State University. He received his Ph.D. degree (1990) from the Ohio State University in public policy and management.

He received the Best Dissertation Award for 1990–91 from the Academy of Management's Public Sector Division for his comparative, experimental study of risk-assessment methods in an emergency services agency.

Robert T. Golembiewski is research professor at the University of Georgia, Athens. He received his Ph.D. degree (1958) from Yale University in political science. His recent books include *High Performance and Human Costs* (1988), *Organization Development* (1989), *Ironies in Organization Development* (1990), and *Handbook of Organization Consultation* (1992).

Howard J. Ishiyama is a doctoral candidate in public policy and management at the Ohio State University. He received his M.P.A. degree (1986) from the Ohio State University in public organization theory and strategic management.

Marisa Kelly is a doctoral candidate in political science at the University of Kansas. She received her M.A. degree (1984) from San Francisco State University in political science. An article she coauthored with Steven Maynard-Moody appeared in *Public Administration Review.*

Steven Kelman is Albert J. Weatherhead III and Richard W. Weatherhead Professor of Public Management in the John F. Kennedy School of Government, Harvard University. He received his Ph.D. degree (1978) from Harvard University in political science. His publications include *Making Public Policy: A Hopeful View of American Government* (1987) and *Procurement and Public Management: The Fear of Discretion and the Quality of Government Performance* (1990).

Donald F. Kettl is professor of public affairs and political science at the University of Wisconsin, Madison. He also serves as associate director of the La Follette Institute of Public Affairs. He received his Ph.D. degree (1978) from Yale University in political science. Among his books are *Buying Smart: Public Governance and Private Markets* and *The Politics of the Administrative Process,* (with J. W. Fesler).

John Leslie King is professor in the Department of Information and Computer Science and the Graduate School of Management, University of California, Irvine. He received his Ph.D. degree (1977) from the University of California, Irvine, in administration. He is coauthor of *Managing Information Systems* (1989, with K. L. Kraemer, D. E. Dunkle, and J. P. Lane). King's articles have appeared in *Computing Surveys, Public Administration Review, Telecommunications Policy,* and *Informatics in the Public Sector.*

Heidi O. Koenig is a doctoral candidate in public administration at Syracuse University and earned a J.D. degree (1989) from the University of Nebraska. She has work forthcoming in *Research in Public Administration.*

Kenneth L. Kraemer is professor in the Graduate School of Management at the University of California, Irvine, where he is also director of the Center for Research on Information Technology and Organizations. He received his Ph.D. degree (1967) from the University of Southern California in public administration. He is coauthor of *Technological Innovation in American Local Government* (1979, with J. L. Perry), author of *Public Management: Public and Private Perspectives* (1983), and coauthor of *Managing Information Systems* (1989, with J. L. King, D. E. Dunkle, and J. P. Lane). Kraemer's articles have appeared in *Public Administration Review, Computing Surveys, Telecommunications Policy,* and other journals.

Laurence E. Lynn, Jr., is professor of social service administration and public policy studies at the University of Chicago. He received his Ph.D. degree (1966) from Yale University in economics. He is author of *The State and Human Services* (1980), *Managing the Public's Business* (1981), and *Managing Public Policy* (1987).

Eugene B. McGregor, Jr., is professor of public and environmental affairs at Indiana University, Bloomington. He received his Ph.D. degree (1969) from Syracuse University in political science. He is author of *Management of Human Knowledge, Skills, and Abilities: Workforce Decision Making in the Postindustrial Era* (1991).

Steven Maynard-Moody is associate professor of public administration at the University of Kansas, where he is a research fellow in the Institute for Public Policy and Business Research. He received his Ph.D. degree (1981) from Cornell University. He is writing a book tentatively titled *Fall from Grace: Moral Politics and Fetal Research* (forthcoming, with D. Nelkin).

H. Brinton Milward is director of the School of Public Administration and Policy at the University of Arizona, where he is also associate dean of the College of Business and Public Administration. He received his Ph.D. degree (1978) from the Ohio State University in public policy and management. He and Keith G. Provan have received a major research grant from the National Institute of Mental Health to study the relationship between service implementation networks and clinical outcomes among seriously mentally ill people.

Rosemary O'Leary is professor in the Department of Public Administration at the Maxwell School of Public Affairs, Syracuse University. She received her Ph.D. degree (1988) from the Maxwell School at Syracuse University in public administration. She and Charles Wise are joint recipients of the 1991 William E. and Frederick C. Mosher Award for best article by an academician published in *Public Administration Review.* O'Leary is author of *Environmental Change; Federal Courts and the EPA* (forthcoming) and is on the editorial boards of *Public Administration Review,* the *Journal of Public Administration Research and Theory, Policy Studies Journal,* and *Natural Resources and Environment.*

James L. Perry is professor in the School of Public and Environmental Affairs, Indiana University, Bloomington. He received his Ph.D. degree (1974) from Syracuse University in public administration. In 1986, Perry received the Yoder-Heneman Research Award from the Society for Human Resource Management. In 1991, he received the Charles H. Levine Memorial Award for Excellence in Public Administration. His books include *Technological Innovation in American Local Government* (1979, with K. L. Kraemer), *Labor-Management Relations and Public Agency Effectiveness* (1980, with H. A. Angle), and *Public Management: Public and Private Perspectives* (forthcoming, with K. L. Kraemer).

Keith G. Provan is professor of management and Ashland Oil Research Professor in the College of Business and Economics, University of Kentucky. He received his Ph.D. degree (1978) from Vanderbilt University in organization theory and behavior. His work has appeared in the *Academy of Management Journal,* the *Academy of Management Review, Administrative Science Quarterly,* the *Journal of Health and Social Behavior,* the *Journal of Management,* and the *Journal of Management Studies.* He serves on the editorial board of the *Academy of Management Review.* He and H. Brinton Milward have received a major research grant from the National Institute of Mental Health to study the relationship between service implementation networks and clinical outcomes among seriously mentally ill people.

Hal G. Rainey is professor of political science at the University of Georgia. He received his Ph.D. degree (1978) from the Ohio State University in public administration. He is author of *Understanding and Managing Public Organizations* (1991).

Nancy C. Roberts is associate professor of strategic management and an associate of the C3 Academic Group at the Naval Postgraduate School, Monterey, California. She received her Ph.D. degree (1983) from Stanford University in education, with a specialization in organizational change. Roberts is coauthor of *Innovation and Entrepreneurship: Radical Change by Legislative Design,* (forthcoming, with P. King).

R. F. Shangraw, Jr., is president of Project Performance Corporation and a specialist in large-scale project and program planning. He received his Ph.D. degree (1986) from Syracuse University in technology and information management. Shangraw has been a consultant to the U.S. Department of Energy's Office of Environmental Restoration and Waste Management and has held a joint faculty appointment in the Schools of Public Administration and Engineering at Syracuse University.

Jeffrey D. Straussman is professor of public administration and senior research associate in the Metropolitan Studies Program, Maxwell School of Public Affairs, Syracuse University. He received his Ph.D. degree (1975) from the Graduate School and University Center, City University of New York, in political science. He was a Fulbright Scholar at Budapest University (Hungary) in 1992. He is coauthor of *Public Management Strategies: Guidelines for Managerial Effectiveness* (1990, with B. Bozeman).

Barton Wechsler is associate professor in the School of Public Administration and Policy at Florida State University, where he teaches graduate courses in public management and policy. He received his Ph.D. degree (1985) from the Ohio State University in public administration. His articles have been published in *Public Administration Review, Administration & Society, Journal of the American Planning Association, Public Productivity and Management Review, Review of Public Personnel Administration,* and other journals.

PUBLIC MANAGEMENT

INTRODUCTION:
TWO CONCEPTS
OF PUBLIC MANAGEMENT

Barry Bozeman

One place to begin is at the beginning—even if the beginning is murky and fog-shrouded. The murkiness of public management's origins contrast with those of public administration and bureaucratic theory. As a self-conscious field of study, public administration seems to date back to Woodrow Wilson and his fascinatingly ambiguous notions about the politics-administration dichotomy. The study of formal bureaucracy seems to begin with Max Weber and his archetype.

The origins of public management are obscured by the fact that the field is more a creature of institutional evolution than of intellectual development. Identifying the locus of origin is easier than identifying the time-of-origin primal causes. Public management, both as a field of study and as an educational enterprise, seems to have sprung, probably in the late 1970s and early 1980s, from two very different institutions—collegiate schools of business and schools of public policy. The latter seem to have contributed more to the evolution of public management, and the former to have contributed more to its initial substance. What about public administration programs? Probably most faculty in graduate public administration programs would say that they have been doing public management all along, and that others are still discovering it. There seems to be some truth in that assertion.

Two Concepts of Public Management

Generally, an understanding of theory requires some knowledge of the people and, particularly, the institutions from whom and from which it arises. This is an introduction to the institutional context of public management studies and, as such, to public management theory also. The chief point is that there are two rival public managements—the public policy school

1

version, and the business school version. In the late 1970s, almost simultaneously, there emerged two significantly different approaches to public management, one derived from a public policy school orientation (the P-approach),
and the other influenced by business school approaches and developments
in public administration (the B-approach).

Down from Public Policy: The P-Approach

As a concept, but not so much as an activity, the emergence of public management in schools of public policy and administration has followed trends
in business schools. Business schools, one after another, changed their names
during the 1970s from schools of business administration to schools of management. This change was most often rationalized as entailing an emphasis
on strategy and business policy, as opposed to the mechanics and processes
of internal administration. The changes were more than terminological and
cosmetic. The requirements of the American Assembly of Collegiate Schools
of Business (the accrediting group for business schools) shifted gradually,
emphasizing strategy and business policy. Demand for courses in these fields
accelerated, and, on the research front, new journals emerged (for example, *Strategic Management Journal*), while a division of the Academy of Management (a leading professional group for university business faculty) was
reorganized to focus on strategy. Developments in schools of public policy
and administration followed close behind, but with different emphases, in
a much more fragmented fashion, and with few immediate accreditation
implications.

    The public policy schools (for example, Harvard's Kennedy School,
Michigan's Institute for Public Policy Studies, Minnesota's Humphrey Institute, Berkeley's School of Public Policy) were founded in part as a direct
repudiation of old-style public administration. The policy schools were much
more oriented toward formal quantitative analysis, particularly applied economics. Increasingly, however, policy schools began to recognize a serious
limitation: there was little demand in the public sector for either formal quantitative analysis or "grand design" of policy. But there was much demand
for management. The policy schools needed something that was akin to public
administration but not identified with this "old-fashioned," craft-oriented field.
Public management was invented as a solution. In the mid 1970s, faculty
at public policy schools began to use the term *public management* and to muse
about (if not yet implement) public management curricula.

    Since policy school–oriented public management — the P-approach —
was more a response to a problem than an idea or an opportunity, it remained a fuzzy concept. Somehow, it was understood, it should be a management complement for policy analysis; but, beyond that, there was little
initial agreement.

    It is significant that virtually none of the individuals who emerged
in the policy school as "public management scholars" had a background or

even an identification with public administration. Some were "defrocked" economists. Some were more practitioners than academics. Some were institutionally oriented political scientists.

Since its haphazard beginnings, public policy school–oriented public management has begun to crystallize and to have its own identity. The approach has centered on so-called high-level policy management. The concern is not with the day-to-day administration of agencies, or even with the strategic management of agencies, but rather with the role of the manager (or political executive) in high-level policy. Case studies used in P-approach public management courses often focus more on political executives than on senior civil servants. As one might expect, this approach places strong emphasis on the political aspects of public management.

The literature that has emerged from the P-approach is largely atheoretical and nonquantitative, oriented toward practice-based prescriptive rules. The preferred research method is also the preferred teaching method — immersion in case studies. Indeed, even Ph.D courses in public management sometimes involve case interpretation. It is easy to see why the P-approach is often seen as representing the "soft" side, while policy analysis represents the "hard" side.

Up from Business: The B-Approach

A public management concept identified with a different group of scholars, a group closer to traditional public administration, is business school–oriented public management (the B-approach). As one might expect, the individuals most closely associated with this approach either have taught in business schools or were trained in business schools or in "generic" management programs.

The differences between the B-approach and the P-approach to public management are stark. First, the B-approach is much more favorably disposed to concepts in the business disciplines. Second, whereas the P-approach is best summarized by an often repeated Wallace Sayre dictum — "Public and private organizations are alike in all *unimportant* respects" — the B-approach makes less stringent distinctions between the public and private sectors, or it recasts those distinctions. The B-approach has stronger links to public administration, whereas the P-approach runs away from public administration.

The B-approach is much more concerned with developing empirical theory, and much of the research has centered on identifying and explaining empirical differences between public and private organizations. The P-approach tends to assume the differences, or to examine practitioner case reports to distill differences.

Despite its increasing concern with strategy and interorganizational management, the B-approach remains much more process-oriented. Thus, topics related to organizational design, personnel, budgeting, and so forth, are of interest to the adherents of the B-approach. Process receives short shrift in the P-approach, which emphasizes policy and politics instead.

Among adherents of the B-approach, the case study is not the preferred method (although it is in evidence). They are more likely to use quantitative techniques, both for analysis of aggregate data and as a complement to experimental designs. But the B-approach does make extensive use of case studies for teaching predoctoral public management courses.

The two approaches have different institutional and professional anchors. The P-approach is very much in evidence in the Association for Public Policy Analysis and Management. The B-approach is perhaps most dominant in the public sector division of the Academy of Management (although it is also prominent in the American Society for Public Administration). Similarly, while the leading P-approach literature is found in the *Journal of Policy Analysis and Management,* the somewhat more extensive B-approach literature is more often encountered in *Academy of Management Review* and the *Academy of Management Journal,* the *Journal of Public Administration Research and Theory,* and the *Public Administration Review.*

A Possible Synthesis

The P-approach and the B-approach have some common points, more than one might suppose from the preceding discussion, and each approach has unique strengths. The common points include the following:

- Concern with something more than internal administration of agencies (an interorganizational external management focus)
- Respect for the role of politics in management
- A prescriptive orientation, and concern with improving managerial effectiveness
- Appreciation for experiential learning, as reflected in the use of case studies in teaching public management

Despite these common points, the merits of the two approaches diverge considerably. The P-approach's strengths include the following:

- Recognition of the importance of policy analysis to public management
- Learning based on practitioners' experience
- Concern with distilling lessons and conveying them in an easily understood manner
- Promotion of dialogue between senior managers or political executives and public management scholars

The B-approach has the following strengths:

- Greater orientation toward research and theory
- Ability to adapt and diffuse methods, techniques, and theory from a variety of disciplines

- Incorporation of increasingly well-developed, empirically based comparisons of public and private management
- Orientation toward strategic management
- Concern with process issues
- Greater focus on the career public manager than on the political executive

Most of the advantages of the respective approaches are not, in principle, mutually exclusive. A synthesis, one taking the best from each approach, might be feasible. The Maxwell School is particularly well positioned to enact such a synthesis in that it includes people who would identify with each approach and has a strong orientation toward policy analysis.

Implications for Public Management Theory

Both the P-approach and the B-approach seem to be well represented in this book (maybe there are a few "X-approaches" as well). Rather than risk potentially offensive classification errors, let us leave it to the reader to do the sorting. More to the point, many of the chapters presented here seem to represent the beginnings of a synthesis. A synthesis of the predominant approaches to public management inquiry might have the following characteristics:

- Concern with both strategy and process, but an externally focussed orientation
- Increased emphasis on the "hard" side, with continued focus on the "soft" side
- Orientation toward senior public managers, at both the middle and upper levels
- A broader definition of the "public" in public management, to include nonprofit organizations, public aspects of private enterprises, and hybrid organizations
- Attention to theory, prescriptive theory, and prescription

From an intellectual standpoint, the synthesis just outlined would pose few problems in implementation, but institutional barriers are often more formidable than intellectual ones. At this point, reasonably powerful educational institutions have a stake in intellectual questions. For some programs, the nature of the distinction between public and private management is not a "mere" matter of intellect; it is a matter of program (that is, business) rationale. For others, the focus on middle- or upper-level managers is not so much an intellectual choice as a matter of who has enrolled.

For the present, let us leave the academic politics on the shelf and, as these chapters so commendably do, ponder public management theory on intellectual terms. We can sort out the institutional implications tomorrow, or the day after, or the day after that.

Part One

IMAGES OF
PUBLIC MANAGEMENT

What is public management theory? "What is" questions often stump us momentarily but, after some reflection, give us little difficulty. Thus, if someone asks us, "What is an organization?" we may stutter a bit, mentally at least, and then provide a reasonably good working definition, perhaps citing such components as structure, mission, resource conversion, coordination mechanisms, and durability (among other possibilities).

Most of us could provide an answer to the question "What is public management theory?" But the answers provided by a group, even a group of experts, might vary considerably. As long as that is the case, the question will be worth asking.

For this volume, several experts were asked to provide an answer to that question and, if they wished, to consider what public management theory might be and what it should be. The task was to be provocative, direct, and succinct. These experts responded well, and the result is an interesting and perhaps even representative set of images of public management.

Hal G. Rainey sets an appropriately iconoclastic tone by declining to answer the question, on the grounds that it is time to stop musing about theory and start producing it. He goes on to suggest some theoretical puzzles that public management researchers might address.

Laurence E. Lynn, Jr., focuses on five interrelated concepts that, he argues, should provide the theoretical foundations for both the study and the practice of public management (thereby latching theory and practice together in a way that most of the authors in this section seem to applaud). Lynn follows his own advice and employs many of these concepts in a later chapter.

James L. Perry adopts Waldo's medical metaphor (1968), suggesting that the relationship between public management theory and practice is a clinical one. He also reminds us that public management theory should be for the public management masses, not just for the elites in top-level positions.

Lee Frost-Kumpf and Barton Wechsler use the "five blind men and an elephant" fable to illustrate the confusion and disarray in contemporary public management theory. They explicitly reject the model of the natural sciences, suggesting that the theory-practice dichotomy give way to a more interactive, collective approach to theorizing about public management practice.

IMPORTANT RESEARCH QUESTIONS

Hal G. Rainey

I decline to comment on what public management theory is and should be. Many capable scholars have devoted time, energy, and ink to the discussion of what public administration is and should be, and to related questions, such as whether the field has an adequate fund of research and theory. Much of that discussion has value, but it also brings to mind the literary character—one of J. D. Salinger's, I believe—who said he longed to stop *becoming* and start *being*. One wonders whether public administration scholars might do better in advancing both the identity of the field and its research and theory if fewer of us ruminated on these topics and more of us simply identified important theoretical and research questions and worked on providing useful answers to them. So be it with the emerging topic of public management.

I have written elsewhere on sources, implications, and directions of this public management rubric (Rainey, 1989, 1990, 1991), and an altruistic concern for readers who have endured those discussions, and who deserve relief, adds yet another reason not to go into those matters here. I have pointed out that public management is in some ways a time-honored rubric but has recently been granted a new cachet by various scholars and experts. As this topic develops, many scholars can offer to guide that development through discussions of the is-and-should-be issue. I hope, however, that many will also press forward untrammeled by such edicts and develop research programs to provide useful answers to the questions that they consider important. By way of illustration, here are some research issues on which progress would be valuable.

1. *What are the variations among types of public organizations and managers?* With some important exceptions, our literature on public bureaucracies tends to overgeneralize, often concentrating on common properties of public or-

ganizations and managers and deemphasizing variations among them. We could use more systematic knowledge of such variations. Typologies have achieved little real success in the social sciences and, like a will-o'-the-wisp, can beckon researchers into the mire. Several studies have produced useful efforts at typologies, however, and other studies have reported differences among public agencies in structural characteristics, employee values, agency culture, and other important dimensions. More studies comparing public agencies and managers — by agency, functional type, policy area, and level of government — could help us understand the variations within the "public" category.

   2.   *What do we mean by the political context of public management, and how does it influence organization and management? What are key dimensions and variations in this context?* We can look for important variations and issues by pursuing anomalies and contradictions. One of these arises from differing perspectives on the role of politics. Public management supposedly takes place within a distinct political and institutional context, and our literature on bureaucratic politics, bureaucratic power, public leadership and entrepreneurship, city management, and related topics contains a fund of knowledge whose value we probably underestimate. It offers rich observations about this context and case illustrations of public managers dealing with congressional committees, the media, interest groups, oversight agencies and their rules (civil service, procurement), and the policy process.

   Yet we also know that many public managers work in virtual isolation from direct political intervention and pressure and from media scrutiny. Against our frequent depiction of public management as management in a goldfish bowl stands the obvious aversion of many elected officials — and of most reporters, newscasters, and talk-show gurus — to serious consideration of administrative issues except when some instance of bureaucratic bungling can be gleefully pounced upon. Many organization theorists and general management experts have pointed to such conditions as evidence that management in government and in business differs little, if at all. This apparent contradiction is also closely related to a frequently noted divergence in the literature on public bureaucracy: between those who claim that the bureaucracy possesses inordinate power and autonomy, and those who depict bureaucrats as cautious and subservient eunuchs.

   Many paradoxes are not paradoxical but just seem that way, pending further analysis. We could use clearer and more systematic conceptualizations of the political environment, to clarify its dimensions, their variations, and how they influence organizations and managers in government. A number of assertions about these influences are ranging around in the literature, and efforts to clarify and validate them could prove very productive. For example, one very important research objective would be to identify the conditions under which public managers and organizations attain certain degrees of autonomy or self-containment (Simon and Thompson, 1991). We also need a better understanding of the variations in how different public managers experience and respond to the political and institutional environments in which they operate.

3. *What do we mean by "vague" goals in the public sector, and how do they influence public organizations and management?* Another anomaly: the most frequently repeated observation about the distinctive nature of public management is that public organizations and managers pursue goals that are particularly vague, multiple, and mutually conflicting, as compared with goals in the private sector. We all have a sense of what this assertion means, since we know that statutes instruct government agencies to do such things as conserve the environment, enhance economic well-being, and regulate business activity in a just and reasonable manner that upholds the public interest (Woll, 1977, pp. 10–12; Wilson, 1989, pp. 32–33). Business firms, we think, build and sell things — they have a bottom line. Yet we also know that the building and selling of things does not always amount to a very clear goal. Moreover, we know that many public managers spend their time on such concrete matters as selling lumber by the board foot, trying to reduce the processing time for social security claims, and making sure that tax forms are removed from their envelopes and properly distributed; the "wicked" problems that the public sector allegedly confronts often turn out to be not very wicked.

To complicate the matter still more, we now have a few surveys of managers in public organizations and business organizations. In responses to questions about clarity of goals, objectives, and performance expectations, it has been found that public managers differ little from private managers. Apparently, the public managers have stubbornly refused to read our literature about them, so as to know how they should respond to such questions. In addition, many organization and decision theorists would take the position that all managers and organizations pursue vague, multiple, conflicting goals, and so it becomes hard to maintain that public managers and organizations face distinct contexts, in this sense. Rather than belabor the matter any more, I shall simply assert that clarifying the nature and applicability of this common assertion about public sector goals would constitute a very significant contribution to our understanding of public management. It could also contribute to our understanding of societal control and direction through political processes, as opposed to control through economic markets.

These questions represent only a few among many other useful research directions that those interested in public management could pursue. The questions reflect my own orientation and background, and no doubt my colleagues will generously help in identifying these questions' limitations. Since they are perceptive, they will observe that, while I have declined to comment on the is-and-should-be matter, these research questions still advance some strong implications for it. They reflect an interest in organizational behavior and theory, as well as positivist and empiricist inclinations. (But not too much, I think; some economists and formal modelers could say that these questions reflect too little clear positive theory.) Some will argue that we ought to spend more time asking public managers what troubles them; others will contend that we should avoid entanglement with fuzzy behavioral issues and advance management of the palpables, such as cash, inventories, and production processes. Nevertheless, through a variety of methods, we can make progress on such questions as those suggested here and thus contribute to a significant and valuable body of knowledge.

2

THEORY IN
PUBLIC MANAGEMENT

Laurence E. Lynn, Jr.

*T*he role of theory in the professional field of public management is to assist managers and their advisers in bringing a critical, analytical intelligence to bear on the design and choice of institutional arrangements for achieving the goals of public policy. Theories enable managers to say (or hypothesize) why observed actions, behaviors, and results occur (or may occur) and to prescribe arrangements that may lead to intentionally better governmental performance.

Theory in public management will make full use of the experience of public managers (on the basis of the notion that public managers will do a better job if they have studied the actual experiences of other managers in similar circumstances). It will also draw on academic disciplines concerned with explaining behavior and choice (on the basis of the notion that administrative reality is usually too complex to be seen adequately with the unaided eye). The following five interrelated concepts are among the essential theoretical foundations for the study and practice of public management.

Agency

Public managers are both principals and agents. In both capacities, they must contend with asymmetrical information, conflicts of interest, and aversion to risk. Public managers must grasp the essential problems associated with establishing and maintaining principal-agent relationships.

Markets, Hierarchies, and Clans

Managers make choices about reliance on marketlike mechanisms, hierarchical arrangements, and social relationships for accomplishing the goals of public policy. They must know how to recognize when each choice is appropriate, and why.

Bounded Rationality and Cognitive Style

Managers must recognize and contend with cognitive limits on performance (their own, and that of others with whom they deal) and with differences in cognitive or learning styles. Understanding one's strengths and limitations as a learner and communicator is often essential to promoting learning and communication within and among organizations.

Executive Discretion and Bureaucratic Supply

Is the public manager merely a role player, or do public managers have autonomy, within which they may exercise discretion? Duty or choice, and how much of each? Specific theories delimit the range of discretion and constraint inherent in executive and managerial roles (in general, and in particular contexts) and identify incentives that motivate managerial and bureaucratic behavior. Public managers can use these theories in formulating their strategies.

Logic of Collective Action and Game Theory

Interactions, both within and between organizations, can be understood as problems of achieving cooperation in single and repeated encounters. Public managers must know what methods can be used to secure cooperation (for example, to overcome free riding or defection) in the face of disincentives (such as prisoners' dilemmas and deadlocks).

Five additional concepts that can be applied to materially improving critical analysis among public managers are as follows.

Reframing

Bolman and Deal (1991) have suggested that organizations can be viewed through four distinct lenses. Public managers must understand the logic of different analytical frames, or lenses, for interpreting the activities of organizations and must be able to apply several to the problem at hand (that is, to reframe the problem).

Networks

Heclo (1978) has articulated the notion of issue networks. Sociologists have developed more formal models of networks, which show how public actors are linked to one another, and why that matters. Public managers must be able to identify the networks in which they are or should be involved and to use networks to accomplish their objectives.

Psychological Type

Several psychological theories identify systematic differences in how individuals function as learners, decision makers, and managers. Individuals of different types will not function in the same way in given managerial situations. Public managers should know their own "typical" tendencies and should know how to interact successfully with people of other types.

Garbage Cans

Policy making and execution are characterized by fluidity, serendipity, and spontaneity. Cohen, March and Olsen (1972, for organizations) and Kingdon (1984, for policy formulation) have applied this concept, with important implications for public managers. Recognizing and creating "windows of opportunity" can be an invaluable pair of managerial skills.

Tools

Salamon (1981) has suggested the value of understanding the distinct advantages and disadvantages of different tools (or specific configurations of institutional arrangements) for accomplishing public purposes. In a related vein, Rosenthal (1982) has identified different models of operations management, each with its strengths and limitations in specific contexts. Public managers are involved in choosing and using institutional tools and must understand the logic of their design and application.

An appreciation of such concepts as these enables public managers to make such statements as "It is better, in these circumstances, to do this than that" or "Doing this or that is likely to have these consequences and pose these risks" or "We are faced with this kind of problem, rather than that kind of problem." Of absolutely vital importance, theory enables public managers to offer reasons for these kinds of statements, reasons powerful enough to overcome doubt, skepticism, or timidity. Theory-based or analytical practice of public management will not always be superior to instinctive practice, value-driven practice, or "rules and checklists" practice, but it offers the best hope for systematically transcending the often stifling effects of ego, ideology, inertia, ignorance, and the unexpected on governmental performance.

3

Public Management Theory: What Is It? What Should It Be?

James L. Perry

*T*en years ago, I co-edited *Public Management: Public and Private Perspectives* (Perry and Kraemer, 1983), which sought to define the relatively new field of public management. That book, along with the contributions of a small number of other scholars (many of them represented elsewhere in this volume) was influential in articulating dissatisfaction with traditional public administration and generic management and initiating an identifiable field of public management.

The present volume marks a passage in the development of public management. A good part of the last decade was devoted to legitimizing public management — with all that entails — and to convincing other scholars that public managers did and should make a difference, eliciting testimonials from practitioners about the need and value of public management as an identifiable enterprise, and establishing that our knowledge about how managers make a difference is largely not random. The period of legitimizing has ended, and we are now entering a more serious stage, in which valued knowledge must be developed.

This new stage will be much more demanding than the first. What should public management theory aspire to provide? In brief, public management theory should provide useful and practical generalizations about how public managers should behave in varying situations. The phrase "useful and practical" is intended to suggest that public management theory must be relevant and problem-oriented. I also firmly believe in Kurt Lewin's often repeated adage, that there is nothing so practical as a good theory. Thus, the injunction that theory be useful and practical is limiting, but not substantially.

Appropriate action by public managers may differ according to circumstances; no "one best way" exists for responding to every situation. At the same time, scholars must be attentive to developing theory about particular facets of situations that define the domains of managerial action. These domains include the organizational and interorganizational context, the institution and institutional rules, incentive structures, and role sets (including public expectations and ethical frames). The important facets of the domains of managerial action are probably quite limited. Public management theory should strive to systematize the description of situations and of how effective action on the part of public managers varies across them.

Suggesting that public management theory provide practical insights into how public managers "should" behave implies a need for knowledge of or competency in both behavioral and normative theory. Behavioral theory can help public managers understand or explain the dynamics of the contexts in which they are situated and the efficacy of potential interventions. Normative theory gives public managers the capacity to think about and recognize how they ought to act in light of the values contending for expression in a given situation. Behavioral and normative theory represent two different logics that must be joined under the umbrella of public management theory.

The relationship that I envision between public management theory and public management itself is epitomized by the patient's relationship with the physician. (This analogy with medicine is not new; years ago, Waldo argued that public administration should identify itself as a profession analogous to the field of medicine; see Waldo, 1968.) The process of healing a patient typically involves diagnosis, treatment, observation of the effects of treatment, and, depending on the success of the initial treatment, either cessation of treatment or initiation of a new cycle of diagnosis and treatment. Like the physician, a public manager searches for patterns in the situation, establishes a model of cause-effect relationships, identifies appropriate interventions, selects an intervention, and implements it. For the public manager, the process is likely to be fraught with considerably greater uncertainty than the physician faces. The important point is that theory contributes to effective performance, but not in completely predictable ways. Argyris, Putnam, and Smith (1985) have referred to this way of thinking about the relationship between theory and practice as "action science."

Even if we are successful in developing public management theory along the lines just suggested, there are barriers to its effectiveness that must also capture the attention of public management scholars. One barrier involves translating knowledge about how to respond to a situation into effective behavior. A simple example will illustrate the point. Suppose that a public manager is engaged in legislatively authorized negotiations with constituents about rerouting an expressway through an urban neighborhood. The negotiations reach a critical stage, where the manager, given what she knows about interest-group dynamics, sees that she has the opportunity to obtain agreement from a winning coalition of the affected parties, *if* she can display an irrevocable commitment to the settlement option on the table. Let us assume that her estimate of the situation (the opportunity for a winning coalition) and her understanding of the appropriate intervention (a display of irrevocable commitment) are accurate. Her success still depends on her skill in *communicating* her irrevocable commitment to the option on the table.

This example shows that managerial skills are essential to realizing the promise of useful and practical generalizations about public management. It also implies that part of the research agenda attendant to the development of public management theory will involve identifying the skills necessary to utilize theory successfully. Boyatzis (1982) and Perry (1989) have identified such skills in a general way, but further research must extend these initial efforts.

Public management theory must speak to all public managers, not just those at the strategic apex of public organizations. Much of what I read — and, I confess, some of what I have written — is slanted toward these higher-level positions. The jobs of assistant secretaries and bureau chiefs are more glamorous than those of first-line supervisors and middle managers. On the face of it, incumbents of top-level positions also have more influence and are more "public" than their colleagues who are camouflaged by layers of administration. But to ignore public managers who do not reside at the top of organizational hierarchies is to overlook a large and important clientele. Public management theory must be as attentive to developing useful knowledge for the large mass of managers in the middle as it is to developing theory relevant to the managers at the top.

4

A Metaphor
Rooted in a Fable

Lee Frost-Kumpf,
Barton Wechsler

*A*ttempts to define the term *public management theory* bring to mind the hoary (and by now, perhaps, overused) fable of the five blind men of Hindustan who happened upon a large elephant blocking their path. Each of the five blind men described the thing that lay in their path, using the limited sensory data available to them to interpret and guide their conclusions. Not unexpectedly, they each made very different discoveries about the nature of the impediment. Since each one swore that he alone possessed the true description, they were unable to achieve any satisfactory agreement about its true nature. Without an effective intersubjective agreement to guide their inquiry, the five blind men were unable to act together in a meaningful way. Like the five blind men, scholars and practitioners attempt to understand and act on something called *public management* by using different frames of reference, different powers of observation, and different tools of inquiry and practice.

There is some danger that attempts to define the term *public management theory* will yield results not much different from the fragmentary discoveries of the five blind men of Hindustan, but members of both the scholarly and the practitioner communities must also be concerned about including disparate, unrelated, incommensurable things within a common yet ill-defined concept. This problem was cleverly expressed several years ago in a cartoon in *The New Yorker,* which had each of the five blind men claiming that he had discovered an elephant, even though they had really detected a snake, a leaf, a wall, a tree, and a blade of grass. This is the central paradox of

---

It has been pointed out to us that we are among the many who have tried to illustrate the condition of public administration and organization theory through this fable. Our research suggests no definitive genealogy. Gareth Morgan refers to the fable, but without attribution, in his book *Images of Organization* (1986) and Dwight Waldo uses it twice in book reviews in the *Public Administration Review* (1961, 1978) but cites Mason Haire (1959) as his source. Whether the fable originated with Haire or was used by someone before him was not possible for us to determine.

inquiry in the design sciences. We constantly confront the gap between theory and practice. Scholars, who seek to understand the nature of public management from a "theoretical" perspective, strive to minimize Type II errors
(that is, to minimize the probability of not rejecting the null hypothesis when
it is actually false). As a result, scholars tend to focus on the power of the
experiment, test, or measurement method(s) to detect true differences. Most
practitioners, by contrast, are more interested in minimizing Type I errors;
that is, practitioners tend to concentrate on minimizing the probability of
rejecting a null hypothesis that is actually true. The basis of their concerns
is reasonable: namely, the need not to expend scarce resources for new policy
or programmatic initiatives posed by the alternative hypothesis until and
unless the evidence compels decisions for collective action that is likely to
change the circumstances subsumed by the null hypothesis. In their zeal to
preserve the integrity of judgments defined by radically different professional
standards, both scholars and practitioners, like the blind men of Hindustan,
run the risk of committing a Type III error, in which they would define
and solve the wrong problem, but in very precise terms. While they are prone
to committing the same error, it is not surprising that scholars and practitioners do so in vastly different directions, and for vastly different reasons.

At any rate the question left unanswered by our recourse to the fable—
and the critical issue for the task of defining public management theory—is
why, like the five blind men, we have been unable to accurately define and
act on the phenomenon (public management theory) that we have encountered. Is our failure to integrate individual observations into shared knowledge and effective collective action due to limited observational capacity,
faulty interpersonal communication, or inexperience with empirically based
theory? Answers to this question are hard to find because individual descriptions of what public management theory "is" or "should be" are likely to vary
along a rather large, complex, and changing set of dimensions, yielding many
different ideas, concepts, propositions, measures, and tests.

Highly specific statements about the nature of public management theory, like the idiosyncratic descriptions offered by the five blind men, are
unlikely either to produce desired improvements in theory and practice or
to generate more consistent and longer-lasting intersubjective agreements
about the defining characteristics of public management as a field of professional practice or a domain of scholarly inquiry. In fact, the history of our
field provides strong evidence of our inability to establish a distinctive intellectual domain. Past efforts at domain definition have served only to am-
plify the dissonance and discord of our disparate voices and to produce disputes that often denigrate the positions, goals, and purposes ascribed by
practitioners to scholars and by scholars to practitioners.

By contrast with the situation in traditional disciplines, theories of public management are constructed, tested, and applied in practice. Public management theory is, should be, and cannot help being embodied in the practice
of public management. Therefore, while theories about public management

and the practice of public management may be kept separate, as representing different forms of collective social activity, the two cannot be separated in their substantive content or in their mutually interactive influences. This means that the scholarly and the practitioner communities are much more than inextricably linked; they are inseparable forces bearing directly on the construction, testing, and application of public management theory. Ideas, concepts, propositions, and hypotheses cannot be neatly separated into domains of theory or practice; the actions, decisions, and culture of one community defines and redefines the actions, decisions, and culture of the other (Barley, Meyer, and Gash, 1988).

Our inability to achieve substantive theoretical progress stems at least partly from deep personal differences in how each of us goes about developing categories and classifying thoughts, observations, and life experiences under the label *public management*. Because our blind spots and preconceptions prevent us from embracing the dynamic forces that shape public management as a field of professional practice and a domain of scholarly inquiry, our attempts to define public management are likely to generate much hope while producing great disappointment for scholars and practitioners alike.

The persistence of these blind spots and preconceptions raises questions about strategies for building and effectively utilizing a definitive theory of public management. How can we overcome the obstacles that we bring to our study and practice? What models of the inquiry process should we follow? How can practitioners and scholars develop the practices of public managers into a field of inquiry and action?

What public management theory "is" or "should be" cannot be discovered along the well-worn path of the natural sciences. There are now many reasons to question, if not directly reject, the post hoc, reconstructive descriptions of the inquiry process found in the natural sciences. The natural sciences model is an inappropriate guide to public management theorizing because it fails to take into account, among other things, the prescriptive, action-oriented, future-directed nature of public management as a design science (Simon, 1969). This means that the scholarly community's efforts to construct, test, and suggest applications of theories to the practice of public management will not, in scholarly isolation, produce much substantive progress in our knowledge or understanding, or much improvement in our management practices. Scholars must go beyond the relatively simple acts of producing definitions, concepts, propositions, and measures and testing hypotheses about what we collectively label *public management*.

We believe that there is great potential for unifying the claims made by practitioners and the results of reflective and systematic scholarly inquiry, yet many continue to insist on the theory-practice dichotomy, to distinguish the domain of inquiry from the field of action. In doing so, scholars denigrate the "theories" of practitioners while aimlessly searching for a Rosetta stone that will allow them to decode the practice of public management. The theory-practice dichotomy must be rejected in favor of a more interactive, collective approach to theorizing about public management practice, an approach that would include the work by scholars and practitioners alike.

Efforts to define what public management theory is must seek to inquire into, learn about, and act through the practice of public management as a shared, collective endeavor. As such, public management involves socially active people engaged in interpersonal encounters that are created by, and that create, highly personal and subjective interpretations about publicly sanctioned, organized, collective social action (Harmon, 1981). Adopting this perspective allows us to recognize that practitioners operate as scholars in their own right—as "personal scientists" who seek to make sense of the world that surrounds them even as they attempt to act upon it (Kelly, 1955). Practitioners, in common with their scholarly colleagues, develop and utilize personal theories to create highly subjective and personal interpretations, which serve as a basis for the continuity of interpersonal exchanges. From these highly subjective positions and extended dialogues, a shared understanding can be developed and used as the foundation for organized collective action.

Our position argues for a more holistic approach to theory construction. Such an approach would require a far deeper appreciation of the dynamic links between theorizing about public management practices and carrying out public management theories in practice. This means that scholars and practitioners must learn to appreciate and even act more like each other. It implies that members of both communities must develop more extensive mutual interests and seek out greater opportunities for collaboration in building, testing, and applying public management theories—from personal experiences and observations, interpersonal exchanges and dialogues, and formal communications between and within the two communities.

What public management really "is" and "should be" can be defined only by action taken on the issues of our time (ideally, with some knowledge of how similar issues were managed or mismanaged in earlier times). The discussion so far offers few clues to the important issues toward which members of both communities could direct their attention while beginning the process of collaborative inquiry, prescription, and action. It must surely be recognized, however, that the central issues confronting scholars and practitioners of public management, like the elephant confronting the five blind men of Hindustan, are perceived in many different forms and present many different aspects.

We face issues that are extremely difficult to frame for research and action, and working on them means that we, scholars and practitioners alike, must substantially improve our capacity to manage organized complexity, operate in the presence of persistent and irreducible ambiguity, and negotiate fundamental and lasting agreements in spite of deep, historically based value conflicts. We must embrace the paradoxes, puzzles, and problems of public management practice. These are the exemplars through which public management theory serves as the central instrument for gaining greater mutual understanding and fashioning more equitable, effective, efficient social action. We must be willing to create new and more broadly based interdependencies, coalitions, and collaborative forms of organizing while eliminating the old and narrow interests, compacts, and agreements that have yielded fewer benefits for all and greater benefits for a few. How members of the scholarly and practitioner communities come to terms with these issues and attack the theory-practice dichotomy may comprise one of the central challenges in the development of democratically based institutions and societies in the fast-approaching century that promises so much to so many but could deliver so little to us all.

ISSUES IN
PUBLIC MANAGEMENT
THEORY DEVELOPMENT

*A*ppropriately, "big picture" issues dominate Part Two, which comprises full-length, formal chapters. Barry Bozeman offers the minority view, at least in this volume, that public management theory should not be guided chiefly by practice and "tacit knowledge." He contends that practitioners' and researchers' theories are not commensurate and that the form of knowledge possessed by practitioners, while arguably more valuable and valid than primitive theoretical knowledge, is inherently different from theoretically oriented knowledge. Bozeman argues that while there have been many advantages to the close ties between public management researchers and practitioners, theoretical progress is not, by and large, one of them. After providing a rough-hewn categorization of public management knowledge, he discusses the "external/integrative" problem, which is related to the processes for adjudication, organization, and valuation of knowledge. He finds that the inclusiveness, openness, and breadth of public management knowledge — laudable in themselves — have led, unnecessarily, to diminished standards for evaluating theory and theoretically oriented research. In the rush to accommodate practitioners, Bozeman argues, academic researchers have abrogated responsibility for their own research agendas and, worse, have evaluated theoretically oriented work by narrow and often inappropriate standards. In sum, there may be nothing so practical as a good theory (views espoused by Lynn, Perry and, originally, Kurt Lewin) but perhaps only after it has been allowed to gestate.

Action theorists who find that the first chapter in this section is a bitter pill to swallow will find the remaining two chapters much more palatable. In Chapter Six, Robert D. Behn presents a strong argument for the centrality of case analysis as a core method for public management research. He discusses case analysis within a taxonomy of managerial research, including experimental research, questionnaire research, practitioner-thinker research, "gedanke" (great mind) research, and observation research (in the tradition of Mintzberg (1973). Case-analysis research, Behn's métier, is illustrated by Kaufman's (1960) and Selznick's (1949) groundbreaking work.

According to Behn, case analysis is more than storytelling and more than theory; it is a useful amalgam of the two.

Donald F. Kettl, in Chapter Seven, tries to determine the essential elements of public management. He sees public management not as a part of public administration but as a rejection of it. By contrast with the implementation tradition with respect to political science, public management is more optimistic about the possibilities for prescription and improving practice. Kettl also notes that public management has tended to focus on top-level managers but, like Perry in Part One, he wonders whether public management research should be confined to top managers. Kettl would also like to see more attention to different levels of government and different levels of bureaucracy.

Kettl seems to agree with Behn on the preferred research method for public management. Public management, according to Kettl, has advanced on the basis of the deductive method, insights derived from business school–style forced-decision cases, and the personal experience of public managers, in stark contrast to the methods used in many social sciences. This point is certainly valid in many respects, but it is perhaps worth noting that the case-study method has had rough sledding in the mainstream business journals (it remains quite popular in business school pedagogy). This observation does not undercut Kettl's argument; much like Behn and many other public management scholars, Kettl sees a strong interrelation between the research and instructional agendas in public management.

5

Theory, "Wisdom," and the Character of Knowledge in Public Management: A Critical View of the Theory-Practice Linkage

Barry Bozeman

*I*f recent assessments (Kraemer and Perry, 1989) of public management research and theory are valid, then the field is not yet ready to take its place alongside more mature and theoretically rich social science disciplines. As a field of study, public management is variously described as being on the "soft" side (policy analysis is on the "hard" side) and as more a craft than a discipline (Liebman, 1963). Public management research and theory usually receive higher marks for practicality and utility (Graziano and Rehfuss, 1974), but not since the formative years of the scientific management era have there been strong claims for its scientific potential.

Two interrelated problems, endemic to public management research, stand in the way of its progress. The *internal/technical (I/T) problem* concerns well-accepted technical standards for scientific research and theory building, involving such issues as testability of hypotheses, proper specification of models, and logic of explanations. The term is new here, the problem is familiar and has been addressed effectively in critical reviews of public management literature (Kraemer and Perry, 1989; McCurdy and Cleary, 1984; Perry and Kraemer, 1986; Stallings and Ferris, 1988; White, 1986; Perry and Rainey, 1988). The *external/integrative (E/I) problem,* the focus of this chapter, concerns not the production of knowledge but its adjudication, organization, and valuation. This term is used for the problem because it is concerned with how to integrate the knowledge created by those external to the public management research community. Critiques of the public management literature have given little attention to the social and institutional aspects of knowledge production.

The following questions are suggested by the E/I problem:

1. How should the public management theory and research community make use of knowledge produced for reasons having little or nothing to do with conventional theory or research objectives?
2. To what extent is "unsystematic" knowledge about public management useful for theory development?
3. Are there ways in which such unsystematic knowledge is inimical to theory building?
4. How should one go about integrating and exploiting knowledge diversity as one seeks to develop explanatory theory?

In addressing these questions, it is useful to consider them in connection with particular public management theories and theoretical problems. Since the public management literature is diverse and fragmented, it is convenient to focus on one central research question: the differences between public and private management. The arguments presented here, however, even those presented in the context of public-private management research and theory, are viewed as valid for public management research in general.

The Character of Knowledge in the Comparative Public-Private Management Literature

The question of differences between public and private management is quite important in its own right. The "publicness puzzle," (Bozeman, 1987)—how the public aspects of organizations affect their management—is the core conundrum of public management theory. Without some understanding of the differences between public and private management, public management has no intellectual rationale as a field of study; without theories of public management, the public in management is easily viewed as a minor measurement problem—an error term, an uninteresting anomaly, a residual, or, at best, an intervening variable.

Despite rapid proliferation of research and theory on public-private management differences, progress has been slow. The best-known critical assessments (Perry and Rainey, 1988; Rainey, 1989; Golembiewski, 1987; Fottler, 1981) range in tenor from pessimism to cautious optimism. Perry and Rainey (1988, p. 192), after noting the increased attention to public-private management differences, conclude, "The studies have been very diverse in design and focal variables, and often they have been exploratory and not clearly related to available theory. [The studies] have not been cumulated into an acceptable explanation of how and why public organizations differ from private ones."

Why, after all the intellectual energy invested in the topic of differences between public and private management, do so many gaping holes remain in our knowledge? Why is there so much disagreement on fundamental issues? Why is there so little confidence-inspiring theory of public management?

Several outstanding reviews of the public-private literature have noted technical problems with research and internal flaws in theory construction (Perry and Rainey, 1988; Rainey and Perry, forthcoming; Rainey, Backoff, and Levine, 1976). While the validity of these criticisms must be granted, another set of issues needs attention. If problems in the production of theory are well known, problems in the evaluation and codification of theory are not so well explored. Since many such problems flow directly from the character of public management knowledge, let us begin with a broad classification of the knowledge types in studies of public management.

A Classification of Public Management Knowledge

Despite the fact that our chief concern here is with the development of explanatory, "science-like" theory—complete with axiomatic statements, bridge principles (Hempel, 1966), and testable hypotheses—much of the knowledge reflected in the public management literature is not scientific in method, tone, or intent; rather, it is theoretical, craftlike, descriptive, or personalistic. This literature—which, for convenience, can be included under the general heading *wisdom literature*—is much more vast and, in many ways, more influential than the body of conceptual and empirical work captured by the term *theory-seeking literature*.

Consider the case of the literature on public-private differences. Much of what is believed about public-private management differences comes from the wisdom literature: practitioners' reports of personal experience (Blumenthal, 1983); suggestive anecdotes (Allison, 1979); "ordinary knowledge" (Kennedy, 1983); prescriptive studies of various types (Bozeman and Straussman, 1990; Nutt and Backoff, 1992); rhetorical exchanges (Moe, 1987, 1988a; Bozeman, 1988); and polemics (Goodsell, 1983). The influence, positive or negative, of such work on theory development sets the stage for the E/I problem—how to sort out, for use in explanatory theory, the knowledge produced for various purposes.

Table 5.1 shows a typology of the management literature on public-private differences, beginning with the separation of ordinary knowledge from wisdom literature and theory-seeking literature.

Ordinary Knowledge

Ordinary knowledge is an encompassing term for a diverse set of knowledge streams that share the characteristics of (1) being largely informal communication, (2) relying strongly on personal knowledge, intuition, and common sense, (3) requiring limited or no credentials, and (4) being culturally and socially circumscribed. Ordinary knowledge includes not only our direct, personal experience but also those of others. If Uncle Harry has an unusually interesting experience (either bad or good) with the Division of Motor Vehicles, its telling can contribute to his and others' views of public and private agencies. Ordinary knowledge also includes the notions transmitted

Table 5.1. Typology of Knowledge in Public-Private Management.

Category of Knowledge	Subcategories	Example
Ordinary knowledge	1. Unreported practitioner/ client experience	Individual's experience with public and private hospitals
Guarantor: personal experience; faith; plausibility; none	2. Culturally pervasive notions	"Business is more efficient because it has a bottom line"
	3. Institutionally embedded knowledge	Limited government
Wisdom Literature	1. Reports of practitioner experience	Blumenthal (1983)
Guarantor: book-review apparatus; traditional peer review; highly diverse standards	2. Noncomparative case studies	Warwick (1975)
	3. Polemical analysis	Goodsell (1983)
	4. Prescription	Bozeman and Straussman (1983, 1990)
	5. Value theory	Benn and Gaus (1983)
	6. Syntheses; criticisms	Perry and Rainey (1988)
Theory-seeking literature	1. Empirical comparisons of public and private management	Rainey (1983, 1989)
	2. Imputed comparisons	Lau, Newman, and Broedling (1980)
Guarantor: book-review apparatus; traditional peer review; less diverse standards	3. Positive axiomatic models	Downs (1967b)
	4. Nonaxiomatic conceptual models	Wamsley and Zald (1973)
	5. Syntheses; criticisms	Perry and Rainey (1988)

within a culture or subculture — such notions as "The private sector is more efficient because there is a bottom line" (this notion is questioned by Weinberg, 1983, and by Bozeman and Straussman, 1983) or "Public agencies are less self-serving and have more regard for their clients" (much of the property-rights literature — see De Alessi, 1980, for an overview — questions this notion). These notions may contain a great deal of truth or none whatsoever. Ordinary knowledge also includes "reflected" knowledge embedded in social institutions (for example, limited government, corporate socialism, and other such institutions that, by their very presence, affect the way people think about differences between public and private).

Wisdom Literature

One of the chief distinguishing features of wisdom literature is simply the fact that it *is* literature, whereas ordinary knowledge is by definition informal and informally communicated. The term *wisdom literature* is neither a term of derogation nor one of praise. It simply refers to studies that seek to contribute to public management knowledge not by gathering empirical data or providing frameworks for the formulation and analysis of empirical data but by relying on synthesis, impressions, systematically reported personal experience, dialectics, and other approaches that may be characterized as systematic but not as theoretical (at least in the narrow definition of the word *theoretical*). The wisdom literature, while having its own methods, is less concerned than the theory-seeking literature with intersubjective validation of knowledge through consensual standards. Despite the fact that much of it is reviewed by the same social mechanisms (journals, book reviewers) as the theory-seeking literature, its standards are more variable, and traditional, sciencelike criteria are less relevant.

Theory-Seeking Literature

A theoretically oriented literature has begun to emerge in the study of public-private management differences, and this literature closely resembles that of other social sciences at similar stages of technical mastery and theoretical development. While the subcategories shown in Table 5.1 differ considerably from one another, they also have much in common. The theory-seeking literature on this topic tends to have the following characteristics: (1) it provides explicit and testable hypotheses or propositions, (2) it develops analytical devices for explanation, (3) it aspires to generalization, (4) it assumes that aggregation is meaningful in analysis, (5) it provides for some degree of analytical separation between fact and value, and (6) it assumes that theoretical progress is not illusory but is real and demonstrable.

In experimental physics, theory-seeking literature is more valuable than wisdom literature; public management theory, however, is not demonstrably superior to ordinary knowledge or wisdom literature. Therefore, even though our primary concern here is the development of theory-seeking literature, this emphasis is not accompanied by any claim that theory-seeking literature is intrinsically more valuable than ordinary knowledge or wisdom literature. The apologia for public management theory is modest: explanatory theory is one of several important routes to public management knowledge, it is underdeveloped, and it is undercut in ways that are detectable and remediable.

The E/I problem involves the integration of extraordinarily diverse sources of knowledge. Particularly troublesome for the theoretician is ordinary knowledge. The guarantor of ordinary knowledge—the means of verifying it—is either nonexistent or based on faith, plausibility, or personal experience (Polanyi, 1958, 1967). The role of the researcher and theoretician is not to debunk common sense and personal knowledge but to maintain skepticism about "the obvious." Indeed, "organized skepticism" is a recognized norm of science (see Merton, 1969, 1973).

In sum, personal knowledge and other forms of ordinary knowledge are extremely important but should entail different rules for their adjudication than those required for theory-seeking literature. The E/I problem emerges if the guarantors of the three types of knowledge begin to converge.

The Nature and Scope of the External/Integrative Problem

Every theoretically oriented public management researcher knows that contributions to the literature come from a wide variety of sources, including not only academic researchers but also nonacademic researchers, practitioners, popular writers and journalists, and scholars from fields far removed from public management.

There is much virtue in focusing only on work ("internal knowledge") produced by a community of researchers, with shared values and norms, who are pursuing explanatory theory. This is one meaning of the term *discipline*. But most critiques of the research on public-private differences are inconsistent in dealing with external knowledge. Traditional (that is, naturalistic, neopositivist) evaluative standards are used, but they are applied to literature produced with little or no thought to those standards. Worse, much of the research comparing public and private management proceeds with no critical posture at all toward the explanatory status of various components of the literature: all propositions are equal. Blumenthal's ruminations (1983) about working in the Department of the Treasury are given essentially the same treatment as the Wamsley and Zald ownership/funding typology (1973), which is treated no differently from Lau and Pavett's empirical comparisons of public and private managers (1980). Field studies of public-private differences in motivation and job satisfaction (see Rainey, 1983) are considered alongside experimental studies on the same topic (Solomon, 1986; Rhinehard and others, 1969), and both are compared to property-rights theories of displaced public sector incentives (Alchian and Demsetz, 1973; Davies, 1971, 1977). Value theories (Benn and Gaus, 1983), prescriptive theories and prescriptive applications of theory (Backoff and Nutt, 1992; Bozeman and Straussman, 1990), and rhetorical treatises (Goodsell, 1983) are all thrown into the same wash.

It may seem fair and open-minded to embrace the many styles, approaches, epistemologies, fashions, techniques, intentions, research norms, values, disciplinary perspectives, and mundane biases brought to public-private management research. One result, however, is that criticism and synthesis of the literature on public-private management differences will require inhuman patience or a coarse-grained filter.

Why is this all-embracing orientation so pervasive in public management? Political scientists specializing in Congress might certainly read Richard Bolling's *House Out of Order* (1965) or Tip O'Neill's *Man of the House* (1987). They might even look to these accounts as possible sources of hypotheses, but they would never confuse these works with the research literature. It is even more difficult to imagine economists integrating such books into the literature as *Liar's Poker* (Lewis, 1989) or *Brokers, Bagmen and Moles* (Greising and Morse, 1991). While economics is not unified by a single paradigm, it is almost never "paradigmless." Whether researchers begin from neoclassical assumptions and develop production-function models, or from neo-Marxist assumptions and develop dialectics, there is disciplinary form and exclusivity in the economics literature.

Why Is Public Management Research So Inclusive?

One of the most important reasons for our literature's inclusivity is an appropriate humility. As already mentioned, public management has yielded little confidence-inspiring theory and is therefore not a sound basis for application or prescription. Philosophers speak of the "cash value" of theory (Rosenberg, 1988); the cash value of public management theory and research may be no greater than the experiential knowledge of practitioners, or "working knowledge" (Kennedy, 1983).

One should not expect theoretical mastery in a field that is relatively immature. There is no paradigm for public management research and theorizing; rather, ours is a preparadigmatic field conforming closely to Ravetz's model (1966) of an "immature and ineffective field of inquiry." Ravetz's diagnostics for such a field include the following:

1. There is an absence of facts achieved through the results of research.
2. The field is based more on a "folk science" than on a set of verified scientific principles.
3. Educational programs are based as much on the exchange of personal impressions and reflections as on a body of widely accepted standard theory and concepts.
4. Research and scholarly activity is inconclusive.
5. Application of "theory," if it is to be successful, requires common sense and wisdom as much as familiarity with the field.

There are many telltale signs of the "immaturity" and "ineffectiveness" of public management research. One of the best practical tests for level of theory development and paradigmatic consensus is the standardization of textbooks. Those in public management are extremely varied and exhibit only modest overlap in coverage, citations, and even style. Not only do "craftsmen" (practitioners) play a role in the education process, NASPAA standards encourage the use of practitioner adjuncts in graduate programs.

The relatively impoverished state of public management theory and research is not the only reason for the E/I problem. In addition to the supply problem, there is one of demand. There is no census of such matters, but it is surely true that the number of people in public management whose professional careers are chiefly devoted to systematic research and theory development is relatively small; there are probably no more than a few

hundred. The self-conscious academic community is not large or homogeneous enough to generate its own demand.

There is an amorphous demand for public management knowledge
among practitioners. Nevertheless, this community not only is unlikely to
have much interest in the technical matters surrounding knowledge production but also may have a strong (and understandable) bias against rigorous,
technically proficient studies. Evidence from the knowledge-utilization literature (Mandell and Sauter, 1984) shows that rigor and application are rarely
allies and often enemies.

The academic community, in abrogating demand to the practitioner
community, often accepts (sometimes eagerly, sometimes reluctantly) the
knowledge standards of the practitioner community. These standards rarely
include the generalizability and technical criteria required for theory development.

Advantages of Inclusivity

While the objective here is to identify problems entailed in the inclusivity
and divergent standards of public management knowledge, it is also important to recognize that this inclusivity offers some significant advantages. From
the standpoint of providing links between the research and practitioner communities, inclusivity certainly has merit. Research is more likely to be tailored
to practitioners' agendas. It is more likely to be communicated in a style
that promotes its utilization, and it is more likely to be used. (It may or
may not be more useful, however.)

If the current openness of the public management literature seems to
enhance practice, what are its advantages (if any) for theory development?
Four advantages seem clear.

Reality Check. In some fields, the distance between the observer and the
phenomenon observed has a deleterious effect on theory and research; the
"detached scientist" problem has not plagued public management research.
The close ties of public management researchers to practitioners may foster
less rigorous, watered-down theory and research, but it is not at all clear
that this is the case. Evidence from sociology (Lodahl and Gordon, 1972)
even indicates that a strong connection between theory and applications can
strengthen both.

Expanded Idea Stream. Paradigms establish the "acceptable" ideas for research (Kuhn, 1970). By determining and legitimating particular theoretical puzzles, communities of researchers in strong-paradigm fields begin to
agree on definitions of "important" research topics. Paradigm consensus, taken
along with the methodological standards set by disciplines, sharply constrains
the range of research ideas pursued. This constraint has a number of advantages, most of which are discussed elsewhere (MacLeod, 1977); but the

same restrictions that keep fields of inquiry on track can sometimes prove stultifying, especially in fields where disciplinary consensus is high but paradigm strength is relatively low.

Research Support. One of the reasons why public management research and theory have not flourished is that the amount of support for research is minuscule. There is almost no research funding for "pure" (that is, purely theory-oriented) public management research. Funded public management research almost always begins with a social, managerial, or policy problem and usually ends with a contribution to the problem's solution. Sometimes, but not often, intellectual problems are solved along the way. Moreover, if it were not for the openness of public management research and its literature, there would be almost no money available for research.

Competition. The "social control of science" is a concept used by sociologists of science (Blume, 1974; Knorr-Cetina, 1981; Zuckerman and Merton, 1971) to examine the social factors governing legitimation of scientific knowledge, credentialing, setting of critical standards for science, and evaluation of scientific contributions. The public management research community exerts comparatively little social control over knowledge production; social control is weak and dispersed.

   One result is competition, not only for journal space but also for the attention of the constituency for public management research. The need to compete with other, systematic approaches, however — for example, agency theory (Mitnick, 1980), property-rights–based interpretations (De Alessi, 1969; Demsetz, 1967), and political economy–based political science research (Chubb and Moe, 1985) — may have the desired effect of sharpening explanations.

The External/Integrative Problem as an Obstacle to Theory Development

The E/I problem presents a great number of obstacles to the advancement of theory. The external production and social control of knowledge (E) and the integration of knowledge (I) both pose problems.

Social Control of Knowledge and Setting of Standards

As already mentioned, the inclusive and amorphous nature of the field of public management means that there are many "players," most of whom are viewed as equally legitimate. The result is that social control of knowledge (Blume, 1974) is very different in public management than in most disciplines.

   It is not at all clear that researchers' competition with practitioners for social control of the formal literature is healthy. For example, in the study of public-private differences, it may be useful for public management theories to compete with economic theories, but competition with either ordinary knowledge or the wisdom literature probably does more to confuse than to clarify. Public-private differences research based on data from systematic field studies is not necessarily strengthened in having to refute, explain, or rationalize "counterfindings" in Blumenthal's reports of his experiences in the Department of the Treasury (1983), or in Allison's secondhand accounts (1979) of Costle's experiences in the Environmental Protection Agency and Chapin's experiences at American Motors.

Papers submitted to the *American Economic Review,* even papers on policy-relevant topics, are reviewed by referees who are professional economists—usually research specialists in the field examined in the paper. They are largely playing the same "game" as the submitting researcher, a game in which there is much agreement on the rules for research, if not its substantive outcomes. Social control in public management is very different. Papers submitted to the *Journal of Policy Analysis and Management* or *Public Administration Review* are likely to be reviewed by practitioners, who may or may not be playing the same game and who may or may not have much sympathy for the enterprise of theory development.

It is not surprising that social control of knowledge in public management differs from what exists in economics, which is a more self-conscious discipline. Its level of theory development is higher, and its credentialing is more formal. But what about the field of business studies? A paper submitted to the *Academy of Management Journal* or *Management Science* is not likely to be reviewed by a nonresearcher, or by one who has limited sympathy for the development of explanatory, "sciencelike" theory. Social control in business management, inherently no less "applied" or "relevant" a field than public management, is much stronger.

For the objective of theory development in public management, the sharing of social control with practitioners and noncontributors to theory has the effect of mixing signals in the evaluation of knowledge and, in some cases, constraining methods and techniques. It may be true that "there is nothing so practical as a good theory," but perhaps only after the theory has been allowed to gestate.

Credibility Versus Validity, and Knowledge in Use Versus Knowledge for Its Own Sake

The stylized, often formalized approaches offered by theoreticians appeal to people steeped in the ethic of the research community. Among practitioners, however—and virtually everyone who is not part of the specialized research community—theory-seeking studies may seem stilted, counterintuitive, jargon-laden. The propositions of theoreticians may seem too qualified and overburdened with caveats. Few outside the specialized research community are likely to gauge credibility and plausibility by the same criteria as the researchers themselves use. Such issues as statistical significance, use of the counterfactual, testability of propositions, operationalism, and criterion stability are crucial to theory development; but, as studies of human judgment have shown (Einhorn and Hogarth, 1981; Hogarth, 1981; Wright, 1974; Kahneman and Tversky, 1982), these issues are not compatible with the ways in which most people make decisions about information.

Policy makers and public management practitioners pay less attention to internal and technical criteria and more to such factors as the credentials of the researcher, the style of presentation (Brown, Braskamp, and Newman, 1978) and the extent to which personal experience is consistent with the propositions being advanced (Landsbergen and Bozeman, 1987; Bozeman and Landsbergen, 1987; Coursey, 1990, 1992). The use of personal experience as the *primary* test of credibility is beneficial to the application of knowledge but inimical to the development of theory.

Failure of Critical Standards: The New Proverbs of Public Management

The research/theory community is so intermingled with the practitioner community (and with other public management knowledge constituents) that it is difficult to implement screening mechanisms that allocate status to contributions. From the standpoint of theoretical advancement, this means that propositions are extremely hard to disconfirm. This point is best demonstrated by a case in point. Consider the following proposition: *Public management differs from private management in that public managers' goals and objectives are more ambiguous than private managers'.* This proposition permeates popular thinking (ordinary knowledge) about public-private differences. Rainey (1989, p. 238) contends that it is "the most frequent observation in all the relevant literature." Almost all the wisdom literature dealing with goals also advances this proposition (Baker, 1969; Weiss, 1974; Mainzer, 1973; Allison, 1979; Lynn, 1981; Blumenthal, 1983). Nutt and Backoff (1992), in a study distilling and applying findings from the literature, note that "the most obvious and crucial difference between public and private organizations is captured by goals. . . . Public organizations often have multiple goals that are both vague and conflicting." They go on to observe, using a line of reasoning found in almost all the literature on public-private differences, that there is no "bottom line" in public agencies, and that this fact results in goal ambiguity. The theory-seeking literature is equally enamored of this proposition; indeed, it is a centerpiece of property-rights theory and a common explanation for the alleged inefficiencies of public management (De Alessi, 1969; Demsetz, 1967).

The problem is that field research provides almost no support for this proposition. In separate studies using diverse organizational data, Rainey (1983), Lan and Rainey (1992), Bozeman and Loveless (1987), Baldwin (1987), and Coursey and Bozeman (1990) all found that public and private managers do not differ significantly in their perceptions of goal ambiguity.

What should we make of this? It is not safe to conclude that the research studies are right and that the wisdom studies are wrong. It may be that each type of study views the question differently — most field studies focus on perceptions. It may be, as Perry and Porter (1982) suggest, that public agencies translate objectives (clear or not) into standard operating procedures. It may be that much of the wisdom literature is focusing on high-level public managers, whereas the survey-based field studies are focusing on middle managers. The empirical research may suffer from selection bias, inadequate samples, or instrumentation effects.

The point is not that the question of goal ambiguity is easily resolved by empirical evidence, but that insufficient attention is given to sorting out incommensurate types of evidence, even when there is a striking conflict between theory-seeking field research and other sources of knowledge. Moreover, this is exactly the type of dispute that should fuel progress in research and theory. But the strength of ordinary knowledge and of the wisdom literature is such that the theory-seeking literature seems to have little hope of playing one of its most important roles — providing a check against "common sense" and "the obvious."

Inadequate Assessment of Progress

Not everyone agrees that theory is cumulative and that progress can be charted (Laudan, 1977; Kuhn, 1970). All fields of study are subject to fashion (Crane, 1969), subjective interpretation (Mitroff, 1974), and social mediation of knowledge (Knorr-Cetina, 1981). Because of their breadth, as well as the impossibility of objectively verifying their most fundamental axioms, paradigms (and preparadigmatic general organizing models) may not be comparable. Nevertheless, even the more radical critiques of the notion of theoretical progress seem to agree that progress is possible within the framework of *particular* theories and paradigms. In explanatory theory, assessment of progress depends on accepted standards of criticism. When there is no clear difference in the criteria applied to ordinary knowledge, wisdom literature, and theory-seeking literature, there is little hope of gauging progress. In the absence of clear-cut assessments of progress, any field is likely to buckle under the weight of its own "truths." In such cases, intellectual discourse gives way to anecdote swapping, rhetoric, and, worse, authority.

Conclusions

The central thesis of this chapter is that the advancement of theory in public management has been hindered by the *external/integrative problem,* a term referring to the inclusiveness of the literature, the lack of standards for the certification of knowledge, and the failure to distinguish adequately between the sometimes conflicting and sometimes compatible needs of applied and theoretical knowledge.

In public management, there is no reason to isolate the development of explanatory theory from the development of applied and prescriptive theory, nor is there any reason to separate theory from practice. Explanatory theory may or may not be ill, but it is not in need of quarantine; it is in need of some recognition that the requirements of practice and application are not *invariably* salutary for the development of theory. Public management theory needs its own credo, which might include the following articles:

1. Practicality and prescriptive richness are not the acid tests of explanatory theory.
2. Theory needs time to develop. The rush to prescription can prematurely transform burgeoning theory into "wisdom."
3. The research and theory community should be wary of abdicating control of research agendas to practitioners. Social importance and theoretical importance are not identical.
4. Social control of knowledge in public management needs to be strengthened; otherwise, theory will not be able to compete with ordinary knowledge.
5. In public management theory, there is currently no higher function than criticism and synthesis. The research and theory community, amorphous as it is, must, at every opportunity, deliberate about standards for the acceptance of knowledge.

Ironically, one of the ways in which public management theory can both advance and maintain a healthy relationship with practice and application is to continue employing a fuzzy definition of the term *theory*. It is not productive now to argue over the requirements of theory or to resurrect positivist-antipositivist debates. What needs recognition is that much of the public management literature is not theoretical, has no theoretical pretensions, and is nevertheless quite useful. Nevertheless, by opening the specialized literature to avowedly atheoretical work and advancing its propositions as readily as they advance those from the research and theory community, public management scholars do themselves a disservice.

6

CASE-ANALYSIS RESEARCH AND
MANAGERIAL EFFECTIVENESS:
LEARNING HOW TO LEAD
ORGANIZATIONS UP SAND DUNES

Robert D. Behn

Case-analysis research is designed to show what can work — to help us discover what combinations and permutations of managerial tactics, approaches, strategies, concepts, and ideas can help managers in different situations produce useful results. Through the careful examination of effective public managers in action, case-analysis research can uncover how particular leaders are able to cope with particular problems so as best to achieve their organizations' missions. Then, from the broad repertoire of managerial activities defined and illustrated by such case analyses, other public managers can, on the basis of the particulars of the situations that they face, select, reselect, and adjust a combination of activities that will increase the chances that their organizations will accomplish useful social purposes.

A Taxonomy of Managerial Research

Scholars and practitioners who have sought to think systematically about management have employed a variety of approaches, most of which reflect one of six distinct research strategies.

Experimental Research

Experimental research is the most truly scientific of these strategies, for it comes the closest to our concept of science (that is, physics; Behn, 1992b). In reality, little experimental research has been conducted on management, although the work of Mayo (1933) and Roethlisberger and Dickson (1939) clearly fits into this category.

The Hawthorne experiments were undertaken to test whether the intensity of lighting influenced workers' productivity. The manufacturers of light bulbs and of electricity wanted to sell more of their products and thus hoped to prove that employees were more productive if they had more light. The National Electric Light Association convinced the National Research Council to sponsor the studies, and Western Electric volunteered its plant in Hawthorne, Illinois. The rest is social science history.

It is significant that the conclusions about human behavior, and thus about management, that emerged from the Hawthorne experiments were not what the researchers had explicitly sought to study: the impact of illumination, as well as the impact of hours of work and rest periods. Indeed, the objectives were only indirectly related to management. But out of this research came new ideas about individual motivation, interpersonal relations, and the behavior of work (social) groups. If the researchers had attempted to test these new ideas with a new experiment, they would have had a very difficult time developing a research design to do so (Behn, 1991a). Thus, quasi-experimental research is employed more frequently than pure experimental designs. The work of Woodward (1965) and of Lawrence and Lorsch (1967) fits into this subcategory.

Questionnaire Research

Experimental research (and even quasi-experimental research) about the effectiveness of managerial actions is difficult to do. Consequently, there has evolved in public management a tradition of questionnaire research, for it offers the opportunity to do the same type of statistical testing that makes experimental research appealing.

The approach is simple: ask a group of public managers a question, organize the answers, and do some statistical tests. For example, a researcher might ask state agency heads about the managerial concepts they have used and then compile the results, organizing them into tables and testing for statistical significance (see Brenneman and Kittredge, 1983; Poister and Streib, 1989; Cutchin, 1990).

How does this help the public manager? If 75 percent of managers report that they use management by objectives (MBO) and only 25 percent say that they use zero-base budgeting (ZBB), and if this is statistically significant at the .01 level, should a manager drop ZBB and adopt MBO? Questionnaire research says absolutely nothing about what concepts are proving effective, or why. (Are managers using ZBB because they find it helpful, because the budget office made them do it, because this is how they have convinced the legislature to give them more money, or simply because that is what all "good" managers are doing these days?) Nor does questionnaire research examine the principles behind these concepts or the circumstances in which these principles may work.

Mintzberg (1979a, p. 583) offers this critique of questionnaire research: "A doctoral student I know was not allowed to observe managers because of the 'problem' of sample size. He was required to measure what managers did through questionnaires, despite ample evidence in the literature that managers are poor estimators of their own time allocation. Was it better to have less valid data that were statistically significant?"

It has been said that all science is divided into two categories — butterfly collecting, and physics. Questionnaire research looks very much like butterfly collecting. Unfortunately, too much of what passes for public management research does not merely identify and count new butterflies; it actually invents whole new species. Such research has only intrinsic interest; it is of no help to managers. Nevertheless, questionnaire research has a long tradition. It fills journals and gets people tenure.

Manager-Philosopher (or Practitioner-Thinker) Research

Many managers have sought not only to write about their experiences but also to reflect on them, in an effort to develop ideas that will be of practical value to other managers. The long lineage of philosopher-managers includes Taylor (1914), Cooke (1918), Fayol (1949 [1916]), Dennison (1931), and, of course, Barnard (1938).

"Gedanke" Research

All research has some kind of empirical base, but those who practice "gedanke" ("great mind") research rely as much on logic as on specific, detailed empirical work. Such big-think research is often an effort to summarize and synthesize the individual scholar's own empirical work or a body of such work done by many others. In other situations, however, the emphasis is on the logic. Max Weber, Herbert Simon, and Charles Lindblom all did empirical work, but they are perhaps best remembered for their theoretical ideas, which they developed (and explained) as much through reason as through observation.

Weber's concept of the "ideal bureaucracy" pursuing rationality has provided the intellectual groundwork for the value of large organizations. Weber readily states that his ideal bureaucracy is nothing more than an ideal — or, as he calls it, a "selective reconstruction" of reality. Nevertheless, over half a century later, Weber's concepts of how the ideal bureaucracy should function continue to shape our thinking (Gerth and Mills, 1946).

Simon (1946a) attacks Weber's notion of rationality, but not his approach to thinking about how large organizations behave. Simon concludes that organizations are not rational because they cannot be; that they do not maximize because they cannot maximize; that they "sacrifice" because that is all that is left. But Simon did not develop these ideas from detailed empirical work; rather, they are the results of systematic (rational) thinking.

Lindblom (1959) takes Simon's descriptive ideas and makes them prescriptive, yet the concept of "muddling through" is built on Lindblom's logic, rather than on a specific empirical base. Indeed, Lindblom's classic article contains not a single detailed illustration, and his footnotes refer to only one such example.

Weber, Simon, and Lindblom established the "gedanke" approach to research on management. The "great minds" of the field can think hard, systematically and rationally, about how large organizations do behave—and should behave—and then write their analyses up convincingly. Weber's ideas fit with our hope for how a large bureaucracy will behave; when we personally confront a bureaucracy, we want it to behave rationally. Simon's ideas fit with our understanding of how a large bureaucracy does behave: the concept of "satisficing" meshes well with our personal observations of the behavior of the large (irrational) organizations with which we deal daily. Lindblom's ideas reflect our grudging acceptance of the best that large organizations can do: we hope that the large organization will at least make several successive, limited comparisons. In the field of management, "gedanke" research gets as much attention as anything else does.

Observation Research

Mintzberg (1973) asks a basic question: What do managers really do? Even for those who are not managers themselves, obtaining an answer to this question is relatively straightforward. One has only to watch some managers in action.

Despite the simplicity of this research strategy, the approach is not as popular as either questionnaire or "gedanke" research. Nevertheless, the school of observation research also has a long tradition, from Babbage (1832) and Ure (1835), over a century ago, to today's practitioners of this approach, who include Mintzberg, Kotter (1982), and Kaufman (1981).

Researchers undertake to observe a number of managers at work, to question them about their jobs, and to report the results. Sometimes these researchers set out to determine what managers in general do; they make little effort to screen out ineffective managers or to distinguish between the characteristics and behavior of successful and unsuccessful managers (note that Mintzberg, 1973, p. 3, emphasizes that his "is not a book about what effective managers do"). Sometimes the researchers (Kotter, 1982) consciously focus on successful managers, attempting to limit their observations to managers who have a reputation for success or whose organizations have a record of success, or to rate the effectiveness of the managers they observe.

Case-Analysis Research

Observation research can take many forms, of course. Sometimes the researcher takes a quick look at a large number of different managers. Sometimes the researcher takes an in-depth look at one manager or one organization. There are all sorts of possibilities in between. For example, the work of Kanter (1983), Peters and Waterman (1982), Peters and Austin (1985), and Peters (1987) falls somewhere in the broad middle of this continuum.

At one end is case-analysis research. The scholar examines a single example of management, in significant depth. Sometimes such research focuses on an individual leader. Sometimes it focuses on a management team. Sometimes it focuses on an entire organization. Regardless, the objective is to do more than tell an interesting story; rather, the researcher seeks to learn how the individual or team or organization has dealt with specific problems, to identify the underlying principles that explain why a combination of specific activities interacting with particular circumstances produced the observed outcomes, and to describe those principles so that they can be applied to other situations. Kanter (1983), for example, looks for examples of innovation being encouraged and helping American companies prosper. Examples of case-analysis research include Kaufman's examination of the U.S. Forest Service (1960) and Selznick's study of the Tennessee Valley Authority (1949).

Experimental and Nonexperimental Research

Observation and case-analysis research are nonexperimental—strictly second-class citizens in the social science world. Indeed, such research is often dismissed as "casual empiricism." According to Simon (1946b), "There are two indispensable conditions to successful research [:] that the objectives of the administrative organization under study be defined in concrete terms [and] . . . that sufficient experimental control be exercised to make possible the isolation of the particular effects under study." Observation and case-analysis research *proves* nothing.

Unfortunately, experimental research on those managerial actions that really matter in public agencies simply cannot be done. Organizational reality precludes both of Simon's indispensable conditions. As he would readily recognize, the objectives of most public organizations are rarely defined in "concrete terms," and it is almost impossible to exercise the experimental control necessary to isolate the important factors under study.

We can experiment with some factors and do statistical tests with the resulting data, but such work inevitably concerns factors that are trivial. Subtle actions—and, more important, subtle combinations of actions—cannot be specified in sufficient detail. Therefore, one action cannot be used (or forgone) by different managerial units, while every other managerial action and environmental condition is kept the same, so as to test the impact of the only action that has been permitted to vary. Real conditions cannot be controlled so as to tease out the effect of any single managerial action. Moreover, any circumstances in which conditions could be controlled would be so artificial as to prevent any serious generalizations about the complex world in which public managers function.

Traditional experimental research seeks to determine whether a specific, single factor (called the *treatment*) is important. But managers do not do only one thing; they are not looking for the single key factor that makes the difference. Managers know that no single factor *ever* makes the difference. The impact of any single factor is undetectable. Thus, the manager's challenge is to create a combination of factors—not *the* combination, but *a* combination—that produces the desired results.

Contingency theory suggests that the effectiveness of specific managerial actions or leadership styles depends on the situation. For some situations, some leadership styles work best; for other situations, other styles are appropriate (Fiedler, 1967, 1974). The most effective approach is contingent on the situation. Still, Taylor's work on "scientific management" created a lasting legacy. People who have never heard of Frank B. Gilbreth, who would never use his phrase "one best way," and who would laugh at the idea of doing a time-and-motion study (Gilbreth, 1912) nevertheless implicitly use the operating assumption that there actually is "one best way," and such managers and scholars are constantly searching for it.

Why should one approach be optimal for a specific situation? Why could several approaches not work equally well for the same set of conditions? Since the manager must undertake not just one activity but rather a combination of activities, there is little reason to believe in "one best combination of activities" for the current situation. The manager is not engaged in a search for optimality (and that is not only because the manager is willing to "satisfice"); rather, he or she has no reason to believe that there exists a single "best" combination of actions that is significantly superior to every other possible combination.

Sand Dunes and Church Spires

People with a background in operations research may have, in the back of their minds, some unstated, unvisualized sense that the search for the right management strategy is like a search for a church spire in a prairie: once you find it, you can clearly see that it is much taller than everything else. The manager, by contrast, knows (again, this knowledge is unstated and unvisualized) that the search for an effective strategy is more like a search for the way to get a group of people to the highest point in the sand dunes. Each dune has its own broad crown, but it is not clear which of the higher dunes is really the highest, even when everyone is already on top of it. The manager is not merely trying to identify one (or several) of the highest or higher dunes; he or she is trying to get the organization to the top. But the dunes are not peaked, but broadly sloping, and so the task is made more difficult and its outcome more unclear. There are also many paths to the top. A new manager can get to the top by taking a completely new path, one that others have never tried. He or she can take one that others have tried but failed to follow. The new manager can also start out on a well-worn path and never make it to the top. Perhaps the wind has changed the pattern of the dunes, and the well-worn path now leads nowhere. Or perhaps all the previously successful managers turned right at the clump of sea oats, but none of them realized or bothered to record that this is what they were doing. The sea oats may not be covered by sand, but the new manager may fail to understand the importance of this marker and may fail to take an important early action.

In an environment of constantly changing sand dunes, traditional research design and the concepts of statistical validity make little sense, for several reasons:

- Being near the top of one sand dune is just about as good as being near the top of another sand dune, and it is difficult if not impossible to tell which is better.
- There are lots of different ways to get to the top of one of these dunes.
- Each approach has its own unique obstacles.
- Different managers and different organizations find different obstacles easy or difficult to overcome. The amount of work required to get to the top of a sand dune depends not only on the characteristics of the approach taken but also on the match between the characteristics of the approach and the characteristics of the manager and the organization.
- An approach that worked for one manager last year may not work for a second manager this year. In fact, an approach that worked for one manager yesterday may not work for the same manager tomorrow. Another important feature of sand dunes is that one cannot tell, from the bottom, where the top is or what the best way is to get there; thus the manager has to grope along toward the top (see Behn, 1988).
- Getting the organization to decide which dune to climb may be a more challenging leadership task than getting it to do the climbing.
- The route chosen may be less important than engaging the brawn and brains of all the organization's members in the task of climbing the dune.

For these reasons, the research needed to help managers lead their organizations up sand dunes is qualitatively different from the research needed to help them identify the highest spire.

Research on Climbing

The purpose of public management research is (or at least should be) to help the public manager produce results. To continue with the sand-dune metaphor, the purpose of public management research is to help public managers lead their organizations to the top of useful sand dunes.

The purpose of the research is *not* to map the sand dunes. By the time the map is printed, it will be obsolete.

The purpose of this research is *not* to determine the highest sand dune. Again, the dunes themselves are constantly changing. What was an important dune last year may be inconsequential this year. (The leader may, however, find some quick analysis, which organizes the current dunes into broad categories by height, to be quite helpful.)

The purpose is *not* to discover the characteristics of sand. (How big are the grains? How much silicon? How much oxygen? How many impurities?) As a question for basic research, this one may be intellectually intriguing, but it has little value in helping a manager lead an organization to the top.

The purpose is *not* to count the grains of sand, to ascertain how many grains are bigger than .7 millimeters, or to determine how many are spherical, how many are ellipsoidal, and how many are tetrahedral. It may be possible to ask which kinds of sand behave in what ways in the presence of wind, rain, or sun, and the results may even be statistically significant, but that will not help the manager get an organization to the top.

The purpose is *not* to discover how the sands move with the winds, how vegetation inhibits the migration of the sand, or what happens when a hurricane washes waves over the dunes. In some forms, some of this information may be quite helpful to the manager; in and of itself, however, this research is not useful. To be useful, it has to be translated into helpful knowledge.

The purpose of public management research *is* to enhance the professional repertoires of managers who wish to lead public organizations up meaningful sand dunes, and to do this, scholars have to say *how* the task is accomplished. Case-analysis research, particularly case analyses of successful managers, teams, and organizations, can prove helpful (Allison, 1979). As Yin notes (1989), the case-study research strategy even has a distinct advantage.

The Challenge to Leaders

The challenge facing the public manager (really, the public leader) is to lead the organization to the top of a sand dune. This requires a wide variety of skills.

The leader needs to select a dune to ascend, and to convince his or her organization to accept it as a worthy challenge. (The leader never does any of these things alone; key members of the organization help decide which dune to ascend, and they help persuade others.) At first, it may appear that the legislation authorizing the manager's organization states explicitly which dune to climb. In fact, however, the preamble to this legislation may list a large number of dunes; and, since its passage, numerous stakeholders have added other dunes to the informal yet politically important list. (The legislation is much more likely to specify what equipment to use, or what path to follow. This is the problem of government management being "tight-loose" rather than "loose-tight"; see Behn, 1991a). Thus the task of selecting dunes is not trivial. It is an important challenge of leadership.

Having made sure that the members of the organization understand which dune they are trying to climb, the leader needs to get the organization to set off toward the dune. Every day the organization has to make some decisions about potentially useful paths. The leader has to keep reminding the members of the organization why they are climbing this dune and encourage individual units in the organization to discover barriers, to determine how to get around them, and then to do whatever else is necessary. The leader wants to engage everyone in the organization in the challenge of figuring out how to get to the top of the dune. The leader is not out there alone; the entire organization is trying to climb the dune. To accomplish this purpose, the leader needs all members to contribute not only their muscle but also their intelligence.

Sometimes the leader has to stop and caucus with key staff members or key line managers. The organization may have reached the top of one dune, but it may not be obvious to everyone that other dunes present new challenges. The leader may recognize that, for whatever reason, the organization will never reach the top of the dune it originally set out to conquer. Or it may be that the original dune, because of the vagaries of the political winds, has simply disappeared. In each case, the leader and the organization have to redefine their purpose and set out for new dunes. And sometimes, having reached a useful spot (but not the real objective) the leader has to declare victory and get everyone down safely to the bottom before the hurricane strikes.

An Example of Case-Analysis Research: Peter Drucker and Management by Objectives (MBO)

Drucker (1954) is considered to be the inventor of management by objectives, yet Drucker did not conceive MBO through quiet contemplation in his office. Rather, he developed the concept through his work with Alfred Sloan at General Motors (GM) and Harold Smiddy at General Electric (GE). Nor did Drucker test MBO in GE by randomly assigning some units to employ the process while withholding the idea from others and then comparing performance (Greenwood, 1981). Rather, Drucker evolved the concept of MBO through active observation of (and advice for) the management of GE.

Drucker built on what he had done and what he had learned with Sloan and GM. He observed how Smiddy's "management letter" worked and, through his consulting work for Smiddy and GE, affected Smiddy's managerial philosophy. At the same time, Drucker's work with GE was affecting his own thinking. Indeed, Smiddy and others at GE read the first draft of *The Practice of Management* and commented on it. From this iterative process between theory and practice, Drucker developed the concept of management by objectives. According to Greenwood (1981, p. 230), "Many other managers probably 'invented' and used an MBO concept before 1954, but it took Drucker to put it all together, think through its underlying philosophy, and then explain and advocate it in a form others could use."

Management by objectives is not the only approach, one that will produce the best results for every management task, private or public. Management by objectives is not even an essential component of every management strategy. Rather, management by objectives can be—in some, perhaps in many, situations—a useful component of an effective management strategy.

The MBO approach taken by any particular manager does not have to follow precisely the process employed by Smiddy at GE, or even the process as outlined by Drucker. There are some fundamental concepts behind management by objectives, concepts that can help managers motivate people to accomplish specific tasks. These concepts are what a manager can effectively use to accomplish particular purposes.

Again, every management task is slightly different. Even a specific manager cannot simply repeat a specific, previously successful strategy in a new situation. Every new management task requires a different combination of tactics, approaches, strategies, concepts, and ideas.

The most effective leader is the one who knows not merely the recipe for management by objectives but also the concepts behind the recipe. Through many experiments, a chef can develop a superb recipe for chocolate cake. Having developed the recipe, the chef can follow it in the wonderfully controlled environment of the restaurant kitchen day after day. Indeed, once the details of the recipe are written down, a sous-chef can be trained in its nuances. Then the sous-chef will also be able to reproduce the same cake day after day. Unfortunately, the public manager's world is constantly changing. Yesterday, this "chef" had three skilled and motivated assistants; today, he or she has forty-seven unskilled and unhappy ones. Yesterday, the kitchen was full of knives, spoons, pots, and pans; today, it contains only scalpels, shovels, thimbles, and wheelbarrows. Yesterday, the kitchen was stocked with flour, sugar, yeast, and chocolate; today, it contains only lemons and seaweed. Yesterday, all the patrons wanted cake; today, they are demanding apple pie. The public manager never has the luxury of simply reproducing yesterday's recipe. The public manager must constantly improvise.

In jazz, similarly, the musician's ability to produce a melodious improvisation depends on her having previously studied, learned, and practiced the fundamental principles of music on which the written score is based. Likewise, the public manager's ability to improvise on the management-by-objectives tune—to blend its melody into a larger composition—depends on his intellectual and practical understanding of the principles on which this particular management concept is based.

Practice from Theory, or Theory from Practice?

Many of the early ideas about management were developed either by the managers themselves or by close observers of management. According to Duncan (1989, p. 4), "Until the Hawthorne studies, most of the contributors of significant books in the field of management were people who either ran business firms or acted as consultants to those who did run companies. Frederick Taylor, Frank Gilbreth, Henry Gantt, Henri Fayol, Lyndall Urwick, James Mooney, Chester Barnard, Mary Parker Follett, and Henry Dennison were all actively engaged in the day-to-day management of businesses or served as consultants." The first of the great management ideas that Duncan presents are Babbage's division of labor and Ure's substitution of capital for labor. The division of labor resulted from the ten years Babbage spent traveling around Europe, observing and studying factories; Ure developed the concept of substituting capital for labor from careful studies of factory districts (Duncan, 1989).

At least until the 1920s or 1930s, concepts of management were not developed by theoreticians or academics. Rather, many of the great ideas of management "were first formulated in the steel mills of Pennsylvania, the factories of Detroit, or the quarries of France." Unfortunately, those who developed the ideas were often unable to articulate them: "Sometimes the managers who so beautifully orchestrate the operations of large organizations find it difficult to verbalize underlying concepts. Often these managers do not have the words, terms, or vocabulary necessary for such a discussion of ideas" (Duncan, 1989, p. xi). Conceptualizing, defining, and explaining the underlying concepts that have proved effective is the role of the scholar.

Of course, scholars — and their conceptions, definitions, and explanations — have not always been critical to the transfer of knowledge. In the past, the master taught the apprentice: "Apprenticeships were an effective means of ensuring an adequate supply of skilled workers. Learning by doing was the official teaching method, and the accomplished worker was an adequate teacher. It was an interesting system when viewed from the biases of today. We, for the most part, teach theory and delay practice. Historically, by contrast, theory was inferred from successful practice" (Duncan, 1989, p. 53). The question is, Which comes first — theory or practice. Should we deduce practice from theory? Or should we induce theory from practice?

In science, inductive reasoning has a long and distinguished history (despite its Popperian disparagement). For example, Isaac Newton, moving from the specific to the general, induced his laws of motion from his observations of how specific objects in motion behaved; only then could he use deduction to test those laws (Spielberg and Anderson, 1987). Case-analysis research is based on the assumption that if we want to develop a theory about effective practice, we have to understand many observations of effective practice. What makes an individual an effective manager in a particular situation is not at all obvious — or logical. If we really want to know what is the best way to lead an organization to the top of some sand dunes, we have to observe many organizational efforts to climb sand dunes. Then we have to cull out the commonalities of success — at least of particular kinds of success in particular conditions — and attempt to develop a theoretical framework to explain such limited and conditional successes.

The Nature of "Theory" About Effective Practice

Can there be a theory about leading an organization up a sand dune? If so, what would such a theory look like?

To be helpful to the public managers, the theory must link activities to outcomes: if the manager does A, the result will be B. Unfortunately, there are unlikely to be many definitive links, with single managerial actions producing single outcomes (at least there are not likely to be many such links with *desirable* outcomes). We may be able to determine that if the manager goes around kicking all the employees in the shins, the employees will revolt. But can managerial scholars identify any single action that will guarantee an increase in output of 50 percent, or even of 1 percent? "Chase's law" sounds wonderful: "Wherever the product of a public organization has not been monitored in a way that ties performance to reward, the introduction of an effective monitoring system will yield a 50 percent improvement of that product in the short run" (Allison, 1979, p. 38). But how many managers will have any faith in the numerical precision with which it is expressed?

The effectiveness of managerial actions in producing desirable outcomes is inevitably contingent on other factors, usually many of them. In fact, the number of other factors on which the effectiveness of any single managerial action will be contingent is so great that the concept of contingency becomes meaningless. Researchers will never be able to determine all the conditions on which the effectiveness of a managerial action is contingent. Even if they could, managers would never be able to replicate all those conditions.

An honest statement of the theory behind Chase's law must include caveats — for example, "Wherever the product of a public organization has not been monitored in a way that ties performance to reward, the introduction of an effective monitoring system will — *if nothing else is out of order* — increase the output by a small amount (and perhaps by a large amount)." Of course, no public manager believes in the 50 percent promised by Chase's law; even the neophyte knows that the word *law* is inaccurate.

Any real law is much less definitive than its clever expression as a "law." The dramatic phrasing of Chase's law captures both the reader's attention and the general point. But people read Chase's law as really saying, "Look, if you have not been monitoring what you want to produce, start monitoring this desired result, and you ought to quickly get some meaningful jump in production." There is nothing very fancy about such a theory. It lacks the mathematical elegance of physics. But that is not the test; rather, the test is whether it actually helps managers in their efforts to improve the performance of their organizations.

But how does a manager know that this theory "works"? How does a scholar know that this theory is "true"? Where is the proof? The "proof" of any such "theory" lies in its having been observed to work just once (see

Neustadt, 1975). If the theory has worked once, it can work again. The only question is, Under what contingencies is such a theory most likely to work, and is it easy for the manager to reproduce those conditions, or will the manager be almost incapable of creating the environment in which the theory can prove effective?

The value of such a "theory" comes from the details of case analysis—the description of the various important contingencies (at least as identified by the researcher) that interacted with an action to produce the desired results. The objective behind case-analysis research is not only to induce general theories from specific cases but also to provide enough of a context to suggest the conditions in which other managers can use a general theory to produce results.

Case-analysis research offers more than stories and more than theories. It offers both general theories and specific stories to illustrate them. It suggests what has worked, why it has worked, in what conditions it has worked, and how it may work in the future.

Dilemmas of Case-Analysis Research

When looking for a case of successful management to analyze, the researcher faces an important question: What is success? Case-analysis research seeks to discover what has produced success, but how does the scholar "know" that the managers in the case *were* successful? What definition does the researcher apply in order to determine whether particular managers or organizations are worthy of detailed analysis?

Consider Gordon Chase's ability to get New York City's Health Services Administration (HSA) to test 120,000 children for lead poisoning in one year. Was this a significant success? Twenty years after Chase's massive lead-poisoning program, children with the disease still make front-page headlines (Waldman, 1991). If Chase had really been effective, would the problem still exist today? Compared with the organization's previous track record—8,000 children tested per year—120,000 annual tests is quite an accomplishment. But that is only an "output" definition of success. After all, Chase always measured his staff not by the number of memos they wrote or meetings they attended but by another criterion: he asked them, "Whom did you make healthy today?" (Chase and Reveal, 1983, p. 177). How many of the 120,000 children who were tested became healthier because of HSA's program? Some certainly did, but neither Chase nor we know how many. Ten healthier children would hardly be a big success; what about 1,000? Is that enough for us to conclude that Chase's efforts were a success, and that his monitoring efforts produced significant results? Or do we require 10,000 healthier children? If so, *how much* healthier? If the case-analysis researcher concludes that Chase's effort was a success—that the testing of 120,000 children for lead poisoning produced a significant outcome—then the researcher's task is to answer the question of *how* Chase produced these results. What combination of environmental conditions, specific activities, and luck contributed to his success? How can the researcher identify which specific activities were important and be sure that it was *these* activities that contributed to Chase's success? After all, pure luck — the null hypothesis of case-analysis research — should certainly be considered.

The scholar must use experience to sort out alternative explanations. Nathan (1988, pp. 126, 130) argues that to evaluate "an ongoing government program once it has been adopted," researchers must use an inductive approach and "model the counterfactual on the basis of available facts and experience and their knowledge of organizational behavior. They observe the behavior of an organization or group of organizations under conditions in which a new policy is in effect and compare that behavior to what they predict would have been their behavior without the new policy." The same approach must be applied to managerial research. Scholars observe the behavior of an organization under new leadership and compare that behavior to what they predict would have been its behavior without that leadership. Other scholars then read the case analysis and test it against their own experiences. Still others analyze other cases, testing whether the theories from the original case fit the new cases. Rival hypotheses develop, and — as in the natural sciences — a consensus emerges as some theories fit the facts better than others do.

The practitioners of case-analysis research will never be able to prove that they are right. They will not even be able to prove that their work is helpful, for even the testimony of managers who find the insights of case analyses useful does not constitute proof. But at least those engaged in case-analysis research will know that they are asking important questions.

Helping to Build Public Managers' Repertoire

The concept of "managing for performance" that I outline elsewhere (Behn, 1991b) was not derived solely from what was done in one state agency in Massachusetts; it resulted from a pattern of thinking shaped by my knowledge of other cases (Behn, 1992b, n.d.). The concept of managing for performance is presented in one particular case analysis, but it reflects a broader intellectual tradition in management research, one that concerns using goals to motivate people and organizations — a tradition that goes back at least as far as Drucker's management by objectives. Ideas related to managing for performance can be applied by public (and private) managers in a wide variety of situations. The ideas may prove useful when the task is to get a state welfare department to educate, train, and place 50,000 welfare recipients in jobs (Behn, 1991a). They may prove useful when the task is to test 120,000 children for lead poisoning (Neustadt, 1975). They may prove useful when the task is to get an Air Force squadron to fly 17,000 sorties (Behn, 1992b). And they may prove helpful to the manager in a welfare agency who must significantly increase the number and amount of collections (Rosenthal, 1984; Behn, 1991b). Any time a manager wants to get a large organization to achieve a specific goal that requires a large number of similar actions, the concept of managing for performance may prove useful.

It will not be useful to all managers in all situations, however. Management for performance would not have helped Miles Mahoney struggle with the political conundrum represented by Park Plaza (Diver, 1975), nor would it have helped David King, the principal of Robert F. Kennedy High School, deal with the vicious interpersonal conflict among his faculty (Gabarro, 1974). Management for performance would not have helped Elizabeth Best convert a pseudo-management position into something valuable and productive (Skinner, 1975). There is no "management concept for all seasons."

Like any other professional, the effective manager needs a large repertoire of managerial concepts (Behn, 1987). Some of these concepts prove helpful in some situations; others prove useful in other circumstances. None alone is sufficient. None may even be necessary. But the larger the manager's repertoire (and the more analytical the manager's understanding of the value of each item in that repertoire), the greater the opportunity the manager has to combine appropriate actions.

A case is more than an intriguing story. The story is important, of course: it becomes the metaphor for the managerial concept, and the contents of the story can provide a useful mnemonic for remembering it. But, in addition to the specifics and the drama of a well-told story, the scholar has to provide an analysis that answers *how?* How did the manager produce results? How was the manager successful (or unsuccessful)? How did her actions contribute to her success? More important, how do the principles underlying her actions explain how they contributed to her success? Most important, how can those principles be adapted to similar situations by other managers, perhaps with different personal characteristics? A case is the vehicle for uncovering and describing new (or redefined) managerial concepts, as well as for analyzing general principles concerning those interactions between managerial activity and organizational and individual behavior that may prove helpful to future managers.

This, then, is the value of case-analysis research: it broadens the professional repertoire of public managers and their understanding of when and how each item in that repertoire may prove helpful. If scholars can develop not only cases that illustrate new items for the well-educated manager's repertoire but also analyses that explain the principles underlying each item, those scholars will be providing a useful service. They will be helping public managers figure out how to get their organizations to climb to the top of sand dunes.

7

Searching for Clues About
Public Management:
Slicing the Onion
Different Ways

Donald F. Kettl

Public management research, as a term to describe the study and practice of making government work, has become the refuge for all sorts of scoundrels. There are those who find public management much more alluring than the traditional study of public administration. There are analysts who seek in public management research a more positive approach than implementation research has yielded. There are organization theoreticians who find the search for practical solutions to management problems attractive. There are those who have migrated to the study of public sector phenomena from business schools, those who seek answers to problems that the analysis of decisions leaves unanswered, and those who seek generalizable theories from the insights their own practical experiences have produced.

As the public management movement has grown under its large umbrella, however, three important issues have followed. First, although scholars from many different disciplines have contributed to its growth, there has been very little disciplinary cross-fertilization. They have much to contribute to each other, yet sharing of ideas has been meager. Second, each of the branches of public management has been fundamentally shaped by what its students have chosen to study. Looking at different units of analysis often yields sharply different insights. Third, even though the primary thrust in public management scholarship has been the search for common tactics that work for most managerial problems, public management often has surprising variations, by kind of program and level of bureaucracy. We can learn as much by studying such predictable variations as we can by looking for shared elements.

Distinctive Features of Public Management

Some students of both public administration and implementation express amazement, even annoyance, at the public management movement. Many political scientists, for example, believe that they have been studying public management for more than a century and point back to Woodrow Wilson's famous article (1887) as proof. Other political scientists claim that implementation research is really public management research under a different name. The public management movement itself, however, has politely but firmly rejected both traditions in developing new theory.

The public management movement, especially the part that has grown out of the study of corporate strategy in business schools, claims a new approach, which shares little with these older traditions. It has been nurtured in the public policy schools and has borne fruit in the Association for Public Policy Analysis and Management. Its students seek to tease broadly applicable lessons from case studies and personal experience; and, in developing their message, they borrow little from the work of public administration research and implementation research. Given the traditions of both these fields, however, it is worth asking whether the new branch of the public management movement truly offers something new, or whether it is simply a conceit of those who have developed it. Is public management research simply public administration or implementation research, rediscovered and relabeled? What innovations does it introduce? Do the old traditions have anything to contribute?

Public Administration, Implementation, and Public Management

The public management movement does indeed develop a new perspective on the administration of public programs (Kettl, 1990). Public administration research is the oldest body of scholarship devoted to the question. As its basic unit of analysis, it has focused on the behavior of *bureaucracies*. It has also been devoted to the search for prescriptions, seeking to uncover basic principles of bureaucratic structure to guide administrative action. After World War II, however, this search for principles came under harsh attack. In part, the attacks came from critics who suggested that the "proverbs" had borne little fruit and, in fact, had often led to contradictory prescriptions (Simon, 1946; Dahl, 1947). In larger part, the attacks came as part of the behavioral revolution in political science, which stepped back from the study of institutions to examine the behavior of officials within them and voters outside them. Public administration continued to be the forum for much important research, but it unquestionably lost its central seat at the table in its home discipline of political science. Increasingly, moreover, those who researched and taught public administration distanced themselves from political science and sometimes found more hospitable homes in other disciplines — or simply constituted public administration as a discipline in itself.

At the same time, political science gravitated to the search for why the performance of public programs so often seems disappointing. Unlike public administration research's focus on bureaucracies, implementation research has focused on *programs*. Many implementation scholars have contended, therefore, that the implementation puzzle was something new and that there ought to be a body of scholarship devoted to its important questions, but that none yet existed. In one provocative passage, Pressman and Wildavsky (1974, p. 166) wrote, "There is (or there must be) a large literature about implementation in the social sciences. It must be there; it should be there; but in fact it is not." In launching the implementation movement, they shifted from the bureau to the program as the basic unit of analysis. The critical question about bureaus was not their importance in their own right but rather how they contributed to—and, more often, hindered—the performance of public programs. "Domestic programs virtually never achieve all that is expected of them," according to Ripley and Franklin (1986, p. 3). It is the program, not the actor, that became the basic focus of study.

Public management research has different and more recent roots. When the public policy schools began developing, they typically launched separate tracks for policy analysis (economics-based approaches for identifying the best decisions) and for public management research (how best to carry those decisions out). Some work that marches under the public management banner is nothing but older public administration and implementation research, with a new appeal to a different audience.

Defining Characteristics of Public Management Research

The key work in public management research that flows out of the public policy schools has several distinctive characteristics (see Behn, 1987, 1988; Heymann, 1987; Lynn, 1987).

Rejection of Public Administration and Implementation. Public management research begins by implicitly rejecting both traditional public administration and implementation research. It is instructive, for example, to note that few of the leading scholars of public management at the policy schools are political scientists or public administrationists. They tend to come from much different disciplinary backgrounds, yet they tend to push past their disciplinary training in the search for new insights. They also tend to push aside the traditional work of public administration research, which seems to present weak policy guidance, and the newer work of implementation research, which presents a discouraging picture of programs that rarely work right. In fact, public management research does not seem to grow from any other identifiable base than the strategy approach of the business schools.

Development of a Hopeful, Prescriptive Field of Study. In sharp contrast to implementation research, which is devoted to the difficulty—indeed, it sometimes seems, to the impossibility—of achieving a program's goals, public management research is devoted to producing results. Instead of saying, "It's amazing that federal programs work at all," as Pressman and Wildavsky do (1974), public management scholars say, "Political executives are central to the performance of government" (Lynn, 1981).

Focus on Strategy Setting by Top Managers. The basic unit of analysis for public management researchers is the behavior of top managers in public bureaucracies. The fundamental problem they face, according to the public management literature, is setting strategies for their agencies and programs. One book's first sentence is "The jobs of the government's senior departmental executives are surprisingly difficult" (Lynn, 1987, p. 1). The cover graphic of another book is a gallery of public managers: Wilbur Cohen, David Stockman, Caspar Weinberger, Anne Gorsuch, William French Smith, Joseph Califano, Les Aspin, Mike Pertschuk, Ed Meese, and Griffin Bell. Not one is a career bureaucrat, as might be true in the case of the cover of a book about public administration. Many (but certainly not all) of these managers, moreover, made an important positive difference in their arenas (as certainly would *not* be the case in most books on implementation). The job of these top officials is to set strategy: "The government manager's primary job thus becomes steering the organization into the production of a desirable set of services" (Heymann, 1987, p. 4). In fact, Heymann sees his contribution as picking up where more traditional public administration and political science research leave off: dealing with "how an effective political actor thinks about getting results in the short run and the long run" (p. xiv). Whereas public administration research has often seemed to its critics like a search for principles that leaves managers few clear guidelines, and whereas implementation research has seemed like an argument that managers are unlikely to be able to make a difference, public management research is devoted to the firm hand that public managers can take in producing outcomes.

Development of Knowledge Through Cases. Public management research has advanced through a rough-and-tumble deductive method, seeking insights through business school–style forced-decision cases and the personal experiences of public managers. Nothing could be farther from the behavioral methods of many social sciences. Public management researchers sometimes contend that we do not know enough to make predictions or develop models; instead, we ought simply to observe what works and what does not, and to draw from those observations some propositions that managers can employ. The goal, ultimately, is a set of prescriptions to drive the behavior of managers.

Struggle to Put the Study of Management on an Equal Footing with the Study of Decisions. Within the policy schools, the analysis of public decisions — both what they ought to be and how well they have worked out — has reigned supreme. In part because economists have often dominated these schools (and therefore have found administrative issues to be of little interest), and in part because decisions were thought to be the more important problems (which drove program administration), public management research has often played a distinctly secondary role to decision analysis. Indeed, one study of successful policy innovations shows that they rarely spring from the comprehensive analysis favored by policy analysts; rather, "management matters most" (Sanger and Levin, 1991, p. 9). The public management movement is singularly and self-consciously devoted to achieving parity with economics and decision analysis.

Questions Unanswered

This approach is both intriguing and valuable. It helps rescue the search for positive outcomes in public programs from the discouraging cynicism of implementation research. It puts a special spotlight on key institutional actors, as traditional public administration research often has not. Because of its very orientation, however, this approach to public management has several critical gaps.

Can Public Management Questions Properly Be Confined to the Behavior of Top Managers? While top managers unquestionably play a critical role in the performance of public programs, they most certainly are not the only actors within a bureaucracy that affect performance. Any theory of public management must be able to distinguish how different actors at different levels affect performance. Public management research needs to grapple far more carefully with how the tasks of management vary by level in the organization.

Is Public Management Similar in Most Government Programs? Or are there systematic variations among different kinds of programs? Public management research has been devoted to the investigation of generic management issues in government agencies. It tends to assume that management is management, regardless of the policy area. It is important to consider, however, whether differences among programs may be even more revealing than similarities. Public management research needs to develop a theory of how the tasks of management vary by kind of program.

Is Public Management Similar at All Levels of Government? Or are there important variations among federal, state, and local managers? A corollary to the pursuit of generic management issues is the assumption that the tasks of public managers are similar, regardless of setting (including level of government). Both the political environment and the nature of the public program, however, may vary by level of government, and so may the problems of public managers. Public management research must distinguish how management tasks vary at different levels of government.

By slicing the "onion" of public management in these three ways, we get important new insights into its basic issues. There is a core of public management that *is* the same, regardless of setting, but there are also likely to be important variations in management — by type of program, by level of government, and by level of bureaucracy. Investigating these variations is critical and may well offer even greater insights.

Variation by Kind of Program

Public management research is largely deductive — it comes from the personal experience of researchers, and from the insights that instructors and students alike glean from cases. The results are uncommonly interesting, full of shrewd and practical wisdom. In fact, the intellectual energy and obvious practicality of much public management research separate it from more traditional political science and public administration research, as does its basic method. The more fundamental point, however, is that the method matters. Nothing makes this point better than a comparison between how case-selection bias has plagued implementation research and how public management research has largely avoided this trap.

Case-Selection Bias in Implementation Research

Deductive insights gleaned from evidence are limited by the evidence under study, and nowhere has this been more true than in implementation research. Implementation research is largely a study of why things go wrong. The predominantly negative focus comes because implementation scholars have been drawn irresistibly to delicious tales of government programs gone sour. Moreover, implementation research has largely (but not exclusively) been based in intergovernmental programs, where organizational interrelations are even stickier than usual, where goals are always harder to define than usual, and where success therefore seems especially elusive. Since the goals of many intergovernmental programs include the sharing of power between federal and state or local governments, disagreement over goals is the norm, not the exception.

One interesting test is a review of the topics contained in a leading implementation textbook (Ripley and Franklin, 1986). Of the eighty-five programs and agencies listed in the book's index, sixty-seven — 79 percent of the total — have an important intergovernmental dimension, according to my count. The index reflects the emphasis that intergovernmental programs have had on the implementation literature. Given such a base, it is little wonder that so much of the implementation movement has been preoccupied with the problem of defining goals, the complexity of joint action, and the difficulty of achieving success. Shared decision making on goals, and joint action to achieve them, have been the very hallmarks of such programs. Had the implementation researchers examined other programs, from the air traffic control system to the National Park Service, they might well have come to much different conclusions.

Public management research has largely avoided the case-selection bias that has plagued—and continues to trouble—implementation research. Its evidence has tended to come from a far richer variety of sources: from defense and domestic programs, from intergovernmental and directly administered programs, from transfer programs and regulatory programs, and from programs managed at the federal, state, and local levels. The central works of public management research have been far freer of case-selection bias. Insights have been more positive and devoted to the possibility that managers can make a difference. Given the findings of public management research to date, as well as the positive, goal-oriented perspective of public management researchers, it is little wonder that public management research finds little of value in implementation research.

Tools of Public Management Research

Especially compared with public administration research and implementation research, the principal contribution of public management research has been the argument that good managers can produce successful results. Public management research sees the key to success in having the manager define strategy and mobilize support for it. Public management research thus focuses centrally on leadership and on the way a leader relates to his or her political environment: the environment outside the agency (including congressional committees, the White House, and interest groups), and the environment within the agency (especially bureaucrats, who can be a help or a hindrance according to whether the manager can win their support). The relationship between political strategies and program results is the central question of public management research.

The critical issue for public management research is whether the problems of strategy are similar in all programs, or whether there are systematic variations that managers (and researchers) ought to discover. An important line of research, the "tools" approach, argues that there are important variations according to the tool a program uses (see Hood, 1983; Salamon, 1989). The relationship between a government manager and his or her clients, on the one hand, and especially the relationship between the manager's agency and what it produces, on the other, is often very different.

Consider the federal government's programs. The tools vary significantly, and federal outlays vary considerably by tool. In fiscal year 1990, payments to individuals accounted for 40 percent of all federal spending. Net interest was the next largest category (at 15 percent), along with procurement (also at 15 percent). Federal grants took 11 percent of the budget, followed by defense expenditures for operations and maintenance (7 percent) and defense expenditures for military personnel (6 percent). Only 6 percent of the entire federal budget went to programs that the federal government

itself directly administered, as Mosher perceptively pointed out long ago
(1980). The federal government has also become increasingly involved in
indirectly managed programs, such as those involving tax expenditures, loan
programs, and other activities from the government's "quasi-world," including
government corporations and quasi-governmental organizations (see Seidman and Gilmour, 1986; Moe, 1988b).

The federal government is largely in the business of writing checks:
to individuals, for transfer payments; to investors, for interest on the debt;
to contractors, for procurement; to state and local governments, for grants;
and to soldiers, sailors, and airmen, for their salaries. Any careful theory
of public management at the federal level thus has to begin with an understanding of the federal government's role as check writer. It must then proceed with an understanding of how different programs and different tools
present very different management problems. The political environment of
each tool is different; so, too, is the relationship between the manager and
the bureaucrats working for him or her, or the relationship between the
bureaucracy and those with whom the bureaucracy works. The nature of
public management therefore varies significantly according to the tool of
government employed.

Variation by Level of Government

Public management also varies by level of the intergovernmental system —
not so much because the tasks of managers themselves are different at the
federal, state, and local levels, but rather because different tools predominate
at different levels of government. This argument is thus a corollary of the
previous point. Both research and training in public management must therefore take account of the systematic variations that follow the patterns of
American federalism.

Spending at the state level, for example, mirrors the federal government's role as banker in the intergovernmental system. Nearly three-fifths
of state government spending in 1987–88 went for check-writing functions:
grants, mostly to local governments (31 percent); welfare (14 percent); trust-
fund expenditures, mostly for retired employees (9 percent); and interest
on state debt (4 percent). State government ran colleges and the criminal
justice system, and it built roads, but its banking role was paramount (U.S.
Bureau of the Census, 1989).

Local government spending, by contrast, is largely devoted to direct
delivery of public services. Education, through local public schools, accounts
for more than one-third of the total (36 percent). Police and fire services
account for another 7 percent, and utilities account for a surprising 12 percent. Another one-third of the total goes to a set of miscellaneous programs,
from local parks and recreation to sanitation, most of which are delivered
directly. A small share of local government spending is accounted for by
check writing, through welfare programs (4 percent) and interest on local

government debt (5 percent), while much road construction occurs through contracting.

Just as public management varies by government tool, government tool varies by level of government. The lower the level of government, the more direct the managerial strategies tend to be. Most directly administered government programs are concentrated at the local level. The federal government concentrates on transfer programs, procurement, regulation, and "quasi-programs," while state governments play the critical intermediate role. An effective and useful theory of public management must account for variations in tools among the different levels of the intergovernmental system. The tasks of public management vary significantly by level of government.

Variation by Level of Bureaucracy

Just as public management varies by kind of tool, it also varies by level of the bureaucracy. As important as strategy setting by top managers is for bureaucratic performance, the behavior of top managers most certainly is not all there is to public management. Indeed, it may not even be the central issue in public management. Organization theorists have developed a substantial body of work that establishes the difficulty of controlling organizations from the top, as well as the tasks that work best in improving performance. The century of development in public administration theory, in fact, has been devoted to the understanding of linkages between policy makers (usually elected officials and political appointees) and those in the chain of command down through the bureaucracy, who are responsible for carrying those policies out. Looking at public management simply as policies and strategies imposed from the top is like concentrating solely on the pitcher in a baseball game. How the ball is put into play is critical, but what happens *behind* the pitcher determines how many runners cross the plate.

Bureaucratic Roles and Public Management

Organization theorists have also discovered that, in addition to the remarkable variation in public bureaucracies, there are uniformities in bureaucracy that are attached to the level of each bureaucrat's position (see Appleby, 1949; Parsons, 1960; Thompson, 1967). We can borrow from Parsons to suggest that three different levels of the bureaucracy are especially critical.

First, there is a *technical* level, where bureaucrats deal with the details of the bureaucracy's work. Technical competence and solid coordination are the important elements of management here. Furthermore, as more governmental activity occurs through third parties, the job of many technicians is not so much to deliver government's services as to supervise the third parties (contractors, grantees, regulatees, and so on) who do so instead. As the government's tools have become more intricate and complex, so has the job of the government's technicians.

Second, there is a *managerial* level. The government's midlevel managers occupy a critical position between top-level political appointees and elected officials, on the one hand, and technicians, on the other. Managers spend most of their energy on two critical tasks (Thompson, 1967). From higher officials they must obtain the resources (budgets, staffing, authority) required to complete the bureaucracy's task. From lower officials they must solicit the behavior needed to get the job done. Both tasks involve mediating. They require not only great technical expertise, to understand and control what the technicians are doing, but also considerable political sophistication, to deal with the often conflict-ridden political environment around them.

Third, there is an *institutional* level, peopled by the top-level political appointees who are the focus of much public management literature. The job of the institutionalist is to build political support by charting the best strategy (as, indeed, the public management literature recognizes). Without such support, it is impossible to perform the bureaucracy's task or to manage programs effectively. Top-level managers — institutionalists — thus play a critical (but not the only) role in public management.

Parsons's most important insight is that these roles disrupt the traditional bureaucratic lines of authority. Each of these three levels of the bureaucracy tends to demand characteristic kinds of behavior. At each level there are predictable tasks, which tend to be performed in certain ways, and these tasks vary significantly at each level. Parsons also argues that the presence of these different roles leads to important breaks in the chain of command as it moves down through the bureaucracy. Behavior from level to lower level does not simply involve spelling out, in progressively greater detail, the decisions of higher-level officials; rather, public management is a characteristically different enterprise at different levels of the bureaucracy because bureaucrats fill distinctively different roles.

Levels of Bureaucracy and the Challenger Disaster

Examples of the importance of these three levels of management abound, but none is more famous than the example of the fatally troubled management that led to the *Challenger* disaster (see Rogers Commission, 1986; Committee on Science and Technology, 1986; Romzek and Dubnick, 1987). Technicians at NASA's lower levels, along with technicians at Morton Thiokol, NASA's contractor for the shuttle's solid-rocket booster, were worried about the effects of cold weather on the booster's O-ring seals. (The launch, as we know, was scheduled for a cold day in January.) When they warned upper-level officials about the danger, however, managers at both NASA and Morton Thiokol rejected the alarms. Both sets of managers were deeply worried about the shuttle's previous performance problems, and they were not convinced that the technicians had made a strong case about the O-rings. NASA's solid-rocket booster manager, Lawrence Mulloy, was furious with the Morton Thiokol technicians and exclaimed, "My God, Thiokol, when do you want me to launch, next April?" The deputy director of the Marshall Space Flight Center, George Hardy, was also "appalled" by the recommendation not to launch (Rogers Commission, 1986, pp. 94, 96). Morton Thiokol's managers joined with Mulloy and Hardy to overrule the technicians. The fatal result was based, the Rogers Commission concluded, "in a serious flaw in the decision-making process leading up to the launch" (p. 104).

The technicians and the managers saw the problem different ways. For the technicians, in both Morton Thiokol and NASA, the perspective was from engineering: they worried about how the unprecedentedly cold weather would affect the O-ring seals, which had already been demonstrating problems as the temperature dropped. For the managers, in both organizations, the perspective was from performance: NASA was already getting bad press for its failure to make the shuttle into a regularly scheduled "space truck," and Morton Thiokol officials were worried because their contract was up for review. The management perspective won the argument, but the technicians, unfortunately, were proved right.

The *Challenger* story does not stop here, however. There were two communication breakdowns in the disaster. First, top-level NASA officials—the institutionalists—were not informed of the lively debate the night before the fatal launch. Whatever role they might have been able to play in averting the disaster, they never had the opportunity. They could not set a strategy because the issue was never presented to them. The second problem is even more interesting. It turns out that, months before the tragedy, top-level managers in NASA were fully briefed about the O-ring problem. They had plenty of time to take action, but they did not. Why? Although they had the information, it came "always in a way that didn't communicate the seriousness of the problem" (Committee on Science and Technology, 1986, pp. 172–73). Here, they could not set a strategy because a haze of technical issues obscured the importance of the O-ring problem. Public management at this level thus failed twice: first, in not recognizing a serious problem when it arose; and, second, in not establishing a system to ensure critical decisions reached them, and reached them in time.

The NASA case (and there are many others like it in government) yields several important insights into public management. First, much current public management research misses important issues of public management. The NASA case is very different from what is found in much of the public management literature. Second, while the role of top-level public managers—the institutionalists—is important, it is not all there is to public management. The failure of the technicians' warning to reach top officials the night before the *Challenger* disaster demonstrates how much richer public management issues really are. Third, to neglect the issue of lower levels of the bureaucracy is to miss problems that often critically affect performance. Fourth, as Parsons (1960) points out, problems at the lower levels tend to be characteristic ones, differentiated by role. Therefore, they can be studied, and theories can be constructed to examine them. The corollary is that a robust theory of public management must be able to explain the behavior of lower-level as well as top-level officials. The tasks of public management vary according to the role the public manager fills.

Implications

The approach to public management taken in this chapter leads to two broad observations. First, public management encompasses far more than the behavior of top agency officials. Public management includes a far larger set of issues, and to concentrate solely or even principally on top officials is to miss important issues that critically affect agency performance. Second, public management does not present a uniform set of issues; rather, the issues differ systematically. Understanding and coping with the differences may well advance us farther and faster than seeking the elements common to all public management. The search for systematic variance leads to four observations with important implications for both public management research and public management education.

1. *The study of public management has been shaped, far more than is generally recognized, by who and what analysts have chosen to study.* Public administration research encountered grave problems as a discipline because its search for the principles that would produce efficiency missed the critical effects of environmental politics. Implementation research was crippled for years because its concentration on intergovernmental programs, many of which seemed to have failed miserably, yielded the conclusion that hardly anything ever works. Had early implementation research focused instead on programs that operated by predictable routines, with clear goals (such as the Postal Service, or the Army Corps of Engineers), its conclusions might well have been very different.

Likewise, public management research has been shaped by what its researchers have chosen to study. Analysts have wisely avoided the case-selection bias that has plagued implementation research, but the singular focus on the behavior of top officials and their search for strategies has raised other problems. Strategy setting at the top is certainly critical: the nation will be spending more than $100 billion (and a whole generation) cleaning up toxic and radioactive waste around nuclear-weapons plants, because of poor strategies set by top officials. But the focus on strategy can blind managers and analysts alike to critical issues at other levels of the bureaucracy. Furthermore, just as there are similarities in the tasks that all managers must undertake, there are also important variations with which different managers in different situations must deal. To focus only on similarities is to impoverish public management research and education. The variations can be just as interesting.

2. *Public management is different according to different kinds of governmental tools.* One of the biggest weaknesses of traditional public administration re-

search is that it is based on notions of command and control through a system of authority. It presumes that the agency's output is produced by agency officials — that when top officials make decisions at the top, the bureaucracy will carry them out through the chain of command. But important parts of government, and the vast majority of the federal government's bureaucracy, simply do not work that way. Public management research must study different governmental tools to understand how they work and, even more important, how effective management varies according to different kinds of tools (see Kelman, 1990; Salamon, 1989; Seidman and Gilmour, 1986; Donahue, 1989; Moe and Stanton, 1989; Derthick, 1990). The management of important policy tools (especially contracting out and "quasi-world" agencies) has been especially neglected.

3. *Public management is different at different levels of government.* The corollary of the previous argument is that both research and training must vary considerably by level of government. The emphasis on different tools varies substantially by level of government, and so should public management research. We tend to call on different levels of government for different tasks. There are few public management jobs at the federal level that match the front-line nature of management in a public-works program, a local school, a fire department, or a police department. A combination of interpersonal skills and dexterity with performance indicators is required for work on the front lines, but the tasks at the state and federal levels are likely to be different. This argument, of course, simply echoes the last one: different tools have different managerial and analytical requirements; because different levels of government tend to be dominated by different tools, however, both research and training in public management need to recognize this critical fact.

4. *Public management is different at different levels of the bureaucracy.* In public management research and training, we need to remember that the behavior of a manager tends to be differentiated by the role that manager plays (Parsons, 1960). This observation raises important warnings against attempting to generalize about all public management from the issues surrounding top-level managers. It also suggests the danger of focusing on top-level managers in the training of beginning public managers. Few graduates of policy or administration programs will ever ascend to the highest level. They will probably begin as management or budget analysts and gradually advance, usually to important managerial positions. The typical career path will not ultimately take them to the positions occupied by those who are the focus of most public management cases but, instead, to the ranks of the bureaucracy directly below those positions.

At entry-level positions, beginning public managers will not have to think about strategy (and will be rebuffed if they try to). Instead, their job will be to see that tasks are managed effectively. In short, they will typically begin as technicians. After five to ten years, they will usually advance to the ranks of managers, where they will be responsible for the critical mediating tasks within the bureaucracy. All too often, they will face both roles without having had much training for either one. To make matters worse, having been trained to think strategically, as if they were top-level officials, they may well become exceedingly frustrated by the different requirements of their positions, which they will not be well equipped to fill.

Future managers, especially those who will be working with third parties, need to know how to negotiate carefully and effectively. Moreover, they need to know the basics of governmental accounting, so that they can spot small problems of performance while they can still be solved (and before they become big disasters). Valuable teaching tools are available to cover these approaches, and students must know them if they are to become effective technical managers (see Swiss, 1991; Anthony and Young, 1988).

Upper-level management positions require different skills. Upper-level managers often must design the performance management tools that technicians use. They must maintain technical mastery of the subject areas they are managing, but they must also acquire sophisticated interpersonal skills and an understanding of organizational theory. They need to develop keen insight into the political environment where they are operating, even though they will have little opportunity to become players in that environment. So different are their requirements, in fact, that the best way to serve them might well be through midcareer education, to help them understand and cope with the changing roles they will be playing in the bureaucracy. An understanding of how the tasks of public management vary at different levels of the bureaucracy is critical to the study and practice of public management, as well as to the education of future public managers.

The research and instructional agendas of this approach to variations in public management are interrelated. They begin with an attempt to understand what public managers actually do, how they do it, how what they do changes over time, and how what they do varies according to different kinds of problems they manage. The study of public management is still in its infancy, and those who teach and practice it have an unparalleled opportunity to shape this area of scholarship. They also have an important chance to improve the way government is managed. The answer lies in slicing the public management "onion" in different ways, for the onion's layers reveal important perspectives on the problem of making government work.

Part Three

THEORIES OF
PUBLIC MANAGEMENT

*T*he chapters in this section take seriously Hal Rainey's suggestion in Part One: to quit talking so much about theory, and just do it. To be more precise, two of the chapters are theory-development enterprises; the third provides something just as valuable but perhaps more rare — a thoroughgoing criticism of extant theory. Steven Maynard-Moody and Marisa Kelly offer one of the most original chapters in this volume. Focusing on one of the most time-honored questions in public administration — the politics-administration dichotomy — the authors rely on public managers' stories as a data source. These are not the case-study "stories" referred to by Behn, Kettl, and others in this book; they are not elicited in the same manner or organized in the same way. As Maynard-Moody and Kelly explain, they looked for existing stories with "an organizational life longer than gossip." The authors were not even particularly concerned with the accuracy of the stories, since they were less interested in a historical record than in developing insights into public managers' thinking. After relating several illustrative stories, Maynard-Moody and Kelly describe recurring dimensions of stories. They used a computer program to analyze the structure of the stories they gathered, and the program produced diagrams for the basic scripts. Each script was then analyzed. Analysis of managers' perceptions of elected officials was of particular concern. The stories often indicate negative views of elected officials, who are perceived as rude, pompous, and deceitful (perhaps these views are not unlike the general electorate's perceptions of politicians).

Robert T. Golembiewski takes on the "Blacksburg Manifesto" produced by Gary Wamsley and his colleagues under the title *Refounding Public Administration*. Wamsley and his colleagues argue that a stronger, activist public service should replace the existing neutral competence and protection, which, in their view, has limited the effectiveness of public managers. Golembiewski develops a set of criteria to evaluate the premises of *Refounding*. Among the several criticisms Golembiewski aims at *Refounding* is that it does not seem amenable to empirical test. A related criticism is that it provides no operational guidance for its implementation.

In the final chapter of Part Three, Laurence E. Lynn, Jr., presents a model of social policy implementation. His model draws on many of the concepts he advances in his commentary in Part One of this book, particularly the notion of public management "games." Lynn presents the prisoner's dilemma in social welfare administration, depicting games from the standpoint of the service worker, the public manager, and the policy maker. Lynn argues that sound prescriptive advice is likely to result from a public management research agenda that focuses on hierarchical relations in public bureaucracies and on the bases for participants' assessments of payoffs in the various policy and management games.

8

STORIES PUBLIC MANAGERS TELL ABOUT ELECTED OFFICIALS: MAKING SENSE OF THE POLITICS-ADMINISTRATION DICHOTOMY

Steven Maynard-Moody,
Marisa Kelly

*I*ncreasingly over the past two decades, organizational scholars have stressed the importance of "sense making" and culture in understanding public and private management (Weick, 1979, 1987; for reviews, see Harmon and Mayer, 1986, chap. 11, and Palumbo and Maynard-Moody, 1991, pp. 64–67). But what kind of sense are managers making and passing on? We examine this question by interpreting a set of stories, or folk tales, collected in several state government organizations.

Not all organizational activities require the same amount of organizational sense making. Attention here focuses on problems that are at once ambiguous and important (Feldman, 1989, chap. 1). For that reason, this study examines stories about the interrelationship between agencies and elected officials. The basic legitimacy and the continuing resources of public organizations are derived from elected officials (Bozeman, 1987, chap. 1), but the only normatively consistent guide for this most basic relationship—the politics-administration dichotomy—does not describe the inner workings of the administrative state. Belief in the separation of politics from administration has deep intellectual roots in the theory and practice of public administration (Wilson, 1887) but is the source of ongoing controversy: "Everyone 'knows' that policy making and administration should be kept distinct. At the same time, everyone 'knows' that policy making and administration cannot be kept distinct and that the distinction itself is difficult to make precise" (March and Olsen, 1989, p. 141).

We would like to thank David Heise, Dvora Yanow, Martha Feldman, and the conference participants for their helpful suggestions.

Thus the relationship between politics and administration is both important and ambiguous. Public managers are preoccupied with elected officials. They are continually pleading for resources, fending off improper requests, nurturing constructive relationships, and providing or withholding information. Relationships with elected officials are central to the work of public organizations; working relationships between public managers and elected officials are the foundation of successful policies, programs, and careers. In short, this relationship is the stuff of good stories.

This chapter examines a set of stories, told by public managers, about working with elected officials. Although they are often brief, they provide a glimpse into the complex and cloudy world of public management. They cannot easily be reduced to one-dimensional norms of behavior, but that does not mean that these and other stories have no practical impact on public organizations. However diverting, they are not just diversions. The articulation and communication of views and beliefs is central to organizations. As March asserts (1984, p. 32), "We live by the interpretations we make, becoming better or worse through the meaning we impute to events and institutions."

Stories, of course, are not the only way organizational members interpret and communicate. Weick and Browning (1986) observe that argument is also central to organizational communication. March and Sevon (1984) note that gossip is the most prevalent form of intraorganizational communication (see also Eder and Enke, 1991). Nevertheless, stories may hold particular interest. For example, earlier research has shown that stories are important in socialization. Van Maanen (1978) describes how "war stories" told to police academy students play a central role in preparing recruits for life on the streets.

In this research, we looked for stories that bureaucrats tell each other, not stories that were invented for researchers alone. We also looked for stories that have existed for some time, stories with an organizational life longer than gossip. These stories did not have to be true, in the sense of accurately recalling events; in fact, the older the story, the more likely it was to be embellished. To the extent that we succeeded in collecting such stories—told and retold in the organizations, independently of our effort to collect them— we collected living artifacts of organizational sense making, stories that are true in a *subjective* sense. Such stories are "impressionist tales" told by the native, not by the researcher (Van Maanen, 1988, chap. 5).

Before analyzing these stories and discussing methods and prior research, we will repeat four of them as illustrations for the reader, one story from each category that guided our analysis. We have given each story a descriptive title.

Story 1: The Impractical Joke

John, a social worker in a large state agency, was at his desk, trying to complete his paperwork when he received a call.

"This is Governor Smith. I'm calling to find out why you haven't helped the Jones family with their adoption."

Smith had recently taken office and had campaigned on the promise to be an accessible and involved governor.

John, although he had worked for twelve years in the state agency, had never met this or any previous governor. He was a government employee, but he had rarely seen or talked to any elected officials. That was for "the people upstairs." John was sure that one of the other social workers had put somebody up to this, as a joke. His office was full of pranksters; maybe that was how they kept from going crazy.

"Who is this again?" John asked.

"I'm Governor Smith."

"Yeah, right!" John said.

The governor became very irritated.

"You're going to be hearing from Secretary Martin," he said, "and you'll learn not to forget who's boss."

Secretary Martin was the head of the department.

"Yeah, sure!" John said again.

The governor did call Secretary Martin, who sent a memorandum warning that the governor did sometimes call caseworkers. The memo instructed the caseworkers to politely direct all such calls to the secretary's office. No disciplinary action was taken.

Story 2: Trying to Out-Politick the Politician

Several years ago, during the gubernatorial election, a high-ranking public employee union official became frustrated with the incumbent governor. The official sent out eight hundred letters to members of his local, employees of one of the maximum-security prisons. He asked the members to vote for the challenger and gave detailed reasons why the incumbent was unfit for office. The incumbent governor won the election, however.

Within the first year of his new term, the state faced a severe budget crisis. The governor began to reduce funds appropriated for staff and supplies throughout the state. In addition to imposing hiring freezes on the agency where the union official was employed, the governor surprised most people in the state by his recommendation to shut down the maximum-security prison where the union members were employed.

The news media, of course, began coverage of the governor's recommendation. Union members in the town where the institution was, as well as the local chamber of commerce, called for rallies, wrote letters to the editor, and wrote to elected officials. (In their efforts to put pressure on the governor, the union members and the union leader did not want to go public with the information that the union leader had used official stationery, mailing privileges, and tax dollars to try to defeat the governor in the recent election.) The governor ultimately changed his official position on closing the institution, but he continued to impose hiring freezes on the agency until the union official resigned.

Story 3: Do What I Want, Not What I Ask

The county commissioners called me on the carpet one day. It was because a woman had come through town with five or six kids and had wanted to be put on welfare.

I had said, "We just ran out of application forms. The best I can do is take you across the street and get you $25 worth of groceries, a tank of gas, and out of town."

Well, I didn't know that the NAACP had put her up to it. It was a setup. She went to the county attorney, the county commission, and the director of the welfare agency. That's when they called me in.

I said, "Commissioners, I've never lied to you before, and I'm not going to start now. I told the woman that we were out of forms simply because I could tell she was a troublemaker. But I also told her I'd get her kids some milk and get her some food and a tank of gas. I didn't think you'd want her in the county."

They said, "Thank you, Jim. Thank you."

Two or three days later, it appeared in the newspaper, and I was fired. They had no choice, but the day they fired me, the state director of the welfare office called me and offered me a job that paid better. That's how it works.

Story 4: Swallowing the Whistle

Legislators are always coming out here on tours. The top administrators always prep us on what to say; they don't want anyone complaining to anybody about being short of money or not doing the job or whatever. So they bring the legislator on the ward.

The legislator looks at an employee when the boss is standing right there, and he says, "Is everything fine?" And we say, "Yup." That happens all the time. It frustrates employees no end.

The legislators go back downtown and they think they've seen an objective view. They come out for reviews, and it's a very canned tour.

Earlier Research

The current literature on organizational stories falls into three categories: epistemological argument, text studies, and storytelling process studies. Providing an example of the first group, Hummel (1990, 1991) argues that managers tell stories to socially construct and then comprehend their world. He also argues that stories conform to standards of accuracy and intersubjectivity that are as rigorous as the more commonly accepted social science standards of reliability and validity (see also Van Maanen, 1988, chap. 2). He implores scholars to pay attention to these stories. Others have argued strongly for the importance of stories in understanding organizational communications (Weick and Browning, 1986) and culture (Ott, 1989, pp. 32–33; Dandridge, 1985). These epistemological claims lay the groundwork for empirical studies of stories, such as this one.

The studies that examine specific texts take several forms. Fiol (1989) has applied semiotic analysis to corporate reports, which are official stories written to bolster public image. Martin, Feldman, Hatch, and Sitkin (1983) examine several stories that, paradoxically, define the unique culture of specific organizations but are remarkably similar to stories told in other, very different, organizations. Mahler (1988) examines stories told by Agency for International Development officials. She finds archetypal myth themes, such as the heroic quest, in these bureaucratic stories. Mitroff and Kilmann (1975, 1976) have studied stories told by managers about their ideal organizations, finding that managers with similar personality types tell similar stories. They have also found that these different personality types explain a wide variety of organizational characteristics, and that paying attention to organizational stories can aid problem solving.

Boje (1991, p. 107) writes, "Text research does not capture basic aspects of the situated language performance, such as how a story is introduced into the ongoing interaction, how listeners react to the story, and how the story affects subsequent dialogue." Since the meaning of any story is based on the joint interpretation of tellers and listeners, Boje examines not the isolated text but the storytelling process. He argues that the context is especially important, since most organizational stories are terse and incomplete; their meanings depend largely on the shared context that tellers and listeners bring to the storytelling process.

Story performance is important, but Boje's point does not negate the value of text research. The stories that are useful in understanding the basic relationships being explored in this chapter are not abstract canvases, open to infinite interpretation. While they evoke diverse interpretations from different listeners in different situations, they are not blank slates. Despite their diverse interpretations, texts are interesting because they are grounded in common, underlying experiences and beliefs (Fiol, 1989, p. 278). Interesting stories must restrict possible meanings so that they can communicate across times, places, and people. The problem of text-based research is to uncover and describe the tacit meaning or meanings *implied* in a given story but *realized* only through such processes as those described by Boje (1991).

Nature of Stories

To varying degrees, stories are composed of two elements—details, and scripts. Each will be discussed in turn.

Details. Details are the unique elements of a story—added information about setting, character, or events that make the particular story subtly different from others with the same basic events and roles. Details give stories richness and flavor that make them memorable and complex. Details provide what Schank (1990) calls "multiple indices," which allow us to recall the same story in response to different cues; perhaps a detail about setting or character brings the story back to mind. Schank argues that stories are the basis of memory because of such multiple indices.

Details also communicate a level of complexity beyond the basic story line. For example, in "The Impractical Joke," the detail that the social worker was at his desk reinforces both the image of his isolation from elected officials and his diligence, which made the governor's call even more disrupting. The detail that his co-workers were always playing practical jokes to leaven the routine adds dramatic credibility to the social worker's rudeness to the governor. To embellish a story, storytellers often add details to events and characters, although they may not be consciously adding or deleting details for effect. Storytellers and listeners (including outsiders, such as researchers) may interpret details differently. However rooted they may be in historical events, stories are fictions created (and recreated) to convey meaning; accuracy is less important than interpretation. Nevertheless, details are tangible text elements that storytellers choose, however unconsciously. "The Impractical Joke" would communicate very different meanings if it began with John playing solitaire at his desk rather than completing his paperwork.

Scripts. Scripts are the more generalizable elements of a story. They are the bones that support the flesh of details. A script is a structure that describes an appropriate sequence of events. It gives a stereotyped sequence of actions that define a well-known situation (Schank and Abelson, 1977, chap. 3). A script is composed of roles, a set of standard events, and causal statements. There can be simple, straightforward sequences or complex structures with various optional or contingent branches. Schank and Abelson describe a restaurant script, which includes the roles of waiters and diners and such common event sequences as ordering and serving, which are relatively constant across similar settings. In general, a script, like a story, is defined by a particular point of view. Our stories are told from the point of view of state bureaucrats; elected officials would tell very different stories.

A script sets up a set of expectations about what will happen next, and this is important to the script's role in sense making. To borrow from Schank and Abelson, as we enter a restaurant we attend to certain cues, to discern which script is appropriate. Is this a traditional or fast-food restaurant? Do we wait to be seated or jockey for a place in line? Which script do we follow?

Interruptions

Standard expectations are important because many of the more interesting stories violate them. The standard-violating script startles the listener and focuses attention on specific details — a character flaw, an unusual event — that help explain the unexpected. Schank (1990) describes two forms of script interruptions: interferences, and distractions. Interferences include unexpected obstacles or errors committed by actors. Often the response to such an interference is a self-corrective loop (keep trying until it works), a self-defeating loop (repeating the same mistake, making things worse), or an emotional outpouring (such as frustration). Distractions are events that temporarily or permanently take the action beyond the script. Someone's choking on a fish bone, for example, will change the restaurant script. Distractions, like details, add complexity to stories but are meaningful only because of the expectations established by the script.

Truncated Stories

A joke repeated by Schank (1990) raises an important question about stories. In the joke, a warden shows a visitor around the life-sentence cellblock. One prisoner says, "Eleven," and all the others laugh. When the laughter dies down, another calls out, "Twenty-seven," again cracking up the inmates. The warden explains that the prisoners have been together so long that they have numbered their jokes. All they need to do is repeat the index number; the inmates remember the rest.

This joke raises a serious question. How short can a story be — how terse a script, how few the details — and remain a story? As the joke underscores, members of the same subculture bring to their stories extensive shared understanding and need only cues to fill in the blanks. Many of the stories collected for this research are little more than barren scripts adorned with a few details. Some are fragments, with no real beginnings or conclusions. Ironically, the more truncated the story, the more it may tell us about the social context of its telling (Boje, 1991). Interpreting the meanings of highly truncated stories is more difficult, however, and may require the help of insiders. One advantage of studying a number of stories on the same subject is that common scripts can suggest what elements have been left out of a truncated story.

Methods

Story Collection

This research is exploratory, in the fullest sense of the term. We contacted twenty storytellers who worked in eight different state agencies in two states. Most of the storytellers were career civil servants; three had recently retired. We found the storytellers by starting with individuals we knew — most were past or present master's in public administration (M.P.A.) students — and then asking them to nominate potential storytellers. Our twenty storytellers told a total of fifty-four usable stories. Most told one to three stories; one told thirteen. The stories were collected by the authors and thirteen graduate students.

We asked for stories about interactions between agencies and elected officials. We sent a letter defining the term *stories* and providing an example of a story that we had collected several weeks earlier. We met our storytellers at their offices or homes and recorded the interactions on audiotape. After they told their stories, we asked them (if these points were not already obvious) who told the story, who heard the story, the occasions for telling, and their views of the main theme. We then coded each story as one of three types, based on Schank's typology (1990): (1) firsthand stories, or stories based on the storyteller's personal experiences; (2) secondhand stories, or stories handed down from a known source; and (3) culturally common stories, or stories shared by members of an organization. (Culturally common stories may start out as firsthand or secondhand stories, but the links to the original storytellers get lost.)

Story Interpretation

Story interpretation followed several steps. Each story was entered into the computer program ETHNO (Heise, 1988a). (For another example of the use of ETHNO, see Eder and Enke, 1991.) ETHNO analyzes event structures, such as those described in stories. Unlike content-analysis programs, ETHNO guides the user through a sequence of questions to describe the logical relations between events. It then defines a "production grammar" that is guided by a sequence of "if-then" rules (Heise, 1988b, p. 186). The production grammar is hierarchically organized and assumes, as a default, that earlier events are necessary preconditions for later events, and that later events use up or "deplete" earlier events. The program does allow, however, for nondepletion and loops. In addition, ETHNO helps the user develop levels of abstraction and generalizations. After the events in the story are described, the user can add branches that illustrate more general versions of events, such as scripts that are related to several stories.

Analysis with ETHNO imposes a constructive rigor on the interpretation of these diverse stories. It requires the user to examine how events are linked and identifies when sequences violate rules of logic. It is important to stress that the researcher, not the computer program, makes the decisions about the story structure: ETHNO asks questions; the researcher provides the answers. ETHNO then produces diagrams that summarize the researcher's decisions. The primary advantage of ETHNO is that it focuses attention on the interrelationships among story elements and makes the researcher's judgments explicit.

The program also encourages the user to identify logical steps left out by the storyteller. Heise (1988a) argues that ethnographic researchers should consider adding or ignoring text elements so that interpretations correspond to general models. He does not suggest changing the stories but argues that interpretations cannot be restricted to any particular story rendition. Heise observes, "Quantitative researchers, with their elaborate theories of error, do something like this routinely; any particular observation is presumed fallible" (p. 7).

Unfortunately, ETHNO diagrams are not easy to summarize for the large number of stories examined here. ETHNO analysis is more useful in guiding the author's interpretations than in presenting and summarizing observations. Therefore, we will not present ETHNO diagrams for the individual stories; we will, however, provide ETHNO diagrams for the seven basic scripts and interruptions in the next section.

After the basic story structure was defined, we completed two levels of interpretation. First, we defined a more general restatement of the individual story. For example, the restatement of "The Impractical Joke" is "Street-level bureaucrat is isolated from politics. Elected official contacts street-level bureaucrat. Street-level bureaucrat rejects political intrusion. Elected official threatens street-level bureaucrat. Elected official contacts upper-level administrator. Political executive protects street-level bureaucrat." This version of the first story is retold in terms of roles and stereotypical events, not in terms of individuals and specific events. The details that make this story unique are stripped off, but they are not forgotten; they remain important to the interpretations discussed in the next section. The remaining roles and stereotypical events are elements in other stories; they occur in various combinations in many of the stories collected for this research. The restatement is a script, not a story, that is related to the specific events of the individual story.

Second, we then examined the individual scripts for more generalized scripts that might refer to a number of stories. Individual stories do not correspond directly to these more generalized scripts; some leave out crucial details, while others violate the script expectations. The imperfect correspondence is crucial to the interpretation. Violation of script expectations is a central element of the meaning of stories — an element that is understood only through comparison with similar stories. It is important to note that the way a script is written determines the interruptions: if rude waiters are the norm, then politeness violates (or interrupts) the restaurant script. We wrote the generalized scripts to describe a positive outcome from the perspective of the public manager–storyteller. We used this decision rule to identify story interruptions that correspond to the narrator's point of view. (The generalized scripts are described in the next section.)

We also coded descriptive information for each story. Approximately three-fourths of the stories were told by midlevel career civil servants; the others were told by political appointees. Half the scripts involve political meddling or the intrusion of elected officials into routine or properly administrative decisions (from the point of view of the storytellers). Fifteen percent describe conflict, and another 15 percent describe cooperation between administrative agencies and elected officials. Ten percent of the stories address whistleblowing, and 10 percent cannot readily be categorized. Forty percent of the stories are firsthand, 20 percent secondhand, and 40 percent culturally common. Sixty percent of the stories include some form of script interruption. In 15 percent, the principal actor faces and overcomes an obstacle; in 22 percent, the actor makes an error; in 18 percent, the actor is forced, by others or by events, to break with the script. In a small number of stories, the script is interrupted by a loop. The specific interruptions are discussed with the specific scripts.

Findings: Interpreting the Scripts

This summary of our interpretations of fifty-four stories will proceed through two steps. First, we will examine each script in terms of setting, actors, events, interruptions, and common interpretations. Second, we will describe patterns across scripts that suggest how bureaucrats make sense of their relationships with elected officials.

Political Meddling

Approximately half the stories involve political meddling or the intrusion of elected officials into what agency officials see as their own legitimate realm of authority. These stories include two different scripts.

Script 1: Political Meddling in Service Provision. "The Impractical Joke" is an example of script 1. In this script, the street-level bureaucrat is at work, far from political actors and pressures. What is implied in this setting — remember, these stories are told from the perspective of administrators — is that the street-level bureaucrat is diligently doing what he is hired to do (in this case, social work). The actors include an elected official (usually a state legislator or governor), who is responding to a constituent's request (although this is only implied in some stories); a service provider; and the service provider's supervisor.

As shown in the first panel of Figure 8.1, the script begins when the elected official directly requests that the street-level bureaucrat provide either

Figure 8.1. Political-Meddling Science.

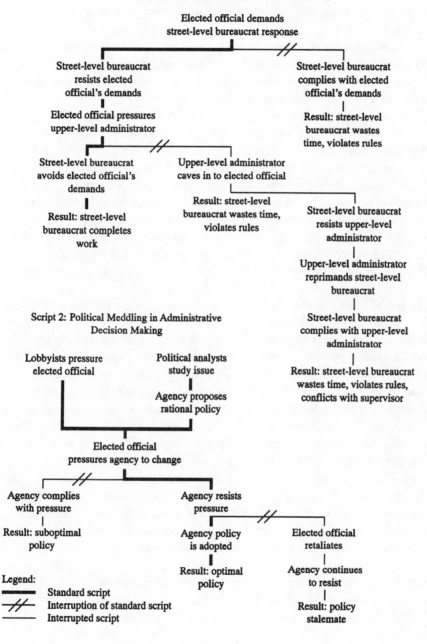

Script 1: Political Meddling in Service Delivery

Script 2: Political Meddling in Administrative Decision Making

Legend:
Standard script
Interruption of standard script
Interrupted script

unusual or inappropriate service to a client. The street-level bureaucrat resists, and the angry elected official pressures someone higher up in the hierarchy. In the standard script, as in "The Impractical Joke," the supervisor protects the street-level bureaucrat, who goes on about his business.

Figure 8.1 and the remaining figures depict the scripts and interruptions. The standard script is identified by the dark line, and the interruptions are identified by the // mark and the lighter line. Bear in mind, however, that any given script can be interrupted in many ways. The interruptions shown here were identified from our sampled stories.

This script has two interruptions. In the first, the supervisor caves in to the pressure, forcing the street-level bureaucrat to comply with the elected official's inappropriate request. Thus the street-level bureaucrat's shell of isolation is broken, and he or she complies. This interruption has an interesting variation. In one of the stories, the service provider resists his supervisor's pressure by writing into the case record that he is putting the ineligible person on food stamps because his supervisor requires it. The supervisor removes the offending passage and reprimands the service provider, leaving little doubt about who is in charge. This version of the story underscores the dependence of street-level employees on the supervisor; they are the buffers.

In the second interruption, the street-level service provider complies directly with the improper request. (Remember, interruptions are defined in relation to the standard script.) The result of this compliance is generally negative: a policy or rule is violated, or the service provider wastes time that could (at least implicitly) have been spent providing needed service. There are three reasons for this direct compliance. In some stories, the elected official seduces the service provider, often by complimenting his expertise. In other stories, the agency head encourages everyone to "drop everything" to respond to elected officials. In all the stories, such hyperresponsiveness results in considerable inefficiency. In one, for example, a social worker "drops everything" when a legislator wants special consideration for a client; after several home visits, the social worker discovers that the mental health client really had no unmet service needs but merely wanted to meet the governor. In this story, the trivial and inappropriate request costs considerable time and even requires the attention of the agency head.

Script 2: Political Meddling in Administrative Decision Making. The second script describes a different form of what bureaucrats consider political meddling: the intrusion of political criteria into technical decisions. These stories are set in the upper, policy level of agencies and involve upper-level career officials, elected officials, and, usually, lobbyists. Script 2 begins with policy analysts carefully studying a decision, weighing costs and benefits. The decisions tend to be technical (for example, involving a pay plan or the selection of a new computer system). After careful study, the agency makes a rational choice, one that is technically sound and not extravagant.

In the meantime, lobbyists pressure elected officials for the less preferred choice. Elected officials in turn pressure the agency to change its policy. In the standard script, the agency resists the political pressure and implements the more cost-effective policy. As in the first script, the bureaucrat and the agency are the heroes.

This script is interrupted in two ways, both of which lead to policy failure in the eyes of the administrative storyteller. The more straightforward interruption involves the agency's giving in to political pressure; it accepts the political choice without much resistance. In other instances, the interruption presents an insurmountable obstacle; but, rather than give in, the administrator continues to resist a choice, leading to policy stalemate. Sometimes the resistance is eventually rewarded, as when an agency, year after year, makes a reasoned request for new cars. The request is denied until the governor's son opens a dealership, which then supplies the cars. This detail underscores bureaucrats' view that politicians are fundamentally corrupt.

Conflict

Eight of the fifty-four stories describe several forms of conflict between public managers and elected officials.

Script 3: Elected Officials' Efforts to Control Bureaucrats. The third script is similar to the first two but is not tied to any specific decision. It describes the more general efforts of elected officials to get bureaucrats to comply with their wishes, and these power plays set up the conflict. These stories are generally set in agencies and involve career civil servants and either elected officials or political appointees. The typical story begins with the political actor trying to assert control over career officials, who resist this power play. In the standard script, the career officials outsmart the political actors. For example, in one story, a demanding and unpopular political appointee carefully monitors the work hours of the staff. Especially annoying is his criticism when staff members do not work weekends (something their political boss *never* does). This detail underscores the unreasonable character of the criticism that bureaucrats are "lazy" because they do not work weekends. Eventually, the staff discovers that the janitor closes doors late on Friday and the boss comes in early on Monday to count open doors. The staff then assigns someone to open doors on Sunday, to trump his ploy. In our sample, no stories interrupt this script; in all cases, the bureaucrats in these tales outsmart their elected overseers (see Figure 8.2).

Script 4: Bureaucrats' Efforts to Control Elected Officials. In this script, bureaucrats are less successful in trying to control elected officials. The setting for these stories is the legislature, usually a hearing room—a change of venue that signals a shift in authority and outcome. Once again, the actors

Figure 8.2. Conflict Scripts.

Script 3: Elected Officials Try to Control Bureaucrats

Elected official tries to
assert control

Upper-level administrator
outsmarts elected official

Result: upper-level
administrator controls policy

Script 4: Bureaucrats Try to Control Elected Officials

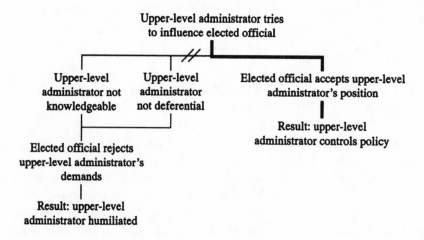

Upper-level administrator tries
to influence elected official

| Upper-level administrator not knowledgeable | Upper-level administrator not deferential | Elected official accepts upper-level administrator's position |

Result: upper-level
administrator controls policy

Elected official rejects
upper-level administrator's
demands

Result: upper-level
administrator humiliated

are career and elected officials. The script begins with the career civil servant trying to influence elected officials, usually through exercising expertise or control over information. In the standard script, the elected official accepts the agency position, and the bureaucrats retain control over policy. (Recall that we define the standard script on the basis of a positive outcome from the storyteller's point of view.) In contrast to those in script 3, interruptions of script 4 are more common than noninterruptions. In five of the seven stories, the scripts are interrupted: the efforts of bureaucrats to control elected officials fail, which often leads to humiliation and loss of influence.

The interruptions are based on two basic errors committed by the bureaucrats. In several stories, the bureaucrat proves to be ill informed, which allows elected officials to regain control. In other instances, the bureaucrats do not show proper deference to elected officials. For example, in response to a question during a hearing, one career official asks the legislator a question. In this story, the committee chair silences him and scolds, "We're the ones who ask the questions."

Cooperation

Although conflict could be defined as interrupted cooperation, cooperation scripts focus on events different from those in conflict scripts. They are not different versions of the same story.

Script 5: Help for the Good Elected Official. Script 5 is introduced not by a specific location but by a statement indicating that the elected official has earned the respect of the bureaucrats. The story may not specify why; it may merely state that the governor is a good governor. Several of these stories take place in nonwork settings, such as after work or on a fishing trip, where place-defined roles no longer constrain the relationship between bureaucrats and elected officials.

The script begins in the same way as the political-meddling scripts, with the elected official contacting a bureaucrat for information or help. Often this request is, strictly speaking, inappropriate. In this script, the bureaucrat admires the elected official and therefore complies willingly. The script is interrupted when, despite the popularity of the elected official among his or her fellow bureaucrats, the protagonist sticks to the rules and does not comply. In these stories, the follower of the rules is punished. In one story, for example, top career officials are asked, in a closed room, to contribute to the campaign coffer of a popular governor. One of them resists, pointing out the obvious impropriety of such pressure. He is punished by being transferred to a regional office. The details from one story in this group illustrate how these stories convey complex messages:

> Oftentimes, legislators aren't friendly to agency people. The normal legislator would call me up and *demand,* not ask. Once in a while, a legislator I know real well will call and *ask* about something: "Could you please give us some information?" Totally different. One legislator is a little worm. He cannot get anything out of an employee of state government, because he's so demanding.

This story contains the basic script: bureaucrats cooperate with good elected officials — the polite legislators — and do not cooperate with bad elected officials (those who are impolite and demanding).

Script 6: Implementation of an Unstated Policy. "Do What I Want, Not What I Ask" is an example of script 6. This script is set in the agency and involves careerists and elected officials. As shown in the second panel of Figure 8.3, the events are simple: the careerist takes actions that are against stated or formal rules of policy and gets caught but eventually is rewarded. In the "Do What I Want" story, the social services director is faced with an obstacle: public exposure of his denying a woman welfare. He responds truthfully about his wrong actions and is promoted, both for supporting the un-

Figure 8.3. Cooperation Scripts.

Script 5: Helping the Good Elected Official

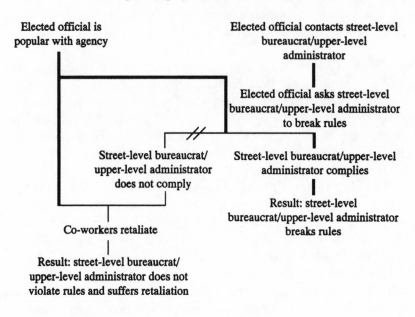

Script 6: Implementing Unstated Policy

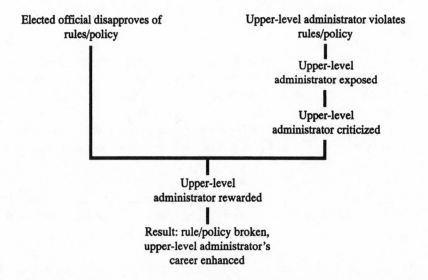

stated policy of discouraging poor families from moving into town and for his truthfulness. He is diligently implementing the wishes of elected officials even while he is violating rules and laws. It is also worth noting that this story is quite old. The event takes place in a county social services office, and these offices were eliminated over twenty years ago. The message, however, remains timely.

Another, simpler example of script 6 involves an agency taking on an important program that is outside its own mandate. Because this program is successful and important to the governor, the agency is eventually rewarded, and funds are shifted from another agency. No stories in our sample violate this script.

Whistleblowing

Script 7: Blowing the Whistle and Bearing the Consequences. Five of the fifty-four stories deal with whistleblowing. Whistleblowing stories are examples of both conflict and cooperation, involving conflict between career bureaucrats and their supervisors but cooperation, at least implicitly, with elected officials. What complicates this analysis is that none of the five whistleblowing stories turn out positively for the whistleblowers. They either suppress their dissent or suffer retaliation from supervisors and are ostracized by their co-workers. The script is based on this norm, although this negative view may be the result of the relatively few stories collected. The prominence of retaliation as an element reinforces other research on whistleblowers (Parmerdee, Near, and Jessen, 1982).

Whistleblowing stories involve at least two levels within the bureaucracy: the central tension is between the lower-level worker, who either goes public with concerns or considers doing so, and his or her boss, who tries to suppress the disclosure and retaliates if the worker goes public. Elected officials play the role of either encouraging or receiving the information from the whistleblower. All five stories are set in agencies. The standard script begins with the upper-level official insisting on conformity and compliance. Elected officials require some inside information, which the whistleblower provides. The upper-level official retaliates, and co-workers ostracize the whistleblower.

The most common interruption, as in "Swallowing the Whistle," is that the whistleblower conforms to the pressure from above and does not give the information to elected officials. These stories that bureaucrats tell each other give voice to the pressure in public organizations to stifle dissent, cover up, and restrict information in public organizations. However heroic, whistleblowing rarely leads to a positive end, at least in these stories (see Figure 8.4).

Discussion

We began by asking what kind of sense public managers are making of their interactions with elected officials. What do their stories tell us about the storytellers, about their point of view? In these stories, descriptions of elected officials are generally negative. They are seen as always ready to help powerful constituents but are more often portrayed as corrupt than as responsive. Elected officials are seen as often rude and self-important and as assuming that government workers are hired to do their bidding. The few positive

Figure 8.4. Whistleblowing Script.

Script 7: Blow the Whistle, Bear the Consequences

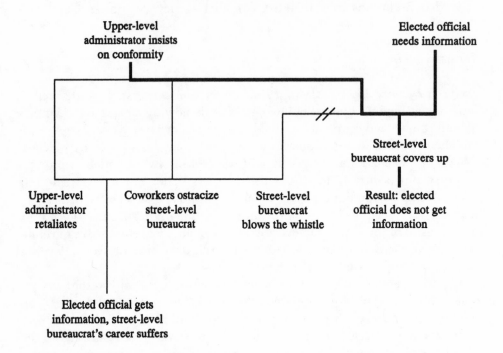

portraits emphasize character flaws (the good governor who drinks too much, the polite but deceitful legislator). Elected officials in these stories cave in to pressure from special interests and disregard or are indifferent to the effects of their decisions on average citizens. In these stories, elected officials serve their own financial or electoral interests even while doing good. For example, an elected official in one story intervenes to help get extra services for a homecoming queen who has been badly injured in a car accident. The intervention helps a suffering constituent, but the storyteller adds the detail that the legislator owns the nursing home that provides the extra services.

These stories paint a very different picture of public managers, who are generally shown as rational, diligent, expert, and concerned about the public and the proper implementation of policy. These stories describe lower-level officials as removed from legislative politics and relying on their supervisors to preserve their independence. Upper-level bureaucrats, who must routinely interact with elected officials, are generally diligent and patient experts, trying again and again to serve the public; they struggle against the wall of electoral indifference. With examples of success and failure, the stories admonish bureaucrats to preserve their expertise and observe proper protocol: the official who has not shown proper deference to elected officials loses influence and career opportunities.

These stories also tell of the pressure to conform within public organizations. On the most trivial matters, upper-level officials assert control over those lower down. The singular message in these stories for would-be whistleblowers is "Don't." Not only do supervisors demand compliance and punish dissent, but co-workers also ostracize colleagues who pass information on to the press or elected officials. The stories describe this conformity pressure as a major problem for government: elected officials do not learn of policy problems until they become a crisis. Conformity pressure separates agencies from elected officials, a separation maintained by upper-level officials.

On several dimensions, these stories are self-serving. Clearly, public managers are not as competent, nor are elected officials as corrupt, as these stories suggest. On a superficial level, these stories are self-flattery. While it is perhaps necessary in the assertion of a positive self-image against the backdrop of disdain on the part of elected officials and the public, on a deeper level this self-flattery reinforces the insularity of government agencies. Although the distinction between politics and administration is intellectually untenable, as most scholars assert, these stories both reveal and construct a conceptual barrier between political and administrative agencies and actors. The politics-administration dichotomy remains important to the culture of public organizations. It serves as an interpretive guide to public administrators (and, we suspect, to elected officials), even though it does not accurately depict the work of public organizations. Stories such as those we have discussed sustain this normative fiction, a fiction that guides everyday interaction between elected officials and administrators and provides a gloss of legitimacy to public organizations.

Study of these stories also tells us about the organizational culture prevalent in public administrative agencies. The literature on organizational theory has emphasized, over the past decade, the cultural dimension of modern work organizations. Bureaucratic organizations have shared norms, values, and beliefs that are understood by organization members and define the context in which they operate, but bureaucratic culture may prove one-dimensional. Our stories lack rich characters, multilayered meanings, and aesthetically powerful renditions. They are generally one-dimensional "if-then" stories underscoring the prosaic nature of government. Despite encouragement from the researchers, no storyteller repeated stories about founders or highly successful public managers; they stuck to the more mundane matters of service provision and routine policy making. In other words, while organizations may not be the instrumental work settings implied by traditional management theory (and feared by critics of modernity), these stories depict an organizational culture that reflects the deep internalization of the rationalized bureaucracy.

The telling and retelling of organizational stories is a vital aspect of organizational sense making, and story texts are intriguing artifacts of organizational culture. There is a great deal to be learned from such stories. We need to examine more stories, told from a wider range of perspectives about a wider range of topics. For example, stories that elected officials tell about working with agencies would add an important dimension to this analysis. Comparison of our story interpretations with those of public managers themselves might also prove fruitful and allow us to gain more insight into these organizations, as well as adding to the methodological debate over the use of such stories. Finding ways to link text research and storytelling-process research could also add a great deal to our understanding of organizational sense making. One procedure would be to find insiders to record stories when they occur naturally in their organizations. These insiders could also describe the settings and the circumstances of the telling.

9

A Critical Appraisal of Refounding Public Administration

Robert T. Golembiewski

Refounding Public Administration (Wamsley and others, 1990) extends and refines an earlier effort (Wamsley and others, 1983) to provide new conceptual roots for federal public management, and the goal is commendable, even vital. The public service has been vilified as the source of our problems of governance, far from being their solution, and the once sturdy ideational basis of the legitimacy of the public service has been severely compromised. Sadly, perhaps tragically, no convincing answer now exists to this question: By whose warrant does the public service manage the affairs of the republic?

Hence, from one perspective, *Refounding* (as I shall call the book here) requires the best that is in all of us, to test what is in it—no holds barred. From another valid perspective, however, critical attention may be viewed as "piling on," as giving comfort to the antagonists of the public service, rather than as contributing to a needed reformation. With the hope that earlier work (Golembiewski, 1977, 1985) establishes my benign intent in this crucial regard, that risk will be taken.

Basically, the ways in which *Refounding* engages its useful intent complicates (if it does not preclude) success in dealing with the broader scientific and practical challenges of regaining the legitimacy so recently depreciated (if, fortunately, still not lost). *Refounding* solves some problems by generating other and more intractable difficulties.

Thus this chapter and *Refounding* reflect a difference-in-similarity. Both start from a common point: that the public service's legitimacy has been significantly eroded, and hence that we need a "new public management," which rests on its own ideational basis. *Refounding* and this chapter differ profoundly, however, on what provides a satisfactory ideational base.

Eight Assessment Criteria

Table 9.1 shows a minimal checklist of eight criteria for the new public management, and the bulk of this chapter tests the adequacy-of-fit of *Refounding* to this general but useful template. *Refounding* often falls short. A rationale for the criteria appears elsewhere (Golembiewski, 1977), and *Refounding* is not given singular treatment in being tested against this criterial template (or, as some might say, being crucified on a cross of criteria). Earlier, I exposed my own work to the same treatment (Golembiewski, 1977), and so I can perhaps be accused of masochism, but not of selectivity.

Table 9.1. Criteria for Assessing Ideational Bases for A New Public Management.

Reestablishing the legitimacy of "public management" will be facilitated by ideational bases that have the following effects:

- Relate directly to prevailing practical challenges facing public agencies
- Avoid resolutions-by-definition
- Support the development of a field, linking analysis and application
- Respect both task and maintenance aspects of a field
- Are tied to values external to public agencies, at constitutional, cultural, and organizational levels
- Frame useful attention to multiple organizational and analytical levels (individuals, interpersonal relationships, small groups, and large organizations)
- Take advantage of a "law of tactical convenience" in prescribing reasonable "next steps" for both application and analysis
- Require and permit testing of empirical covariants, as well as the empirical consequences of value aspects, and this open-system perspective implies a self-correcting potential

Source: Adapted from Golembiewski (1977), pp. 221–235.

Using the Criteria to Confront *Refounding*

The eight criteria are interactive, and the discussion of none of them can be fairly begun, let alone concluded, until all the criteria have received substantial attention. The separate sections that follow work their way through the criteria shown in Table 9.1, even though this sometimes makes for an awkward flow. But no alternatives do better. For each criterion, the text sketches *Refounding*'s position and also usually generates two separate evaluations — the attractions of that position, and its limitations.

Relevance to Prevailing Challenges

A satisfactory ideational base should remedy public management's fading legitimacy, and here *Refounding* fails as it wears its heart on its sleeve. Far more, rather than less, *Refounding* proposes (1) that "Public Administration" is and should be something special in American governance (p. 270), with the capitalization of *P* and *A* leaving no doubt; (2) that civil servants have been unjustly blamed, over the past few decades, for causes and consequences (involving a mixture of freedom and justice with capitalism and state intervention) far beyond public administration; and (3) that this vulnerability is inherent in the basic but effete concept of a "neutral and protected" public service, which *Refounding* (p. 43) refers to as "nonpartisan instrumentalism" and proposes to change, as the solution to the crisis of public managerial legitimacy.

This more robust concept is called The Agency Perspective (TAP) and seeks to blend verbal and operational senses. At its base, TAP builds on a commonsense definition of *agent* as "one who acts for, or in place of, another by authority from him." The authors explain this lexicographical industry as follows:

> These definitions begin to approximate the kind of concepts needed in the agential perspective we advocate; a perspective requiring the individual public administrator to see him or herself as a citizen agent standing in place of other citizens (principals), exerting power *for them and in their stead* to achieve an end, a collective purpose; but always consciously *responsible to them and acting by their authority*. The Public Administrator is thus a "special citizen"; not one with special status or privileges but rather one with special skills and responsibilities; standing in place of and acting for fellow citizens [*Refounding*, p. 117; emphasis in original].

Looked at from an operational perspective, The Agency — sometimes *Refounding's* ideal, sometimes its estimate of the reality, but always essentially the existing administrative apparatus — is "better situated and equipped than any other actor" in the following two main aspects of developing the "public interest": (1) shaping the interactions among major stakeholders so as to urge them toward "a higher notion of the public interest"; and (2) developing programmatic representations of the "public interest," and especially of those subinterests involving functional clusters of stakeholders (p. 143).

Refounding leaves no doubt about this well-situatedness, whether references suggest an "is," a "should," or both. As the text notes, "The *only* possible source of governing impetuses that might keep our complex political system from either a dangerous concentration of power on the one hand, or impotence or self destruction on the other, is a public administration with the necessary professionalism, dedication, and legitimacy to act as *the constitutional center of gravity*" (p. 26; emphasis added). *Refounding* acknowledges this is a "stark statement that some will find shocking."

Less obtrusively, *Refounding* also proposes — on the basis of a similar rationale — a kind of ratcheting-upward of Administration into what was once Politics. Thus the text urges generally that "we should acknowledge, elucidate, and extend the distinction" (p. 43). A sharp distinction was useful in legitimating public administration around the turn of the present century, *Refounding* acknowledges (p. 450), but that distinction never was well grounded

constitutionally, the argument continues, and it has grown woefully inadequate for present challenges.

Attractions. In framing its essential challenges, *Refounding* presents three major
attractions. First, the book's basic intent is to shift the negative political dialogue directed at the public service, essentially by upgrading the common
terms of reference. Success in changing that vocabulary implies a concept
of "high administration" that is less vulnerable to attack, to put it simply.

Second, some breathing room is welcome. Briefly, normal processes
caught up with the upper levels of a work force that grew substantially from
1935 to 1965 and then stabilized. An ideological sea change just happened
to occur along with this aging, and the combined dynamics involving numbers and philosophies served to distort some elementals. Even under the most
stringent conditions there always will be a very large public sector, and it
probably will grow over time.

Third, *Refounding* proposes an "institutional grounding" for "rethinking the role of public administration in constitutional governance." Substantial
attention had been directed at the latter "end of the structural-individual
continuum," as via "radical humanism," but *Refounding* sees these efforts as
"far more useful in rethinking human relations and the role of management
in organizations" than for the focus on constitutional governance (pp. 20–21).
Refounding acknowledges that its institutionalist or structuralist approach has
both positive and negative features (pp. 22–23) but is unavoidable because
we are all social beings and hence "individual responsibility and commitment [cannot serve] as the basis for action and social change" (p. 20).

Limitations. Major limitations outweigh these three attractions. Consider
only three points, one practical and the other two conceptual. Practically,
Refounding is so unrelievedly positive about the public service and The Agency
Perspective as to encourage polarization — one is either "with 'em or agin'
'em." This encourages the forfeiting of a very valuable middle ground, as
I have argued elsewhere (Golembiewski, 1989a). Broadly, that middle ground
has a positive view of the public service as an ideal, while it also consciously
seeks to extract motivational impetus to change from real concerns about
existing structures, policies, and relationships ("no pain, no gain"). By contrast, *Refounding* prefers to redefine "the public service" and hence to avoid
pain, at the possible expense of motivational energy directed toward necessary change.

Conceptually, and more significantly, *Refounding* requires several very
long reaches. Should public agencies play the special role in defining the
"public interest" credited to them by *Refounding*? And if agencies do have
such a special role, do the advertised salubrious consequences occur, on
balance?

Basically, *Refounding* often suggests the discouraging or disconcerting
word but resolutely rises above it on towering waves of enthusiasm. For ex-

ample, the volume at once rightly warns readers about accepting "grand theories" while curiously offering one. Moreover, *Refounding* closes with an appendix of mixed testimonials, including strong concerns (pp. 313–315) about the argument from constitutional, conceptual, and practical perspectives, but leaves those challenges unattended. What is perhaps most revealing, one of the coauthors surveys an approximation of The Agency Perspective in action and directs attention (p. 289) to the "dark side of the strengths associated with a vigorous agency perspective." The text nevertheless almost always walks on the sunny side of the street.

Refounding also offers no compelling contrasts among — indeed, no analysis of — alternative approaches to dealing with the crisis of legitimacy facing the public service. Several approaches to skinning that particular cat do exist, however. The Volcker Commission (1989) gives a broad-ranging critique of current public management, makes numerous recommendations for changes in policies and practices, and especially urges a major salary increase for senior managers as the strategic opening move in moderating the crisis of legitimacy. Golembiewski (1985, 1989, 1990) proposes a values-*cum*-technology approach to improving productivity and satisfaction in the public sector, with such improvements contributing to a heightened sense of excellence, which, over the long run, will constitute an expanding claim for managerial legitimacy, based on the meeting of both personal and organizational ends at work. And Ostrom (1973) sees legitimacy as an intellectual crisis in public administration, due to the acceptance of the centralized views about organization and management that he associates with the Wilsonian school, which he proposes to replace with the "federal philosophy" of Hamilton and Madison.

Unlike these three alternatives, *Refounding* fatally fails both to describe the existential challenges and to prescribe relatively specific ways of moving beyond the present condition. With only general exceptions (for example, pp. 164–177), *Refounding* does not linger over the analysis of what ails public administration (beyond the political assaults it has suffered). Thus *Refounding*'s sense of "here" — of the present state of public management — does not have the specific (if often dour) character of the recent Volcker Commission report (1989). Perhaps *Refounding*'s authors wish to avoid even the appearance of adding to attacks on the federal service; or, as the next section emphasizes, perhaps *Refounding* simply rises above "managerial" concerns. In any case, *Refounding* remains quite general about what specifically is broken and how to fix it. Indeed, *Refounding*'s sense of "there" seems essentially defined by the status quo.

Avoiding Resolutions-by-Definition

The study of public management in the past has been stunted by definitional conveniences. For example, the politics-administration dichotomy was rooted in definitions that promised separate preserves for political science and public administration, as well as a stout linkage between them that also subordinated public administration to political science. Such a deal today's public administrationists do not need (Golembiewski, 1977).

Refounding rejects the major product of this past but retains its method. Indeed, self-consciously and even exuberantly, *Refounding* revels in verbalisms and definitions. Perhaps in its essential form, the focus on "Agency" and "Agential Perspective" is intended "to change our language, and therefore our thinking, to embody, in a more positive and prescriptive voice, the multiplicity of expectations and attitudes we have of public administrators" (p. 116).

Attractions. This approach has something to recommend it, of course. At the prescriptive level — that is, as a "normative guide for the cultivation of public virtues" (p. 115) — it is useful to develop the sense of the "autonomous agential role." Ideally, such analysis could elaborate the character of the prescribed condition, present a convincing picture of how to get there, and identify the likely empirical consequences of approaching or attaining that state.

Beyond ideals, sometimes in practice we can create our own reality by suitable "enactments" (to rely on Weick's seductive term). At base, indeed, this may be what *Refounding* seeks. In this exuberant view, we have nothing to lose but the chains of our ideation — which, since we ourselves forged them, we might just as well now replace.

Limitations. This approach constitutes a very slippery slope, and *Refounding* lacks the required conceptual sure-footedness. Consider only four senses in which the argument exceeds, and even gallops far beyond, its prescriptive boundaries as it tries to avoid recalcitrant realities.

First, few of even the most attractive prescriptions can be enacted, for two basic reasons: the wit and the will to do so may be lacking, and, regularities in nature can withstand even energetic and well-targeted attempts at planned enactment. These issues do not preoccupy *Refounding*. It is suggestive that the basic choice of *agency* derives from "searching for a word and concept with positive connotations" (p. 116).

Second, *Refounding* does not encourage the perception that proposed enactments are well targeted, as in the case of the "public interest." *Refounding*'s argument is sometimes reasonable, as in the passage that says, "Agencies are repositories of, and their staff are trustees of, specialized knowledge, historical experience, time-tested wisdom, and most importantly, some degree of consensus as to the public interest relevant to a *particular societal function*" (p. 37; emphasis added). The basic issue in the "public interest" concept is not in "particular societal functions," however, but in wholistic estimates. *Refounding* (p. 37) does refer to the "parochialisms" endemic in all organizations but unhelpfully dismisses them as mere "perversions of the Agency Perspective." One coauthor deals with the "Defense Department as a test case" and shows that this best analogue of an "autonomous agential role" raises significant issues with respect to whole-part linkages (*Refounding,* pp. 297–303). The volume refers only casually to this demonstration as "interesting" and indicative of the "problems of operationalizing the prescriptive concept" (p. 29).

Third, *Refounding* is clearer about direction than about degree. For example, the traditional politics-administration dichotomy is seen as limiting The Agency Perspective, and the volume urges unspecified new formulations that permit "Administration" a greater "share in governing wisely and well the constitutional order that the framers of the Constitution intended." *Refounding*'s verbalisms get in the way, however. Thus the reader is told — "descriptively and conceptually" — that there is "no dichotomy." However, "again [sic] speaking descriptively" but at another "level of meaning," at least a "considerable distinction" between "Politics" and "Administration" now exists and always has. This latter distinction is the one that *Refounding* proposes that we "should acknowledge, elucidate, and extend." How, and especially to what degree, do not appear obvious (pp. 43, 47).

Fourth, *Refounding*'s specific tactical expressions of degree cover a broad range. "*The* normative guide" urges a special and "autonomous agential role" (p. 115), but the proferred calibrations include the following statements: "[Multiple] subordination [provides] the opportunity to shape events" (p. 81); "The link between subordination to constitutional masters and freedom to choose among them preserves the instrumental character of Public Administration and the autonomy necessary for professionalism" (p. 82); and "Public administration [is] the constitutional center of gravity" (p. 26). This range encourages different reactions; but, on balance, *Refounding* seems to solve one problem by risking even more intractable ones. For details, see the "Selected Responses" at the volume's end, and especially those by Cooper and Kaufman (pp. 311–315), where Cooper asks (p. 313), "Why not simply surrender and declare for bureaucracy over democracy?" (One such approach builds aspects of democracy into administration, and this avoids the conceptual issues emphasized by Cooper; see Golembiewski, 1985, 1989, 1990, where the basic goal is more limited than that of *Refounding*.)

This illustrative catalogue of problems with *Refounding*'s reliance on flexible verbalisms and definitions establishes that the volume's method does not support the comprehensive action research necessary for getting from here to there. Ideally, mutually heightening synergy develops between working aspirations and practical ways and means, as the former provide guidance and the latter reflect appropriate grounding.

One way *Refounding* inhibits itself as it seeks to define a distinctive turf (p. 36) involves acceptance of Wallace Sayre's catchy conclusion that business and public administration are alike in all unimportant respects. What is paramount, however, is that the judgment of whether all generic management features are "unimportant" should be based not on "in/out" definitions but on situational analysis, which neither Sayre nor *Refounding* provide.

Some solid generic foundations for analysis and action do exist. Consider "trust," for example. Its conceptual linkages to central organizational dynamics have long been accepted (see Gibb, 1972). Research has replicated trust's significant network of associations at work, in both public and private work settings (Boss, 1978). Trust dynamics have significant implications for a broad range of organizational features — for interaction and structure, as well as for policy and procedures. Trust-related efforts have been successful in developing organizations with high involvement and quick-reaction capabilities (see Golembiewski and Kiepper, 1989).

Further, *Refounding* seeks to rise above testing itself against such foundations through inflexible distinctions between "institutions" and "management," with (I suppose) interpersonal trust being assigned to the latter and *Refounding* focusing on the former. This definitional segmentation has serious costs. Directly, strong evidence indicates that the long-existing institutions of public administration are trust-inhibiting (see Golembiewski, 1979). This requires some crucial choices. One can specify the costs and choose to bear them. One can retain the basic institutional framework while providing various buffers for its effects. Or one can variously change or modify institutional arrangements to reduce the costs.

Refounding defines such issues as beyond its scope, or it merely neglects them. The text proudly notes its being institutionally grounded (pp. 20–22), but the volume is nowhere very specific. This implies retaining existing agency policies and practices while upgrading the image of the civil servant, which presents dual difficulties. Practically, this may be awkward or even impossible. For example, portraits of public administrators as heroic (Glazer and Glazer, 1989) feature their institutions as common obstacles, and even as predators. Theoretically, moreover, reinforcing the status quo inhibits taking advantage of features like high-trust formation that seem central in the organizations of the future (Golembiewski and Kiepper, 1989; Perkins, Nieva, and Lawler, 1983).

Linking Analysis and Application

Insistently, and even curiously, earlier approaches to public management have been uncomfortable about being seen as praxis — that is, as an interaction of analysis and application. At the pejorative worst, Simon was criticized for running a fire station instead of contributing to a theory of flame. On balance, *Refounding* not only continues that tradition but, in the process, also contributes to major double binds, even as the volume prominently (pp. 6–7) raises its "pracademic" colors.

As noted, the volume's basic focus is on changing the vocabulary and the nature of the political dialogue of the previous decade or so. Consequently, the view of "application" is quite narrow, and "analysis" has been largely restricted to providing support for the prescriptive model proposed by *Refounding*.

Attractions. Paradox aside, if widely enacted, the proposed prescriptions imply a much more robust "Administration" than exists today, and that (by definition) would help solve *Refounding's* view of the ongoing crisis of legitimacy.

Limitations. Two perspectives highlight how the volume's linkage between analysis and application underwhelms in numerous particulars. First, *Refounding* basically focuses on a "grand theory" whose direct implications for application are both indirect and (usually) unclear. Consider the major obscurities associated with the "public interest" and the politics/administration dichotomy or distinction. Second, *Refounding* insistently but only generally grounds itself in public sector institutions, and it lacks the empirical grounding that a solid analytical frame would provide. Thus *Refounding* deals with the negative evidence of its only empirically grounded contribution by shrugging it off as "interesting" and as indicative of problems with "operationalizing" its prescriptive model. An alternative approach to negative evidence, of course, requires changing the model.

Balancing Task and Maintenance

Earlier definitions of the field of public management have been eccentric rather than balanced in a critical regard. All too briefly, every field is a complex network that requires values-*cum*-technology for why and how to do its work, as well as a social-psychological nexus of references, loyalties, and satisfactions of membership that keep aficionados committed. Conventionally, students of systems distinguish "task" and "maintenance" aspects, respectively. Ideally, the two aspects reinforce one another in self-heightening spirals of growing competence.

 Refounding provides little hope that its prescriptive model strikes a useful balance. In sum, it is largely maintenance-oriented. As such, *Refounding* may seem to provide what so many yearn for in this age of splintering allegiances, but the volume does not provide a solid basis for task.

Attractions. Public managers — especially at the federal level — have been in retreat (if, fortunately, not in rout) over the last decade and more, hence the obvious relevance of maintenance. *Refounding* clearly articulates both its concern and its identification (p. 10) and circles the wagons against largely Nixonian and Reaganesque predations as *Refounding* expresses its authors' feeling-tone: "What depressed us as students of government were the chaos, confusion, the delegitimation of our institutions of government — those things upon which the capacity to govern hinges, regardless of who occupies the [presidency and executive roles]" (p. 11).

Limitations. Bluntly, the issue is: maintenance for *what*? The character of the specific maintenance linkages must dominate. Many alternative ideational networks can inspire maintenance, and these can have a range of effects on task—very positive, very negative, or anywhere in between. Thus the politics/administration dichotomy once provided for the maintenance needs of both political science and public administration, but it did little to facilitate the latter's task activities and, arguably, thwarted both methodological and substantive development (see Golembiewski, 1977). *Refounding's* approach to maintenance complicates task. Indeed, paradoxically, the greater the acceptance of *Refounding's* prescriptive model, the more deleterious the probable impacts on task.

Illustrations suggest the fuller evidence supporting *Refounding's* awkward character. First, so great is the perceived threat to maintenance that *Refounding* implies (even demands) a polarization: one is either with the federal service, or against it. This polarization is understandable under the circumstances, but that does not dilute its negative effects. Basically, the polarization reduces the motivation to change generated in the middle ground. There exists a dynamic tension deriving from the gap between the ideal and the existing (which gap I believe is substantial in all contemporary management). As I have shown elsewhere (Golembiewski, 1985, 1989, 1990), tension can motivate needed changes in public managerial structures, policies, and interaction. These changes relate both to participative values and to operational designs that are substantially tried and tested in both the public sector and the business sector (Golembiewski, Proehl, and Sink, 1981; Nicholas, 1982). *Refounding* acknowledges now and again, that public sector management might be improved, but the overwhelming bias is positively and avowedly protectionist, as if any discouraging word would only add to the already too painful bureaucrat-bashing. This buffers the motivation to change.

Second, *Refounding* reinforces reliance on the existing apparatus of public management—structures, as well as policies and procedures—which many see as part of the present crisis of legitimacy (Golembiewski, 1985, 1989, 1990; Volcker Commission, 1989). Revealingly, *Refounding* advertises "no brief for any particular organizational form" but then emphasizes its unmoving focus on public administration "as an institution of government rather than of bureaucracy as an organizational form."

This analysis through attempted avoidance of practical ways and means does not satisfy when it comes to dealing with our crisis of legitimacy. Although they differ in many other regards, the three alternative views identified earlier—Ostrom's, the Volcker Commission's, and my own—all prescribe major changes in organizational forms in the public sector. *Refounding* could either be explicit with regard to such ways and means or explain why each is irrelevant. Instead, basic reliance is placed on definitions and distinctions that distance *Refounding* from probable and attractive working solutions.

Third, *Refounding* (see pp. 129–130) is very insistent on the uniqueness of the public sector. This insistence constitutes another variety of polarization, of course, and it distances *Refounding* from much useful work with "organizational forms," as in testing whether the public-private distinction is too coarse to encompass reality. Diagnosis is critical in dealing with all organizations, and interprivate as well as interpublic variations can be as great as those postulated between the sectors. Depending upon level, mission, history, culture, and so on, private versus public organizations may differ fundamentally or not much at all (Rainey, 1991). This insistence also removes *Refounding* from the need to deal with (or deny with better data) the generalization that business versus government applications of various innovative "organizational forms" have similarly high success rates (Golembiewski, Proehl, and Sink, 1981; Nicholas, 1982).

Disciplining by External Values

A central tenet of the Western tradition—hard-learned and at times slippery—prescribes tethering collective life by values external to the social unit in question. For example, code words like *Nuremberg* and *My Lai* represent a powerful standard: one has a positive responsibility not to obey illegal or immoral orders. The ideal is not always manifest in behavior or sanctioned in courts of law, but it remains deeply imbedded in our religious and organizational consciousness.

Refounding's normative attention wanders. At points (p. 20), the text locates itself in the normative tradition of the first Minnowbrook Conference: "We hold important the same values as those often attributed to the so-called New Public Administration." These include a commitment to greater "social equity"; wider participation; "a desire to move values and norms to a central position in theory and practice"; a focus on knowledge and action; and a critical view of pluralism, logical positivism, and empiricism. At other points (p. 7), *Refounding* seems to prefer not being bothered: "Doubtless there were philosophical bases for the Manifesto, but in our view it was wrong to spend time trying to dredge them up retroactively."

Attractions. This looseness about values permits definitional sweeps and darts. The volume seeks to be "unapologetically positive" (p. 116) about "Agency," which expansively prescribes that the public service should not only "satisfy or balance the most powerful interests" but also "represent the unspoken interests of unwitting stakeholders," "act as an agent for those citizens *not* present and . . . for all citizens of the nation, perhaps even those of future generations," and "pursue a common good—one that is *distinguishable from what a society* (even one faithfully represented) *thinks it wants*" (p. 117; emphasis in original).

Limitations. One cannot be generous with regard to how values discipline the volume's intended reach and then, three additional points further, support this dour conclusion. Consider the loose tethering of the "public interest," which is so crucial in The Public Administration. *Refounding*'s bottom line is bold to begin with: "Public bureaucracy is . . . *the* leading institutional embodiment and proponent of the public interest in American life" (p. 107; emphasis added). The text grants that this argument "will strike many as unjustified and even ludicrous," but this does not deter a section on "The Public Interest as Public Administration." Indeed, at points, the text almost substitutes an "equals" sign for the "as."

Bluntly, this treatment requires an enormous benefit of a grave doubt. Earlier, *Refounding* restricts its attention to the public interest as an ideal or even gentle metaphor and—most specifically, it appears—as a "process" (p. 40). The "content" of values and preferences encompassed by the "public interest" gets only distal and indifferent attention (p. 41): that content "might yet to some degree be definable." This is cavalier, as one contribution to *Refounding* (pp. 299–300) even emphasizes, and especially because resource scarcity—so much a part of our present and future—highlights content issues.

Moreover, *Refounding*'s consideration of authority is both bold and normatively fuzzy. Many can share the text's expressed need for a "fuller appreciation of the positive role of authority in administration," but not only because it is "essential for dealing effectively with the problem of compliance" (p. 39). It is not clear from the text what this "fuller appreciation" entails, but some details suggest a narrow view. Authority for *what*? Clearly, *Refounding* wishes a more robust sense of agential authority to increase that "compliance" which will add muscle to "The Public Administration," but with no clear sense of what holds are barred. This gives little comfort to those who see basic managerial problems in conventional views of authority. Witness the prevalence of a "surplus regression," the need for "whistleblowing," or (better said) "ethical resistance" (Glazer and Glazer, 1989), and so on.

To be sure, *Refounding*'s longest chapter (pp. 182–245) deals with reframing the authority/participation debate; but that, on balance, muddies value issues. The chapter concludes that the true role of authority is to facilitate human development (as defined in Jungian terms, emphasizing individual consciousness). The "public interest" is said to be "public consciousness"; and, although both forms of consciousness are "undefinable in concrete terms," they can exist as "people live [them] out with each other." As the public interest is sought in this way, the chapter author expansively advises, we can "achieve *isonomy,* the highest form of government: *rule by all in relationship*" (p. 239; emphasis in original).

What all this means is at least debatable, but *Refounding* seems to offer a kind of value-free or value-relative authority. By definition, the "public interest" becomes "consciousness," which evolves for each individual out of a "value transcendent . . . unconscious." Life gets simplified thereby, in one sense. Here is the clear bottom line:

> Any value system is in principle as good as any other because
> *under the proper relation of ego to self* it is not the value commit-

ments of an individual that shape his or her actions. Rather, actions derive from and are conditioned by the relation of the individual to the self . . . . What counts — in terms of good and evil . . . is how energy is mediated as it moves from its source in the unconscious into action. Evil occurs when [energy in transition] either erupts or becomes blocked (which is simply prelude to eruption) [p. 215; my emphasis].

Here again, *Refounding* does not provide an external normative constraint on management. Indeed, at least in the central chapter on authority, *Refounding* frames (some or all) normative issues in terms of an individual's relation to self — as energy from the unconscious somehow freely results in action when the ego and self are in "proper relation." This neglects conceptual issues, such as the transformation of individual consciousness into the public variety, which constitutes the public interest. Empirically, *Refounding* also neglects crucial issues: how likely are the ego and the self to be "properly aligned"? What happens when they are not?

Such issues, and the ideation underlying them, are hugely consequential. They support a neo-Simonian politics/administration dichotomy, with the latter's province being that of "effective social process" and (apparently) the "rational." Politics deals with the "collective" and the "irrational" — "alternative names for the unconscious" (p. 236).

Furthermore, at the micro level, *Refounding* rests the "Agential Perspective" on values while curiously defusing its own insight. Given a "bad" organization, in essence, sanguine processes and outcomes seem unlikely; and *Refounding* acknowledges at one point (p. 120) that its argument lacks "the developed normative dimension required by our theoretical needs."

The point is equally clear when *Refounding* (pp. 121–122) deals with three "important normative aspects of an institution" (generally identified as a public agency like the U.S. Department of the Treasury; let us overlook that, here, *institution* becomes *agency,* which undercuts *Refounding*'s other efforts to distinguish the "institutional" from the "managerial"). The three normatively loaded aspects of organizations are *mission,* expressed "in institutional language and associated with powerful, positive symbols"; *constitution,* or "aspects of the normative order that have to do with the 'rules of the game' . . . and the rules ordering internal conflict"; and *culture,* which is broader than "constitution" and involves "shared beliefs toward [sic] internal and external phenomena." These three value-loaded aspects can cut both ways, *Refounding* briefly realizes (pp. 122–123). Depending upon specific value loadings, the three aspects can lead either to ennobling or to "disturbing manifestations." So far, so good; but *Refounding* provides little direction for an agency's normative aspects, and that underwhelmingness is accomplished in very revealing ways. The timing is said to be inopportune for such detail (p. 123): "A national security crisis that has the world on the brink of Armageddon is not an appropriate circumstance to make judgments about whether or not institutional cultures have negative versus positive valences." Then our general constitutional design is said (p. 123) to still serve as a "powerful antidote to parochial tendencies stemming from institutional culture." Thus the separation of powers, or the system of checks and balances, can encourage or force more systemic perspectives from self-preoccupied agencies. Finally, and in curious juxtaposition to both preceding points, readers are told that we can "depend on the dynamics of institutions." Specifically, "no institutional normative order is monolithic, static, or homogeneous. Most often they are multidimensional, rife with factional conflict over mission emphases, and laced with distinct subcultures in various states of congruity or tension with the dominant culture" (p. 123). Precisely—hence this element of *Refounding*'s rationale for neglecting the "valence" of institutions constitutes the best reason for concerted attention to value-loaded features.

Life can get complicated in organizations, of course, and so all-encompassing normative perspectives represent a challenge beyond our capabilities. For a start toward such directed normative attention, see Golembiewski (1985, 1989, 1990).

Framing Multiple Analytical and Application Levels

The systems perspective reminds us of a profound elemental truth that we often forget: reality is ineluctably multilayered; hence the criticality of consciousness about suboptimization. Many solutions "work" at one or another subsystemic level but are inoperative or even seriously counterproductive in other subsystems. Therefore, ideal solutions should be self-consciously targeted and tested at multiple levels.

Attractions. The shifting of political dialogues is no mean feat, and sometimes it can even be the very best thing. Thus—although I believe that the worst is behind us in connection with bureaucrat-bashing, and although I see *Refounding*'s approach as neither strategically nor tactically suited to long-run remediation of our crisis of managerial legitimacy—I can empathize with the intent of *Refounding*'s authors and even wish them well in dialogue shifting.

Limitations. This chapter urges two conclusions: that *Refounding* may or may not serve to replace the terms of the bureaucrat-bashing character of recent political dialogue, and that it is in either case ill equipped to guide useful attention to multiple levels of analysis and application.

Generally, *Refounding* has a determinedly limited focus, and the most striking evidence of this point relates to the distancing of a central conceptual chapter (pp. 182–245) from the large available empirical literature. *Refounding* expresses no preference for organizational forms. Such large-bore concessions, in effect, reflect a presumption favoring (or a resignation about) conventional arrangements—relationships, policies, and procedures, as well as structures. And that in turn rejects the weight of evidence of virtually all the relevant literatures—in organization behavior, organization development, quality of working life, and so on—that "organizational forms" matter profoundly (see Golembiewski, Proehl, and Sink, 1981; Golembiewski and Sun, 1989, 1990). In sum, *Refounding* emphasizes self-sealing argumentation.

Consider also a convenient summary of how *Refounding* often actively, and in significant particulars, avoids multiple levels of analysis and application. *Refounding* uses the following devices, when it could have dealt with major issues related to interacting levels of analysis and application:

- *Attempted avoidance,* as in the case of "holding no brief" for any particular organizational or structural forms. Consequently, it remains unclear how and why existing structures and managerial practices can meet the requirements of the participation/authority mode that *Refounding* proposes.
- *Occam's razor,* as in several definitional disclaimers that such-and-such is out of bounds for *Refounding*—for example, the position that the focus is "institutional" rather than "managerial," thereby encouraging the neglect of interactions between the two, which many observers see as substantial.
- *Hasty homology,* as in the substantial identification of personal development and the public interest: both involve consciousness, are undefinable in concrete terms, are apparently transnormative, and so on (pp. 238–239).
- *Inferential leaps,* as in proposing a strong—indeed, virtually exclusive—emphasis on "process" while defining the public interest (and the strong "Agential" role in it) while lamely proposing "to remain open to the idea that [the "content" of the public interest] might yet to some degree be definable" (p. 41).
- *Whole/part confusions,* as in numerous assertions that, because some lesser proposition is arguable or even reasonable, it follows that a very much broader version deserves or demands support. The "Agential" role is said to be supported or legitimated by the lower-octane position that the "unique task and experience [of specific public agencies] is worth far more than we have been willing to acknowledge up until now" (p. 37).
- *Claims of allegedly inopportune timing,* as in "this critical juncture in world affairs is not the time" to assess the normative character of agency cultures (p. 123).

Taking Tactical Advantage

The common wisdom rightly observes that if we do not know or care where we are going, any approach will do. But such clarity about "there" does not suffice, perhaps most of all when the vision is especially attractive or even noble. Without a relatively clear map for getting from "here" to some proximate "there," the prognosis is poor, however ennobling the proposed locus.

Attractions. Refounding takes a global approach and is basically preoccupied with supporting its grand theory. Therefore, its overriding concern is with "going all the way," rather than with taking a convenient next step. To be sure, *Refounding* (see pp. 12–13) does, at points, characterize its argument as having tentative, organic, and even serendipitous qualities, but these caveats do not deflect, much less deter, the self-sealing character of the ideational enterprise.

Limitations. Refounding pays infrequent attention to tactical convenience and charts few or no reasonable next steps for getting from "here" to "there." In sum, its verbalizations about "there" can soar and inspire, but its prescriptions for how to move from "here" typically are rare and incomplete. The chapter on authority and participation is neither sufficiently linked with nor differentiated from those large and growing literatures (in organization development and quality of working life) that provide the most explicit available theory and experience with participation and with associated nontraditional organizational forms and behaviors. In general, *Refounding* does not build on the existing literatures or even engage them. This does not bode well for *Refounding:* numerous evaluations show high success rates for a broad family of participative applications, taking into account methodological features of the research designs (Golembiewski and Sun, 1989, 1990). A chapter that provides an effective constitutional exegesis is learnedly clear about "there" but, at its base, reflects only a hopeful sense of decreasing the distance from "here." Revealingly, its author urges at one point (p. 81) that "by grounding our thinking about the Public Administration in the Constitution, we can transform erstwhile lackeys, leakers, obstructionists, and whistleblowers into administrative statesmen." This may occur, and perhaps even because of what *Refounding* proposes; but *how* remains far from clear, granting the attractiveness of the ideals and the forcefulness of their statement. Finally, the volume's most serious effort to provide operational guidance has mixed and even ironic features. *Refounding* professes rootedness in today's institutions but provides only a single test case. Thus one coauthor focuses on the Department of Defense as a favorable test-prototype of "agency" but quickly comes (pp. 285 ff.) to dwell on the "worrisome aspects of the case."

Testing via an Open-System Perspective

An ideal ideational base for the new public administration will require and permit empirical testing. This reflects an open system, in the critical sense that such testing implies a potential for self-correction. An ideal ideational base will help generate the motivation and discipline to actuate this potential, which is no simple task in that self-fulfilling tendencies commonly characterize human affairs.

This open-system perspective operates in two related ways that are often practically and conceptually at odds. First, and more directly, empirical features of public management models require testing for any regularities in nature. In sum, under what conditions does X covary with Y? Second, the empirical aspects of associated values also require open-system attention, and this poses greater challenges. Thus core values require explicit attention, in terms of choice making, specifying facilitative conditions and the probability of inducing them, and assessing these facilitative conditions normatively as well as empirically.

Refounding neglects such open-system perspectives — not totally, but far more rather than less. The chapter on authority and participation illustrates this tendency as it responds to its key question (p. 182): "whether and/or to what extent *participation* is 'better' or 'worse' than centralized or unilateral decision processes." However, the analysis unhelpfully ends just where that literature begins. The chapter's author merely observes (pp. 231-232), as he concludes his argument, that participation requires some degree of maturation and development; that maturation and development in turn depend on an authoritative institution, as well as on the exercise of authority appropriate to their existing levels; and that "effective participation requires authority" and "effective authority requires participation."

Conclusions

Refounding does not measure up well to the eight criteria serving here as a template for the development of public administration as a field of application and analysis. *Refounding* may influence our political dialogue, but it leaves much else undone or awkwardly framed.

10

Policy Achievement as a Collective Good: A Strategic Perspective on Managing Social Programs

Laurence E. Lynn, Jr.

*A*n important type of legislation directs public bureaucracies to increase social welfare by producing changes in individual attributes and behavior thought to have unacceptable social consequences.[1] For example, such federal legislation as the Family Support Act, the Education for All Handicapped Children Act, the Foster Care and Adoption Assistance Act, the Child Support Enforcement Program, the Family Violence Prevention and Services Act, the Americans with Disabilities Act, and the Job Training Partnership Act seek to change people and organizations in order to obtain collective benefits, such as a more just distribution of opportunity and obligations, greater security from undeserved or unforeseen adversity, and fuller utilization of a society's human potential.[2]

The results of bureaucratic activity on behalf of such ambitious legislative mandates are mixed at best, however, and usually disappointing, both to their sponsors and to the public. The hoped-for changes in attributes or behavior do not occur or are of insignificant extent or effect. There may be unintended, adverse consequences. Public managers, service workers, contractors, and clients complain of constraints and coercion. Monitoring and oversight are unpredictable or inattentive. Dissatisfaction with specific programs becomes a general dissatisfaction with inefficient and unaccountable bureaucracies. Subsequent efforts are made to strengthen accountability and improve results, but these efforts too yield less than satisfactory results.

Why is the record so dismal? One reason is that the vagueness of collective benefits has ambiguous implications for social program implementation.[3]

This chapter has benefited from the criticisms of Evelyn Brodkin, Laurence O'Toole, Paul Peterson, Paul Quirk, John Schuerman, Jack Stevens, and David Weimer.

If the intended benefit is a more productive work force, for example, then job creation, day-care, schooling, training, or wage-rate subsidies might be authorized, each having different costs and consequences for those with a stake in implementation. Suppose that job-readiness services are chosen; there is still ambiguity. Is the objective of job services the mere availability of the service? the effective use of the service by the group whose behavior is to be changed? the altered behavior or altered economic status of that group? the public's approval of the behavior of the beneficiaries? Another reason is the value-laden and controversial nature of the very process of changing people on behalf of societal goals. Service delivery inevitably has moral implications, and intense conflict concerning the definitions of need, appropriate treatment, and desired outcomes is likely.

For these reasons, participants in social policy implementation will have different preferences among the choices that must be made. They will all prefer strategies that satisfy their own interests at the lowest possible cost and exposure to risk. Thus ongoing conflict among participants in social policy formulation and execution is virtually guaranteed.[4]

In the light of this ambiguity and conflict, and of imperfect monitoring of bureaucratic activity and outcomes by stakeholders, some theorists of the state would predict relatively weak policy control of the bureaucracy. The administrative units of the state, according to Skocpol, possess at least some measure of autonomy within which to "formulate and pursue their own goals. . . . [P]olicies different from those demanded by societal actors will be produced."[5] Lipsky argues, "Street-level bureaucrats . . . exercise wide discretion in decisions about citizens with whom they interact . . . . [W]hen taken in concert, their individual actions add up to agency behavior . . . . In general, lower-level workers have different job priorities than managers."[6] Dunleavy suggests that "rational officials in decision-making ranks characteristically adopt a *bureau-shaping strategy* designed to bring their bureau into a progressively closer approximation to 'staff' (rather than 'line') functions, a collegial atmosphere and a central location." In other words, they choose self-serving rather than collective goals.[7]

Yet the literature also reports virtually the opposite conclusion: that statutes and policy guidelines are binding, and goal displacement is complete, right down to the street level. On the basis of their study of methadone-maintenance programs, for example, Attewell and Gerstein conclude that "under certain specifiable conditions, federal policy can be seen to directly determine local program behavior even down to the microsociological level. The 'failure' of local efforts is seen to flow *systematically from the structure of policymaking,* especially insofar as contradictory interests, embodied in policy, undermine crucial resources which local agencies require to gain the compliance of their clientele on a day-to-day basis."[8] Weisner and Room report that changes in public policies concerning the financing of alcohol treatment have altered the nature and rationale for treatment.[9] Financing requirements have led agencies to increase their emphasis on "client gathering," especially from the criminal justice system, and to pressure providers to shift their emphasis from clients' motivation and voluntary treatment to "breaking through denial" and keeping clients out of the criminal justice system. Providers' loyalties have necessarily shifted from clients to the sources of clients: employers, unions, and probation officers.[10]

Thus, depending on the case and the perspective of the observer, policy control of the bureaucracy ranges from loose or nonexistent to oppressive and pernicious. The possibility of such divergent results raises important issues for both the theory and the practice of public management. How can public management research be of greater value to the designers and executors of social policies? How should participants in social policy implementation choose and carry out goals?

The purpose of this chapter is to present a theoretical framework to account for the divergent and often unsatisfactory outcomes of social policies and to suggest directions for public management research. This framework draws on game theory, principal-agent theory, and positive political theory to identify systematic features of social policy implementation and their implications for social policy design and management.

In the first section, I sketch the conceptual approach. Then I discuss the strategies and incentives available to participants at various levels in the process of social policy implementation. Next, I discuss possible approaches to securing greater cooperation from these actors on behalf of the collective goals of social policy. This discussion leads into a discussion of the managerial dilemmas suggested by this approach. Finally, I discuss the implications of this type of analysis for public management theory and research.

A Model of Social Policy Implementation

Assume that social legislation has as its goal a net collective benefit for members of the enacting coalition.[11] The most concrete expression of such a social policy occurs at the point of contact between individuals, here termed *service workers,* and groups of citizens or actors, who may be termed (depending on the context) the *target group* or the *clients.* Interactions between service workers and clients are, however, the culmination of a series of formally hierarchical relationships: between service workers and their supervisors, between supervisors and middle managers, between middle managers and senior levels of management, between officials at the state and local levels and officials at the federal level of government, and, ultimately, between executives and enacting coalitions in legislative bodies. Cooperation and coordination up and down the line can be assumed to be necessary in securing a full measure of the collective benefit anticipated by the legislation.[12]

Each party to an interaction—say, a service worker and a client— may be assumed to have a choice of strategies and a preference among those choices, depending on their consequences or payoffs. Further, the payoffs depend on the strategy of the other party to the interaction. Thus behavior at each level of interaction is strategic and has the characteristics of a game. To simplify matters, I assume initially that each game is played once — for example, an individual applies to a public agency and is either awarded or denied benefits — and that each party to the interaction chooses between two strategies: cooperation and noncooperation. Further, to explore the implications of hierarchy in social policy implementation, I assume three levels of interaction: between clients and service workers, which I call the Service Delivery Game; between service workers and their managers, which I call the Public Management Game; and between public managers and political executives, which I call the Policy Game.

It is obvious that these games are not isolated from one another. The payoffs and strategic choices of the participants in one game may be influenced by events or outcomes of other games. Service workers, for example, are simultaneously engaged with their clients and with their managers. The service worker's choice of strategy in the Service Delivery Game will no doubt be influenced by activity in the Public Management Game, such as definition of job responsibilities. Payoffs to public managers are affected by events in the Policy Game, such as budget allocations. Thus these games may be regarded as "nested," that is, as having interdependent payoffs.[13]

Assuming that a nested-game framework captures the reality of social policy implementation in at least some important cases, a number of empirical questions arise. What is the structure and the magnitude of the payoffs in these games? How and to what extent are the payoffs in particular games influenced by activity in other arenas? Under what circumstances will each party choose to cooperate with the other on behalf of the goal of securing collective benefits for the enacting coalition?[14]

Evidence on social service delivery processes suggests that the games are often Prisoner's Dilemmas, thereby ensuring noncooperation. The enacting coalition (and the public) must therefore forgo the additional collective benefits that cooperation would bring.[15] The public management issue in such cases is whether the losses associated with noncooperation can be avoided. Participants may (if they do not already) come to relate to each other formally, as principals and agents, and seek to achieve cooperation through performance contracts.[16] Achieving cooperation through performance contracts may prove infeasible, however. There may be other strategies available at a given level of administration for inducing a greater degree of cooperation among participants in social policy implementation. The fact that payoffs are interdependent and that games are repeated may present opportunities for participants to cooperate through means that are other than contractual.

Games and Payoffs

In this section, I discuss evidence bearing on strategies and payoffs available to participants in the Service Delivery, Public Management, and Policy Games.

The Service Delivery Game

The most concrete expression of social policy occurs, as already noted, during routine transactions between would-be or actual beneficiaries and a direct service worker. In the simplest of circumstances — say, establishing eligibility for social security (which does not, incidentally, presume that the attributes of the recipient are to be changed) — the transaction between service worker and client is relatively straightforward. Transactions are usually more complex, however, and what happens during an interaction defines the service actually delivered.

Ambiguity, combined with self-interest, influences behavior by both participants in the Service Delivery Game. Each party to the transaction has limited information about the other's intentions and objectives, and, although they communicate directly and may respect each other's roles and situations, neither can necessarily be assumed to trust the other.[17] Service workers and clients alike may have an incentive to avoid or defect from cooperative understanding.[18] Thus a strategic problem exists.

In their exercise of discretionary judgment, service workers and clients alike presumably act in their own interests.[19] Moreover, they seldom have identical interests. The implied fiduciary role of service workers requires them, at the very least, to be on the alert for fraudulent claims. Moreover, the inclination on the part of service workers to control clients is often strongly ingrained in professional norms. On the other side of the transaction, applicants for service may believe their need to be greater than what is apparent to service workers. To the extent that services and assistance are free, clients have incentives to overstate their needs. Thus the divergence of interests between service workers and clients is often rather wide.

Strategies. There has been little systematic research on client strategies in dealing with service bureaucracies. A client's objective is to obtain the service or support he or she wants from the service worker, but how best to do so — how much information to divulge, how much effort to put forth — may be problematic.

Clients are not without advantages in their interactions with service workers. At least to some extent, service workers must trust clients' representations of their own circumstances, needs, and behavior. Misrepresentation may be advantageous: "Client strategies include passivity and acquiescence, expressions of empathy with workers' problems, and humble acceptance of their own responsibility for their situation."[20] Deferential styles of interaction may raise the likelihood that clients will gain the benefit of any doubt about their eligibility or probable compliance with program requirements. Many analysts of social policies nevertheless view clients as relatively powerless in their relationships with service workers because service workers are in a position to grant or withhold benefits and to define the terms of their relationships with clients, and so control lies largely with them.[21]

For clients, therefore, cooperation may be defined as making reliable or honest claims and representations based on respect for and trust in the program and its service workers, and noncooperation may be defined as making evasive, exaggerated, or unreliable representations concerning eligibility or compliance with directives and expectations.[22]

For service workers, cooperation may be defined as helping clients obtain the services and assistance they want (and to which they appear, on reasonable grounds, to be entitled) and interpreting rules so as to give clients the benefit of any doubt. Noncooperation may be defined as administering procedural requirements in a self- or bureau-serving manner, in such a way as to force clients' acceptance of program protocols, or even in a way that suggests a presumption of ineligibility.[23] The former strategy — which may be termed a *social service* or *client* or *empowerment* orientation — implies promptness, personal attention, and assisting clients with problems. The latter — which may be termed a *police* or *case load* orientation — implies deliberate withholding or manipulation of information, selective treatment, impersonal administration, and self-conscious efforts to control and restrict clients' autonomy.[24]

Payoffs. What will the structure of payoffs in such interactions look like? Clients and service workers are likely to prefer mutual cooperation to mutual defection. Mutual cooperation implies that clients are truthful concerning their need and compliance with obligations, and that service workers provide services proportionate to need. Mutual defection implies that impersonal or mistrustful but powerful service workers confront clients or applicants who are determined to beat the system.[25] Administration that emphasizes the payment, on reasonable grounds, of honest claims is likely to be regarded as better by service workers and clients alike than administration in which determined bureaucrats rigidly enforce procedures that ferret out dishonest claims.[26]

At the same time, service workers and clients alike can be presumed to rank unilateral noncooperation as the most attractive outcome and unrequited cooperation as the worst. Self-interested service workers usually garner higher rewards when they can demonstrate that they have met procedural goals and prevented waste, and this is a much more rewarding prospect when clients naïvely cooperate. The worst outcome is to be fooled. Similarly, clients' rewards are highest when they can in fact beat the system — when service workers accept their self-serving claims at face value. The worst outcome is to be penalized for honesty.

The Game. A game with this payoff structure is shown as Game 1 in Table 10.1. It is a Prisoner's Dilemma: the dominant strategy for both participants is noncooperation. Thus, although each would gain through cooperation, the conflict of interest inherent in the gains to both from unilateral defection leads to a Pareto-inefficient outcome.

Table 10.1. Prisoner's Dilemmas in Social Welfare Administration.

	Game 1	
	Client	
	Reliable Claims	Unreliable Claims
Service Worker — Emphasize Client Access	3,3	1,4
Compel Procedural Compliance	4,1	2,2

	Game 2	
	Service Worker	
	Full Disclosure of Actions	Distorted, Self-Serving Compliance
Public Manager — Delegation of Authority	3,3	1,4
Emphasis on Controls and Monitoring	4,1	2,2

	Game 3	
	Public Manager	
	Active Cooperation with Political Authority	Passive Compliance with Directives
Policy Maker — Delegation of Authority to Career Managers	3,3	1,4
Visible Exercise of Managerial Control	4,1	2,2

Note: The numbers represent a preference ordering of the four payoffs, with 4 representing the highest and 1 the lowest.

The Public Management Game

The countless field sites that comprise social service delivery systems are agencies for a higher level of administrative oversight (typically a human service organization, such as a state department of social services) whose mission is seeing that the outcomes produced by service workers reflect the values, policies, and objectives of the organization.[27]

Strategies. Managers in human service organizations are formally bound by a regime of rules and other constraints on their autonomy.[28] Although the literature on discretionary behavior by public managers in social welfare bureaucracies is not extensive,[29] evidence suggests that public managers are able and, under appropriate circumstances, willing to exercise discretion in supervising service workers, and that supervisors are not prone to unquestioning conformity to managerial rules. On the basis of his survey of studies bearing on bureaucratic rule rigidity, Foster concludes that "the 'bureaucracy yields rote rule adherence' aphorism should be dropped."[30]

The strategic choices for managers and service workers alike seem clear enough. Cooperation with service workers on the part of the public manager might be defined as promoting justice, responsiveness, and autonomy in service delivery by allowing service workers discretion in applying professional judgment in each case. Noncooperation takes the form of close monitoring of service workers, to ensure compliance with explicit rules designed to eliminate and punish discretion and to produce particular kinds of behavior, both toward clients and toward superiors.

Cooperation on the part of service workers in the Public Management Game may be defined as honest reporting on cases and candid exercise of discretion in case dispositions (perhaps conceding the benefit of the doubt to supervisors). Noncooperation may be defined as some combination of reporting only what is required, self-serving distortion of information, and concealment of nonconforming, self-protective actions. Noncooperation with management by service workers may or may not favor clients.[31] Justifications include protection of clients' interests — avoidance of stigmatizing labels, for example — and maximization of reimbursement or capitation income and discretionary resources available to the field.

Payoffs. If anecdotal and other evidence is to be believed, participants in the Public Management Game can be assumed to prefer mutual cooperation (which implies the achievement of results through fundamental justice and autonomy in the disposition of cases) and a regime of mutual trust over mutual defection (which implies self-serving reporting of information, documentation of agency actions to ensure compliance with procedural requirements, and mistrust). Moreover, as in the lower-level game, unilateral noncooperation has a clear advantage for both parties over unrequited cooperation. For public managers, unilateral noncooperation (penalizing supervisors for divulging information contrary to their interests) redresses an information disadvantage. For service workers, unilateral noncooperation (dissembling to a trusting superior) may redress a resource disadvantage. Successfully exploiting the other is unambiguously more rewarding than being exploited by the other.[32]

The Game. Following this formulation, the interaction between public managers and service workers can be conceptualized as a game with the payoff structure shown as Game 2 in Table 10.1 — another Prisoner's Dilemma. The public manager compels compliance for the good of the organization and chooses this course instead of creating broad areas of discretion for service workers. Service workers choose to beat the system instead of complying straightforwardly with rules. As in the lower-level game, noncooperative behavior dominates cooperative behavior, and the higher level of social benefit that might have resulted from mutual cooperation is thereby sacrificed.

The Policy Game

Public managers are subject to administrative oversight by political executives, who are appointed by elected executives to provide policy direction to their agencies. The literature bearing on the relationships between political executives and senior career managers, such as program directors, is not particularly analytical.[33] The analytical literature on the supply of goods and services by bureaus contains little in the way of systematic treatment of intraorganizational relationships.[34] There is a strong presumption, however, that participants in these interactions behave strategically.

Strategies. The strategies of political executives are rather more complicated than those of career employees because of their extensive prior, present, and likely future involvement with a variety of constituencies outside their organizations. For a political executive, cooperation with subordinate public managers may be defined as substantial delegation of control to subordinates and reliance on their experience and their reports of program effectiveness in meeting the statutory expectations of the enacting coalition. Noncooperation may be defined as retention and exercise of authority through, for example, establishment, monitoring, and enforcement of requirements for formal procedural compliance by subordinates, to ensure that their behavior conforms strictly to expectations or to actually prevent cooperation (construed as *collusion*) between managers and self-serving service workers and undeserving clients. Noncooperative strategies enable a political executive to demonstrate, symbolically, that control over the bureaucracy has not been relinquished.

　　For a subordinate public manager, cooperation with a political executive may be defined as accurate reporting of relevant data on program activity, costs, and effectiveness and as willingness to identify and solve problems in program administration as they arise. Cooperation means helping a political superior look good. Noncooperation takes the form of self-serving reporting, avoiding controversial or risky actions, concealing (or, alternatively, self-servingly revealing) performance and cost problems or successes, and passively (or maliciously and aggressively) complying with expectations.

Payoffs. A political executive may or may not share with agency employees a commitment to the agency's mission. Agency employees may or may not share a commitment to the political executive's priorities. Strong conflicts of interest seem likely. Thus, while mutual cooperation may outrank mutual defection, for political executives and career public managers alike, it cannot be assumed as readily as in lower-level games. Indeed, it is not implausible that hostile confrontations between political and career executives are preferable to mutual accommodation.[35]

　　It does seem likely that the rewards are greatest for officials who can demonstrate short-term retention of control over a bureaucracy for which nothing is hidden, and worst for officials who "go native" and seek long-term relationships of trust and cooperation with dissembling bureaucrats who have seen political appointees come and go and know how to fool them. By similar reasoning, bureaucrats may believe they will fare better if they can seduce the political appointee, and fare worse if they are coopted. It is likely, then, that as in the other games, unilateral defection is the better outcome, and unrequited cooperation the worse for both.

Thus the game between political executives and their subordinates may be a Prisoner's Dilemma; but, if the ranking of mutual cooperation and mutual defection is reversed, it may also be a game of Deadlock. In a Deadlock, as in a Prisoner's Dilemma, both participants have noncooperation as their dominant strategy; unlike the Prisoner's Dilemma, however, the Deadlock is Pareto-optimal, and neither party has any incentive to seek cooperation.[36]

The Game. For the purposes of developing this argument, interactions between policy makers and public managers are assumed to take the form of Game 3 in Table 10.1 — yet another Prisoner's Dilemma. The consequences of other payoff structures are discussed in the following paragraphs.

Interdependent Payoffs

It should be evident that these games are not isolated from one another;[37] their payoffs are likely to be interdependent, and the games may be said to be nested.[38] If participants are able to communicate with or signal to each other, and thus correlate their strategies, the outcomes of other games may affect the likelihood of cooperation in the game in question, even to the extent of inducing cooperation in Prisoner's Dilemmas.[39] In general, the likelihood of cooperation increases along with increases in the payoffs for cooperation and reductions in the payoffs for defection. In a Prisoner's Dilemma, cooperation is more likely when the attractiveness of defection, relative to cooperation, declines.[40]

The direction of influence may be from the top down. Take the Service Delivery Game as an example. Suppose that the outcome of the higher-level Public Management Game is noncooperation — that is, the public manager chooses a strategy of self-serving, risk-averse compliance and hidden action with respect to policy makers. Such an outcome may affect the relative and absolute values of payoffs for both participants in the Service Delivery Game by reducing the payoffs for cooperation and increasing the payoffs for defection (or both), thus reducing the probability of cooperation in service delivery.[41]

Influence may also flow from the bottom up. Physical proximity and interpersonal contact with clients and peers at service delivery sites in the field may override rigid conformity to rules on the part of service workers, leading to "organizational behavior by cliques, employee noncompliance, sabotage, and small group pressures."[42] Indeed, where service workers are governed by process-oriented controls, clients can influence these workers' success rates by granting or withholding cooperation, ensuring some reciprocity or even collusion in the relationship.[43] Thus outcomes in the Service

Delivery Game may increase service workers' perceived payoffs for defecting in the Public Management Game.

  Which interdependencies will have greater influence on service workers' strategies in the Public Management Game? The answer may differ among policy domains and bureaus, but the presumption is that interdependence with higher-level games will be stronger because of subordinates' dependence on higher-level funding, authorization, surveillance, and rewards. Because accountability is typically upward, noncooperation tends to drive out cooperation from top to bottom.[44] Thus, for example, if action in a higher-level game greatly restricts budgets in lower-level games, then payoffs for mutual cooperation will be reduced, and payoffs for unilateral defection will be increased. The interdependence of payoffs ensures that fiscal strain will cause whatever cooperative relationships might exist between service workers and clients, and between service workers and public managers, to deteriorate.

Cooperation by Any Other Means?

The preceding discussion suggests that there are strong tendencies toward noncooperation in the games of social policy implementation. Noncooperation includes the equivalent of moral hazards (clients failing to comply with the spirit of behavioral requirements; subordinates failing to comply with the spirit of procedural directives) and the equivalent of adverse selection (clients misrepresenting need; subordinates misrepresenting competence or effort). Noncooperation tends to be associated with extensive "gaming" of the system, especially in the form of distorted or deliberately misreported information, the one activity in which subordinates and clients often retain substantial discretion. In our Prisoner's Dilemmas, the "subordinate" participant is presumed to have an informational advantage and a potential conflict of interest with the "principal" participant, due to the attractions of unilateral defection and the penalties of unrequited cooperation.

  In Prisoner's Dilemmas, however, the potential gains from cooperation give participants an incentive to find ways of coordinating their strategies. "Generally," Tsebelis argues, "players can develop contingent [correlated] strategies if they can communicate, if they can write down contracts, or if they can enter into repeated interaction. In each of these cases they can use their earlier communication, their contract, or their behavior in previous rounds of the game to coordinate or correlate their strategies."[45] The possibilities for achieving cooperation through performance contracts, and through the development of trust based on repeated interaction, are taken up in turn.

  One possible solution to the problem of noncooperation in Prisoner's Dilemmas is the establishment by superiors of binding contracts, to secure the gains from cooperation and thus end the game.[46] An appropriately specified series of performance-based contracts might be used to secure diligent efforts on behalf of changes in clients' behavior (such as job searching or remaining in a job) that will produce the collective benefits sought by the enacting coalition. Such contracts would involve the establishment of a structure of contingent rewards and, presumably, a shifting of the risks inherent in social service delivery from the more risk-averse service workers (who do not want to be penalized for clients' behavior, over which they have no control) to the more risk-neutral public managers.

Eisenhardt argues that "agency theory is most relevant in situations in which contracting problems are difficult. These include situations in which there is (a) substantial goal conflict between principals and agents, such that agent opportunism is likely, . . . (b) sufficient outcome uncertainty to trigger the risk implications of the theory, . . . and (c) unprogrammed or team-oriented jobs in which evaluation of behaviors is difficult."[47] These conditions virtually define social program administration.

Indeed, widespread efforts to "privatize" the delivery of social services represent a move precisely in this direction. Privatization can be understood as an effort to substitute carefully specified performance contracts for the more problematic employment contracts associated with direct service delivery by public agencies — problematic because they are not binding commitments, relative to social policy goals, and thus permit strategic noncooperation.

The likelihood of optimal contracts increases with the extent to which the agent's behavior can be monitored, measured, and controlled by the principal. The costs of achieving effective agency may be prohibitively high, however — if the agent's behavior is difficult to observe (for example, as in private counseling or treatment sessions), if the agent is protected from sanctions administered by the principal (for example, by virtue of merit-system rules), if information asymmetries favor the agent (as is the case, for example, in professional judgments concerning a client's need for treatment or assistance), and if the nature of the service is inherently ambiguous (for example, as in counseling, motivation, and homemaker or job-readiness services).[48]

Thus there are good reasons for doubting that binding contracts can put an end to strategic noncooperation. Some of these doubts are based on the intractable complexity of the social policy implementation process. As Rose-Ackerman shows, establishment of feasible economic incentives, which effectively align superior and subordinate goals through arm's-length incentive payments and a minimum of interference with individual behavior, require measurable goals, compatibility of aims between superiors and subordinates, observability of output by the superior, and risk-neutrality or risk-indifference on the part of superiors.[49] Thus, she argues, "uncertainty may move an agency away from market tests either toward the use of detailed behavioral rules or toward the professionalization of the lower ranks."[50]

A regime of rules, as we have already seen, has its own problems. "Circumstantial judgments cannot be eliminated by ever more precise behavioral definitions and rules of counting, since the activity of counting itself is circumstantial. They can, however, be well-concealed in presentations of baseline and follow-up data."[51] Records and reports may reflect what

Needleman calls "negotiated reality" rather than verifiable facts.[52] Reporting one thing, agents may in fact be doing something else. Public managers, moreover, may have virtually no incentive to effectively challenge these practices.[53] They are influenced by events in other arenas, and these events are likely to favor non-cooperative strategies. Thus both principal-agent contracts and rules may just as well be intended to secure non-cooperative strategies as to promote cooperation.[54]

More generally, Tsebelis points out, "communication may be limited, signals may be more or less clear, promises may be made but not perfectly enforced, and opportunism may be present,"[55] thus undermining or destroying the prospects for effective performance contracts. As Miller argues of principal-agent theory's potential to solve problems of noncooperation in public organizational performance, "it is logically impossible to design a mechanistic incentive/control system that convinces every individual in the organization that his or her own interests are best pursued by close devotion to organizational interest."[56] In a similarly pessimistic vein, Arrow notes that actual contracts seldom resemble those that would be predicted by principal-agent theory. The applicability of the theory is undermined by the transaction costs of specifying complex relations, by the unmeasurable dimensions of performance, and by the importance of nonpecuniary rewards as motivators of behavior.[57]

For example, participants hardly ever have one-dimensional tasks to perform: managers and service workers have tasks with many dimensions of varying complexity. In an important result for public management, Holmstrom and Milgrom show that paying a fixed salary, regardless of measured performance, can be superior to performance contracts that, because they are incomplete with respect to all relevant aspects of the job, unduly distort agency incentives.[58]

Cooperation Without Hierarchy

A more likely inducement to cooperation is in the repeated playing of the game, that is, in repeated contacts between the game's participants: regular dealings between political executives and public managers, between public managers and service workers, and between service workers and clients. Repetition is important because it creates mechanisms for participants to coordinate their strategies and thereby discover the advantages of mutual cooperation. So long as participants value the future and can recognize the advantages of reciprocal cooperation, mutual defection is no longer inevitable in Prisoner's Dilemmas. Thus cooperation can materialize without centralized intervention.[59]

Repetition might be thought to be a fact of life in social policy hierarchies, but that is not necessarily so. Interactions between service workers and clients, for example, may or may not be repetitious. Eligibility determination may be a one-time process. Monitoring of clients' performance may be infrequent or impersonal. Indeed, in Prisoner's Dilemmas, avoidance of substantive contact and insistence on impersonal documentation may be the essence of noncooperation. It is not uncommon, moreover, for subunits of a bureaucracy to become relatively isolated from, or only loosely coupled to, other subunits and levels; policy makers may isolate themselves from contact with career managers, and career managers may seldom visit the field.

Thus the possibility of repetition does not guarantee the emergence of cooperation. For voluntary cooperation to emerge in repeated play, "a conditional cooperator must be able to monitor the behavior of [other participants] so as to reassure himself that they are doing their parts and not taking advantage of him."[60] As Bendor and Mookherjee conclude, "in real organizations the problems of monitoring, of misperception, of uncertainty about the underlying strategies of one's colleagues, cast doubt on the ability of decentralized strategies of reciprocity to stabilize cooperation,"[61] although this conclusion depends in part on the size of the group; in small agencies, monitoring may be more effective.

Are there any other reasons for optimism concerning the possibility of achieving the extra benefits of voluntary cooperation? Some theorists have suggested that the most likely institutional form for securing the benefits of cooperation is "nested structures that combine strategies of conditional cooperation at local levels and strategies of selective incentives at the global level."[62] In social policy hierarchies, cooperation in the Service Delivery Game may reflect norms of trust that arise between clients and service workers, perhaps reinforced by the ethical commitments of social workers, shared values and experiences, and simple familiarity. Within the bureaucracy, coordinated cooperation in the Public Management Game may be built on material and symbolic inducements available to senior managers (allocation of discretionary resources, access to decision makers, recognition of success) and to subordinates (ability to provide undocumented information, possession of valuable political intelligence, offers of collateral cooperation).

Formal hierarchies may reveal little of the extensive network of interpersonal and intraorganizational relationships that may have some bearing on the behavior of participants in the system. While this informal system may resolve itself into semiautonomous or "loosely coupled" subsystems — field or regional offices, budget offices, the legal staff, networks of interest-group representatives, appointed officials and their staffs, highly affected professional staffs — many of these subsystems are likely to be linked in a variety of nonhierarchical ways (such as through participation in professional or purposive activities, symbiotic relationships that affect behavior). Thus norms of organizational loyalty, accountability to superiors, or professional values may affect payoffs sufficiently to create incentives for establishing relationships of mutual trust and for coordinated, cooperative behavior.

There is no particular reason to expect that participation in these networks reinforces norms of cooperation, however. A political executive's networks may do the opposite: reify the ideology of control. A service worker's networks may reify an ideology of autonomy, resistance to arbitrary bureaucratic authority, and loyalty to the client. A client's network may reify an ideology of distrust of the system and determination to beat it. Thus, perhaps ironically, the interdependence of payoffs may reduce rather than increase the prospects for strategic cooperation on behalf of the collective good.

Managerial Dilemmas

Viewing social policy implementation as a series of nested games has a number of implications for public management. First, if Prisoner's Dilemmas (or Deadlocks) are as prevalent as the evidence suggests, then public managers may have little rational incentive to seek the collective benefits of cooperation with either hierarchical superiors or subordinates and clients. The problem may originate in the higher-level Social Choice Game between members of an enacting coalition and policy-making executives. But the symmetry of game theory suggests that noncooperation can also originate with signals from clients, or from street-level bureaucrats, that there is a high likelihood of defection or noncooperation in the Service Delivery and Public Management Games.

Second, the contractual approaches to cooperation, involving the specification of contingent performance requirements and payments and the monitoring of lower levels by higher ones, may actually compound implementation problems by increasing the likelihood of strategic misrepresentation and hidden action, thus raising the level of mistrust.[63] The good actually produced — observed behavioral changes attributable to the services delivered to categorically eligible clients — may resemble the desired collective good but differ from it in being "distorted" by strategic conflicts among participants. For example, a foster placement may satisfy particular rules imposed by managers on service workers (for example, by achieving a placement within a specified time), but at the expense of the child's prospects for ultimately achieving a stable family relationship.

Third, public managers may have little influence over the structure of incentives within which clients, supervisors, and policy makers calculate where their strategic advantages lie. Payoffs are likely to be strongly influenced by statutory and policy controls, on the one hand, and by the availability and cost to clients of alternative services and the characteristics, competence, values, and relationships of the participants in the system, on the other. Caught in the middle, public managers are unlikely to have much influence over these kinds of factors.

Fourth, attempts by policy-making executives to redesign the economy of incentives within an organization — or, to put it another way, to redesign the organization's culture by manipulating rules and material rewards — may prove costly and uncertain.[64] Creating a culture of cooperation through noncontractual methods, involving symbolic actions and persuasive communication, may prove more effective but at the same time more uncertain, especially if delivery of the promised benefits or cooperation is expected to be limited by an executive's short tenure in office.

Where does this reasoning leave the public manager?[65] The typical economy of incentives in bureaucracies leaves public managers who are committed to cooperative outcomes with three possible strategies: (1) seeking microadjustments to controls intended to produce marginal improvements in programmatic results;[66] (2) establishing norms of trust and cooperation through the kinds of strategies suggested by repeated-game theory;[67] and (3) resorting to "extra-rational" motivations, such as appeals to professionalism and the ethic of service, to induce convergent behavior by subordinates.[68] All these strategies, however, may require the public manager, in effect, to choose defection strategies in the Policy Game. Their dual participation in higher- and lower-level games places public managers in the difficult and stressful position of having to coordinate their own strategies in different games. The difficulties and dilemmas associated with this kind of coordination, and the unpredictable consequences of the resulting choices for bureaucratic performance, constitute an important explanation for the discouragement with social policy implementation cited at the beginning of this chapter.

Significant change, it might be argued, must originate at the national policy level, in the process of social choice; politics at the federal (or state) level often appears to produce Deadlocks, which are deeply inimical to bureaucratic cooperation. To gain a full measure of collective benefit, members of enacting coalitions and authoritative decision makers must be willing to allocate the costs of effective monitoring to the larger collective benefit they seek, rather than to achievement of more self-serving objectives. They must be correspondingly persuaded to choose or allow "alternative institutional designs emphasizing redundancy rather than specialization, delegation rather than hierarchy, flexibility rather than rules, and champions rather than trained experts."[69] Monitoring of such a choice would be based on comparisons between the actual outcomes of efforts to put social legislation into practice (distorted as they are by noncooperative resolution of strategic conflicts) and so-called cooperative outcomes (which, if they could be attained, would provide the optimal level of satisfaction to all participants). The ultimate dilemma is that this optimal level of satisfaction, founded on cooperative team production within bureaucratic hierarchies, is by definition a collective good to which participants in social choice may have little or no incentive to contribute in the form of reduced control of bureaucratic or client behavior.

Self-interested legislators, executives, and others influential in national decision making are likely to choose strategies that yield satisfactory rewards proportional to their interests, whether material or nonmaterial.[70] Policy leadership is often based on promising that kind of reward. Statutory mandates governing public bureaucracies are invariably a product of strategic conflict and compromise among participants in the coalition securing enactment of the legislation.[71] In the end, to transcend factional disputes among would-be principals, legislation and other authoritative directives often embody conflicting principles of action.[72] While circumstances involving "multiple principals" in an enacting coalition may actually enhance the discretion of public managers by enabling them to play interests off against each other,[73] they may also lead to escalating reliance on process-oriented controls and monitoring, so that contending factions can check up on public managers' behavior and, in effect, on each other.

The logic of collective action suggests that strategies of cooperation will require the efforts of an entrepreneur to induce participants in national policy making to contribute—through forbearance, clearer articulation of collective benefits, and relinquishment of existing controls—to the collective good of serving clients in a cooperative manner. Given the strength of the incentives in the current system, however, an extraordinarily effective effort to educate interest groups and legislators will be essential to achieving the necessary change of heart.[74]

It may be objected that achievement of this optimal level of satisfaction is an abstract and arbitrary ideal, an artifact of my analytical framework and my definition of collective benefit.[75] To the extent that self-regarding participants in social policy implementation choose noncooperative strategies, that is simply the price that must be paid to secure any level of collective benefit for the clients of the American welfare state: a highly constrained methadone-maintenance program is better than no program at all. In a Prisoner's Dilemma, after all, mutual defection is not the worst outcome for either participant. Choosing organizational (as opposed to societal) goals as a basis for evaluating social policy implementation, and finding strategies to satisfy the complex and conflicting interests represented in enacting coalitions, are, one might argue, what politics is all about. Searching for strategies designed to achieve incremental improvements in program administration within the present economy of incentives, then (so the argument goes), is both realistic and ethically appropriate.

Even if this conservative point of view is accepted, however, the question facing public managers remains: How best to incorporate considerations of strategic conflict into social program administration, so as to secure more rather than less cooperation? It is an issue that has been explored far too little in public management research.

Implications for Theory and Practice

Academic interest in social policy implementation is well developed. A steadily expanding literature documents disparities between expectations and outcomes, attempts explanations (or apologies) for bureaucratic failure, and offers advice for improving matters. Readers of this literature can learn, for example, that successful social policy implementation depends on the experience and competence of professionals, on the extent of cooperation and commitment among participants, and on identifying and learning from success models. A typical finding is that public managers should promote consistency in reporting requirements and definitions across programs.

Implementation research favors largely descriptive, static, and anecdotal accounts of administrative processes, however, and has little in the way of theoretical foundations. According to O'Toole, "it consists of overly broad assertions regarding how to achieve implementation success, is only loosely connected to coherent bodies of carefully specified theory, and is internally contradictory."[76] The research strategy suggested by this chapter, in contrast, would integrate formal theories of social and individual choice and of preference aggregation to analyze incentives and choices in specified institutional settings and to predict strategic behavior in actual cases of social policy implementation. Such research would lead, ultimately, to prescriptive advice concerning the improvement of bureaucratic performance in particular cases.

Pursuing such an agenda, researchers would model the hierarchical relationships in public bureaucracies engaged in social policy implementation as a series of interactions in which participants choose strategies in light of their consequences. Such research involves identifying the chain of interactions necessary to social policy implementation, the choices (which might be expressed as objectives or goals) actually or potentially open to participants in these interactions, the payoffs that participants associate with each choice, and the actual strategies or objectives chosen by participants.[77] Researchers would also identify the bases for participants' assessments of the magnitude and the ranking of payoffs or consequences in each interaction. Here, one is attempting to discover the system of incentives within which participants function. Of particular interest is the relative influence of factors internal and external to particular interactions or games. Internal factors might include information asymmetries and their origins, the way actors choose to interpret and exercise discretion, and the results of prior interactions. External factors might include the influence of various policy controls (such as budget constraints), the objectives of politically appointed executives, and the requirements of administrative guidelines and of norms, beliefs, and professional affiliations.

In empirical work, an investigator might focus on all relevant levels of interaction or only on an equivalent level of interaction (say, the Service Delivery Game) in a number of different organizations, either in the same or in different policy domains. An investigator might gather comparative data for organizations widely regarded as successful, for organizations in which leadership transitions have occurred (for example, at the beginning of an administration), or for organizations adapting to an exogenous change in policy direction (for example, the enactment of a new or amended federal or state statute).

The following kinds of questions might be addressed by such research:

1. What are the extent of and the explanations for goal displacement or selection during the implementation process?

2. In what circumstances does cooperation emerge and stabilize? What kinds of games (what kinds of payoff structures) are characteristic of social policy implementation processes?
3. What is the relative influence of policy structures and informal relationships (either internal or external to the organization) on policy outcomes? What is the influence of statutory mandates, relative to policy controls initiated by the executive branch? Under what circumstances are statutory controls most effective?
4. What is the influence of particular actors (such as appointed executives, middle-level program managers, or first-level supervisors) on the outcomes of social programs, and what are the bases of their influence?
5. How do change agents succeed? What is the influence of appointed executives on social policy implementation, and through what mechanisms is their influence felt?
6. What is the influence on goal displacement and on policy outcomes of "privatizing" or the contracting out of service delivery functions? In general, how prevalent and effective are the kinds of binding commitments necessary for effective principal-agent contracts?

Findings from such research might lead not only to refinements of theory but also to a useful classification of implementation contexts and their implications for the design of social legislation and of bureaucratic organizations, for executive leadership, for the conduct of social audits, for the construction and interpretation of social indicators, and for the evaluation of managerial performance.[78]

Notes

1. Hasenfeld classifies human service organizations by whether they are "people processing," "people sustaining," or "people changing" and by whether their clients are "normal functioning" or "malfunctioning." An organization's classification has important implications for its management. See Hasenfeld, 1983, pp. 4–7.
2. A collective benefit is one for which one person's enjoyment does not reduce or diminish the enjoyment of anyone else and for which, once available, it is infeasible to exclude anyone from its enjoyment. See Hardin, 1982, pp. 17–20.
3. This paragraph draws on the discussion in Lynn (1980), p. 138.
4. In implementation of the Family Violence Prevention and Services Act of 1984, for example, Davis and Hagen note, there were two contending views expressed in policy debate, each with significant implications for the organization of service delivery. Violence against women could be viewed as "rooted in sexism and women's powerlessness" or as "rooted in dysfunctional family dynamics." The former would require abuse-specific interventions and efforts to empower women; the latter would

require services to support functional family relationships and sanctions against domestic violence. An agency adopting one of these approaches will alienate supporters of the other. See Davis and Hagen (1988), p. 650.

5. See Skocpol (1985), pp. 9, 15.

6. See Lipsky (1980), pp. 13, 18.

7. Dunleavy (1984), p. 322; emphasis in original.

8. See Attewell and Gerstein (1979), p. 311 (emphasis in original).

9. See Weisner and Room (1984), pp. 167–184. See also Needleman (1981), pp. 257–260.

10. Weisner and Room (1984), pp. 177–178. In this vein, the consequences of hierarchical policy control and strategic conflict can be extraordinarily subtle. A study of federal farm policies concluded that they effectively discouraged innovation and unconventional practices by farmers, locking them into dependence on programs that, ironically, have as a larger purpose promotion of innovation. See Borchelt (1989), p. 3. The consequences of putting a particular piece of social legislation into effect may include unforeseen but not necessarily undesirable results. For an interesting example of a benign outcome in the case of the Foster Care and Adoption Assistance Act, see Testa and Goerge (1988).

11. Participants in the coalition gaining enactment of the statute may have come to share the belief (persuaded by a political entrepreneur, for example) that costly statutory interventions in private behavior are justified because they prevent even more costly social problems from emerging, or because they substitute less costly for more costly interventions. See Hardin (1982), pp. 35–37; Margolis (1991), pp. 83–105. Of course, there may be no incentive to cooperate among potential participants in an enacting coalition, and a Prisoner's Dilemma may result. For the essential equivalence of Prisoner's Dilemma games and problems of collective action, see Hardin (1982), pp. 25–30.

12. This interpretation of public policy as taking concrete form in a culminating transaction between a client and a public official is in the tradition of Carl Friedrich: "Public policy, to put it flatly, is a continuous process, the formulation of which is inseparable from its execution." See Friedrich (1940), p. 6. See also Lipsky (1980), pp. 13–25; Elmore (1982). In a related vein, I argue elsewhere that the interpretation that stakeholders place on governmental actions that affect them is the only useful way of defining public policy for analytical purposes. See Lynn (1987), pp. 28–32.

13. See Tsebelis (1990), pp. 10, 52–91.

14. For a discussion of collective action problems within bureaucracies, see Dunleavy (1984), pp. 299–328. For a discussion of collective-action problems, conceived in a spirit similar to the argument in this chapter, see Crozier and Friedberg (1980), pp. 1–13.

15. In other words, their choices produce a Pareto-inefficient outcome,

forgoing the gains from cooperation. Apart from applying to a great many real-world situations, Prisoner's Dilemmas are analytically interesting in public management applications because the dominant strategy is unstable, given the potential gains from cooperation. See Tsebelis (1990), p. 10.

16. See Mitnick and Backoff (1984), pp. 62–63.

    On agency theory, see Arrow (1985), pp. 37–51; Bendor (1990), pp. 383–398; Eisenhardt (1989), pp. 57–74; Levinthal (1988), pp. 153–185; Moe (1984), pp. 739–777; Perrow (1986), pp. 224–236.

17. See Cox, Brogan, and Dandridge (1986), pp. 603–618; Pesso (1978), p. 311: "As a general rule, intake workers did not develop rapport with applicants."

18. See Attewell and Gerstein (1979).

19. Hoch and Hemmens (1987) report on efforts to incorporate informal helpers into a formal helping system. Formal helpers associated with an agency conceived of service as an instrumental relationship with a client, whereas informal helpers (often friends, neighbors, or parishioners) conceived of service in terms of reciprocity and relationship.

20. See Lipsky (1980), p. 59.

21. See Lipsky (1980).

22. Cox, Brogan, and Dandridge (1986, p. 616) report that three-fourths of client errors in their study "seemed to involve the willful withholding of eligibility information."

23. Police officers and health care personnel become involved in a "coordination game" in deciding how to process mentally ill offenders. The behavior of each party must take into account the strategic choices facing the other: if a police officer escorts a mentally ill offender to a hospital, will he be tied up in a long delay while waiting for a doctor to release the offender? If a medical staff member returns a homeless alcoholic to the street, does he or she risk alienating the police? Mentally ill offenders often end up in jail, instead of in appropriate treatment, because jail is the nonconvergent solution to the Prisoner's Dilemma facing police and health care workers. See Finn (1989).

24. A general discussion of client-helper interactions is in Bisno (1988). See especially his distinction between "helping" and "instrumental" professional actions (pp. 19–24). For a good discussion of AFDC administration, see Schorr (1986), pp. 96–104, and sources cited therein. Of the second type of strategy, Schorr notes that clients "are tormented by being made to queue up, to come and go, to fetch and respond, and to struggle anxiously to understand what is going on." (p. 96). Prottas (1979, chap. 2) discusses the employment of noncooperative strategies by managers of public housing projects. Pesso (1978, pp. 305–330) contrasts ideal with actual intake processes in local public welfare offices. See also Zimmerman (1983), pp. 237–266; Tweedie (1989).

25. "This lack of reporting appears to be done without malice. The fact that AFDC recipients respect the professionalism of the county DFCS workers does not outweigh the perhaps overwhelming need for income resulting from Georgia's tiny monthly AFDC payment levels" (Cox, Brogan, and Dandridge, 1986, p. 616).

26. There is empirical evidence to the effect that "role ambiguity and skill variety," rather than rote adherence to administrative protocols, are the best predictors of job satisfaction among human service workers. See Glisson and Durick (1988), pp. 61–81.

27. Field sites may be units of public sector organizations or private contractors of public sector organizations, a distinction to be discussed. For a discussion of issues in this section, see Friedson (1989), pp. 71–92.

28. The very existence of the organization implies the existence of employment contracts, which regulate management-employee relationships. The issue is the extent to which managers are subject to additional rules in the interest of outcome control.

29. See Lynn (1990). For an interesting general discussion of managerial strategies, see Hargrove and Glidewell (1990), pp. 28–46. See also Meier (1989); Crozier (1964).

     A possible example of managerial discretion is described by Schuerman, Stagner, Johnson, and Mullen (1988), pp. 50–51. Under an imperative to engage in permanency planning for children in foster care, managers might encourage structured placements early in a child's experience or, alternatively, proceed gradually, from less structured to more structured placements. This might be regarded as a choice best left to professional judgment or as one to be governed by a rule.

30. See Foster (1990), p. 235.

31. See, for example, Kirk and Kutchins (1988); Buckholdt and Gubrium (1980); Stern and Epstein (1985); Steinwald (1987).

32. Service workers' attitudes toward administrators are addressed by Halachmi (1980); Rose-Ackerman (1981); Hardin (1991).

33. See, for example, the classic studies by Heclo (1977) and Kaufman (1981). See also Lynn (1981).

34. See, for example, Lynn (1991). The best analytical treatment of intraorganization issues is Dunleavy (1984).

35. See, for example, Randall (1967); Nathan (1975).

36. See Tsebelis (1990), p. 63.

37. In game-theory terms, they are not subgames.

38. It is interesting to note that the original formulation of the Prisoner's Dilemma implied interdependence with a game in which criminal penalties are established. The district attorney describes or interprets these payoffs to the prisoners.

39. See Tsebelis (1990), pp. 10, 58, 68–72: "In order to develop [correlated] strategies, promises, threats, or credible threats, punishments are required" (p. 72). Coordination is necessary to achieving cooperation

in such games as Prisoner's Dilemma, Stag Hunt, and Chicken, where unilateral defection is preferred to unrequited cooperation. See Oye (1986), p. 6. It is doubtful that cooperation will arise in a single play-ing of a Prisoner's Dilemma unless the game with which its payoffs are interdependent is played first and information on the outcome is available to both participants. Thus the sequence of play matters (Tse-belis, 1990, p. 72).

40. See Tsebelis, 1990, p. 72.

41. Outcomes in a client's other arenas may likewise affect perceived payoffs in the Service Delivery Game. Kane makes the interesting argument that "repeated experience with lack of control or being labeled as in-competent makes it less likely that people will recognize potentially effective actions later." Clients' perceived payoffs for cooperating with service workers may, in other words, be affected by their experience of control or efficacy in other arenas of their lives. See Kane (1987), p. 411.

42. See Foster (1990), p. 235, 237. The symmetry of the Prisoner's Dilemma illuminates the power and incentives of clients to exploit ser-vice workers. Symmetry also accounts for principal-seeking behavior by potential agents, such as nonprofit agencies' seeking sponsorship sympathetic to their missions. See Sosin (1985). The economics of a related phenomenon, "influence activity," are discussed in Milgrom and Roberts (1987).

43. Lipsky (1980), pp. 58–59: "If one party seeks to control the other, the second party may increase the costs of the first party gaining or exer-cising control, even if the first is unquestionably more powerful."

44. "The prospect of bureaucracy moving into [informal helping] relation-ships to require, monitor, or contract for specific exchanges may vio-late the rules by which such relationships function, and in the long run destroy rather than support the informal system" Chapman and Pancoast (1985), pp. 61–62. Alternatively, a Prisoner's Dilemma might be reproduced from the field to the top if it is assumed that clients will invariably cheat. See Davis and Hagen (1988), pp. 649–667, for a par-ticularly clear-cut example of how the exercise of strategic choice at the national level affects service delivery. A more general formulation is put forth by Knott and Miller (1987, p. 256): "Organizations that are closely monitored to guarantee their accountability seem often to create incentives for individuals to behave in a way that results in in-efficient organizational behavior."

45. Tsebelis (1990), p. 69.

46. The implication here is that hierarchical relationships founded on em-ployment contracts, the terms of which are independent of performance, do not constitute the establishment of agency. A principal-agent rela-tionship requires that a principal be able to make credible binding com-mitments to agents. Such commitments are possible in cooperative

games but not in noncooperative games, such as Prisoner's Dilemma, which, I argue, are the kinds of games characteristic of social policy implementation (Bendor, 1990, p. 387; Tsebelis, 1990, p. 70, n. 10). Thus as the likelihood of mutual cooperation in a Prisoner's Dilemma increases for any reason (to be discussed), the prospects for the emergence of effective principal-agent relationships likewise increase, but if the likelihood is low, the prospects for performance contracts are low as well. Miller's attempts to explore the value of principal-agent theory within the context of Prisoner's Dilemmas reaches interesting and important conclusions. See Miller (1987).

47. Eisenhardt (1989), p. 71.

48. A related argument is put forth by Ouchi. Hierarchical or bureaucratic control is most appropriate or efficient when individual behavior can be controlled through the kinds of procedural devices and formal evaluation associated with employment contracts: "In order to use a rule . . . , a manager must observe some actual performance, assign some value to it, and then compare that assigned value to the rule in order to determine whether the actual performance was satisfactory or not. All of this consumes a good deal of administrative overhead. If the rule is expressed qualitatively rather than quantitatively, the cost of administration can be expected to be even higher" (1979, pp. 835–836).

49. Rose-Ackerman (1981), pp. 144–134.

50. Rose-Ackerman (1981), p. 150. Miller (1987, p. 22) shows that "a fundamental problem of hierarchies is to find an appropriate incentive system even when monitoring is perfect."

51. Buckholdt and Gubrium (1980), p. 285. See also Needleman (1981).

52. Needleman (1981), p. 255.

53. For an interesting analysis of the conflicts between technocratic rationality and human intentionality in human services administration, see Caputo (1988).

54. Introducing multiple agents into the analysis affects control strategies to the extent that agent payoffs are jointly rather independently determined. See Levinthal (1988).

55. Tsebelis (1990), p. 69.

56. Miller (1987), pp. 4–5.

57. Arrow (1985), pp. 48–50.

58. Holmstrom and Milgrom (1991).

59. Bendor and Mookherjee (1987).

60. Taylor (1982), p. 53.

61. Bendor and Mookherjee (1987), p. 131.

62. Bendor and Mookherjee (1987), p. 144; Simon (1969).

63. Attewell and Gerstein (1979) report that pressure to comply with the detailed protocols established by the Food and Drug Administration created intense role conflicts for service workers torn between preventing

the abuse of methadone and changing addicts' behavior. Ironically, an important source of service workers' building trusting relationships with addicts and influence over addict behavior became their willingness to make exceptions to the rules. The discretion exercised by program staff "became a crucial organizational resource for compliance" (p. 325).

64. Compare Dunleavy (1984, p. 303): "There is very little likelihood that [bureaus] are ever completely dominated by one individual or even a small leadership group with cohesive interests. . . . The realization of collective benefits for bureau members is likely to require concerted action by a number of officials which may be quite large." For an optimistic view, see Wilkins and Ouchi (1983).

65. A useful discussion of managerial control in social program administration is in Williams (1980). An analytical approach to the problem of promoting cooperation is that of Oye (1986). See also Mitnick and Backoff (1989).

66. This kind of strategy is similar to Dunleavy's "bureau-shaping strategy" (1984, p. 327).

67. "Managers who can induce norms of cooperation and trust among employees can realize more of the gains from team [i.e., cooperative] production than can managers who rely on formal incentive systems" (Miller, 1987, p. 50). For a more comprehensive discussion of promoting cooperation in games involving dilemmas, see Hamburger (1979), pp. 179–192.

68. Ouchi (1979) refers to the deliberate use of socialization processes to control organizations when bureaucratic methods of control fail as "clan mechanisms."

69. Knott and Miller (1987), p. 267. For additional discussion of legislative control of bureaucracy, see Ingram and Schneider (1990); Weiss and Gruber (1984); Gruber (1987). See also Lynn (1991).

70. Heckathorn and Maser (1990); McCubbin, Noll, and Weingast (1987, 1989); Horn and Shepsle (1989). See also Gauthier (1990).

71. Calvert, McCubbin, and Weingast (1989); Macey (1991); Mitnick (1975); McCubbin and Schwartz (1984); Ingraham and Ban (1986); Halachmi (1989).

72. A study of services for victims of child abuse and neglect pointed out, for example, that the choice of whether to take protective custody of a child, in contrast to leaving the child at home with in-home services to prevent further abuse, was virtually never considered by the Illinois Department of Children and Family Services, because the investigative and service provision functions were the responsibility of separate organizational units, rendering cooperation between the two highly problematic (Schuerman, Stagner, Johnson, and Mullen, 1988).

Consider the requirements the Family Support Act imposes on the states, as agents of national social policy. State officials must, among other things, offer Aid to Families with Dependent Children (AFDC) benefits to children who live with two parents if the principal earner is unemployed; extend year-round Medicaid coverage to many now ineligible; require parents under the age of age twenty, without a high school degree, to participate in education programs; establish a Job Opportunities and Basic Skills (JOBS) program, with four required and two optional components, and require nonexempt AFDC recipients to whom the state guarantees child care to participate, within reason; guarantee safe, healthful child care to individuals for whom such services are necessary to program participation, and reimburse other work-related costs; inform all applicants and recipients of their rights and obligations under the Act; involve the private sector in JOBS planning and program design; withhold child support from earnings in all cases in which there is a court order; issue paternity-establishment standards; issue (and require judges and other officials to use) state child support award guidelines; require persons in contested paternity claims to submit to genetic testing (unless there are good reasons for not doing so); and develop and implement statewide automatic data-processing and information-retrieval systems. States are allowed discretion in carrying out these new mandates, but overall effectiveness levels for official performance are prescribed in the law, and federal evaluation of the results will be conducted.

73. Compare Ferejohn (1986).

74. Miller (1987, pp. 48–50) suggests that an ethical imperative to "cooperate in prisoner's dilemma situations, even if every other player in the dilemma is defecting," perhaps must be introduced into the concept of effective leadership. See also Sen (1985); Higgs (1987). For an excellent discussion of promoting cooperation in the presence of Prisoner's Dilemmas, see Axelrod (1984), pp. 124–141.

75. A more technical expression of this criticism is that, within the process of social choice and social policy implementation, all goals are endogenously determined. The goal of public management theory is to model the process of goal determination and to predict the consequences of changes in the parameters of the model and of the values of its variables on managerial strategies.

76. O'Toole (1986; 1991, p. 2).

77. For an interesting empirical study of goal and strategy selection, see Anspach (1991).

78. Such a classification and its implications could supplement other synoptic approaches to policy implementation, such as those of Meier (1989) and Salamon (1989).

Part Four

STRATEGY AND
PUBLIC MANAGEMENT

While there is little consensus on the nature of public management as a field of study, most contributors and chroniclers seem to agree that public management involves strategy. Those who seek distance between public administration and public management often point out that public administration has been concerned with tactics and internal operations, and thus there is a need for a field centered on strategy. This criticism does not seem altogether fair — there have long been at least some strategic elements in public administration studies — but it has boosted interest in public management nevertheless. The three chapters in this section are concerned, in different ways, with strategy.

Most sanguine about the possibilities for strategic public management are Lee Frost-Kumpf, Barton Wechsler, Howard J. Ishiyama, and Robert W. Backoff. Their chapter is an intensive and detailed study of a single agency and of its strategic management and transitions. Rooted in case-study traditions, the study uncovers nine thematic patterns among the 120 strategic actions in the agency.

Nancy C. Roberts's chapter is a breath of fresh, cold air. She challenges the applicability of strategic management concepts and practices to public agencies, especially large, multiorganizational systems. There are four areas in which the transfer of tools from enterprise strategy seems to break down: policy formulation, adaptation to the external environment, policy implementation, and bureau-level decision making. In short, it breaks down in almost every respect. Drawing on extensive experience with the Department of Defense, Roberts provides specific instances of the breakdown of strategy. After observing that the failure of enterprise strategic management in public agency settings is not so much an agency failure as a failure of the inappropriate tools, she concludes by suggesting some alternative conceptions for organizational design, planning, and management.

Eugene B. McGregor, Jr., is likewise concerned about the prerequisites of public management success, arguing that public management needs a theory of success and seeking to provide one. Public management has been dominated by failure and the theoretical expectation of failure, according to

McGregor; its success depends on achieving three strategic positions: an intervention cannot be technically flawed, an authoritative governance coalition must be prepared to stay the course with the intervention, and there must be operational clarity concerning the required tasks.

The three chapters in this section contrast in interesting ways. One implies that strategic public management, as traditionally conceived, does not work. Another documents success. A third discusses the meaning of success.

11

STRATEGIC ACTION AND TRANSFORMATIONAL CHANGE: THE OHIO DEPARTMENT OF MENTAL HEALTH

*Lee Frost-Kumpf, Barton Wechsler,
Howard J. Ishiyama, Robert W. Backoff*

Public sector strategies and strategic management processes have received considerable scholarly attention in recent years (Backoff and Nutt, 1990, 1991; Bozeman and Straussman, 1990; Wechsler, 1989; Wechsler and Backoff, 1986, 1987; Weinberg, 1977). The theoretical focus of much of this research is "patterns of non-routine decisions, choices, and actions that set the public agency's direction into the future" (Wechsler and Backoff, 1987, p. 34). The relatively few empirical studies that have been conducted demonstrate that public leaders can and do engage in strategic choice and action taking, and that there are interesting and important variations in the patterns of organizational strategy found in specific agencies (see Wechsler and Backoff, 1987, 1986).

Some scholars have suggested that the study of strategy in public agencies might serve as a foundation for constructing a distinct theory of public organizations (Backoff and Nutt, 1990, 1991; Rainey, 1989; Perry and Rainey, 1988; Poister, 1988; Nutt and Backoff, 1987; Wechsler and Backoff, 1987; Ring and Perry, 1985; Allison, 1983; Evered, 1983). If strategy is to play this central organizing role, we will need to understand more fully the processes by which different patterns of strategy emerge and the various methods and tactics that strategists use in crafting strategies to guide public organizations. While there are several ways to approach this research problem, one of the most promising remains the critical case study (Yin, 1989), which provides a "thick description" (Geertz, 1973) of the circumstances, contexts, and settings in which organizational strategists pursue particular strategies of action.

In this chapter, we examine the case of a public agency that fundamentally changed its basic mission and goals, mix of services, service delivery arrangements, operating characteristics, and resource allocation patterns. This pattern of fundamental change, one of several found in previous studies of public organization strategies, has been defined as a transformational strategy (Wechsler and Backoff, 1986). A transformational strategy consists of individual and collective commitments to making significant changes in the fundamental qualities of a public agency and in its relationships to key elements of its external environment. The emergence of a transformational strategy is based on an explicit, shared vision of the agency's future. This vision is guided by a set of core values that enables key stakeholders and constituencies, both inside and outside formal organizational boundaries, to engage in mutual and interdependent acts. Collective action that gives rise to a transformational strategy occurs through collaborative activities in organized and active social settings (Denhardt, 1984; Harmon, 1981), based on a set of core values that support a shared vision of the agency.

Transformation of the Ohio Department of Mental Health

The Ohio Department of Mental Health (ODMH) provides a case study of a state-level public agency that purposefully engaged in a fundamental transformation of its mission, operations, management functions, services, and service delivery arrangements. Although we focus on a single agency, this research is part of a larger project, under way since 1983, to investigate strategic management and leadership transitions among a much larger set of state government agencies in Ohio. This particular study allows us to explore, more fully and more intensively, a specific agency's strategy in action and to understand the processes and dynamics of a transformational strategy as pursued by the leaders of this agency.

Methods

Our methodology is based in the case-study approach (Yin, 1989; Lincoln and Guba, 1985). In this more naturalistic approach to inquiry, intensive analysis is made of primary and secondary source documents, including interpretations of events and actions by those involved. Among the documents reviewed in the preparation of this account were transcripts of interviews with key agency personnel, strategic management studies conducted by teams of graduate students in 1984, 1986, and 1988, videotaped presentations by the director of ODMH, and transcriptions of audiotapes in which the director reflected on changes in the agency at various points in the change process. Numerous other documents were content-analyzed, including speeches, idea papers, and descriptions of key events written by the director during the effort. Annual reports, planning documents, and performance reports were also reviewed, especially for data describing trends in key indicators. Several secondary sources were consulted, including other case studies of Ohio's mental health reforms (Robinson, 1991; Schaff and Goodrick, 1988; Kates and Roberts, 1987).

The Ohio Department of Mental Health

ODMH is a general-purpose government agency responsible for ensuring that people with mental illnesses receive necessary services. Between 1983 and 1990, ODMH worked with a broad coalition of stakeholders to develop and implement a series of strategic initiatives that significantly changed the mission, goals and objectives, operations, services, and service delivery arrangements of the agency. These efforts were guided by a new vision of the department and its role in Ohio's mental health services system, culminating in the passage of the Ohio Mental Health Act of 1988. This landmark legislation resulted in a massive shift of programmatic responsibilities, mix of services, and methods of service delivery from ODMH to community-based mental health boards and local mental health services agencies.

Fiscal and human resources shifted from the state and state-operated hospitals toward community mental health boards and local mental health agencies. Program and service delivery responsibilities were decentralized to community mental health boards, which served as the primary conduits for state mental health funds and became the primary contractors for local mental health services in the community. Service planning, reporting, and evaluation functions became a shared effort among consumers, service providers, community board members and staff, and departmental managers and staff. New information flows were developed to support these activities. Strategically important planning, reporting, and evaluation functions were developed or improved within the department. New resources were acquired from federal and foundation sources and repackaged as new program initiatives to consumers, community boards, and mental health service providers.

The way in which mental health and mental health services were conceived also changed in fundamental ways. People with mental illnesses were no longer viewed as patients to be placed in treatment programs. Instead, they were seen as consumers of mental health services, with those services "wrapped around" the clients in their own communities. The quality of the mental health care system in Ohio was transformed as well. Between 1983 and 1990, Ohio's reputation for mental health care shifted from one of the worst in the United States to one of the best. Moreover, some of the strategic and program initiatives pursued during this period became nationally recognized and served as models for other states. Through these changes, the department moved away from attempting (and largely failing) to manage a dual system of mental health services and toward providing central staff support services in a complex, community-based network of mental health services and service providers.

Understanding the Transformation Process at ODMH

The strategic transformation of ODMH and Ohio's mental health system can best be understood through a detailed analysis of the more than 120 strategic actions initiated and implemented by the leaders of the department between April 1983 and December 1986. The sources used in identifying these actions included numerous departmental reports, memoranda, speeches given by the director, and studies of the change process by students and researchers.

Our analysis reveals several thematic patterns among the strategic actions taken during the change process. Detailed action maps of these streams of strategic action (Thompson, 1967) show nine distinct patterns of coalignment that make up ODMH's transformational strategy. Each of the nine patterns involves, to some degree, coalignment of internally or externally directed strategic action initiatives, policies, and programmatic thrusts taken by the department's executive leaders. Broader coalignments are also evident when strategic actions are assessed over time and across the nine patterns. An analysis of the streams of action across these basic patterns provides some sense of both the content and process aspects of a transformational strategy. It also suggests how the strategic context and operational bases of mental health services in Ohio were restructured in fundamental ways over the five-year period.

Gaining External Support

Building support among key stakeholders was the first strategic pattern we identified. ODMH leaders received considerable support from both internal and external stakeholders at critical points in the transformation process. The most important supporter outside the agency was Governor Richard Celeste, who provided personal, moral, and political support for strategic initiatives taken by the leaders of ODMH. His interventions helped to preserve the overall strategic direction taken by the leaders of the department, allowing it to continue developing policies and programs that brought fundamental changes to Ohio's mental health system. This was especially true during the early stages of the change process, when opponents of the department's initiatives became particularly vocal, both in the legislature and in the media. Celeste's support continued even when the opposition included important power brokers of his own political party. The governor also worked to allay the concerns of various mental health groups outside the agency, who questioned the director's credentials as a mental health professional.

One of the most important ways that Governor Celeste demonstrated his support was by appointing the director and members of the department's top management to several task forces and cabinet-cluster working groups. Participation in these venues increased both the visibility and the credibility of the departmental leaders among other agencies and constituencies.

Interagency cabinet clusters and task forces enabled the leaders of ODMH to gain cooperation from those agencies whose policies, programs, and services had an impact on Ohio's mental health system and its consumers. Cooperative efforts among agencies were crucial to the success of the transformation of ODMH, since many of the consumers of mental health services lived in communities and depended, to varying degrees, on the social, economic, psychological, and medical support services provided by state and local agencies other than ODMH. These clusters also allowed policy and programmatic ideas to be developed and shared among different sets of state agencies. This led to cooperative demonstration projects and other ventures, which sought to coordinate and coalign new and existing policies, programs, and services in ODMH with the policies, programs, and services of other agencies having statewide or local jurisdictions. In this way, the multiple needs of people with mental illnesses could be met more effectively through coordinated interagency and interjurisdictional actions. It is clear that the support for the ODMH's leadership and its strategic direction, initially provided by the governor and eventually extended by other stage agencies and key constituency groups, was essential to the transformation of Ohio's mental health services system.

Building Internal Capacity

Building analytical, administrative, and management capacity was the second strategy we identified. ODMH took several strategic actions to build internal organizational capabilities. Significant changes were made in top staff assignments and responsibilities. Early in her tenure, the director brought key people into the agency. Top-level staff were organized into an executive planning council, which met weekly to help develop policy and programmatic initiatives, as well as to share ideas and information about the impact of strategic actions, events, and other changes as they unfolded. Midlevel managers were brought into the strategic change process through monthly planning councils; these councils also served to identify individuals within the agency with specialized expertise and knowledge who also exhibited strong commitment to changing mental health policies and programs in Ohio. Eventually, the growth in staff ability to manage strategic change processes became institutionalized. Internal ability developed in two distinct ways.

First, as a result of a failed attempt to redesign the organizational structure of ODMH, much of the effort to remake the department proceeded in an evolutionary fashion. Starting in late 1984, various policy and programmatic initiatives emerged as part of a grander scheme to transform Ohio's mental health system. Some of these initiatives were begun by ODMH's leaders; others were mandated by the governor, the state legislature, or external stakeholders (such as hospital accreditation and funding agencies). Many initiatives, especially later in the process, were created in response to constituency demands for new administrative functions within ODMH.

As these new initiatives took shape, offices were created to manage policies and programs and to provide insight. By the time these initiatives were in full swing, capacity had developed to the point that new offices could be staffed quickly and managed effectively. By 1988, most of the planned changes in the organizational structure of ODMH were completed. Many of the changes that were implemented reflected the modifications that had been sought during the failed reorganization attempt in 1983. Initiatives to improve technical systems within ODMH, such as information-processing systems and training centers, were begun in 1986. These technical changes were made only after most of the structural changes had been successfully implemented.

Second, a top-management team was assembled, and this action was followed by efforts to develop managerial and administrative skills among this group and the department's middle managers. Next, new policy and program initiatives began to appear, requiring specific and limited adjustments to the agency's structure. As the strategic changes broadened in scope and deepened in impact, departmental leaders began fulfilling new administrative and programmatic functions. These newly acquired functions required more substantial changes to the agency's structure, and these in turn brought about new offices and altered responsibilities. Only then did changes to the technical systems in the department begin to emerge. This type of top-down or outside-to-inside approach provided the staff the learning experiences necessary to better understand both the limits and the applications of technical systems.

Developing Technical Expertise

The third strategic pattern involves the development of technical expertise and knowledge among agency personnel. At ODMH, this expertise was developed by encouraging top staff and midlevel management to make changes in departmental policies, programs, and operations. Several important sets of strategic actions supported the development of such expertise among the staff and midlevel management in ODMH.

A consultant was hired to provide special expertise and to help organize and manage change processes both within ODMH and among key external constituency groups. As noted earlier, the activities of the consultant enabled the leaders of ODMH to share ideas and information with one another and to extend participation in the change process to several constituency groups.

Constituency groups were empowered to engage in the change process through relatively frequent planning conferences held throughout the state. These conferences allowed the leaders and key managers of the agency to carry on a dialogue with members of the various constituency groups. For instance, one specific set of conferences enabled consumers and their families to gain a voice and become actively involved in the change process. By deliberately sharing power with consumers and other constituency groups, the leaders of ODMH gained access to new information and ideas. This led to new insights regarding actual and perceived barriers to adequate services throughout the mental health service delivery system. Such actions also promoted greater commitment among ODMH professionals, consumers, and other constituency groups to changing the mental health system in Ohio.

Utilizing Training

Another set of strategic actions was based on training programs designed to transform the service delivery system. Some training programs enabled departmental and community-based service providers to learn new skills, such as case management, outpatient care, and local and regional services planning. Other programs were developed to help educate consumers about their roles and responsibilities as representatives on statewide and local task forces, commissions, and boards. The training activities even extended into Ohio's colleges and universities, with the department taking a very active role in helping to reform the curricula used in training mental health professionals. New academic programs were designed to reflect changes in the knowledge and skills required of mental health professionals, who eventually would be operating under a vastly different system in Ohio.

Taking Symbolic Actions

Symbolic actions signaled a break with the past and the transformation of the department. Chief among these actions were the giving of speeches and the creation of documents that detailed the guiding philosophy, ideas, program and service plans, and performance of the agency while changes were being made in the mental health services system. These actions communicated new concepts and values while emphasizing the possibilities for real and effective change in the future. The director's language expressed a new vision about what Ohio's mental health system could become and marked an irreversible break with past policies, service philosophies, and operating procedures. Rejecting many of the issues of the past as irrelevant and simultaneously presenting a vision of what a new system of mental health care could be, the director gave momentum to the change process and portrayed a new role for ODMH in a transformed system.

Developing New Program Thrusts

Yet another set of strategic actions focused on programmatic thrusts developed by ODMH in conjunction with various stakeholders and constituency groups. Some of these groups—the National Institute of Mental Health, the Robert Wood Johnson Foundation, Nationwide Insurance, and the National Council of Churches—provided significant funding for new policies, programs, and demonstration projects. Other groups—the We Care Network, the Alliance for the Mentally Ill, and the Ohio Departments of Human Services, Health, Youth Services, and Rehabilitation Services — provided personnel and expertise to help the ODMH staff plan new policies and programmatic initiatives, develop new services or service definitions, and formulate state and local legislation to codify the changes in the mental health services system. Still other groups — community mental health boards and mental health services agencies in Cleveland, Toledo, Dayton, Portsmouth, and Cincinnati, as well as the directors and staff of selected state mental health hospitals — provided sites and staff to help develop, operate, and manage demonstration projects.

Many of the programmatic thrusts initiated during this period represented large-scale experiments involving the development of new types of services for the mentally ill. One of the most significant features of the strategic transformation of ODMH and Ohio's mental health system were those programmatic initiatives in which services were developed and operated by members of key constituency groups, including services operated by consumers of the mental health system.

Empowering Key Constituencies

The empowerment of key constituency groups, especially consumers and their families, was also a theme of strategic action. Between 1983 and 1986, the leadership of ODMH worked strenuously to develop, involve, and empower key constituency groups. For example, numerous regional, statewide, and national conferences were held, involving members of various constituency groups throughout Ohio. During these conferences, ideas and information were shared, to build the capacity of the constituency groups to participate in planning changes in the system. People of all backgrounds, interests, and experience were encouraged to attend and to take an active role in guiding the development of strategies, plans, and actions to effect the transformation of Ohio's mental health system.

The language used by the director and her top staff at these conferences evoked empowerment, choice, participation, community support, and "independence from dependency" to the maximum possible extent. Over time, the participation of various constituency groups became institutionalized in formal policy-guidance groups, such as the We Care Network. ODMH then promulgated new policies to formalize their participation as required representatives on all statewide boards, commissions, and task forces. Ultimately, constituent representatives were required on each community mental health board in Ohio. In this way, key constituency groups were given the power to take control of the agenda for change in Ohio's mental health system.

Developing Alternative Sources of Revenue

Programmatic initiatives and participation by key constituency groups alike required new departmental resources. With the severe budgetary constraints then current, few additional dollars were available, at either the state or the local level, to help fund programmatic initiatives or cover the cost of statewide planning conferences. From 1984 to 1986, ODMH became increasingly successful and sophisticated in obtaining money from a wide variety of external funding sources, generating yet another pattern of strategic action. As its strategy of seeking funds to support the transformation of Ohio's mental health system took shape, the department assumed a new role — as repackager of ideas, information, and funds — to support the strategic initiatives of community boards, service agencies, and consumers and other constituency groups. In this way, the department began to move away from its traditional role as a direct service provider and toward a new role as a policy, planning, and management support system to community mental health boards, local mental health service providers, and consumers.

Responding to Opposition

Some constituency groups opposed ODMH's strategic direction and programmatic initiatives. There were four episodes in which key constituency groups actively — and, in some cases, quite publicly — opposed ODMH.

The first two involved reactions to philosophy and idea papers that identified problems and issues in Ohio's existing mental health system and expressed the need to move away from a dual system of mental health care. A key idea in these documents was that state funds should be spent in local communities, where the clients were. Predictably, employees of the state mental hospitals and their union reacted quite negatively to these ideas; shifting state funds to communities presented a clear threat to job security and to their future income. Some community mental health board members and directors also reacted negatively, suspicious that these ideas were simply an attempt by the state to transfer even more mentally ill people from the state mental hospitals to communities, whose resources were already stretched far beyond their capacity to serve the current population of mentally ill people. A related concern, of vital interest to many directors of community mental health boards, was the issue of who would decide whether someone received outpatient care in the community or inpatient care in a state mental hospital. Liability questions were extremely important here. These issues were resolved, to some degree, through negotiations leading to the passage of the 1988 Mental Health Act, but significant media attention was generated by these conflicts and portrayed the director of ODMH as less than competent.

The third episode involved a proposal to contract for the operation of one psychiatric care facility (operated by state mental health employees) with a private group of local physicians. The bargaining unit for the state employees quickly mobilized, killing the proposal. The unit's success was due in part to support from the powerful speaker of the State House of Representatives, who was also a key member of the governor's political party.

The fourth episode concerned efforts to pass the Ohio Mental Health Act of 1988. This legislation codified the strategic changes in the policies, programs, and operating rules of ODMH and Ohio's mental health system. The bargaining unit for the state employees fought the proposal by trying to delay consideration of the legislation until after the state legislature recessed in 1988, and thereby to delay its consideration until the next biennium budget and the last full year of the Celeste administration. Nevertheless, eleventh-hour negotiations produced an agreement among the leaders of the department, the state employees' bargaining unit, and community mental health boards. This ensured passage of the 1988 legislation in the closing hours of the legislative session.

Coaligning Streams of Strategic Action

ODMH was able to counter tough, well-financed, well-organized opposition to the proposed changes because its leaders pursued an overall strategy in which several actions and programmatic initiatives were developed and coaligned over time. This pattern of coalignment represents the final and most important pattern of strategic action in ODMH — the essence, really, of a transformational strategy. Figures 11.1 and 11.2 illustrate how key strategic actions taken by the leaders of ODMH created opportunities to coalign several strategic actions and programmatic initiatives over time. They did this by developing new internal policy, administrative, and management abilities; empowering key external constituencies; breaking with the past and generating new models for the service delivery system; and blocking or overcoming opposition.

Figure 11.1 illustrates strategic coalignments that occurred during the five-month period between October 1983 and March 1984. Actions begun in late 1983 culminated in the commitment of the ODMH leaders to establish the Community Support Program, a new and innovative programmatic thrust, which emphasized community-based provision and delivery of mental health services. This commitment, expressed in idea papers and at various planning meetings with key departmental constituencies, symbolized a new way of thinking among department leaders with respect to the form and focus of mental health services. What was perhaps more significant, adoption of the Community Support Program's philosophy symbolized a clear break with past service philosophies, administrative and services values, and general ways of doing things in the department, thereby signaling a new strategic direction for ODMH.

The commitment of the department's leaders to the Community Support Program also created circumstances that favored significant new strategic initiatives for improving the case management provided by community-based mental health agencies. The Community Support Program gave visibility to the leaders of the department and to the director, who served as cochair of an interagency task force that the governor's office made responsible for investigating the conditions of Ohio's homeless people, many of whom were eligible for community-based mental health services.

Figure 11.1. Coalignment of Strategic Actions Involving Leaders of ODMH: October 1983 to March 1984.

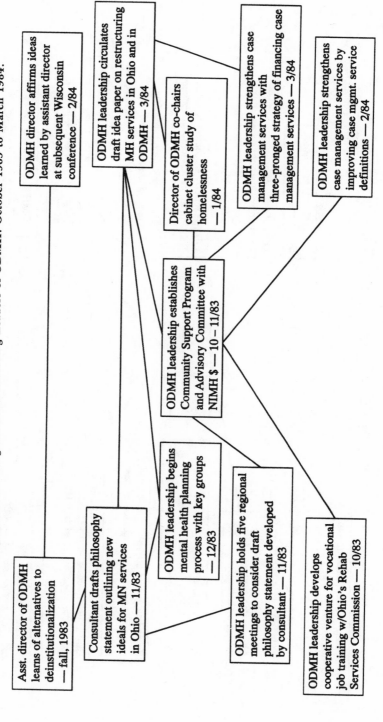

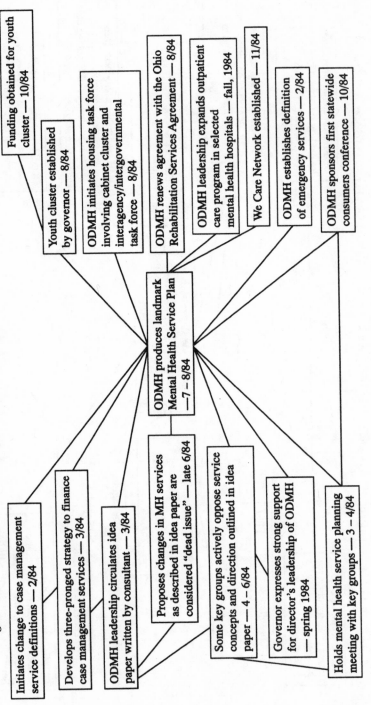

Figure 11.2. Coalignment of Strategic Actions Involving Leaders of ODMH: March 1984 to November 1984.

Funding obtained for youth cluster — 10/84

Youth cluster established by governor — 8/84

ODMH initiates housing task force involving cabinet cluster and interagency/intergovernmental task force — 8/84

ODMH renews agreement with the Ohio Rehabilitation Services Agreement — 8/84

ODMH leadership expands outpatient care program in selected mental health hospitals — fall, 1984

We Care Network established — 11/84

ODMH establishes definition of emergency services — 2/84

ODMH sponsors first statewide consumers conference — 10/84

ODMH produces landmark Mental Health Service Plan —7 – 8/84

Initiates change to case management service definitions — 2/84

Develops three-pronged strategy to finance case management services — 3/84

ODMH leadership circulates idea paper written by consultant — 3/84

Proposes changes in MH services as described in idea paper are considered "dead issue" — late 6/84

Some key groups actively oppose service concepts and direction outlined in idea paper — 4 – 6/84

Governor expresses strong support for director's leadership of ODMH — spring 1984

Holds mental health service planning meeting with key groups — 3 – 4/84

It must be noted that important activities had also occurred in ODMH before this period. These activities set the stage for the first set of significant, systematic strategic actions taken by the leaders of ODMH. Among the more significant activities of the transitional period were the hiring of the new director (March 1983), the recruitment and hiring of people for key leadership positions (April 1983 to August 1983), a comprehensive budget review by the Office of Budget and Management (late spring through summer of 1983), and an aborted attempt by the new director to reorganize key ODMH bureaus and divisions (late summer to fall of 1983).

Figure 11.2 portrays the subsequent phase of strategic action, occurring in the eight-month period between March and November of 1984. Administrative and programmatic initiatives and reforms became the foundation on which additional strategic actions were fashioned and implemented. This led to the first real challenge faced by the director and her top-management team. As the new community-based philosophy emerged, through idea papers and in meetings with key constituencies, some key groups began to actively oppose the new strategic role and direction outlined for ODMH. The significance of Governor Celeste's intervention to support the director and signal his commitment to her leadership cannot be understated. The strategic direction outlined by ODMH's leaders, and the opposition to it from some key constituency groups, served as the catalyst for the landmark Mental Health Services Plan produced during the late summer of 1984. The plan served as a guide to action for the department and signaled the emergence of a new coalition of stakeholders, who had not previously participated in ODMH policy deliberations. With the adoption of the Mental Health Services Plan and the state legislature's tacit approval of the direction that the plan defined, new programmatic initiatives began to appear in the department and in selected demonstration counties. Such initiatives, combined with consumers' opportunity to voice their concerns directly to the top leaders of ODMH at statewide conferences, gave greater power to the consumers of mental health services and built a new coalition to counter those constituencies concerned with limiting the rate of change or preserving the status quo.

Figures 11.1 and 11.2 are only illustrative, but they are consistent with some key elements of ODMH's transformational strategy. At all points in the process, consumers were actively engaged in decision making about their own treatment and in the planning and development of mental health policy. This increased involvement and empowerment, flowing directly from ODMH's new vision, operationalized a new orientation to service delivery and linked the changed values with strategic action.

The model of transformation reflected in these and other strategic coalignments was relatively simple in conception but complex and sophisticated in action. In conception, ODMH's approach was to make a symbolic and public break with the status quo, to make a case for change based on the failures of the present system, to develop new models for a system con-

sistent with espoused values, to build support for the new vision, to legitimate the change, and to implement the transformation. The pattern of strategic action necessary to make the transformation involved complex streams
of action, both purposeful and emergent. In some instances, actions were
carefully sequenced: efforts to develop a strong management team and an
internal consensus preceded externally oriented activities expressing the new
vision, and the building of external support and was followed by further
internally focused action(s). Some actions simultaneously targeted multiple
internal and external constituencies: use of the phrase *mentally ill people,* as
an expression of a new orientation toward clients and services, was targeted
at members of the department, strategic constituents (such as the governor),
and clients and advocacy groups.

     Sometimes transformational action was more emergent and less ex-
plicitly structured: information about reforms in the mental health system
of Wisconsin, as well as the involvement of an outside consultant, triggered
the preparation of a "new ideas" paper that became the blueprint for the
development of community-based services. Experiments provided opportunities for learning, for failing without large cost, and for building support: pilot projects in various Ohio cities provided tests of key elements of
the new delivery system. Actions, blocked at one point, were picked up later
and successfully implemented: a failed attempt to reorganize did hurt the
department politically and cause delay in implementation of community-
based services, but the reorganization was ultimately accepted in the 1988
legislative package, after efforts to build support and diffuse opposition had
succeeded.

Conclusions

This chapter has described and analyzed the transformation, achieved through
deliberate strategic action, of a public agency. In this section, we attempt
to draw out additional learnings from the ODMH case and, returning to
an earlier theme, explore the usefulness of strategy as a basis for public management theory.

Learnings from the ODMH Case

Transformation of the Ohio Department of Mental Health involved new
ways of thinking about clients, about the type and nature of mental health
services, and about patterns of resources and resource allocation. Through
the transformation process, ODMH was changed from a single agency, focused on operations and direct delivery of services, to a service-support
agency, operating in a complex network of community-based mental health
services. The transformation of ODMH was driven by strongly held values
and by a new vision of the agency's role in the provision of mental health
services. This new vision was articulated in a way that changed the terms

of debate in Ohio and empowered agency personnel, clients, constituents, and other stakeholders to collaborate in the effort to improve the quality and availability of mental health services. Complex streams of purposeful and emergent action led to the realization of this new vision.

The first of these streams of action involved the link between the strategic language of the leaders and the strategic actions initiated and sustained to transform the agency and the service system. The strategic language of the director nullified past issues, prior operating philosophies, and traditional practices in the department while giving form and substance to a new strategic direction. Through such language, numerous opportunities were opened for new ideas, actions, policies, and programs. The importance of this particular language cannot be overstated, since it enabled the leaders of the department to coalign strategic and operational concepts and thereby provided a sense of strategic direction to the agency and to the mental health services system (Frost-Kumpf and Ishiyama, 1991).

The link between the development of various constituencies and the internal abilities of the department was involved in the second stream of action. During this period, new planning, management, and participatory abilities were developed, both within the department and among new and existing constituency groups. This occurred in the form of collaborative planning efforts and training initiatives, involving departmental personnel as well as members of constituency groups (such as community boards, service providers, consumers of mental health services, and their families). The use of a variety of forums to get people from different perspectives to talk to one another, to communicate core values, and to develop a vision of the future of mental health services in Ohio helped energize and sustain the massive transformation of ODMH and Ohio's mental health services system.

Cooperative ventures among clusters of state-level administrative agencies constituted the third stream of strategic action. To our knowledge, few administrations have relied so directly and extensively on this approach as Governor Celeste's did. In the case of ODMH, interagency cabinet clusters and task forces provided a wealth of ideas, information, resources, and significant economies of scale in planning and implementing strategic changes in public policies and programs. The cabinet-cluster approach prevented interagency conflicts (over political mandates, legal authority, jurisdictional definitions, and programmatic standards) from erupting into disasters of planning and implementation.

Timing is essential to the success of any strategy. In the case of ODMH, strategic actions were coaligned over time, through regular and consistent sequences. For instance, the publication of an idea paper, philosophy statement, or planning or performance report by the department was regularly followed, within one to three months, by a regional or statewide planning conference. This pair of actions often led to a flurry of new policy and programmatic initiatives, which, given the increasingly sophisticated fundraising efforts by the department, would lead to significant additional external funding of programmatic and administrative experiments as demonstration projects. These actions would then often lead back to the beginning, and to another cycle of reporting, conferencing, programming, funding. Although the content of the actions varied tremendously among iterations, we believe that these iterations provided progressive insights and information to ODMH's leaders regarding which policy and program initiatives would probably work and which ones would not. In this way, fairly rapid and sustained organizational learning occurred at the system, agency, interpersonal, and individual levels of the agency.

This chapter charts one instance of the transformation of a public agency. It demonstrates that transformation requires the coalignment of complex streams of strategic action. While making and sustaining massive change is difficult, strategists can create new possibilities and transform an agency, its mission and goals, its operations, and its external relationships. Through strategic action, public agencies have the power to influence, inform, and alter the fundamental concepts, conditions, and assumptions under which they operate.

Strategy and a Theory of Public Organization

We have described here one pattern of strategic action open to a public organization and its leaders. In previous studies (Wechsler and Backoff, 1986, 1987), we have cited the existence of other patterns of strategy in public organizations. These findings, and the idea of strategy, serve as a useful starting point or organizing concept for public management and organization theory. The dynamic pressures of politics and administration act simultaneously on public organizations, shaping a distinctive context and set of constraints (Ring and Perry, 1985). Effectively managing this tension field of internal and external pressures (Nutt and Backoff, 1987) is the principal and defining task of public management.

Because strategic action occurs at the nexus of politics and administration, description and analysis of the strategies of public agencies can provide valuable insights into the nature and tasks of public management. As we have shown in the case of ODMH, "thick description" allows us to detail the patterns of coalignment that shape organized action. Themes derived from this analysis yield potentially generalizable statements about public management. Of course, much more research is necessary, to go beyond the limited knowledge we have about strategy and strategic action in public organizations. Our research agenda includes the study of additional agencies, to examine other cases of transformational strategies and to explore other strategic patterns (Wechsler and Backoff, 1986, 1987). We hope that this work will permit us to make more extensive and more closely grounded statements about the distinctive nature of public organizations and management.

12

LIMITATIONS OF
STRATEGIC ACTION IN BUREAUS

Nancy C. Roberts

Strategic management is of growing interest to public sector managers (Bozeman and Straussman, 1990; Koteen, 1989). As drawn from traditional business and industry usage, the concept has come to mean a conscious, rational decision process by which an organization formulates its goals and then implements and monitors them, making adjustments as environmental and organizational conditions warrant. Goals are established in light of the organization's resources and its internal strengths and weaknesses, as well as the opportunities and threats that exist in its external environment. Goals are expected to be mutually reinforcing and integrated into a comprehensive whole, so that organizational activity can be coordinated and controlled (Fredrickson, 1983).

Nevertheless, despite the numerous books and articles defining the subject and its practice, there is no agreement on a common definition, nor is there a common approach to the practice and study of strategic management (Cunningham, 1989). Instead, one relies on two general approaches to capture the essence of strategic management: the *synoptic approach* and the *incremental approach* (Fredrickson, 1983). In very basic terms, the *synoptic approach* is characterized by "integrative comprehensiveness." There is a conscious attempt to integrate the decisions that compose the organization's overall strategy, to ensure that the decisions are consciously developed, mutually reinforcing, and integrated into a whole (Fredrickson, 1983). In addition, the objective is to integrate the organization's internal roles, processes, structure, and decisions in order to position the organization for the best fit vis-à-vis its market and environment. Thus, good "fit" or "alignment" describes the compatibility between the organization, its external environment, and its preferred strategy—defined as the means an organization chooses to move it from where it is now to where it wants to be in the future (Digman, 1990). The process is expected to be analytical, rational, and comprehensive. With the *incremental approach,* there is little attempt to consciously integrate individual and organization decisions that affect one another. Strategy emerges from a loose coupling of groups of decisions that are handled individually, without integration (Fredrickson, 1983). Typically, this type of strategic process is directed at some modification of the current state and requires little coordination among various groups and individuals in the organization. While the ultimate objective is to achieve "a viable match between the opportunities and risks present in the external environment and the organization's capabilities and resources for exploiting those opportunities" (Hofer, 1973, p. 3), there is no effort to manage this adaptation in a coordinated and integrated way. Descriptions of the synoptic approach tend to predominate in the business literature, while descriptions of the incremental approach tend to predominate in the policy and public sector literature.

The practice of strategic management, at any rate, is assumed to be transferable to all organizations. While analysts acknowledge constraints in the application of strategic management to public bureaus (see, for example, Wheelen and Hunger, 1986), they nevertheless recommend its introduction and acceptance, with modifications, into public sector practice. In part, these recommendations derive from the assumption that management is a generic process (Baldwin, 1987; Weinberg, 1983). Although the ends of business and government are different, the means of achieving the ends are believed to be similar. Both public and private management have common procedural elements that permit one to view management as a universal process (Murray, 1983). Furthermore, analysts have pointed to a convergence of sectors — government and business organizations are becoming more similar in terms of their functions, management approaches, and public visibility (Bozeman, 1987; Musolf and Seidman, 1980). In fact, recent analyses suggest that all organizations can be viewed as public to the extent that political authority affects their behavior and processes (Bozeman, 1987). These assessments would suggest, therefore, that it is both appropriate and possible to transfer strategic management to public bureaus.

This chapter challenges these assumptions. Strategic management in public bureaus has limited applicability, especially in large, multiorganizational systems. To make the initial argument, the differences between public bureaus and private enterprises are summarized in the first section. The second section examines the impact that unique features have on bureau strategic management. In particular, one finds four major areas where the transfer of enterprise-based strategic management is especially problematic: formulation of bureau policy, the bureau's adaptation to its external environment, implementation of bureau policy, and decision making. The case of the Department of Defense (DoD) is used as an illustration in the third section. Despite extensive efforts toward strategic analysis, decision making, and planning in DoD, a coordinated, integrated effort to strategically manage the department has yet to be realized. Although DoD has some unique features that distinguish it from other large bureuas, the difficulties it has with policy formulation, implementation, environmental adaptation, and decision making are characteristic of other multiorganizational systems. The chapter concludes with the recommendation that those interested in the strategic management of multiorganizational bureaus turn to the generation of innovative organizational images and designs as the most viable option for future strategic management.

Unique Features of Public Bureaus

There is a growing theoretical and empirical literature to document the differences between public and private sector organizations (Rainey, Backoff, and Levine, 1976; Perry and Rainey, 1988; Rainey, 1989). Figure 12.1 displays the major concepts that have been used to differentiate between the two domains.

At the far left of the figure, we see three areas of distinction between public and private entities: ownership, funding (Perry and Rainey, 1988), and mode of social control. There are two forms of ownership, public and private; and there are two distinct forms of funding, public and private. Mode of social control is a dimension that describes the extent to which major components of an organization are subjected to control by markets or polyarchy (Dahl and Lindblom, 1953; Perry and Rainey, 1988). Markets, at one extreme of the continuum, have numerous buyers and sellers, who have no organized intent to control an organization. Control is exerted by the price system in economic markets as participants engage in economic exchanges of goods and services between customers and suppliers. At the other end of the continuum, polyarchy involves bargaining and persuasion among those external to the organization, who have some degree of control over the organization. In Western democracies, polyarchy involves a pluralistic political process: multiple governmental authorities, interest groups, and independent participants contest "the rules" and control through the directives issued by government. And while participants may engage in exchanges, the exchanges are not economic but political. Through their exchange, they attempt to change authoritative rulings by marshaling political support and legal authority (Dahl and Lindblom, 1953; Perry and Rainey, 1988; Wamsley and Zald, 1973).

These three elements — ownership, funding, and mode of social control — produce a complex continuum of organizational structures and processes. Eight types outlined by Perry and Rainey (1988) are summarized in column 1 in Figure 12.1. At the market end of the continuum, enterprises have private ownership and private funding, with markets as a mode of social control. At the other end, bureaus have public ownership and public funding and a polyarchic mode of social control. The organizational types in between are hybrids representing various combinations of ownership, funding, and social control. As an example of a hybrid, a government-sponsored enterprise, such as the Corporation for Public Broadcasting, has private ownership, public funding, and a polyarchic mode of social control, while a state-owned enterprise, such as Airbus, has public ownership, private funding, and a market mode of social control (Perry and Rainey, 1988).

Figure 12.1. Comparison Between Enterprises and Bureaus.

(1)	(2)	(3)	(4)
Institutional Mechanisms for Political and Economic Activity / Organization Types[a]	Implications for Organizational Properties[b]	Implications for Internal Organizational Processes and Systems[c]	Challenges for Strategic Management
1. Bureau	1. Performance Expectations	1. Number of Goals and Objectives	1. Policy Formulation
Ownership → 2. Government Corporation	2. Performance Measures	2. Standards for Evaluation	2. Performance Standards and Environmental Adaptation
3. Government-Sponsored Enterprise	3. Legal and Formal Constrains	3. Authority Relations and Role of the Manager	3. Policy Implementation
Funding → 4. Regulated Enterprise	4. External Stakeholder Influence	4. Incentives and Incentive Structures	4. Decision Making
5. Governmental Enterprise	5. Degree of Coerciveness	5. Performance Characteristics	
Mode of Social Control → 6. State-Owned Enterprise	6. Breadth of Impact		
7. Governmental Contractor	7. Public Scrutiny		
8. Private Enterprise			

[a] Typology from Perry and Rainey, 1988. [b] Adapted from Rainey, Backoff, and Levine, 1976. [c] Adapted from Rainey, Backoff, and Levine, 1976.

These eight organizational types, representing different admixtures of ownership, funding, and social control, are hypothesized to have differential impacts on organizational functioning and management (column 2). Of particular interest for this discussion is the functioning of bureaus. At least seven organizational and contextual properties are expected to be affected: performance expectations, performance measures, legal and formal constraints, external stakeholder influence, degree of coerciveness, breadth of impact, and public scrutiny (Rainey, Backoff, and Levine, 1976; Rainey, 1989). Variation in a bureau's internal processes and systems is also expected. According to Rainey, Backoff, and Levine (1976) and Rainey (1989), variation among the eight organization types is expected to produce an impact on at least five internal organizational processes and systems (column 3): goals and objectives; standards for evaluation; authority relations and role of the manager; incentives and incentive structures; and performance characteristics.

Implications for Strategic Management of Bureaus

This brief overview of the uniqueness of bureaus, in terms of their contexts, properties, and internal processes and systems, has many implications for management in public sector organizations (Rainey, 1989). Of most interest for this analysis, however, is how these differences may affect the strategic management of the bureau. Analysis to date, while scanty and not well grounded empirically, suggests little reason for optimism.

One finds at least four major areas of difficulty in transferring strategic management to bureaus (see Figure 12.1, column 4): (1) the general manager of a bureau is required to share power with other key players (those both internal and external to the organization) when formulating organizational policy; (2) bureaus operate in a political economy, not an economic one, and lack consensually based indicators to measure organizational performance; (3) the bureau's general manager has less autonomy and control, compared to an enterprise's general manager, to induce system coherence, integration, and coordination during policy implementation; and (4) the bureau's strategic decision making, as a consequence of the above factors, is much more complex and uncertain than the enterprise's strategic decision making.

Shared Power in Policy Formulation

The most fundamental difference between bureaus and enterprises stems from the Constitution. In business, the functions of general management (formulation of goals and strategy, management of internal organizational systems, and interfaces with external constituencies) are centralized in the hands of a general manager—the chief executive officer (Allison, 1983). In bureaus, the functions of the general manager are shared among competing institutions: the executive, two houses of Congress, and the courts. The objective of this constitutional arrangement is to preclude the arbitrary exercise of power: with a number of individuals and competing institutions given the right to be involved in a bureau's decisions, each checks the power of the others. As the *Federalist Papers* make clear, "the great security against a gradual concentration of the several powers in the same branch consists in giving those who administer each branch the constitutional means and personal motives to resist encroachment of the others. Ambition must be made to counteract ambition" (cited in Allison, 1983, pp. 80–81). Thus, in most areas of public policy, responsibility is shared among individuals, such as the President and his staff, appointed bureau heads, career officials within the bureau, and members of Congress and their staffs.

Bureau general managers reflect on how difficult this arrangement is for them, especially those with experience primarily in the private sector. As Secretary of the Treasury, Michael Blumenthal could not control the policy-making process as he had when he was president of Bendix. His power to decide what policy was to be pursued, who was to be involved in its development, how it would be developed, and who was going to administer it was severely limited: "No one, not even the President, has that kind of power" (Blumenthal, 1983, p. 30). Instead, he shared policy making with others inside and outside his organization, since "everybody [felt] that he or she [had] a legitimate piece of the action and must be involved" (p. 30). Besides the additional numbers of people engaged in policy debates, the process is complicated by the divergent interests and goals of those involved. In business, Blumenthal's board of directors and shareholders had common interests, which they shared with top management. Members of Congress and government officials, by contrast, represent no monolithic group; they all have very different backgrounds and represent very different constituent interests: "By definition, you cannot please all of them. And whatever policy you follow, you are certain to be attacked and criticized, which is not true in the private sector. So what you learn is that there is no way to please your constituents in this job the way you can please your constituents in the private sector. You have to learn to live with that situation and survive within it" (Blumenthal, 1983, p. 29).

Adaptation to the Environment

Enterprise-based strategic management begins with the assumption that adaptation to the environment is crucial to long-term organizational survival. Refusal to acknowledge competitors and their strategies, to initiate or adopt new technologies, or to monitor and respond to sociopolitical trends can doom an organization to obsolescence. Therefore, monitoring environmental forces, interpreting them as threats or opportunities, and acting on those possibilities are important features of the strategic management process. Fortunately, the market economy provides a useful scorecard for interpreting the organization's capacity for adaptation. As a mechanism for matching supply with demand, gauging consumers' preferences, and monitoring performance, the market allots penalties and rewards via sales, return on investment, profit, and other such indicators. Embedded in the logic of the marketplace is the means of comparing one enterprise with another. Such comparisons keep the enterprise accountable to its environment by revealing the extent to which it has been effective in doing what it has set out to do and by measuring just how efficiently it has gone about doing it. If the enterprise wants to maintain its course or alter its strategy, it relies on market signals to assess how well it has performed with respect to others. Those signals, translated from the buying behavior of consumers, provide the ultimate test of an enterprise's adaptability.

Adaptation to the environment is also of concern to bureau managers, yet bureaus operate in a *political* economy. Bureaus have to rely on oversight bodies as their markets (Backoff and Nutt, 1990). These oversight bodies help establish bureaus' goals and provide the resources necessary to accomplish them. Resources are not allocated by any market mechanism; they require bargaining and negotiating with political authority, such as an oversight body, in order to alter appropriations. Unfortunately, the signals in a political economy, especially in a democratic one with polyarchic centers of control, are weak, contradictory, and difficult to interpret. No clear consensus on appropriate indicators of performance (such as price, profits, sales, or return on investment) exists. There is no "bottom line" to serve as a measure of success. The lack of clear performance measures, and vague and competing stakeholder interests, encumber the forging of a consensus on bureau goals and the allocation of resources. Although mechanisms (elections, political mandates) exist to gather and interpret information in the political economy, they register stakeholders' preferences only periodically, and the results tend to be generalized to a presidential administration, not turned to a specific bureau's policy.

Bureaus rely on proxy mechanisms to keep their managers accountable to their environments. Performance is judged in terms of its compatibility with legal mandates, obligations to a charter, and the interests of current executive and legislative authority. In addition, court rulings, enabling legislation, and newly elected administrations all produce directives that the general manager and his or her subordinates are measured against (Backoff and Nutt, 1990). Unfortunately, these proxy indicators produce a "jurisdictional jungle" (Levine, Backoff, Cahoon, and Siffin, 1975). They represent confusing and often competing sets of expectations. With conflicting signals from the environment on what policies to pursue, and with few "objective" indicators to track and reward performance, it is understandable that general managers may prefer to make incremental modifications in the current system, rather than embark on major changes that require boldness and imagination. Because a bureau's environment is complex, it is preferable not to venture too far into the unknown. Change is risky: it activates the opposition (or creates it where none existed) and has the potential to upset the delicate balance among competing stakeholders' interests. Besides, focusing on the familiar, and deviating only slightly from the status quo, will make it easier to absorb feedback and modify the bureau's operations as one goes along (Mintzberg, 1974). Avoiding disruption and minimizing threats from the environment, then, will be preferable to searching for new opportunities. As long as the general manager's rewards for making marginal adjustments to the status quo exceed the rewards for adapting in more innovative ways, there will be less interest in the organization's adaptive capacity.

Policy Implementation

Given the market mechanism to assess performance and hold the organization accountable, enterprise-based strategic managers are granted greater responsibility for policy implementation than their counterparts in public bureaus. Their responsibility for implementation involves many tasks: designing the organization's structure and culture to match its policy; developing managers and employees to ensure that they have the appropriate background, skills, and attributes to make the policy work; employing the right functional policies to support the organization's overall goals; establishing compatible financial, accounting, information, and evaluation systems to monitor organizational performance; and developing personnel systems to reward performance. These tasks can be left in the hands of general managers because upper managers, boards of directors, and stockholders have market indicators to keep the general managers accountable.

The bureau's general manager, by comparison, does not have the same level of autonomy in implementing bureau policy. The general manager controls neither the personnel system nor the bureau's personnel to the same degree. She cannot change the system to fit with the organization's new direction, nor can she hire and fire people as the strategy changes—both of which are usual recommendations in enterprise organizations. Staffing of high-level positions requires the approval of Congress. The broad outlines of organizational structures are specified in legislative mandates and are difficult to modify and align as policy changes. Incentives to encourage entrepreneurial behavior or support for a new policy are circumscribed by law and operate under guidelines established by the Civil Service and the seniority system. The system is devised more to prevent abuses than to give general managers control over the implementation process. And, as previously mentioned, oversight bodies constitute the bureau's resource base, and they determine resource allocation politically. The bureau does not have an independent say over its budget or finances. Authorizations and appropriations emerge from the give-and-take of the legislative process. This check on resource allocation constrains not only *how* policies can be implemented but also, ultimately, *what* policies can be implemented. No matter how impressive the policy, its implementation is moot without adequate funding.

It should also be noted that organizational coherence and integration are not major goals in bureaus. Enterprise-based strategic management is built on the premise that an integrated approach to policy formulation and implementation is essential to organizational effectiveness and efficiency. The same premise does not hold for bureaus. In fact, policy formulation is constitutionally separated from policy implementation. Evaluation of organizational operations and outcomes is less the concern of the general manager than the responsibility of congressional oversight committees. Therefore, the necessary mechanisms important in coordinating organizational activities and monitoring organizational performance (such as management information systems and financial and accounting systems) are underdeveloped, and in many cases, nonexistent. Bureau systems are not intended to provide coherence; the concern is for "justice, not efficiency; the preservation of liberty, not the best use of economic resources; accountability and legitimacy, not efficiency and effectiveness" (Bower, 1983, p. 174).

Strategic managers in public bureaus are quick to acknowledge their limitations in implementing policy and providing organizational coherence. Michael Blumenthal has compared bureau- with enterprise-based management and concludes that managing a large federal bureaucracy bears little resemblance to running a large corporation. While he was technically Secretary (chief) of the Treasury, he had "little power, effective power, to influence how the thing function[ed]" (Blumenthal, 1983, p. 25): "in government, that kind of control [did] not exist." Limited in terms of hiring, firing, transferring personnel, providing incentives, and structuring his organization, he was judged not on how well he "ran the place" but on what happened with the economy, the budget, inflation, and so forth, all factors external to the bureau and beyond his immediate control. That was not the case when he was in business. There, he was judged on whether he was a good administrator. Another former Secretary of the Treasury, George Shultz, concurs: "In government and politics, recognition and therefore incentives go to those who formulat[e] policy and maneuver legislative compromise. By sharp contrast, the kudos and incentives in business go to the persons who can get something done. It is execution that counts. Who can get the plant built, who can bring home the sales contract, who can carry out the financing, and so on" (cited in Allison, 1983, p. 87).

Decision Making

As a consequence of the unique features of bureau management, general managers resort to a particular process in making decisions. Analysts have characterized it alternatively as "muddling through" (Lindblom, 1959) or "disjointed incrementalism" (Braybrooke and Lindblom, 1963). Caught in the pull of competing political forces, with no one central source of power, general managers establish goals and make decisions as they bargain and negotiate with stakeholders. Rather than having one goal — to "maximize" profits or growth — they have a whole array of goals and decisions that emerge from their interactions.

Since it is difficult to coordinate and reconcile these goals, given their diversity and, in many cases their incompatibility, decisions about goals tend to be made sequentially and not integrated into a whole. Any inconsistencies among them are ignored. Although treating decisions in this disjointed fashion avoids the challenge of coordinating and integrating organizational activity, it opens up a problem of organizational coherence. Subparts of the organization can and do end up working at cross-purposes, undermining the overall effort. But, again, the emphasis is on being responsive and adaptive to multiple and competing stakeholders, rather than being concerned about organizational coherence.

The role of the media is also frequently mentioned as a major factor complicating general managers' decision making (Blumenthal, 1983; Rumsfeld, 1983). Public management is described as a much more open, "fishbowl" experience. Press coverage can be so intense, and leaks of bureau deliberations so pervasive, that many policy initiatives are halted before they get off the drawing board. Enterprise-based general managers deal with the press only under exceptional circumstances (oil spills, product tampering); it is a rare occasion when the press has access to the internal operations of a firm as it formulates and implements its strategies. Its deliberations are not subjected to the same level of scrutiny as in bureaus (Ring and Perry, 1985). The relative openness in buraus leads policy makers to be as concerned with how policies will look to various constituencies as with how the policies will work. In Washington, according to Blumenthal, "appearance is as important as reality" (1983, pp. 22–23). And the press plays an important role in establishing appearances, especially when the bureau's performance indicators are ambiguous and difficult to define and interpret.

Time also complicates a bureau's decision making. A bureau-based general manager's duration in office is usually measured in terms of four-year election cycles (or even less, as the fourth and third year in office are interrupted by reelection campaigns). The length of service of politically appointed top government managers averages no more than eighteen months for assistant secretaries (Allison, 1983). Changing a bureau's policy, which tends to be locked into statutes or regulations, is difficult and time-consuming. Moreover, the continuity of new policies, not to mention the linkage between formulation and implementation, is limited under these circumstances. The process is further disrupted with very specific time frames for legislatively mandated implementation and congressional budget cycles. According to Harlan Cleveland, "We are tackling 20-year problems with five-year plans staffed with two-year personnel funded by one-year appropriations" (cited in Ring and Perry, 1985, p. 281).

The Department of Defense

Given these general difficulties in importing strategic management into bureaus, let us now turn our attention to a specific bureau: the Department of Defense (DoD). DoD receives public funding, operates with a polyarchic means of social control, and is publicly owned. It experiences the same constraints as other public bureaus. In addition, it has unique properties that make the transfer of enterprise-based strategic management even more difficult.

Policy Ambiguity in a World of Shared Power

DoD operates in a shared-power environment, with competing centers of power both inside and outside the organization. The Secretary of Defense does not initiate his own strategy. He participates in a fluid process with a complex set of stakeholders: the President and his staff, the National Security Council and its staff, international allies, other executive departments of the government, and powerful members of his own department. In Congress alone, there are ten Senate committees and eleven House committees that have formal jurisdiction over various aspects of defense policy (Wildavsky, 1988).

These centers of power rarely establish a consensus on national security strategy; with the Eisenhower administration as a possible exception, consensus on national security strategy has been infrequent in the post–World War II era (Brown, 1989). Instead, the President resorts to very global and vague policy statements. Policy ambiguity, rather than clear and direct policy guidance, becomes the norm (see, for example, *National Security Strategy*, 1990). Managers in DoD are left to manage in a vacuum. Forced to build their own interpretations of national security, their choices are substituted for those of "upper management" and quite naturally reflect their more specialized and parochial interests. Under these conditions, it is not surprising to find localized interests predominating over organizational interests, as well as less coordination and integration of the whole.

The reluctance to provide specific guidance is a natural by-product of our constitutional system (Ring and Perry, 1985). There is variation among presidents and their secretaries of defense in providing specific guidance, but the natural tendency is to avoid stating one's policy preferences in clear and precise terms. In fact, there are disincentives for clarity (Hammond, 1988). From the perspective of dealing with Congress, the President's unambiguous articulation of strategy can "give ammunition to [his] enemies" (Hammond, 1988, p. 6). It makes his administration politically vulnerable by setting up priorities to support one strategic need over another—support for one international regime as opposed to another, building ships as opposed to missiles or airplanes. There is a preference for avoiding the mobilization of opposition (both internal and international) and the limiting of one's future options. There is also danger in being too explicit about one's intentions. Revealing what one is going to do suggests (given resource constraints) what one is unlikely, unwilling, and unable to do—information that could be valuable to one's enemies. In addition, a lack of announced goals and strategy, especially those that are fiscally constrained, transfers the hard choices to Congress while the administration avoids the risk of splintering its own coalition and decreasing its own popularity. This is part of the "game that Congress and the President play with one another . . . . The objective of this game is to let the other player make or appear to make the decision" (Hammond, 1988, p. 8).

There are also disincentives for unambiguous policy directives from the President: "Agencies want guidance for a mixture of good and bad reasons. The good reasons are in order to facilitate their design and implementation of effective programs and their accountability. The bad reasons— bad from the standpoint of the President—are to reduce their uncertainty at the expense of the performance requirements of the President" (Hammond, 1988, p. 9). The President may want to change his goals and strategy quickly, to meet environmental exigencies, and do so more rapidly than DoD can support them. He may prefer incremental commitment to programs, given political constraints, rather than the long-term commitments that DoD programs may require. The President may also want to present and interpret his goals and objectives differently to different audiences. There is a "need to be able to say different things to different foreign audiences as well as domestic audiences" (Hammond, 1988, p. 12). Keeping a coalition together with competing objectives, in order to gain passage of legislation, requires some finesse. The opposition can rally, or a shaky coalition can fall apart, if a clear and unambiguous strategy is articulated. Under these conditions, it may be of benefit to the President to be deliberately vague (Nutt, 1979). Thus there are many disincentives for the President to issue clear policy statements to DoD, despite the department's administrative need for them.

Indicators of Performance and Environmental Adaptation

Like other public bureaus, DoD has difficulty in establishing measures to characterize its performance and environmental adaptation. "Readiness to fight" is a DoD measure of performance in times of peace, but it lacks the precision of market indicators. It is difficult to define and it is open to various interpretations among competing stakeholders; no consensus exists on what "readiness" means, much less on how to measure it. To compound the problem, "readiness" is an "input variable," which focuses attention on equipment and supplies and draws it away from operations and outcomes. According to critics, the emphasis on "input variables" rather than "output variables" has resulted in major problems with our military operations in the past (Luttwak, 1985; Senate Armed Services Committee, 1985). Reliance on output measures to gauge DoD's performance also has its disadvantages. Two measures—winning or losing in combat—are indicators that may take long to determine (as is the case in winning) or may be impossible to rectify (as is the case in losing). Reliance on these measures to judge performance is either too time-consuming or too risky. These dilemmas over performance measures led former Secretary of Defense Harold Brown to conclude that "there is no single number that provides a bottom-line measure of how well the DoD or any other governmental agency is being managed" (Brown, 1983, p. 217); it is "not possible to manage the Department of Defense exactly like a business and to try to get to a bottom line that indicates profit or any other single measurable criterion."

Policy Implementation

The Secretary of Defense also lacks control over policy implementation, as do other public managers. The implementation functions of the general manager are not centered in his office but are spread out among competing centers of power. For example, the Secretary of Defense does not control his budget; Congress authorizes and appropriates it. The process of producing the budget is also very complex, time-consuming, duplicative, and difficult to administer and coordinate (Gansler, 1989; Hendrickson, 1988; Jones and Doyle, 1989; Kanter, 1983; Kaufmann, 1986; Wildavsky, 1988). Congressional budget involvement and oversight, for example, involve "some 30 committees, 77 subcommittees, and 4 panels . . . . *Every working day* . . . entails on average almost 3 new General Accounting Office (GAO) audits of DoD; an estimated 450 written inquiries and over 2,500 telephone inquiries from Capitol Hill; and nearly 3 separate reports to Congress *each* averaging over 1,000 man-hours in preparation and approximately $50,000 in cost. Senior DoD officials spend upwards of 40 hours preparing for the 6 appearances as witnesses and the 14 hours of testimony that they provide on average for *each* day Congress is in session" (Cheney, 1989, pp. 26–27; emphasis in original). In addition, as one study has found, just to fulfill statute requirements, Congress requires 319 reports of the DoD (U.S. General Accounting Office, 1988).

    The Secretary of Defense is also restricted, as are other bureau managers, in making organizational changes. Adding or deleting personnel and subunits, at the level of the assistant undersecretaries, requires the approval of Congress and can take months before acceptance is granted. Congress also intervenes to make its own organizational changes and add new units as it deems necessary. Before 1981, it prescribed several functional areas of responsibility, and others were added after 1981. Congress even spelled out the duties of the new officials in statutes, details usually left for DoD directives, and it "broke new ground" when it mandated the establishment of a Unified Command for special operations and prescribed its composition and functions in detail (Office of the Secretary of Defense, 1987, p. A-17). In addition, DoD's request to develop a less rigid personnel management system, with some degree of flexibility in the hiring and pay of specialized personnel, has yet to be authorized by Congress.

Decision Making

Given such constraints on the Secretary of Defense in managing the department, as well as the complexity of departmental management, decision making in DoD has been described as "organized anarchy" (Sabrosky, Thompson, and McPherson, 1983), and a "garbage can process" (Crecine, 1986; Bromiley, 1986). The models of rational decision making on which strategic management is built assume that choice depends on knowledge of alternatives, knowledge of consequences, consistent ordering of preferences, and clear decision rules. Yet these conditions do not obtain in DoD strategic decision-making situations; rather, decision makers are "sharply constrained by circumstances of time, distance, and organizational complexity and self-interest," all characteristics of organizational anarchies (Sabrosky, Thompson, and McPherson, 1983, p. 38).

The planning, programming, and budgeting system (PPBS) initiated in the early 1960s by Secretary of Defense Robert McNamara, was intended to bring some order and rationality to decision making in DoD. The goal was to centralize planning in the Office of the Secretary of Defense, provide guidance on programming, correlate budgets with plans, and use cost-benefit analysis and other analytical techniques to assist in decision making. McNamara believed that the problems of the Department of Defense derived not from lack of management authority "but rather [from] the absence of the essential management tools needed to make sound decisions on the really crucial issues of national security" (Office of the Secretary of Defense, 1987, p. A-8). PPBS was envisioned as such a managerial tool. Within a fifteen-month cycle, it was expected to translate broad national security objectives and strategy into a five-year defense plan and a yearly operating budget. There is intense debate, however, over the efficacy of PPBS. Despite the fact that it has been in a constant state of evolution since its introduction into the DoD, reformers still criticize its inability to couple expenditures with the department's mission, as originally intended. Problems arise, they say, because PPBS has not been properly developed and administered. It suffers from various ailments: ineffective strategic planning; an insufficient relationship between strategic planning and fiscal constraints; absence of realistic fiscal guidance; failure to emphasize the output side of the defense program; inability to make meaningful improvements; insufficient attention to execution and control; and the length, complexity, and instability of the PPBS cycle (Ansoff, 1984; U.S. General Accounting Office, 1985; Senate Armed Services Committee, 1985). In his testimony before the House Armed Services Committee, Charles Bowsher, Comptroller General of the United States, put it most bluntly: "Our evaluations of DoD's practices clearly show that it does not adequately control its resources; provide its managers, the Congress, or the public with a true accounting for the financial assets entrusted to it; or effectively control costs. DoD needs accurate and comprehensive information of costs, assets, liabilities and funding" (U.S. General Accounting Office, 1990, p. 27).

Besides the constraints just summarized, there are unique features that limit the importation of strategic management into DoD. These include the size and complexity of the department, turnover of personnel, and DoD's mission.

Size and Complexity of DoD

DoD is noted for its sheer size: "There is simply nothing in American civil society that begins to compare with its awesome dimensions" (Luttwak, 1985, p. 68). Significantly larger than any business, the DoD has over four million active-duty, reserve and civilian employees who work directly for it, and over three million additional personnel in the private sector who provide services or products (Brown, 1983; Office of the Secretary of Defense, 1987). By comparison, General Motors (ranked by Dun & Bradstreet as the largest private employer in 1986) had only 600,000 employees (Office of the Secretary of Defense, 1987).

Theorists warn that organizations of such size will suffer from the control problems inherent in all bureaus: "No one can control the behavior of a large organization" (the "Law of Imperfect Control"); "the larger an organization becomes, the weaker is the control over its actions exercised by those at the top" (the "Law of Diminishing Control"); and "the larger any organization bcomes, the poorer is the coordination among its actions" (the "Law of Decreasing Coordination") (Downs, 1967b, pp. 132–143). Downs adds that, despite efforts to significantly increase the data-handling capabilities of the organization, to improve the accounting systems, to develop high-speed computers, and to structurally modify the organization for enhanced coordination, little can be done, especially for managers at the top, to "overcome the basic working out of these Laws" (p. 143). As a consequence, "one of the most serious problems of our times is the management of bigness" (Brown, 1982, p. 74).

Transferring the "small is beautiful" logic sweeping business and industry (Gilder, 1989; Peters, 1988) to DoD is fraught with difficulties. Despite its creation as a single entity, in 1947, and despite the evolutionary changes over the last forty years, which have produced greater consolidation in the Office of the Secretary of Defense (Office of the Secretary of Defense, 1987), the Department of Defense is still described as a fragmented, anarchical collection of feudal baronies (Luttwak, 1985). With many powerful internal and external stakeholders, who have great influence on DoD policy, and with poorly developed internal systems for integrating the department, the Secretary of Defense has minimal tools with which to manage. It is difficult to translate strategic management theory into practice for a multiorganizational bureau under such conditions.

Personnel Turnover

DoD experiences regular and rapid turnover of its civilian personnel, particularly presidential appointees, as do other cabinet departments. The average tenure is calculated to be about three years (Collins, 1982). At the end of fiscal year 1986, the average tenure of presidential appointees in the Office of the Secretary of Defense was twenty-four months, and the average tenure of noncareer executives was slightly over thirty months (Office of the Secretary of Defense, 1987). This rapid turnover limits the participation of top officials in the defense strategy-formulation process: "Average turnovers [are] so short that even fully qualified civilians and military men customarily [find] it almost impossible to promulgate cohesive policies and programs, much less pursue them to successful conclusions" (Collins, 1982, p. 105). What compounds these problems is the mandatory turnover in military personnel. While the time period varies, military personnel typically change their billets once every two to three years, to rotate between combat and support functions. This turnover, coupled with civilian changes, challenges institutional memory and continuity. Not only is routine functioning disrupted; significant change projects that require a significant period of time also suffer from lack of coordination. Strategic management theory assumes that organizational adaptation to the environment is vital for organizational survival, but DoD's personnel policies limit the continuity of personnel in managing these adaptations.

Mission and Visibility of DoD

With responsibility for implementing the military strategy of the United States, DoD must be ready to use violence to achieve national objectives whenever peaceful efforts fail. As a consequence, every American (and, some would add, the entire international community) has a stake in how well the department is run. DoD accountability is of great concern under these circumstances, and the public, through presidential elections and oversight committees in Congress, reviews defense policy and its execution. Task forces, blue-ribbon commissions, and special hearings in Congress also investigate various aspects of defense management and provide additional opportunities to examine operations. As we saw in the Desert Storm operation, television opens up new avenues by which DoD performance can be judged. No other bureau is so visible or so important, and no other elicits as much public interest as the DoD does. This interest has increased lately, given the growing cost of supporting the department and its mission. Questions such as "How much is enough?" have surfaced again as defense needs compete with those of other critical services and domestic needs (Fox, 1988). How these questions will be addressed and answered remains to be determined: "There is no rational system whereby the Executive Branch and the Congress reach coherent and enduring agreement on national military strategy, the forces to carry it out, and the funding that should be provided— in light of the overall economy and competing claims on national resources. The absence of such a system contributes substantially to the instability and uncertainty that plague our defense program" (Packard Commission, 1986, p. 472). It is precisely this type of system that strategic management seeks to introduce, and it is precisely this system that will be difficult to introduce, given the limits just outlined.

Discussion and Conclusions

Readers interested in the strategic management of public bureaus are left with a major dilemma, if they accept the arguments in this chapter. The major model of enterprise-based strategic management tends to be more useful and appropriate in smaller organizations operating in fairly stable environments—organizations with consistent routines and fewer changes in technologies, competitors, customers, employees, suppliers, distributors, and relations with other key stakeholders (such as governmental agencies). That model has been less successful in large organizations facing turbulent and complex environments that require adaptation and innovation in response to changing circumstances (De Greene, 1982; Mintzberg, 1990). In fact, strategic management in a chaotic environment is neither well understood nor well practiced (Peters, 1988). Under these conditions, some even question the possibility of any purposeful organizational strategy at all (Astley and Van de Ven, 1983).

Thus, rather than turning our attention to public bureaus that "fail" to transfer strategic management principles from enterprises, we would do better to direct our energy toward the failure of the strategic management models themselves. It is a major premise of this chapter that problems in transferring enterprise-based strategic management to public bureaus occur, not because of the enormity of the task to be accomplished, but because the model itself fits poorly with a bureau's context. What multiorganizational bureaus managing in very turbulent environments need are new images and models to guide strategic choice. But where does one find such images and models? Enterprise-based strategic management provides little guidance. Isolated insights have begun to cast doubt on the assumptions of strategic management models (Morgan, 1983, 1986; Mintzberg, 1990; De Greene, 1982; Gemmill and Smith, 1985), but strategy research has produced no alternatives.

An example will illustrate this point. According to strategic management theory, if a strategic manager were searching for models to guide the strategy process, she would have three alternatives from which to choose: the entrepreneurial model, the incremental model, or the planning model (Mintzberg, 1974). Theoretically, the model selected would depend on the nature of the organization's context, the time needed to make strategic decisions, and the organization's internal task requirements for integration. Figure 12.2 illustrates how these models can be graphically displayed.

The *entrepreneurial model* of strategic decision making is characterized by the search for innovations and new opportunities. Time is of the essence. Quick, bold responses to environmental opportunities can give an organization an edge over its competitors. As a result, decision-making authority tends to rest with an entrepreneur, and complex decision processes are avoided, since they slow down the response time. Imagination, flexibility, and creativity are more highly valued than concern for internal coordination,

Figure 12.2. Decision-Making Models.

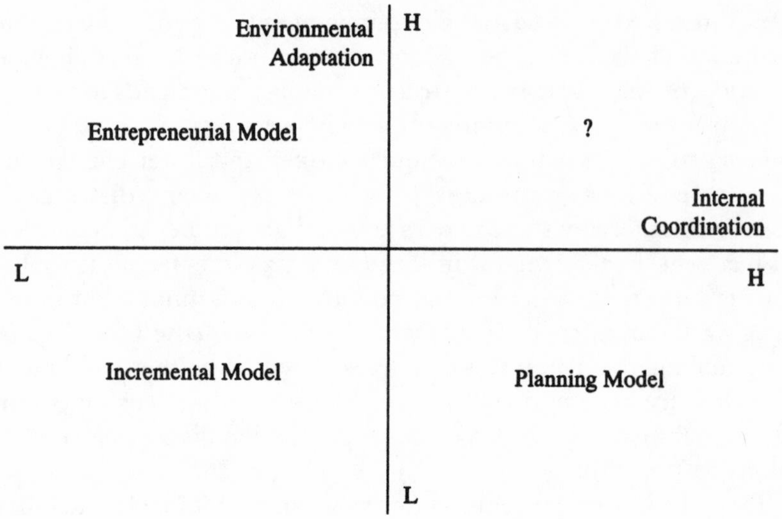

```
             Environmental  | H
               Adaptation   |
                            |
     Entrepreneurial Model  |              ?
                            |
                            |                     Internal
                            |                   Coordination
                            |
     L ─────────────────────┼────────────────────── H
                            |
                            |
      Incremental Model     |        Planning Model
                            |
                            |
                            | L
```

integration, and control. Any coordination that does occur depends on the entrepreneur and on her personal ability to quickly integrate organizational responses to the environment.

The *incremental model* is characteristic of organizations with no one central source of power but rather multiple centers, each with its own goals and objectives. Decisions in this complex environment tend to be made in small, disjointed, incremental steps. The steps are small, to avoid triggering resistance from the opposing factions; disjointed, because no one has the capacity to interrelate and integrate them, given the multiple centers of power and the complexity of the process; and incremental, because it is easier to "test the water," collect feedback, and make adjustments as one goes along. Integration needs are of less concern, since serial adjustments to accommodate competing demands substitute for reconciliation of interests as a whole and for the forging of a coherent entity. Time presses less on decision making, since adaptation to the demands of others is viewed as more important than rapid response for the purpose of innovation and change.

The *planning model* describes the systematic assessment of the costs and benefits of alternative proposals for the future and, through that process, the choice of a desired end state. A comprehensive plan is designed, to interrelate all the organization's decisions and activities. Coordination is paramount, to avoid the inherent conflicts when decisions and actions are made independently of one another. Rapid response to the organization's environment is less important than coordinated action. The organization's environment tends to be stable, and so patterns can be anticipated and built in to cost-benefit analysis. More important to the strategic decision process is the coordination required to implement the comprehensive plan.

The question mark in Figure 12.2 makes the point that no model has yet been identified that can enable decision makers to make strategic choices quickly in response to environmental changes while maintaining the organization's internal coherence and integrative capacity. Yet it is this type of situation that most characterizes the needs of large organizations as they cope with environmental chaos and turbulence. The search is for mechanisms to enhance internal coordination while ensuring continued flexibility in response to the environment. Historically, organizations have not done well at both tasks, at least not for prolonged periods. The tendency has been to focus on one dimension (either coordination or adaptation) to the detriment of the other.

Concentration on internal coordination and integration, for example, tends to make organizations inward-looking, without concern for their external environments. Unaware of their contexts, they often have been unable to adapt if their external environments changed. (The U.S. car companies of the 1970s are a good example of this problem.) Organizational emphasis on flexibility and responsiveness to the external environment usually provokes various types of decentralization: the organization wants to be closer to its "markets" and "customers" than a centralized structure permits; its goal is to be innovative and flexible in response to customers' needs. The danger is that decentralization can produce even greater specialization and fragmentation among the organization's subparts, resulting in less interest and concern for the organization as a whole. Without some mechanism to hold the organization together, subgoals can form, to threaten organizational cohesion.

Thus we are at an important juncture. Models from enterprise-based strategic management do not fit well with organizations that have high needs for coordination and adaptation, and new models have yet to evolve. We are in search of new forms of social organization (Drucker, 1988; Jelinek, Litterer, and Miles, 1986). Current suggestions on how to proceed are provocative but have not produced recommendations developed enough for immediate application. For example, to move us beyond our old paradigmatic thinking, some analysts have encouraged the use of innovative concepts and insights that have emerged from the revolution in physics, chemistry, biology, and the cognitive sciences (Bradley, 1987; Gemmill and Smith, 1985; Morgan, 1983). Other interesting suggestions have come from social theorists, on self-designing organizations and adaptive designs (De Greene, 1982; Jantsch, 1975, 1980). Morgan (1986) recommends the use of alternative images or metaphors of organizations, to help managers characterize the complex character of organizational life; he hopes that this creative exercise can point to possibilities for designing and managing organizations in ways not thought possible before. While intriguing, these concepts and insights have yet to be molded into a coherent epistemology, let alone a comprehensive framework that could guide strategic action in organizations

(Daneke, 1990). And no substitute for the current approach to strategic management exists to guide strategic choice in large multiorganizational bureaus that need to adapt and maintain their cohesiveness. At this juncture, perhaps the best one can hope for is "imaginization" and invention as people begin to recreate and rewrite the strategic maps of their organizations. Finding the logic of "rational," comprehensive action too limiting, the beliefs about management control illusory, and the acceptance of the status quo unimaginative and too costly, one welcomes the discovery of new forms of social organization to open up the promise of the future.

13

TOWARD A THEORY
OF PUBLIC MANAGEMENT SUCCESS

Eugene B. McGregor, Jr.

*P*ublic management needs a theory of success with respect to performance and productivity. The need is both academic and practical. On the academic side, one must wonder how long and in what way a public management business with increasingly strong professional pretensions can maintain itself if its repertoire does not include at least one reasonably strong model of success. On the practical side, a drama is unfolding involving stakes and outcomes that dwarf the significance of the academic play, for the current scale and pace of real-world events have conspired to remove the old stages on which the public management act was presented. At this writing, new stages are under construction, and new plays are being written about the global search for competitive economic development advantage; energy development and allocation; environmental management problems associated with ozone depletion, ocean pollution, toxic-waste disposal, and rain forest destruction; massive population shifts deriving from differential rates of birth, death, and life expectancy; and a miscellany of conundrums associated with such problems as poverty, hunger, ignorance, international drug trafficking, terrorism, and the spread of AIDS.

No theory of public management success currently exists, despite many recent encouraging formulations of public bureaucracy (Metcalfe and Richards, 1987; Heymann, 1987; DiLulio, 1989; Wilson, 1989; Ostrom, 1990; Lynn, 1990) and optimistic soundings (Ukeles, 1982; Rainey, 1991; Wise, 1991; Bozeman and Straussman, 1990). Some of the more important recent probes include public adaptations of the "total quality management" (TQM) prescriptions (Deming, 1982a, 1982b; Gitlow and Gitlow, 1987; Mizuno, 1988; Sensenbrenner, 1991) and useful suggestions for breaking through the staff-line rigidities of public bureaucracy (Barzelay, 1992). In addition, there is a growing body of rich insights into government reinvention (Osbourne and Gaebler, 1992), public sector leadership (Behn, 1991a), and the achievement of public service "excellence" (Peters and Waterman,

1982; Knauft, Berger, and Gray, 1991; Ingraham and Kettl, 1992). Public sector innovations can be found at all governmental levels, including even the most rural communities (Cigler, 1991). Notwithstanding a growing list of encouraging probes and cases, a theory of management success has proved elusive.

Because theory is, by definition, a mental construct designed to permit the analyst to make general statements about specific cases, theory is, in a narrow technical sense, wrong. Yet the practical utility of theory is often overlooked. Theory is what enables the analyst to abstract the essential characteristics of practical problems, to invent alternative proposals that might be chosen to solve problems, to imagine the effects that would occur if one or another proposal were selected, and to understand the complex details that would have to be managed in order to produce a desired effect on public affairs. It is theory that frees the mind both to rearrange the empirical world and to assess the likely outcomes if that world were in fact rearranged.

This means that theories of success require generalizations about two types of problems. One involves design generalizations, whereby a normative framework clarifies goals and problems, depicts alternative ways to reach complex policy goals, and compares choice options. The second involves descriptive generalization, whereby guesses are codified about what will occur when a design option is selected. In both cases, solutions to the problems of design and generalization do not depend on elaborate descriptions of the unique except as they may be useful in anchoring general statements to case applications. Instead, solutions depend on developing powerful abstractions that can be put to practical use.

By contrast to the need, what has often dominated public management discussions is a cataloguing (McGregor, 1991) of program failure, cutbacks, decline, and misadventures of public policy and administration, as well as a theoretical expectation that much public management effort is bound to fail. One potential practical effect of this once "rising business" in "decline" is a potential rejection of public management activities and instruments on the grounds that the public management hand is a weak one and, when played, produces small and unreliable outcomes. The cumulative impact is that one can even imagine scenarios in which a cynical public dooms itself to living out a self-fulfilling prophecy — presumptions of failure feeding underachievement, thereby reinforcing the original presumption — so mistrustful does a public become of public management's capacity to use instruments of public action effectively (Osborne and Gaebler, 1992).

Another Look at the "Moon and Ghetto" Problem

The intellectual question is whether a general logic can be developed that will support public management practice. This is the essence of the "moon and ghetto" problem (Nelson, 1977). Simply stated, the problem is this: if public management has succeeded at one spectacular accomplishment, such as going to the moon, why can it not . . . ? One obvious answer to the "moon and ghetto" question entails the use of an analogy, in which analysis models public management practice on the behavior of a specific "star" program, such as NASA's Apollo program (Webb, 1969). This transfer of case-specific knowledge to a new case works only if the demands of the new case match the reigning "success" offered on the supply side by the old case (Nelson, 1977). Thus, if the problems of cities, public schools, welfare agencies, and solid-waste disposal can be cast as large problems of research and development (R&D), amenable to a NASA-type project management approach, then the lessons of the Apollo program will have a natural appeal. Should a mismatch occur between either the demands of the problem or the constraints placed on its solution (for example, that the solution must be revenue-neutral) and the assumptions of the institutional model, then the analogy is misplaced. Alternatively, should yesterday's success story enter a period of decline (McCurdy, 1991), then the analogy must be defended on the basis of the historical memory of how the success was achieved, rather than on the basis of adapting it to current practice.

A second approach might be to state generally what we think we know about success and failure, and then apply a general formulation (about what works and what does not work) to specific cases. This approach is attempted here. A review of the literature reveals no obvious and complete theory of success, but partial theories of success and failure can be found in abundance and are catalogued in Table 13.1. Theories classified under "failure" represent theorems and arguments about things that went wrong or that pose impediments to effective problem solving and decision making. Thus, to discover that socially unattractive clients, constituent conflict, lack of professional standing, and weak agency mythology can conspire to make certain management jobs "impossible" (Hargrove and Glidewell, 1990), or that public problems resemble "garbage cans" of problems, solutions, and participants (Cohen, March and Olsen, 1972), or that the absence of goals and feedback accounts for programmatic failure (Kettl, 1988), is to add important insights to the stock of knowledge about what does not work or what impedes success. This is not the same as finding that if strategic conditions were obtained, success would follow.

By contrast, theories of success represent accounts of situations in which success is engineered, in the sense that if specific conditions exist, then success is expected. Thus discovery of the conditions under which compliance with executive command is obtained (Barnard, 1938; Neustadt, 1960) and power is exercised (Lynn, 1987; Heymann, 1987) does satisfy the test of theoretical success. The direct implication is that if hypothesized conditions are achieved, a desired and predicted result will occur. The theoretical challenge, of course, is to discover the conceptual "glue" that holds together the two columns of theory from which can be fashioned generalizations about success and failure. As already stated, there is no comprehensive theory of public management success. A list of selected partial theories has been compiled

Table 13.1. Selected Partial Theories of Public Management Success and Failure.

Failure	Success
Cutbacks and decline (Levine, 1978, 1979) (G)	Economy of incentives (Barnard, 1938) (G)
Garbage cans (Cohen, March, and Olsen, 1972) (G)	Presidential power (Neustadt, 1960) (G)
Development of disasters (Turner, 1976) (O)	Strategy and structure (Chandler, 1962) (I)
(Mis)management of goals and feedback (Kettl, 1988) (O)	Implementation success (Sabatier and Mazmanian, 1979 (O)
Permanently failing organizations (Meyer and Zucker, 1989) (G)	Logical incrementalism (Quinn, 1980); tinkering (Sanger and Levin, 1992) (I)
Logic of collective action (Olson, 1965) (G)	Competitiveness and competitive advantage (Porter, 1980, 1985, 1989) (I)
Impossible jobs (Hargrove and Glidewell, 1990) (G)	Politics of public management (Lynn, 1987; Heymann, 1987) (G, O)
Privatizing the public sector (Savas, 1987) (I)	Forward and backward mapping (Elmore, 1982, 1985) (I, O)
Failed governance in public schools (Chubb and Moe, 1990) (G)	Governing the commons (Ostrom, 1990) (G)
Organizational decline (Weitzel and Jonsson, 1989) (I, O, G)	Total quality management (Feigenbaum, 1954; Deming, 1982a, 1982b; Barzelay, 1992) (O)
Resource-hungry bureaucrats (Niskanen, 1971) (O, G)	Effective schools (Chubb and Moe, 1990) (G)
Implementation failure (Pressman and Wildavsky, 1974; Bardach, 1977) (I, O, G)	Public management bromides (Chase and Reveal, 1983) (O, G)
	Leadership (Behn, 1991a) (O, I)

in Table 13.1 to illustrate arguments and allegations about success and failure and help develop a more comprehensive view of success and failure. Review of the table reveals many partial theories of success and failure that provide insights, suggest lessons to be learned, and offer clues about what goes right and wrong in public management. The research challenge is to discover the underlying patterns and subject the derived theory to an empirical test. Fortunately for theory development, repetitive arguments suggest common themes. Indeed, Table 13.1 reveals at least three major problems whose solutions are associated with public management success.

The first is that success is based on a theory of technical intervention, roughly defined as the approval that public policy takes to matching problem demands with the institutional instruments, organizational designs, and work systems required to perform problem-solving tasks. The salience of the intervention issue is evident on the success side of the ledger in the strategic management literature (Chandler, 1962; Quinn, 1980; Sanger and Levin, 1991; Porter, 1980, 1985, 1989) that develops strategies for corporate and national competitiveness. It is also found in the policy analyst's attempts to create "forward and backward" maps connecting problems to problem-solving behavior (Elmore, 1982, 1985). The issue surfaces again on the failure side of the ledger, where alternatives to government production systems — particularly privatized interventions — are offered as more effective, efficient, and accountable than direct government production (Savas, 1987). Partial theories of success and failure that contribute to an understanding of successful and unsuccessful interventions are designated with the letter I.

The second problem involves governance, which refers to the exercise of power. It defines the conditions under which authoritative, winning coalitions are assembled and maintained, so that public action can proceed. The governance issue reminds us that public management designs are not accidents of nature; they are deliberate assignments of resources and work to persons under competitive conditions in which choices get made, goals are embraced and ignored, and winners and losers are created from programs of action. Thus energy is required to create matches of problems seeking solutions and solutions seeking problems (Cohen, March, and Olsen, 1972), and winning political coalitions are required to hold together authoritative matches of problems and solutions. The significance of power is confirmed in an extensive literature documenting that successful public management requires an acceptance of managerial authority (Barnard, 1938; Neustadt, 1960; Chase and Reveal, 1983; Lynn, 1987; Heymann, 1987; Ostrom, 1990; Chubb and Moe, 1990), while unsuccessful public managers either are unable to marshal sufficient power and "energy" to make decisions and establish priorities (Cohen, March, and Olsen, 1972; Olson, 1965) or place power in the wrong locations, so that effective problem solving is rendered impossible (Chubb and Moe, 1990). Partial theories in Table 13.1 that address the question of governance are designated with the letter G.

Third, technically adequate interventions and governance are necessary but insufficient conditions for the creation of public management success. Failure can still occur in many ways, particularly at the operations level of organizations, bureaucracies, and institutions, where operators fail to convert goals and purposes into programs of achievement (Wilson, 1989; Lipsky, 1980). Operations management is sometimes referred to as the "low game of managing public policy" (Lynn, 1987); and, not surprisingly, one measure of executive failure is defined by the inability of political executives to design and install decisions that affect the core operations through which real work is accomplished (Lynn, 1987). The operational literature offers much wise counsel about how public managers can develop routines to deal with bosses and chiefs, cope with staff agencies, and interact effectively with elected officials, special interests, and the media (Chase and Reveal, 1983).

The critical ingredient in operations management is uncertainty. Success requires uncertainty reduction on the part of bureaucratic operators, who must at least cope with the work demands placed on them. Failure, by contrast, thrives under conditions of operational uncertainty (Wilson, 1989). The management failure that arises from operational uncertainty has

many sources. Uncertainty can be generated by unclear goals and interrupted feedback (Kettl, 1987), organizational cultures that ignore signs of
disaster (Turner, 1976), and resource shortfalls that threaten critical operations (Levine, 1978, 1979), to name only a few possibilities. Partial theories
of operational success and failure are designated in Table 13.1 with the letter O.

Evidence

Can a theory of success be derived? A scan of Table 13.1 suggests that, at
the minimum, public management success depends on achieving three strategic positions. First, the proposed intervention cannot be technically flawed.
Given technical feasibility, the second test is one of governance: an authoritative coalition of interests must want an intervention to occur and be prepared to hold its ground, in order to hold strategic program designs together
under competitive conditions. Third, there must be operational clarity and
precision about the critical tasks to be performed. Intervention, governance,
and operational clarity, taken together, form a trichotomy of standards defining what works and what does not.

Does the trichotomy theory work? Useful theory ought to be able to
explain case outcomes of public management success and failure. A classic
problem intrudes, however: experimental and quasi-experimental research
designs might suggest many theoretical possibilities for testing theory, but
research options are limited. For one thing, real management decision making
finds it difficult to establish control groups from which to withhold treatments and interventions widely thought to be successful. For another, interrupted time-series analyses often require extraordinary patience and good
luck to be able to generate enough longitudinal data to state whether management has been effective. Finally, case studies of purported success or failure
confront theoretical problems (Yin, 1982a), for questions can be raised about
the missing complement: If success is the only exemplar, then the conditions under which failure would have resulted from management action become difficult to specify and, in any event, are speculative; but if failure
is the only exemplar, then the requirements for success may also be unclear.
(What could have averted the *Challenger* disaster? It is managerially insufficient simply to say, "It was too cold to launch on January 28, 1986.")

A second confounding problem is that the very definitions of success
and failure are slippery and subject to conflicting interpretations and evaluations. The true goals of public action are often elusive. Furthermore, failure
can produce positive value in many indirect ways. Moreover, it often generates the learning curve that leads to success. Success, by contrast, is rarely
unalloyed. It often contains costs and consequences that either are not reck-
oned at the time closest to the most immediate events or are recorded on
ledgers not widely recognized and circulated. Our approach is more limited,
for we concentrate on "judged success," on which general agreement exists

about success and failure. Thus we search for cases where the public goals were understood, the initiatives were undertaken, and the resulting efforts did what was intended, according to the assessments of analysts and well-placed observers. Here, success and failure are clearly limited concepts that do not require a defense on the basis of "truth." Moreover, the reader is not asked to share the biases and opinions of the author.

Accidental sampling of limited success and failure does hold some promise. For example, if it were possible to sample so that agreed cases of success and failure could be listed and compared, analysis could at least respond to two types of questions. First, what do all the successes and all the failures have in common? Second, what factors can be found under one heading but not under the other? Agreement about success and failure avoids many crippling analytical issues, simply by placing the judgment of outcome beyond debate: success and failure are taken as given. Yet clear answers to these questions are made difficult by accidental sampling, for there is no limit placed on the numbers and types of variables that come into play over uncontrolled space and time. Thus there is the risk that examination of complex cases of success and failure may reveal nothing in common, even among agreed common outcomes.

Caveats notwithstanding, a list of successes and failures is provided in Table 13.2. The list is based on a sampling of cases that have been documented by some form of analysis, rather than on the arbitrary opinions of the author. The list is clearly not exhaustive and, in some cases, may prove controversial. Victories have been found lurking in the midst of apparent disaster. As mentioned, successes often contain hidden costs. Furthermore, many case examples have been omitted, because of their inherent complexity (thus, for example, such reputedly elite government agencies as the Marines, the FBI, the CIA, the Forest Service, and the Social Security Administration are not included, given the difficulties of conducting extensive analysis to demonstrate unambiguous success and failure — a requirement for inclusion in the list). As a result, the list emphasizes well-known and relatively documented cases of the successful management of policies, programs, or crises, and it deemphasizes the evaluation of whole agencies whose handling of complex program portfolios is either impossible or controversial and, in any event, has not been authoritatively assessed.

The following general definition was used to create Table 13.2: *success* and *failure* were defined to be outcome-driven (or end state–driven); that is, cases were sought in which it could be said that public management had achieved a desired final result. The public needs of citizens were met as a result of concerted public management action. Failure occurs when, despite the varying efforts of public managers, the agreed-upon public purposes were not met. Such a definition distinguishes public management success strategically, focusing on the transactions between public managers and organizations and on the final outcomes and effects that justify managerial effort. This approach ignores many examples of supportive management tactics

Table 13.2. Selected Cases of Public Management Success and Failure.

Failure	Success
Policy and Progam Management	
Title I of ESEA (Murphy, 1971)	Marshall Plan (Janis, 1982)
New towns-in-town (Derthick, 1972)	TVA (Lilienthal, 1964–1971)
Urban economic development (Pressman and Wildavsky, 1974)	New York City public works, 1930s–1950s (Caro, 1974)
Americanization of Vietnam war (Janis, 1972)	U.S. Nuclear submarine program (Lewis, 1980)
Bay of Pigs (Janis, 1972)	U.S. Coast Guard, dual-purpose mission (Bragaw, 1980)
Community action program (Moynihan, 1969)	Apollo progam (Webb, 1969)
1986 *Challenger* disaster (Vaughan, 1990; Trento, 1987)	U.S. Bureau of Prisons (DiLulio, 1987)
Methadone-maintenance programs (Nelkin, 1973; Hannan, 1976)	Manpower scheduling system (Mechling, 1974)
U.S. savings and loan crisis (Kane, 1989)	Job Corps (Wholey, 1986; Long, Mallar, and Thornton, 1981)
	Blue-ribbon schools (U.S. Department of Education, 1990)
Crisis Management	
Pearl Harbor (Janis, 1972)	Cuban missile crisis (Janis, 1972; Allison, 1969)
Bhopal petrochemical disaster (Rosenthal, Charles, and t'Hart, 1989)	Three Mile Island (Kemeny Commission, 1979; Cantelon and Williams, 1982)
Chernobyl nuclear disaster (Rosenthal, Charles, and t'Hart, 1989)	Manhattan Project (Groves, 1962; Jones, 1985; Rhodes, 1988)
Irangate (t'Hart, 1990)	

and operations that are internal to the business of public management, such as how to configure and manage the overhead agencies (Barzelay and Armajani, 1990). The idea is to be further distinguished from other terms, such as *entrepreneurship* (Osborne and Gaebler, 1992), *innovation* (Sanger and Levin, 1992), *leadership* (Behn, 1991a) and other important behavior that contributes to but is not congruent with success. Finally, our use of the term *success* refers to end-state conditions, rather than to such processes as "evolutionary tinkering" (Sanger and Levin, 1992), "groping along" (Behn, 1988), and logical incrementalism (Quinn, 1980), which have been said to account for the manner in which certain successes have been produced. In short, the use of *success* refers directly to a summary judgment about advancing the public interest (Clotfelter and Cook, 1990), and it ignores many rich insights and much important management research that are intermediate to a judged final result.

If broad agreement can be said to exist about the success and failure of the cases listed in Table 13.2, then case comparison does have one great advantage: the factors found in one column and not in another are not speculative but are based on the facts of the cases. This means that comparison could reveal something about patterns leading to success and patterns associated with failure. Thus we avoid the theoretical trap in the popular literature on management "excellence" (Peters and Waterman, 1982; Gitlow and Gitlow, 1987), which latches on to putative examples of excellence (no cases of failure admitted), whose properties are examined on the *assumption* that their mere existence "proves" excellence. Another frequent assumption is that lessons from the private sector can be transferred automatically to the public sector (Duncan, Ginter, and Capper, 1991). This assessment of the "excellence approach" to comparative case analysis deserves a short digression because it reveals the dilemma with which theory must struggle.

Suppose one accepts that good public managers must do four things to be successful (Duncan, Ginter, and Capper, 1991): build and keep a vision, provide a coaching and developmental style of leadership, foster innovation at the level of grass-roots creativity, and attend to clients' needs. These are encouraging maxims. They are humane and motivating, and they possess commonsense validity based on experience. They are also, like the "proverbs of administration" (Simon, 1957) examined in an earlier time, problematic and incomplete. If these four qualities are indeed critical to success, then how are the Peters and Waterman eight attributes of best-run companies (1982) to be regarded? Are there now twelve rules (or fewer, once the overlaps are taken into account)? And what about Deming's fourteen points for total quality performance (Gitlow and Gitlow, 1987)? Are there now twenty-six rules? Does one then add the special wisdom and insights of such an experienced manager as Gordon Chase to the list (Chase and Reveal, 1983)? The list of "excellence" attributes can grow long indeed.

The real test of such a list is not length, however, but theoretical generality, which in turn hinges on the necessity and sufficiency of the general rules of "excellence." In the examples just cited, the question is whether given maxims are necessary, sufficient, or both. Is there no success that can be achieved without the "magic four" principles? And, if they are only necessary conditions, what must be added to achieve sufficiency? Must the four principles, for instance, be supplemented with technology? incentives? acts of politics? all three? Or are the principles necessary and sufficient turnkeys (one has only to carry them out, and the results will be ensured)? The reader can easily see the drift of this argument.

Table 13.2 does generate an accidental sample of naturally occurring experiments with which to assess the partial theories derived from Table 13.1. If it is true that a theory of success and failure leads us to expect that intervention, governance, and operations are necessary and sufficient for public management success, then the beginning of a testable hypothesis is in the making.

Some clarification of concepts is necessary, however, before we submit the trichotomy theory to case facts. By *problem intervention* we will mean an agency's or program's basis (or lack of it) in a treatment plan that is technically possible, timely, and of a sufficient scale that a reasonable expectation of success exists. Flawed interventions involve technical treatments that cannot be made to work (interventions requiring that water run uphill are doomed, regardless of governance configurations and operations management). For example, manned space flight is possible only when solid or liquid rocket propellants can be developed to lift the requisite payloads, when plasma physics is developed to the point where heat-resistant materials can be adapted to reentry-vehicle construction, and when computers and guidance systems are sufficiently miniaturized. To take an obvious example of failure, the decision to land insurgents, without air cover, at the Bay of Pigs to face Castro's forces was doomed because the intervention itself was flawed: a small invading force, obliged to move through a swamp to engage its adversary, rarely overwhelms a larger force that has not been surprised by strategic cunning, tactical stealth, and swift application of power. Fatally flawed interventions cannot be redeemed by public support (governance) or by smooth execution and performance of critical tasks (operations).

Governance refers to the application of power and authority in a way that commits relevant political actors to managerial decisions. Authoritatively binding conditions of governance exist when a winning coalition of political interests supports a defined course of action. Governance is not to be confused with substantive problem solving; governance is authorizing and enabling action, without which a commitment required to see a technical intervention through must be regarded as missing. Virtually every example of program success found a way to solve the governance question (although the techniques for doing so varied with circumstances). For example, bipartisan congressional support for the Marshall Plan was ensured through the appointment of a Republican, Paul Hoffman, as program head while resources were funneled through the Democrat-controlled White House. Robert Moses sustained his position as New York City public-works czar through his directorship of the Triborough Bridge Authority and through interlocking board directorships (supported by the strategic management of bond sales to banks and brokerages and by contracts to architectural, engineering, and construction firms). Furthermore, his public-works ambitions were sustained by public opinion, leading newspapers, and civic leaders, who during the 1930s, 1940s, and 1950s strongly supported the Moses vision for New York. Similar stories could be told about the early successes of NASA (Webb, 1969, chap. 6), the Tennessee Valley Authority (TVA) (Selznick, 1949), and virtually all the cases in the "success" column.

Operations refers to the completion of the critical tasks required in program success. Standard operating procedures and daily routines of ordinary people establish the work systems that generate success; more precisely, nothing gets done without a properly organized work system. The modes of operation organized in "response to a legally defined requirement for collective action" can be so powerful that the resulting production systems can take on the characteristics of an "operating ideology" (Sharpe, 1985, pp. 371–372). The effective power of operating ideologies is apparent in the ways in which an operating system develops an internal logic, structure, and culture, which effectively resists change and well-meaning attempts at rational direction until the generally accepted policy rationale for a given public service disappears.

Successful work systems are driven in turn by goal clarity regarding the performance of critical tasks (Wilson, 1989). Goal clarity reduces uncertainty, so that the people who are to carry out an assignment know precisely what is expected and what they are to do. Operational clarity does not require organizations to be harmonious, all organizational goals to be ranked and accepted, and all ambiguity to be eliminated. It merely requires clarity about the daily work to be done. Thus the goal for a man to set foot on the surface of the moon before the end of the 1960s, and the goal for the job to be achieved with the best scientific and technical talent in industry and the universities (Webb, 1969), formed the operational basis for NASA's success. The effect of President Kennedy's commitment to NASA's very operational objective was to produce the implied time, cost, and technical performance objectives for NASA operations for the remainder of the 1960s and the early 1970s. Similarly, the simple clarity of the custodial operational goals in the Texas prison system, contrasted with the complexity and lack of goal clarity in the rehabilitation objectives of the Michigan state prison system (DiLulio, 1987; Wilson, 1989), does much to explain a strategic difference between those prisons that succeed and those that do not. One suspects that an examination of successful schools, police departments, welfare offices, and even universities and R&D centers would reveal similar patterns. A conclusion seems supportable: operational goal clarity is as fundamental to success as the nature of the intervention and the system of governance.

Confirmation of the theory lies in the examination of the cases listed in Table 13.2. Simply put, if the trichotomy theory derived from Table 13.1 is correct, then all the instances in the "success" column should display clear evidence of intervention adequacy, authoritative governance, and operational certainty. Furthermore, the theory leads to the conclusion that if any one of the three conditions is missing, the effort is effectively undone. Examination of Table 13.2 indicates that this is precisely what we find, although we must still arrive at a definitive conclusion about what was missing in the cases that involved multidimensional failure. For example, failed intervention plagued the Bay of Pigs operation and the *Challenger* disaster. Flawed intervention most certainly was a strategic problem in the Economic Development Administration's failed attempt to stimulate economic development and job creation through a series of capital-investment grants to the City of Oakland (Pressman and Wildavsky, 1974), so that the likely result was job destruction, rather than job creation. Long and complex stories of intervention flaws can also be told about the Americanization of the conflict in Vietnam, methadone-maintenance programs, and the U.S. savings and loan crisis.

Lack of governance surely characterizes a second significant class of managerial failures. Lack of authoritative support has doomed such high-minded efforts as methadone-maintenance programs, where majority support for free maintenance of a drug addiction is hard to marshal and maintain. Lack of governing commitment was also painfully evident in the war in Vietnam and in the implementation of such seemingly reasonable programs as new towns-in-town (Derthick, 1972) and a community action program (Moynihan, 1969). Finally, the record of NASA's problems during the space-shuttle program era reveals major problems of governance and control, so that one might reasonably argue that the *Challenger* disaster was symptomatic of flawed governance in the American aerospace effort (Trento, 1987), rather than simply the outcome of disastrously flawed managerial decision making.

Operational confusion has plagued programs with otherwise promising prospects for successful intervention and strong political commitment. The implementation of Title I of the Elementary and Secondary Education Act (ESEA) of 1965 depends in large measure on the administrative capacity of state departments of education to target and administer special funds directed toward disadvantaged persons. The U.S. savings and loan crisis unravelled with accelerating and surprising speed, in part because operational inspection systems and warnings were not timely and sufficient. Whether this was a manipulated result, due to political tampering with the regulatory process, is but a further tantalizing complexity of governance, which does not obscure the enormous operational problems in regulating the savings and loan industry.

These summaries are intended merely as illustrations. The realities require much more extensive commentary than can be supplied here. For example, it is clear that success and failure involve multiple factors. Only in the unusual case of failure does intervention or governance or operations stand alone as the one fatal flaw. Failure is generally multidimensional, and much remains to be done in understanding sequences of success and failure and the precise mechanisms involved.

Conclusions

If nothing else, perhaps this chapter suggests that systematic discussions of public management's successes and failures are not entirely futile. Partial theories can be found in abundance. Cases of success are as plentiful as examples of failure. It is not true that public management has no stunning successes from which to learn, and no theories on which to base improvements in practice. Moreover, these findings neither supplant nor contradict a rich and emerging literature on success, excellence, performance, innovation, and entrepreneurship in public and private management. It can only be hoped that a framework might be established, within which many rich contributions can be appreciated.

One can imagine developing a case literature in tandem with increasingly sharp analyses of successes and failures in public management. The dialogue between theory and cases is a complex matter, much more complex than this brief analysis reveals. More ambitious approaches to success and failure will have to balance the temptation to explore the unique with the need to develop generalizations. To savor the peculiarities of each case enormously enlarges the descriptive base characterizing success and failure, in ways not addressed by this chapter. To dive into both the theoretical and the descriptive findings, in an attempt to reduce size and complexity (as this chapter has done), risks ignoring much rich detail that matters to public management. Paradoxically, the success of the theoretical effort should be found in the ability to develop new case materials useful both to practice and to theory. Cases that embrace the three key dimensions of success would be particularly useful.

Much also remains to be done in showing the connections between the trichotomy theory propounded here and the many other topics with strong links to the success and failure of public enterprises. It remains to be shown how advances in such areas as organization design, leadership, management decision making, and new analytical techniques can contribute to the success of the public management enterprise. The trichotomy approach makes it conceivable, for instance, that leadership involves many functions, and that successful leadership somehow involves solving problems of intervention, governance, and uncertainty in operational areas. Whether the successes of the great executives of American public management—David Lilienthal, Herbert Hoover, Robert Moses, James Webb, Paul Appleby, Gordon Chase, and Charles Atkins, to name only a few—can be assessed and appreciated through the use of such a simple theory remains unexamined. A speculative conclusion is that some acts of leadership fall under each of the three agendas, but truly great leadership may well operate under all three simultaneously.

It was the modest aim here to outline a possible approach to the study of an elusive topic. The approach was a simple one. This chapter merely attempted to abstract only the most basic findings from a diverse literature, and to test some crude theoretical hunches with a random but unscientifically drawn list of public management "successes" and "failures." Simplicity, in this case, merely serves as a vehicle for language and logic to show what a more complete theory of success would require, and to demonstrate that it may be possible to make some progress on one of public management's most difficult subjects.

Part Five

POLITICAL INSTITUTIONS
AND PUBLIC MANAGEMENT

*I*n public management, the politics-administration dichotomy, a point of debate occupying public administration scholars for decades, seems moot. Public management scholars assume that politics infuses virtually every aspect of public management, and much theory and research centers on political institutions and processes. The four quite varied chapters in this section take different approaches to the study of the politics of public management, but each treats politics as primal.

Recently, researchers have become much more cognizant of the public management issues entailed in the administration of the judiciary, long the preserve of political scientists studying judicial politics. Public management scholars have taken a somewhat different perspective—examining managerial issues, but within the distinctive context of the courts. Rosemary O'Leary and Jeffrey D. Straussman are chiefly concerned with research into the impact of the courts on public managers. They argue that many of the propositions about the courts' impact are based on shaky evidence, and that these are composed almost entirely of "wisdom knowledge" (which they define, a bit more narrowly than Bozeman in Part One, as "insider first-person accounts"). They present some of the most familiar propositions about the courts' impact on public managers, grouped into five categories.

Also concerned with legal dimensions of public management, Heidi O. Koenig examines a quite different political-institutional realm. Koenig's chapter focuses on the public management role of the President, with particular attention to the President's influence on the Department of Justice Division of Antitrust. Working within the framework of principal-agent theory, she tests a number of explicit hypotheses about presidential influence, including propositions about the role of deregulation and budgetary change.

Steven Kelman focuses on legislatively mandated restrictions on former government employees' jobs—the so-called revolving-door restrictions, including restrictions under the Ethics in Government Act of 1978 and amendments passed in 1979 and 1989. Kelman considers arguments for and against revolving-door restrictions. Arguments against restrictions include the argument that individuals with experience in both the public and the private sector are likely to make better decisions than those with experience in only one sector, and that legislation inhibiting the acquisition of broader experience is in some respects counter to the public interest.

Finally, Jameson W. Doig shows the relevance of historical analysis to public management research and theory. The New York Port Authority was the first "public authority" created in the United States and represents, among other motives, an attempt to insulate administration from politics. Doig's historical-political analysis shows that whatever else was realized by the Port Authority, political independence was not. Indeed, the early history of the Port Authority can be understood in terms of a "garbage can" model of decision making, in which politics were strewn throughout the can.

14

The Impact of Courts
on Public Management

Rosemary O'Leary,
Jeffrey D. Straussman

*I*t is safe to assert that the world of public management is shaped, to some extent, by the courts. Court decisions affect both the conduct and the content of public management. For example, court decisions determine the liability of public organizations and public managers, which in turn yields changes in operating procedures, to avoid future liability. Judges may influence budgets by mandating expenditures. Courts also shape public personnel practices by enforcing due-process procedures, to protect employees from arbitrary dismissal. The impact of courts on public management is so pervasive that the National Association of Schools of Public Affairs and Administration (NASPAA) recently mandated the study of law and courts by students of public affairs.

The importance of law in the conduct of public affairs is not a new subject. Woodrow Wilson (1887) alluded to the link between law and public administration in his famous essay "The Study of Administration." Similarly, both Goodnow (1900) and White (1926) discussed the role of law in public administration. Yet it was Judge David Bazelon, then chief judge of the U.S. Court of Appeals for the District of Columbia Circuit, who, in his 1971 decision suspending the use of the lethal pesticide DDT in the United States, wrote of a new collaborative "partnership" between judges and public managers in the then-recently created U.S. Environmental Protection Agency (see Bazelon, 1976). Only a few years later, the involvement of the courts in various areas of public policy was attacked as an "imperial judiciary" (Glazer, 1975). The "new partnership" subsequently was labeled a pseudonym for judicial usurpation of administrative power (Melnick, 1985). Today, the debate concerning the impact of courts on public management continues in social science journals, law reviews, and, perhaps most important, among public managers, plaintiffs, attorneys, judges and judicially appointed overseers of agency activities.

189

The purpose of this chapter is to assess the major themes in the literature concerning the impact of courts on public management. The term *public management,* as used in this chapter, includes both elements of public administration (the internal dimensions of bureaucracies, such as budgeting, personnel, and structure) and development and implementation of strategy, which necessarily includes linkages between managers and an organization's external environment.

We raise two questions concerning this body of literature. First, what do we think we know about the impact of courts on public management? By the phrase "impact on," we do not mean to imply that the relationship between courts and public management is only an external one; rather, we acknowledge that law, with its diverse sources, in many instances is the "water" in which public administrators "swim." An example can be found in the field of personnel administration, in which such concepts as due process and equal protection have revolutionized recruitment, selection, and promotion procedures (Shafritz, Hyde, and Rosenbloom, 1986). Public administration is produced within the law and at the same time is affected by the law (see Wasby, 1970a, 1970b). We also acknowledge that courts themselves are public organizations. Second, how do we know what we know? That is, are there any *empirical* foundations to what we know? We define *empirical* as follows: "It must rely on perceptions, experience, and observations. Perception is a fundamental tenet of the scientific approach, and it is achieved through our senses . . . . Knowledge is held to be a product of one's experiences, as facets of the physical, biological, and social world play upon the senses. . . . [It is based on the assumption that] pure reason alone is [in]sufficient to produce verifiable knowledge" (Nachmias and Nachmias, 1987, pp. 9–10). Hence, our concern is primarily with whether there is evidence-based research to support the claims for court-agency interaction in the literature that we have surveyed.

This chapter concludes that, despite spirited debate on the subject of court-agency interaction, the empirical foundations for most of the conclusions concerning the impact of courts on public management are quite weak. While there are some strong conceptual works in the literature, based largely on legal analyses of case law, few scholars have studied the impact of courts on public management through one or more of the standard empirical methods: theoretically informed case studies, comparative case analyses, surveys, interviews, and statistical analyses of quantitative data. Given the paucity of empirically based research, we conclude that much of our "knowledge" of the impact of the courts on public management is based, at best, on thoughtful speculation or wisdom, with few or no data (broadly defined) to support it. Before we begin, a few caveats are in order.

First, the literature cited here is not the only scholarly discourse on the subject. There are numerous studies, for example, of the impact of courts on police practices (Milner, 1970; Stephens, 1973; Wasby, 1973), on school prayer (Johnson, 1967; Muir, 1967; Dolbeare and Hammond, 1971), and on school desegregation (Hogan, 1985; Tyack and Benavot, 1985; Dimond, 1985; Schwartz, 1986) that are of paramount importance, but they may not be broadly applicable to public management as a whole. Therefore, we have selected what we consider to be only those works that address some of the most fundamental issues facing public managers today. These include authority in public organizations, agenda setting, the external environment of public organizations, and the management of resources.

Second, surveying methods of inquiry in the literature proved to be an immense challenge with imprecise results. In most instances, the authors did not articulate in their works what their methods of inquiry or sources of data were. In such instances, we had no choice but to infer methodology from the context of the work.

Third, not all "propositions" presented here are created equal. They were taken directly from the literature, as presented by the authors. Some address very specific and narrowly defined areas of court-agency interaction; others are broader in nature. Some of the authors intended to frame issues and formulate hypotheses, rather than test them. Other authors intended merely to communicate insights or conjectures inspired from a reading of landmark cases. Differences in wording and coverage of the propositions reflect the different approaches to this type of research found in the literature.

Fourth, by assessing the empirical nature of the following works, we do not intend to imply that empiricism is "good" while other types of research are "bad." Our intention is not to judge but rather to map the collective observations and claims of authors in this field. Our hope is that, by our assessing the evidence concerning the impact of courts on public management, both gaps in the literature and future opportunities for research will become evident.

The following are the "top twenty" propositions concerning courts and public managers found in the literature, which we have divided into five broad themes: the legitimacy of judicial intervention into public management; capacity and competence; setting of the public management agenda; bureaucratic strategy; and management of resources.

Legitimacy of Judicial Intervention

The perceived increase in involvement of the courts in public administration has been accompanied by a debate concerning the legitimacy of such involvement and the capacity of the courts to enforce their decisions. On the first issue, negative appraisals have been captured in Glazer's phrase "the imperial judiciary" (1975), which yielded an image of judges unimpressed by suggestions that their intrusions into the business of the executive and legislative branches violated the intent of the framers of the Constitution. Those who focused on the capacity theme purportedly have some empirical evidence on their side. Horowitz (1977), for example, after studying four cases, concludes that there is a large gap between legal doctrines promulgated by judges and their actual administrative implementation. He ends his study with the caution that judicial intervention in the affairs of the other branches would seriously endanger the constitutional role given to the courts. There have been many related assertions concerning judicial intervention in public management in the literature. They are summed up in the following propositions.

1. *Judges have been aggressive and active in their oversight of administrative agencies.* Frug (1978), Melnick (1983), and Rosenbloom (1983) are representative of those authors who maintain that judges have been aggressive and active in their oversight of administrative agencies. Frug, who examines federal courts' attempts to remedy the constitutional violations of public organizations (such as prisons and mental health facilities) by mandating government expenditures, concludes that the lower courts were largely responsible for judicial activism at a time, ironically, when the Supreme Court was emphasizing "the proper and properly limited role of the courts in a democratic society." Melnick, who has studied the impact of court decisions on the U.S. Environmental Protection Agency's (EPA) air pollution control programs in six different scenarios, concludes that judges in recent years have become increasingly aggressive in shaping Clean Air Act regulatory policy, abandoning their traditional deference to bureaucratic expertise. Rosenbloom, analyzing the judicial response to the rise of the administrative state, concludes that the federal judiciary has established sufficient leverage and control over public administration to secure itself a "coequal status" with the other branches of government" (Rosenbloom, 1983, p. 208).

Two immediate problems arise with their first proposition, which are endemic in many that follow: the use of terms that are not adequately defined, and the assertion of conclusions that cannot be tested. What does it mean to be "aggressive" in the oversight of administrative agencies? How does one interpret or test the concept of "coequality?"

None of these three authors attempts to explain his method of inquiry. It is clear, however, that the authors rely on court decisions and on the work of others for their arguments. Of the three, only Melnick mentions having examined other primary or secondary sources of information, such as archival materials and interviews with organization staff. Further, while each of these authors presents interesting examples of aggressive and active judges, one cannot logically conclude whether the illustrations represent significant departures from the past, signaling a new era in judicial-administrative relations, or whether they are merely isolated cases.

2. *Judges may become invested in the outcome of litigation involving public institutions and, as a result, lose their "cloak of neutrality."* In assessing a particular remedy in cases involving public organizations, the focus often shifts from the "rightness" of the issue to a focus that includes "effectiveness." Cramton (1976) argues that when a judge is forced to become an administrator, there is a potential loss of neutrality. According to Horowitz (1983), when judges

become invested in the outcome of litigation, it may jeopardize their typically balanced perspective. This conclusion is furthered by Rosenbloom, who
concludes that "as judges become active in public administration they are
almost certain to lose their cloak of neutrality" (Rosenbloom, 1983, p. 223).

Like the previous proposition, these concepts lack precision. The concept of judicial neutrality is certainly an important one, yet how does one
define and measure "neutrality?" How do we know when a "cloak of neutrality" has been lost? How did these authors come to these conclusions?
Again, none of these three authors attempts to explain his method of inquiry. The primary methods that can be inferred are examination of court
decisions and of the work of others, coupled with pure reasoning. No empirical evidence is furnished to support the conclusions concerning the loss
of "a cloak of neutrality," nor are formal propositions advanced concerning
the consequences of such a loss for the management of administrative agencies. Rosenbloom, however, does offer some informal propositions, predicting
that the impact of courts on public administration will have the following
effects: hierarchy will be undercut, impersonality will be diminished, specialization will be enhanced, formalization will be enhanced, merit-oriented public
personnel administration will be strengthened, and the size of public bureaucracies is likely to grow (1983, pp. 214–217).

3. *Judicial activity can result in "wrong" or "bad" policy.* Two authors, Glazer
(1978) and Melnick (1983) describe judicial-administrative interaction and
conclude that courts may make "incorrect" policy decisions. Glazer asks,
"Should judges administer social services?" and then offers five hypotheses
concerning the impact of the judiciary's administrative decision making on
social policy. One hypothesis predicts that, as judges intervene more often
in administration, theoretical knowledge will be given greater weight by
judges than the practical knowledge of administrators, and such reliance on
theoretical knowledge may cause social policy to be turned in a direction
that is "wrong." Melnick (1983), examining Clean Air Act court decisions,
provides examples of judicial decisions that he deems "bad" policy.

The primary weaknesses of these conclusions are the value judgments
and measurement difficulties inherent in attempting to ascertain "wrong-
ness" or "badness." (Some writers have consciously declined to make such
determinations. For example, Cooper, 1988, in his work on federal courts
and state and local governments, declares his unwillingness to engage in
such debate.) At best, we have in the literature a handful of examples of
what individual authors deem "wrong" or "bad" decisions, examples that are
built on a very thin empirical base and that are not generalizable.

Can progress be made on this proposition? Robert Wood, who was
superintendent of the Boston schools in 1979 and 1980, identifies three adverse impacts of remedial law on public management. First, court orders
are often inflexible because they stand unless and until they are reheard by
a judge—a cumbersome process. This arrangement may even produce unintended and, indeed, counterproductive results. Wood indicates that a 1975

order, creating an outcome-based formula for the racial composition of Boston schools, was infeasible, given the shifting demographies of the city. He offers the following vignette: "At one point, we sought to demonstrate to the court that, as a matter of mathematics, we could not comply with a 1975 formula stipulating the school composition of white, black, and other minority students; a decline in white students after 1975 had rendered impossible the outcome required by the court. The court's response was 'that was a matter for Dr. Einstein.' The 1975 order stood" (Wood, 1982, p. 462). Wood also notes that prescriptive requirements promulgated by the courts may be misguided in light of the actual operations of an agency. Here, he points out how the court's requirement for community participation in administrative hiring (presumably for affirmative action objectives) was easily subverted in practice; nevertheless, the court held to its original requirement. Wood laments that court intervention can blur (and perhaps erode) a manager's accountability: individuals representing plaintiffs and court officials may intrude directly into matters traditionally left to educational administrators (Wood, 1982, pp. 462–463).

Are Wood's observations empirically informed? Yes. Are they rigorous and systematic? No. Wood's observations primarily illustrate the value of wisdom in advancing empirical analysis, because his argument is based on participant observation. But we still lack a generalizable framework from which to assess "bad" policy. Wood's work, however, does provide us with some ideas to construct such a framework, which would be drawn from analyses of implementation and political feasibility.

4. *Judicial interaction with administrative agencies can jeopardize representative democracy.* Rosenbloom (1983) analyzes the judicial response to the rise of the administrative state and concludes that judicial-administrative interaction can jeopardize representative democracy. Federal judges are not elected. They are largely unaccountable to the rest of the political system. Judicial interaction with administrative agencies can establish priorities, leaving the electorate with little recourse. One example in support of Rosenbloom's study can be found in the work of O'Leary and Wise (1991) who have analyzed a court-imposed tax to remedy constitutional violations in the Kansas City school system.

Clearly, any court-imposed order that "usurps" executive and/or legislative authority (such as the power to tax) may be attacked on the grounds that it jeopardizes representative democracy. Without belittling the importance of this insight, however, we can say that its broad sweep offers a challenge to systematic investigation of the impact of the courts on public management. For example, how common are such intrusions? It is also important to distinguish between a court-imposed resolution to a dispute (such as a tax increase chosen by a judge) and a liability judgment that may result in a remedy (such as a tax increase) that the legislature would not have selected in the absence of the judgment. This is not simply a semantic quibble; after all, the role of the courts in our constitutional system has always allowed for the latter scenario. To substantiate this proposition, the frequency and type of intrusions by the courts into executive and legislative prerogatives must be studied. Furthermore, it is important to demonstrate that the political branches are being "forced" to make decisions that they would not make in the absence of judicial intervention. Only then would it be possible to fully debate the significance of court-agency interactions for representative democracy, as well as the precise effects on public management.

Capacity and Competence

The debate over the appropriateness of judicial intervention into the affairs of public agencies rages on, without resolution. Studies have been completed on individual judges (Yarbrough, 1982), as well as on some of the legal battles that have received national attention (such as the battle between the courts and the Reagan administration over the implementation of the social security disability program; see Mezey, 1986). Several policy areas have received scholarly attention, including corrections (DiLulio, 1990), mental health and developmental disabilities (Rothman and Rothman, 1984) and the environment (Melnick, 1983; O'Leary, 1989). A recent gathering of experts, who discussed the impact of the courts in the area of remedial law, illustrates both how far we have come in our understanding of the spectrum of the courts' intervention activities and the continuing propensity to blend empirical statements with sweeping normative assertions (Wood, 1990). A pessimistic prognosis concerning the capacity of courts to influence the essential dimensions of public management competently and predictably is based on four propositions. As in the case of the previous theme, the empirical evidence is thin.

5. *Judges must often rely on other courts and other organizations to supervise the implementation of a court decision.* In their synthesis of the judicial-impact literature, Johnson and Canon (1984) conclude that there is often a wide gulf between a judge's decision and the implementation of that decision. The authors point out that judicial decisions are not self-implementing, nor are judges capable of closely supervising day-to-day operations of government agencies. As a result, judges often rely on other courts (for example, in the case of a remand or an appeal) or on nonjudicial actors in the political system (such as interest groups that threaten to refile lawsuits, court-appointed masters, and oversight committees) to implement decisions. These findings support the early work of Glick (1970), who concludes that state supreme courts, as interest groups, seek access to other political decision makers in order to urge the adoption of policies that they cannot implement themselves.

Evidence about the impact of court-appointed oversight bodies is mixed. Insider accounts by participants who were defendants in remedial cases tend to portray the effectiveness of these bodies as minimal. Wood (1982), in his first-person account of the challenges of managing the Boston school system under a court order, refers to difficulties faced in reconciling procedures required by the oversight committee and to his conception of the realities of managing a large school system. Yarbrough's study (1985) of the *Wyatt* v. *Stickney* case finds that an oversight committee provided a valuable link between a state agency and a judge. This link, according to Yarbrough, was instrumental in the implementation of the remedy.

Insider accounts and single case studies are informative, but no study compares, from a management perspective, the implementation of a court decision under a court-appointed oversight committee with either the "normal" implementation of a judicial decision or the implementation of a policy in the absence of a judicial mandate. (We realize that such a study would involve a comparison that, by definition, cannot actually be made: it is impossible to find two organizations or situations that are identical for the purposes of such a comparison; ideas for minimizing the degree of error in such a study, however, are offered briefly in the concluding section of this chapter.) Further, because the few empirical studies that do exist are all case studies of the implementation of one decision, it is certainly premature to deduce any general principles about the implications of judges' reliance on external bodies.

6. *Judicial decisions concerning public agencies often include detailed judicial supervision of organizations (including ongoing, affirmative decrees), with frequent judicial interaction with agency staff.* It is widely assumed that public-law litigation does not merely clarify the meaning of the law; it establishes a regime that orders the future interaction of the parties (and perhaps also of those who are not parties), subjecting them to continuing judicial oversight (Chayes, 1976; Frug, 1978; Fiss, 1978; Horowitz, 1983). The judge plays an active role in such an endeavor—structuring the suit, assessing the desirability of various potential remedies, and acting as "the creator and manager of complex forms of ongoing relief" (Chayes, 1976). The judge becomes a participant in the affairs of the defendant public organization, its clients, and its whole environment. As Horowitz says, "Monitoring of compliance with the decree becomes essential, liaison with . . . adjunct . . . personnel is common, periodic reporting to the court is generally required, and amendment of the provisions of the decree from time to time may be deemed desirable" (1983, p. 1, 268). While Fiss argues that judicial intervention into public management is necessary to remedy constitutional violations, Frug finds this judicial-administrative interaction particularly troublesome from a management perspective. Court orders can contain hundreds of specifications, which a public manager must implement, that are simply "unworkable." Government agencies are said to be too complex to administer under a court order.

These claims have been deduced through legal analyses of pertinent court cases. Two exceptions are Wood (1982), who mentions the difficulty of dealing with the court in the Boston schools, and O'Leary and Wise (1991), who discuss the same issue with respect to Kansas City. There is, however, only one longitudinal study (O'Leary, 1989), and no comparative empirical study, of the impact of such judicial action on the management of a public organization.

Cooper (1988) applies a "decree litigation model" to five case studies involving state and local governments. Drawing on interviews, as well as on legal documents, Cooper shows that judges do indeed play a major role in the implementation of remedies. But he also points out that the extent and impact of involvement varies significantly from one judge to another. Indeed, his conclusion about the "hard choices" facing judges refers to the balance between ensuring the adequacy of the remedial action and ensuring the prudence of judicial intervention into matters considered administrative, in order to achieve some acceptable remedy. Like other works, however, Cooper's study tells us more about judges than it does about the impact of judges' actions on public management. One is left with the impression that detailed supervision by the courts is supposed to have a negative impact on the management of public institutions, but the paucity of empirical research cautions against sweeping generalizations concerning this phenomenon.

7. *There are often unintended consequences, unanticipated questions, and unforeseen problems in court decisions involving public agencies.* Horowitz (1977), in his study of the role of courts in social policy, asserts that although a particular issue addressed by a court may seem narrow and insignificant, the policy and administrative ramifications of the court's decision are often sweeping: "The lawyers' customary search for the 'controlling issue,' lead[s] the court to a view of the case . . . that is significantly narrower than the innovation the decision actually imposed" (p. 255). Not considered by the courts, yet of paramount importance to the agencies implementing judicial decisions, are such issues as the general feasibility of carrying out court orders, monetary costs, and second-order consequences. In this sense, the judge may become a catalyst for unforeseen administrative change.

This claim has intuitive appeal. But what, exactly, *are* those unintended consequences, unanticipated questions, and unforeseen problems? How common are they? Are they *always* detrimental, and, if so, detrimental to what or to whom? Is the likelihood or incidence of court-initiated unintended consequences different from that of unintended consequences generated from other policy processes? We get a glimpse of some unintended consequences in the works of Wood (1982), O'Leary (1989), and O'Leary and Wise (1991). Yet these studies do not provide a systematic, broad-based investigation of this proposition.

8. *Judges often deal with subject matter outside their areas of expertise.* Cramton (1976), Wood (1982), Rosenbloom (1983), Horowitz (1983), and Melnick (1983) are representative of those authors who maintain that judges often deal with subject matter outside their areas of expertise. The proposition seems quite straightforward: a law degree enhances the ability of a person to be a lawyer, not a public manager. Management, budgeting, personnel administration, and specific policy topics are not taught in law schools. It is inevitable that judges will deal with subject matter outside their areas of

knowledge. (A "generalist" manager, by definition, also lacks specific policy-area expertise.)

Cramton, Horowitz, and Rosenbloom seem to be basing their conclusions on an examination of judicial decisions and on the nonempirical work of those who preceded them. Melnick bases his conclusion on the same materials, as well as on archival materials and interviews. Wood bases his chronicle on his experience as superintendent of the Boston school system.

The problem with this proposition is that it is incomplete. One assumes that lack of expertise has negative consequences; but consequences for what? With the exception of Rosenbloom's informal propositions, the consequences for management are not articulated. Presumably, the consequences would be for the ability of the manager to initiate and implement his or her agency's strategic mission, but this presumption reads more into the proposition than these authors tell us. This area is ripe for exploration.

The Public Management Agenda

Judges do not define organizational missions, but their judgments may alter them. Consider the obvious case of the desegregation of urban schools. No student of courts and public organizations would deny that court-ordered desegregation has influenced the formulation of education policies. Similarly, while the shift toward the deinstitutionalization of mental health patients evolved primarily through a change in professional thinking, the courts served as catalysts (Grumet, 1985). There are clearly some interactive effects. Overall, there is reason to believe that courts have had a significant impact on the shaping of agency agendas. This presumption has influenced the following assertions.

9. *A court order can dictate the issues that must be considered by public agencies.* It is appealing to conclude that a court can dictate the specific issues that must be dealt with by public agencies, but there is very little empirical research on this subject. Johnson (1979a, 1979b) studied the impact of five Pennsylvania Supreme Court decisions on five Pennsylvania state agencies and concludes that the organizations went to great lengths to avoid dealing with the issues dictated by court orders. In her study of the courts and EPA (an agency plagued by lawsuits), however, O'Leary (1989) has found that the major impact of court decisions on that agency was policy-related. She found that from a "macro" or agencywide perspective, compliance with court orders has become one of the agency's top priorities, at times overtaking congressional mandates. The courts shape the agenda at EPA. In an atmosphere of limited resources, coupled with unrealistic and numerous statutory mandates, EPA has been forced to make decisions among competing priorities. With few exceptions, court orders have become the "winners" in this competition. O'Leary's conclusions are based on interviews, as well as

an examination of over 1,400 court decisions, agency memos, archival materials, court documents, budget and personnel documents, environmental newsletters, *Federal Register* notices, congressional hearing reports, and other public documents. She also describes her analysis and data-validation procedures, which were rigorous. Nevertheless, since her evidence is limited to one federal agency—and one that may be sued more often than most other public organizations—generalizations about courts dictating policy require additional research.

10.   *The filing of a lawsuit can confirm and strengthen government policy.* Bullock and Lamb (1984) studied the implementation of civil rights policy and found that the recognition of civil rights by the federal government has created a "slight nudge" toward the implementation objective. More active enforcement, as through lawsuits filed by federal attorneys, was found to be critical, however, to confirming and strengthening such government policy.

Is there additional evidence that lawsuits are effective weapons in an agency's administrative arsenal? O'Leary's EPA study (1989) found that, in the implementation of one policy, the agency deliberately used the courts to gain power and legitimacy over local governments not in compliance with the Clean Water Act. O'Leary also found that positive court decisions substantially strengthened the EPA's Superfund (hazardous-waste cleanup) program as the agency used the courts to establish pro-EPA precedents. Further research is needed.

11.   *Court orders can disrupt processes within scientific organizations.* Court orders can disrupt scientific processes, often with "grave ramifications" (O'Leary, 1989). Scientific processes are often "long-linked" (Thompson, 1967), involving serial interdependence. Certain actions must build on other actions before final products can be issued: scientific studies must be completed, data must be collected, and the data must be analyzed before technical regulations are developed. There is a need for peer review. O'Leary found that, often, the EPA either cannot comply with court decisions, because these foundational steps have not been completed, or skips needed steps and issues poorly conceived scientific standards. Time constraints are exacerbated. This finding has implications for other public organizations (such as the Nuclear Regulatory Commission, the Department of the Interior, the National Aeronautics and Space Administration, and state environmental agencies) that depend on solid scientific analyses as a primary source of information and credibility. Unfortunately, there are no studies on the impact of courts on other public organizations that engage in scientific processes.

Litigation and the Authority of Public Managers

Scattered throughout the literature about the impact of court decisions on public management is the assertion that public managers gain advantages from being the targets of public lawsuits. Consider the following propositions.

12.   *A negative judicial decision can be used by an agency to strengthen its po-*
sition. Litigation has been interpreted as providing administrative leverage
in the face of resistance from legislatures or elected executives. The presumption seems reasonable for managers who occupy "impossible jobs" — mental
health commissioners, social welfare commissioners, and corrections officials
(Hargrove and Glidewell, 1990). The expectation that a negative court decision may be useful, most commonly in the quest for additional funds
through the budget process, comes from the belief that some managers do
not, under normal circumstances, receive sympathetic responses from legislatures (Diver, 1979; Straussman, 1986). The threat of a lawsuit or, even
better, a judicial order is considered a powerful weapon in the budgetary
"game." Allerton (1976), Frug (1978), Hale (1979), Horowitz (1983), and
Straussman (1986) conclude that there are often unforeseen budgetary ramifications of judicial decisions, which may offer opportunities both for en-
hancing agency budgets and for restricting them (see propositions 15–19).
One interpretation is that litigation represents a "crisis technique" (Wildavsky,
1988) that managers try to use as leverage in the budget process. Conceptually, this can be viewed as an element in bargaining and negotiation between an agency and the legislature, where each party adopts a "risk estimate" and negotiates over a budget that may be affected by the risk caused
by the litigation.

Moss (1983) has found that a court decision had a "catalytic" effect
on legislative behavior that was sympathetic to the policy thrust implicit in
the judicial decision. Melnick (1983), in one of his six case studies concerning the EPA's Clean Air Act policy, describes a situation in which the agency
"clutched tightly" to a negative court decision concerning the setting of air-
quality standards, in order to insulate itself from White House pressure to
set standards on the basis of cost-effectiveness. O'Leary (1989), however,
has found that such budgetary enhancement within the EPA has come at
the expense of other programs.

This proposition seems straightforward. It is based on the assumption that public managers are self-interested utility maximizers (where the
budget is the best single indicator of this behavior). Observations concerning selected managers from high-profile remedial cases provide face validity
for the proposition. Consider Rothman and Rothman's interpretation of the
actions of Thomas Coughlin, who was commissioner of the New York Office
of Mental Retardation and Developmental Disabilities when that agency
operated under the Willowbrook consent decree:

> He had an intuitive feel for politics and was ready to follow the
> maxim of many innovative administrators: Ready, Fire, Aim!
> He immediately recognized that his own ambitions were inter-
> twined with the judgment, that fulfilling its provisions would
> bring him additional resources and authority. Although pub-
> licly he complained about the intransigence and pettiness of the

[Willowbrook] panel, privately, in the corridors of executive buildings, he used its threats to pry more money loose. On the back of the panel, Coughlin rode to power. Mental Retardation eventually broke off from Mental Hygiene to become a separate department — the Office of Mental Retardation and Developmental Disabilities (OMRDD) — and he became its first commissioner" [Rothman and Rothman, 1984, p. 137].

Dr. Stonewall Stickney, commissioner of mental health in Alabama during the famous *Wyatt* v. *Stickney* case, was quoted as saying, "Actually, it's kind of exhilarating to see that the courts may get the Legislature going. It's been our experience that they'd rather spend money for highways than mental health" (quoted in Yarbrough, 1982, p. 397).

The empirical basis for the proposition comes from insider accounts such as these (coupled with single case studies), which confirm existing presumptions about bureaucratic behavior. But the "data" are suspect: after all, managers who prefer to continue their tenure in office are not inclined to reveal their strategies and tactics so boldly (in fact, Stickney was removed from office shortly after he made this statement), nor are managers likely to comment publicly that they did not employ this strategy. What is missing from this proposition is a rigorous analysis of bureaucratic behavior in the context of a theory concerning the strategic considerations of judicial-agency interaction.

13. *Judicial activity can lead to reduction in the power and authority of administrators.* Glazer (1978) predicts that judges' intervention into public management will reduce the power and authority of administrators. O'Leary (1989) provides some empirical evidence to support Glazer's hypothesis; specifically, she has found that courts have reduced the discretion, autonomy, power and authority of EPA administrators. First, new programs are sometimes not implemented, because resources are devoted to meeting courts' demands. Second, court decisions affect EPA planning activities, since it is virtually impossible to plan for a court remand. Third, some court decisions concerning the EPA have been found to be broad and vague, affecting more than they need to. O'Leary has also found that court decisions have increased the power and authority of attorneys in the EPA (as Glazer, 1978, also predicts, as do Pfeffer and Salancik, 1978) but decreased the power and authority of scientists.

These two studies represent a good beginning. The next stage is to develop a model of judicially induced change, to determine under what circumstances judicial activity yields a change in power and authority. It will also be important to study the consequences of such changes. For example, what ramifications flow from a shift in authority from, say, scientists to attorneys?

14. *Judges often refuse to defer to administrators' expertise.* Melnick (1983, 1985) has been the primary messenger of the conclusion that judges often

refuse to defer to administrators' expertise. In his study of the courts and the EPA, Melnick chronicles this fact. The primary weakness of Melnick's 1983 work is that all the conclusions are based on a few selected case studies in one narrow statutory area affecting one federal agency. Hence, a concern is raised, not with the accuracy of particular findings, but with the methodology employed, a possible selection bias, and the generalizability of results. Further research is needed.

Management of Resources: Budgets and People

Several authors have studied the impact of court decisions on public organizations' budgets and personnel. Included in this group are Fisher (1975), Allerton (1976), Hale (1979), Horowitz (1983), Straussman (1986), O'Leary (1989), and Ekland-Olson and Martin (1988, 1990), to name just a few. Among their findings are the following propositions.

15. *There are anticipated and unanticipated costs of implementing a court decision.* Hale (1979) concludes that the financial consequences of most judicial decrees are unknown and surmises that court-ordered programs may be financed at the expense of other public agencies. The logic here is straightforward: given a fixed budgetary pie, court-mandated spending necessarily comes from other parts of the budget. Moreover, monitoring requirements may be unanticipated. Yet in a budgetary context any emergency, as a contingency or supplemental appropriation, is unanticipated, at least with respect to timing, precise need, and level of spending. Therefore, the empirical issue, it would seem, is the place of the court-ordered spending on a continuum of unanticipated expenditures. Further empirical research is needed to determine exactly what these unanticipated budgetary effects are, as well as the impact they have had on public management.

16. *Special legislative appropriations are sometimes needed to provide the funds necessary to implement a court decision.* A negative judicial decision, as already discussed, can be used by a public organization as ammunition in its quest for funds from a legislative body, but little empirical research has been done to ascertain the extent of this practice. In fact, O'Leary (1989) concludes that, in its twenty-year history, the EPA has been successful only once in using a court decision to gain a special appropriation from Congress. Once again, O'Leary's work, although longitudinal, concerns only one agency.

17. *Funds often must be taken from other programs and channeled into the program that is the subject of a court decision.* Allerton (1976), who has written about the effects of court decisions on Virginia's mental health institutions, has found that the institutions were forced to reorder their priorities in order to make funds available for complying with court orders. The redistributive consequences of court decisions have also been discussed by Horowitz (1983), Hale (1979), and Straussman (1986). O'Leary (1989) describes the typical EPA response to court orders as "reprogramming," in which funds are moved

from program to program within an office, or even from office to office. An observation by Miller and Iscoe (the former was a commissioner of the Texas Department of Mental Health) is telling:

> Among the several remedies ordered by the court was imposition of a rigid staffing formula (psychiatric aides to patient ratios of 1:5, 1:5, and 1:10 on the three shifts), although no evidence has been presented at the court hearing to support this or any other ratio. As a result of the court order, nursing personnel and supervisors lost their ability to modify employee levels based on changing needs in the department's eight state hospitals. Because the court-ordered ratios for these psychiatric aides are among the richest in the country, the agency's limited funds have been consumed in meeting the mandate, leaving insufficient dollars to hire adequate numbers of professional personnel such as psychiatrists, registered nurses, and psychologists [Miller and Iscoe, 1990, p. 124].

Logically, this condition should apply to all remedial cases where resources are static; and, indeed, a growing body of case studies provides evidence in support of the proposition.

18. *Court decisions may yield a transfer of budgetary power from an administrator to a judge. When this occurs, the budgetary discretion of administrators is decreased.* Fisher (1975) has studied how federal courts have forced the release of funds appropriated by Congress and impounded by the President, severely restricting the latter's discretion. Hale (1979) has found that nearly 50 percent of the largest public organizations operate judicially mandated programs. Among the implications of this study is the conclusion that such action yields a transfer of budgetary power from administrators to judges, decreasing the discretion of administrators. Harriman and Straussman (1983) have studied the impact of court decisions on state correction facilities. While they claim that courts have influenced prison spending, their results show lower spending per prisoner in states that have been parties to such lawsuits. But they also have found that, in fifteen states that were under court order for unconstitutional conditions in one or more prisons, capital spending increased in the five-year period following the court orders. A more recent study by Taggert (1989) has questioned this result. Chilton and Talarico (1990) have examined the budgetary impact of *Guthrie* v. *Evans,* in Georgia. They note a substantial increase in spending (as measured in aggregate terms and in terms of cost per inmate). Nevertheless, no one to date, controlling for other possible explanations, has designed a study to determine the impact of litigation on public organizational budgetary expansion.

19. *Court decisions can frustrate budgetary retrenchment and can encourage budgetary games.* Hale (1979) surmises that many public officials may cooperate freely with judges and plaintiffs, in the hope of obtaining additional

money. Hale provides no empirical evidence to support this statement but concludes that such budgetary gamesmanship occasionally works to management's advantage. O'Leary (1989) documents the fact that court-mandated programs were the only items considered safe from the budget-slashing scalpel during Anne Gorsuch (Burford)'s reign as administrator of the EPA. O'Leary and Wise (1991) provide a case study of plaintiff-defendant cooperation in Kansas City but conclude that the impact on management was devastating. No generalizable empirical research has been carried out, however, to ascertain the impact of court decisions on budgetary retrenchment generally.

20.   *Court orders affect staff morale.* The ability of the public administrator to manage his or her organization is partly affected by morale, which in turn may be influenced by court orders. Here, there is some case-study evidence from corrections and from a study of the EPA. One line of argument, based on interviews and participant observation, is that court orders have eroded the morale and authority of prison staff (Ekland-Olson and Martin, 1988, 1990), but O'Leary (1989) was surprised to find just the opposite at EPA. As EPA workers banded together to accomplish the goal of compliance, they reported becoming more focused and directed. Staff who were interviewed expressed great pride in implementing a court order in a timely fashion.

The prison study and the EPA study, viewed together, yield further important research questions. Under what circumstances do court orders have an adverse affect on staff morale? Under what circumstances do they have a positive affect on staff morale? Clearly, further empirical research is needed.

Conclusions: A New Research Agenda?

This chapter has provided an overview of the "top twenty" propositions in the literature concerning the impact of courts on public management. What do we know?

There seems to be agreement that court intervention can and does alter the activities of public managers. We know this from a small number of case studies. We know, for example, that some public managers use litigation as leverage in their negotiations with legislatures. We also know that some judges maintain extensive oversight of administrative agencies, while others do not. Yet we have no propositions concerning the conditions under which one managerial or judicial strategy is likely to be more or less successful than another. Most important, however, the focus in the majority of the literature has been on the courts, not on the managers of the organizations affected by the courts.

How do we know what we know? We know what we know primarily through analyses of case law, "wisdom," and conceptual thinking. There is little empirical evidence to support most of the twenty propositions. While case-law analyses, insider accounts, and conceptual thinking are necessary prerequisites of sustainable research in this area, they are not sufficient.

Lempert (1970) suggests three ways of determining the impact of laws passed by legislatures, methods that can be modified and applied to discerning the impact of court decisions on public management. The first way is to compare the same public organization before and after the court decision in question, noting any behavioral changes that seem to have resulted. The second way is to compare similar organizations that have been the subjects of such suits and those that have not, assuming that without the suits, behavior in the two would not have been the same (an assumption fraught with difficulty). The third way combines the other two approaches and involves examining behavior patterns in a particular set of public organizations, both before and after court decisions, and comparing these patterns with those found over the same period in a set of organizations not subjected to court orders.

Each of these options is problematic in some way (Levine, 1970). Public management scholars must be aware of the shortcomings of different research design options and take the weaknesses into account in analyzing results. Further, we must be aware that the relationship between court decisions and management outcomes is probabilistic rather than deterministic (Levine, 1970); causation is often difficult to infer.

There is also a need for us to rethink and broaden our concept of "data" to include not only court decisions but also archival materials, court documents, interviews, budgetary and personnel documents, and other government documents, to name just a few sources. We need survey research and comparative case studies that examine not just the spectacular cases but also the normal, everyday cases that affect public management. Moreover, we need long-range longitudinal studies of the impact of courts on public management. Most important, we need an adequate theoretical base from which researchers can predict effects, test them, and ascertain, in a more systematic and rigorous fashion, the impact of courts on public management.

15

THE ROLE OF THE PRESIDENT IN ANTITRUST ENFORCEMENT

Heidi O. Koenig

*T*heorists have long posited the ability of the President of the United States to affect the performance of administrative agencies. The structuring of the federal government makes such an ability very reasonable, since the administrative agencies are generally a branch of the executive branch. (Independent commissions are the exception to the general rule of inclusion of administrative agencies under the executive branch. These commissions, therefore, will not be included here in the term *agency* or *bureaucracy* unless specifically included.) As the study of the power of the President continued, though, the ability of the administrative agencies to escape presidential control became clear. One result of these early efforts at studying administrative agencies was that the bureaucracy became known as the fourth branch of the United States government (Wood, 1988). The federal bureaucracy was portrayed as a renegade force in national government.

Recently, in both economics and political science, the effort to model what the bureaucracy does has become more popular. The work of Terry Moe has been instrumental in shifting the focus of study away from the elements of bureaucracy that cannot be controlled to the forces that do control, or temper, the actions of the bureaucracy (Moe, 1982, 1984, 1985). The purpose of the research reported here is to examine the influence of the President on the Division of Antitrust, which is an enforcement agency within the Department of Justice.

The enforcement of the antitrust laws has long been the responsibility of the Department of Justice, which is part of the executive branch. It has been noted that the Division of Antitrust is isolated from congressional oversight (Sanders, 1986). The President, as the leading force in the executive branch, shapes the policy of enforcement within the Department of Justice. Each president has had at his disposal the ability to shape national economic policy through use (or lack of use) of the special forces of the division. The focus here on the President as the main shaper of policy is therefore appropriate.

Rise of Antitrust as a Federal Economic Issue

The Sherman Act, passed in 1890, was the first federal antitrust law of force in the United States. The purpose of the Sherman Act was to prohibit cartel-like behavior by producers or manufacturers. Enforcement methods within the Sherman Act include criminal sanctions, in the form of jail sentences or fines; dissolution of the corporate act that resulted in a violation of the Sherman Act; and treble damages. The damages provision has been the method of enforcement most readily imposed, making trust behavior very costly. Until recently, Sherman Act enforcement has not been very controversial. There have always been detractors of antitrust law, and believers in the purity of market forces, but the success of the Department of Justice in preventing trusts from developing has silenced all but the most vocal critics.

As the need to participate in the world market became more apparent to the shapers of economic policy in the United States, there was a shift in the argument against antitrust (Wills, Caswell, and Culbertson, 1987). It was argued that removing the antitrust bar to behavior would provide for a more economically efficient use of the resources available to industry. Antitrust was seen as blocking potentially valuable partnerships, combinations that could advance the state of science and help the United States regain its position as a world force in the development of goods (Wills, Caswell, and Culbertson, 1987); this renewed status would in turn lead to a healthier domestic economy. Pressure was created to improve the economic success of the United States within the world economy. One response for the executive branch, while not the only response available, would be to decrease the forcefulness of antitrust enforcement, thereby permitting the argued-for combinations to occur.

Before 1980, antitrust enforcement was not controversial (Sanders, 1986). President Carter was a strong supporter of antitrust enforcement as a method of preventing economic inequality (Eisner and Meier, 1990). The easing of the burden of regulation on the business sector was a significant element of the Reagan "new federalism" (Conlan, 1988). One tool available to Reagan was changing the levels of antitrust enforcement.

The agencies of the federal government have a broad range of duties, from delivery of services to application of the nation's laws. In taking care of these responsibilities, they are largely self-run organizations, similar to all other organizations. At the same time, agencies are subject to the political forces exerted on them by both the executive branch and Congress. In this respect, agencies are elements in the political environment, subject to the demands of elected officials. It is these two factors of bureaucratic structure that have led to the great difficulty in explaining the behavior of agencies. Is the organizational structure most important in determining the outputs of an agency? Is the political force exerted on the agency the determinant of the agency's behavior? Or, as seems most likely, is the true explanation a combination of these two forces? If both forces are active, what statements can be made about the forces that operate?

Role of the President in the Bureaucracy

Theoreticians and practitioners agree that there is some room for presidential control of administrative agencies (Edwards, 1985; Light, 1982). This control may be asserted through appointment powers, budgetary change, or involvement in the legislative agenda that concerns an agency.

Budget

The use of budget as an instrument of control seems very straightforward. In the strongest case, manipulation of the budget will show a direct intent by the President to alter patterns of behavior by refusing to sponsor that behavior. In the weakest case, budgetary change can require an agency to shift the focus of its work. No matter what the strength of the change in the budget, it is clear that, by diminishing resources, the President should be able to alter behavior.

Appointment Powers

The President holds the power to appoint the chairs of agencies. Although the appointment of a political ally will probably have an effect on the agency, it has been suggested that this effect is neither long-lasting nor likely to result in a realignment of the agency's policy (Moe, 1982). The appointment power is more often significant in the ability of the newly appointed chair to make changes in the personnel of the agency and to create organizational incentives that will change short-term behavior (Sabatier and Pelkey, 1987).

Legislative Agenda

The President's policies achieve priority on the legislative agenda (Kingdon, 1984). Kingdon links the ability of the President's concerns to move quickly to the top of the legislative agenda with the President's control over jobs in the federal government and the presence of a more united decision-making capability in the executive branch.

Presidential Policy Statements

The majority of current work fails to consider the role of presidential policy at the time of the President's inauguration and the efforts the administrative agencies might take to shape their behavior around that policy (Wood, 1988, is a notable exception to this majority.) Although this is a difficult variable to quantify, the early statements of the newly elected President provide a good indicator of the direction in which the President will move while in office (Conlan, 1988).

In the process of attempting to understand the influences that shape agency behavior, researchers and theoreticians have developed two distinct lines of theory within bureaucratic politics — principal-agent theory, and bureaucratic autonomy (Bendor, 1988). Each emphasizes one particular aspect of the agency as determining its outputs.

Principal-Agent Theory

The application of principal-agent theory to the relationship between the bureaucracy and the Congress, and between the bureaucracy and the President, is now common. In political science, much of this research has been focused by positivist theory. Bendor and Moe (1985), Moe (1982), and Calvert, McCubbin and Weingast (1989) have all used this theoretical framework to capture some portion of the influence asserted by either Congress or the President on the bureaucracy, or to identify influence flowing the other way. According to Bendor (1988) the minimal components of the principal-agent model are as follows:

1. Both principal and agent are optimizers of their own interests.
2. There is asymmetry of information between principal and agent.
3. The principal knows what action is preferable; the problem is to induce that action.
4. The contrast between principal and agent is self-enforcing for the agent.
5. The contract has a participation constraint, preventing the principal from breaching it.

Moe (1982) has used the principal-agent perspective in an effort to understand the role of the President in relation to three independent commissions — the Federal Trade Commission (FTC), the National Labor Relations Board (NLRB), and the Securities and Exchange Commission (SEC). These commissions were selected to test for the presence of influence by the President because they are, by statute, independent of the executive branch. In his comprehensive review of these commissions, Moe begins by asserting that the impact on the commissions of the presidential powers of appointment, budget, and political leadership will be significant. (The power of appointment, it should be noted, is not merely the recommendation of a candidate for appointment. The Hoover Commission, in 1950, extended the powers of the President by giving him power to remove chairmen and by giving chairmen more control over staffing decisions; see Moe, 1982.) The hypothesized impact of the President is related to the exercise of these powers by the President. Box-Tiao models (Box and Tiao, 1975) are used to estimate the effect of the President on regulatory activity. The data used are annual data on rates of enforcement.

Most interesting here is Moe's investigation of the FTC. The FTC is responsible for regulation of national trade. One of its jurisdictions is antitrust law. The results of this portion of the analysis are particularly interesting in the present context: Moe found that changes in the party affiliation of the President are associated with changes in enforcement; in periods with Republican presidents, there are greater enforcement efforts. This result is anomalous to Moe's hypothesis regarding party affiliation. It was first thought that Republican presidents would represent the interests of their business constituency by calling for less regulation. Further understanding of the enforcement pattern was sought through review of the Division of Antitrust's enforcement rates over the same time periods. (The Division of Antitrust was chosen for its nonindependence from the executive branch.) Moe confirmed the presence of influence over the FTC by showing that the same pattern existed for changes of enforcement rates in the Division of Antitrust as were seen in the FTC. Moe concludes that there is indeed presidential influence at work in the federal bureaucracy.

The relationship between the president and the Division of Antitrust may be appropriately analyzed from a principal-agent perspective. Each of the five components (Bendor, 1988) necessary to the application of principal-agent theory is presented below.

Optimizing Behavior

Optimizing behavior merely means acting in a way that serves one's best interests. Both the Division of Antitrust and the President act in ways that are consistent with their own interests. The division continues to receive a portion of the federal budget, which affects its ability to proceed in cases and enforce the law. The President acts to ensure constituency support for his position.

Asymmetry of Information

Where asymmetry exists, there is imbalance. The asymmetry of information flow merely requires that either the principal or the agent be able to withhold information so that the other participant is forced to behave in a desired way. It is now axiomatic that the bureaucracy and the political branches of government withhold information from one another to gain bargaining position. The relationship between the President and the division falls into this classification.

Principal's Inducement of Behavior

This is the clearest part of the principal-agent model that is satisfied in the present study. The President, merely by changing the budget or by changing personnel, can alter resources to such an extent that keeping the same level of output is not possible.

Self-Enforcing Contract for the Agent

A self-enforcing contract is one that needs no effort by either party to come into existence. Here, the contract providing enforcement of the antitrust laws is self-enforcing for the division, by the mere fact that the division is an institution unto itself. Therefore, the contract between the President and the division is really one between two political bodies. It is this property that makes the contract self-enforcing.

Participation Constraint on the Principal

This requirement means that the principal is not allowed to break the contract. Since, as we have seen, the contract between the principal and the agent is between two political bodies (the President and the Division of Antitrust), there can be no breach of contract by the principal. When the current President leaves, another is ready to assume the contract.

Each of the five "minimal components" is satisfied by the President–Division of Antitrust relationship. Principal-agent theory is not the only way to characterize the relationship, however. Here, as in Moe (1982), the influence of the President and the President's staff may be understood as an alternative explanation to theories of "regulatory independence"—theories that are derived from the perspective of bureaucratic autonomy.

Bureaucratic Autonomy

Work on bureaucratic autonomy emphasizes the organizational factors that determine agency outputs (Eisner and Meier, 1990). This adopts an internal agency focus, identifying the discretionary powers of the bureaucracy and ability to exercise control over the release of information as the predominant factors characterizing the policy interaction that occurs between the bureaucracy and elected officials.

Several researchers have now tied shifts in antitrust enforcement to changes made by President Reagan (Anderson, 1986; Mueller, 1986). Eisner and Meier (1990) suggest that the change in enforcement rates that occurred in 1980 was unrelated to the inauguration of Mr. Reagan. In their investigation of organizational factors that have influenced rates of case filings, Eisner and Meier found that the adoption of the Chicago school of thought in the Economic Policy Office (EPO) of the Division of Antitrust was the predominating factor leading to changes in the rates of antitrust enforcement. Eisner and Meier's study assesses the role of the EPO, and of the Chicago school economists in EPO, by reviewing longitudinal data on case filings. The primary hypothesis was that as EPO gained strength within the agency, the types of cases filed should have shown a change from merger-and-monopoly prosecutions to price-fixing prosecutions. Support was found for this hypothesis. The conclusion drawn is that the shift seen in enforcement at the beginning of the Reagan administration is traceable to the influence of the Chicago school within the confines of the division, and not to the change in the political environment.

The application of autonomy theory to the question raised in this study would be rather simplistic: the Division of Antitrust is part of the federal bureaucracy; therefore, an examination of the division's enforcement activity with an approach focusing on bureaucratic autonomy seems inherently reasonable. There are other reasons that make this case an interesting one from this perspective, however. The Division of Antitrust is staffed by professionals—attorneys and economists (Eisner and Meier, 1990). It is therefore an organizational structure that will be highly resistant to change efforts that originate externally. The division is also isolated from congressional oversight (Sanders, 1986), which makes its exercise of discretion easier. An example of this discretionary attitude may be seen in a recent statement by the director of the Division of Antitrust, James F. Rill. He announced that budgetary changes have had no effect on the division's efforts in enforcing the law ("Antitrust Lawyer Rises to Stardom . . . ," 1990). Although this statement provides no insight into the budget process, it is interesting to note that Rill perceives a primary tool of change to be powerless in his division.

It is clear that the role of the president in influencing the outputs of the Division of Antitrust could be examined from either the perspective of principal-agent theory or that of bureaucratic autonomy. The examples given here of use of the competing models are not meant as a review of the implications of these models, nor are they offered as a resolution of the competing perspectives. Each perspective purports to explain very similar phenomena from very different bases and, in the process, omits an explanation of some portion of the specific phenomenon studied. Eisner and Meier (1990) acknowledge that cuts took place in the budget of the Division of Antitrust. Eisner and Meier also note that President Reagan's budget cuts were disproportionately borne by attorneys in the division. They state, "The ratio of economists per 10 attorneys was 1.0 at the time the EPO was created. By the end of the 1970s, it had reached 1.5. Although the Reagan budget reductions forced dramatic reductions in the Antitrust Division staff, the reductions were not borne equally by the attorneys and economists. Accordingly, by 1987 there were 2.9 economists for every 10 attorneys, almost twice the number as before the reductions began" (p. 279). They continue to maintain, however, that President Reagan had no effect on antitrust enforcement. Moe (1982) compares rates of enforcement in the Division of Antitrust and FTC, to prove that similar changes seen in FTC enforcement data are related to changes in the executive branch. No attempt is made to explore the organizational factors that may have operated, perhaps quite differently, in the FTC and the Division of Antitrust. If both studies had made room for an alternative perspective, the results might well not be subject to alternative explanations.

The advantages that might be gained by having the ability to look to both of these theories are many. Some of these are generation of more precise hypotheses, richer understanding of policy processes, and greater insight into the democratic forces active in modern government. With a combined theoretical model, the shortfalls of each theory may be compensated for.

It is no longer necessary to choose either the principal-agent perspective or the perspective of bureaucratic autonomy in illuminating research questions. Instead, it is possible to see the interconnections between principal-agent theory and bureaucratic autonomy, and to use those interconnections to answer complex questions. One version of this new union between principal-agent theories and theories of bureaucratic autonomy is captured as an "adaptive model" of bureaucratic action (Bendor and Moe, 1985). Another is the theory of political control and agency discretion developed by Calvert, McCubbin, and Weingast (1989). A third is found in the work done by Wood (1988), and it is Wood's style of analysis that guides the present research.

Wood (1988), in an extensive study of the Environmental Protection Agency (EPA), predicted that the budget decreases, changes in political appointments, and deregulatory atmosphere imposed during the early Reagan presidency would result in a significant shift in enforcement efforts. Wood selected the EPA for study, on the basis of its high independence from political control. In this way, the limits of the principal-agent perspective were tested, since the principal-agent perspective is based on the belief in political hierarchies that tie agencies to political actors (Bendor, 1988). Three "interventions" were hypothesized to exist — the inauguration, the first budget effects, and the appointment and resignation of EPA director Anne Gorsuch (Burford). Box-Tiao modeling was used to assess the presence of changes in the levels of activity in EPA monitoring and abatement activity over the period 1977–1985.

Because of the "micro" level of his data, Wood was able to document the fact that the period following the inauguration was marked by an increase in enforcement activity. Moreover, the predicted effects of budgetary decreases occurred nine months after the budgetary changes had been invoked. The ability of the organization to continue, even increase, enforcement efforts in the nine months between the inauguration of Mr. Reagan and the enactment of the first Reagan budget changes is attributed to the careful use of slack resources. This finding, then, supports the perspective of bureaucratic autonomy. Changes in the budget did lower enforcement. This can be understood best from the principal-agent model. The removal of the EPA director had the expected effect of allowing an increase in monitoring and abatement activity. Both the principal-agent perspective and that of bureaucratic autonomy would anticipate this result.

President Reagan's interest in changing the EPA has been the subject of much of the empirical research on President-bureaucracy interaction. EPA was not the only governmental agency affected by President Reagan. The

level of federal regulation of business activities became an issue of importance to President Reagan during his campaign and was part of his "new
federalism," which formed a large part of his agenda (Conlan, 1988). This
focus on business regulation made the manipulation of antitrust enforcement efforts a logical method of achieving a presidential policy goal.

Data and Methods

The study of the bureaucracy is often made more difficult by the absence
of readily identifiable outputs (Wood, 1988). This problem appears in two
forms in attempts to do research on any bureaucracy: is there some behavior
or action by the agency that can be interpreted as outputs, and the behavior
selected by the researcher as outputs may or may not be representative of
the bureaucracy's work. Adopting Wood's criterion, *outputs* are defined as
"interactions . . . intended to secure compliance" (p. 219). In the case of the
Division of Antitrust, then, the output is the effort put toward enforcement
of the antitrust laws.

        The primary source of data for this study is information on the activi-
ties of the federal courts gathered by the Federal Judicial Center (FJC). (These
data are currently available from the Crouse-Hinds School of Management
at Syracuse University.) Data from the FJC encompass all federally filed
civil antitrust cases from 1970 to 1987; 361 cases were drawn from these
data. Cases in the FJC data set not yet complete, and cases not fully reported,
were not used in the present analysis. The data were sorted by quarter, yielding 44 intervals of measurement. In addition, the budget of the Division
of Antitrust was obtained from the executive office within the division.

Dependent Variables

The dependent variable under examination is the rate of antitrust enforcement. Antitrust enforcement is subject to measurement through three dimensions. These are the number of cases filed (CASEFILE), the duration of a case
(DURATION), and the procedural progress made in each case (OUTCOME). The
data provided by the FJC formed the base for this portion of the study.

CASEFILE. Necessary to the enforcement effort is the actual filing of a com-
plaint, or case. Not every case filed will be prosecuted, however. It is highly
likely that the threat of a legal challenge may be enough to cause the individuals charged with a violation of the antitrust laws to rethink their actions. Filing, therefore, constitutes a separate enforcement effort by the division. Values for this variable were gained by counting the number of cases
filed within each quarter.

DURATION. This variable was chosen to reflect the enforcement effort put into
each case by the division. The DURATION variable is defined to be the number of days from filing to the last action taken by the division on that partic-

ular case. For every case in the FJC data set, the date of filing and the date of last action were reported. The value for DURATION was gained by subtracting the date of filing from the date of last action. The value for each case was ordered in the data used in this study on the basis of date of the last action. For instance, a case filed on July 1, 1977, and dismissed on July 1, 1978, would have a value for the DURATION variable of 365 (days). This value would be placed in the data set in quarter 5 of the 44 quarters, on the basis of the July 1, 1978, dismissal date. After the DURATION of each case was calculated and ordered by quarter, the mean of all the DURATION values was taken within each quarter. It is this mean that was used in the statistical analysis.

OUTCOME. The outcome of the case — the level of prosecution after which no further action is taken — is included as an indicator of the enforcement effort of the division. The FJC data include information on the procedural progress of cases when enforcement activity was stopped. The different types of procedural progress identified in the FJC data set are *no issue* (the term *issue*, as used here, is a legalism indicating the existence of a question of law or fact that is appropriate for a judicial forum); *no action; no issue, action; issue, no pretrial, no action; issue, no pretrial, action; pretrial, no trial; terminated during court trial; terminated during jury trial; judgment after court trial;* and *judgment after jury trial.* These categories were recoded for the present study. The recoding scheme used was as follows:

0   no information on case (this was included in the recoding to check for missing values; no missing values were found, and this category was not used; it is reported for the reader's information)
1   no issue, no action; no issue, action
2   issue, no pretrial, no action
3   issue, no pretrial, action
4   pretrial, no trial
5   terminated during court trial; terminated during jury trial
6   judgment after court trial; judgment after jury trial

This recoding of the procedural-progress variable from the FJC data set accomplished two ends. The first benefit of the new coding scheme is the characterization of procedural progress as being preissue, pretrial, trial, or posttrial. Because procedural progress was reported at termination of action on a case, and duration was included in the quarter when the case was terminated, there is no chance that a case is reported in two different quarters for the two variables. The second advantage of the recording is that it generated a scale in which each preceding category was required for the next. For instance, the existence of an issue of fact or law is necessary to the holding of a pretrial conference or a trial; therefore, categories 2 and 3 are necessary conditions to categories 4, 5, and 6. The recalibration of the data into an interval scale enables the use of regression techniques in analysis.

Independent Variables

The data from the Division of Antitrust concerned the line budget for the division within the Department of Justice budget. The budget was reported by quarter, in terms of appropriations. Although this information is available in current dollars, for the purpose of this study the dollar amounts were indexed, to permit comparison across the eleven-year span of the study. Indexing was accomplished with a gross national product (GNP) deflator scale based in 1982. This variable (INDEX) is used as an independent variable by itself and in an interactive term (INTER) that poses a multiplicative relationship between (1) the real-dollar amounts appropriated to the division and (2) time. The values for time are captured in the variable TREND. The theoretical basis of the interactive term is found in the long-term effects of decreasing budgets. As the budget continues in a decreasing pattern over time, people will alter their behavior accordingly (Tarschys, 1981; Wildavsky, 1964).

A second set of independent variables was used in the analysis. These were based on the change in presidency from President Carter to President Reagan. The actual change in office was modeled by a dummy variable (REAGAN). Again, an interactive term (INCUM) was included in the analysis, to capture the effects of the increasing dominance of the President as his term endures. The fiscal-year time period was used in the opening round of analyses, to allow meaningful incorporation of the budgetary data from the Division of Antitrust.

Hypotheses

Hypothesis 1

The policy of deregulation espoused by President Reagan in the early days of his presidency will result in a change of antitrust enforcement rates. This change will be seen in a shortening of duration in cases.

As already explained, DURATION is the amount of time the case is worked on in the Division of Antitrust. OUTCOME is the point of procedural progress at which the case is stopped. CASEFILE is the number of cases filed. It is hypothesized that these three measures of antitrust enforcement will not be subject to the same amount of influence by the president.

DURATION is believed to be most likely to be open to political manipulation. Although direct confirmation of political manipulation is not likely, the existence of political force may be inferred from the existence of a new pattern in the DURATION data. The possibility of influence is greater in the instance of length of a case, primarily because of the effects of decreased budgets. A case that might be pursued for a long time during a period of budgetary slack may get less attention in a period of tight budgets. DURATION will also be subject to policy influence. This influence will heighten any budgetary influence seen.

The outcome of the case is set by the questions of law and fact unique to each case. OUTCOME reflects the differing levels of success of the division in prosecuting antitrust cases. The outcome of each case in this data set should depend on the facts presented and the relevant law and therefore be outside the realm of political influence. It is possible, however, that the levels of outcome attained will change with pressure to decrease enforcement efforts.

The number of cases filed will be less resistant to political change than OUTCOME will, and more resistant to change than DURATION. This relationship is hypothesized to exist on the basis of the amount of control the division can assert over the filing of cases. This amount of control is greater than the amount of control exercised over appropriations or judicial rulings.

Hypothesis 2

The change in budget will alter antitrust enforcement rates differently for each of the three dependent variables. There will be resistance to the policy objectives sought by President Reagan, giving rise to the exercise of discretion based on slack resources (Wood, 1988) or professionalization (Eisner and Meier, 1990; Mosher, 1968; Lauth, 1978).

DURATION will be the most altered, given changes in the budget, since the lack of resources will necessarily limit the ability of the division to actively prosecute cases. As the budget constraints get tighter, less time will be spent on each case.

CASEFILE will be more resistant to changes from budgetary influence than DURATION will be. Just as EPA activity continued after the first budget constraints were placed on it (Wood, 1988), the division's rate of filing cases will not change immediately. This hypothesis of resistance is based on the perspective of bureaucratic autonomy, with professionalization as a source of resistance to political changes.

OUTCOME may be affected by budgetary changes. If the decision to prosecute is changed by the budget, alternatives to prosecution will be used. These alternatives, if used, will lower the values of OUTCOME. It is important to remember, however, that this measure is subject to the pressures of the judiciary and may remain inflexible to the pressures of the executive branch.

Analysis

To measure presidential influence, the method of analysis used was an interrupted time-series design. The inauguration of President Reagan was used to express the intervention. Each dependent variable was analyzed on the independent variables related to the change in President. The general model for presidential influence incorporated the variables of REAGAN, INCUM, and TREND. The method of analysis used to measure budgetary influence was ordinary least-squares regression. The general model for the budgetary influence model was INDEX, INTER, and TREND.

Results

Results of the individual models run are given in tabular form. Some general concerns about the models may be addressed here. Corrections for autocorrelation were not made, since the Durbin-Watson statistic calculated for each model was close to 2.0, indicating minimal problems with autocorrelation (Hanushek and Jackson, 1977). (The Durbin-Watson statistic and value for first-order autocorrelation are reported solely for the edification of the reader.) The estimation process for multicollinearity among the variables resulted in condition index values that varied from 11 to 15. The multicollinearity estimation process was done without consideration of the intercept as a variable in the diagnostics. This path was taken because of the theoretical impossibility of a zero intercept. On the basis of these results, no significant problem with multicollinearity was judged to exist (see Table 15.1).

This element of enforcement was subject to sway by the President. The change in President showed a strong relationship with change in this variable. The significance of the relationship is seen in the significant findings on all of the independent variables. The adjusted r^2 of .5282 also indicates a strong relationship between the independent variables and the duration of the cases.

The plot of the predicted values of the duration of cases against the 44 quarters makes even clearer the existence of a relationship between the change in President and the duration of the cases (see Figure 15.1 and Table 15.2).

These results show that changes in the mean outcome of the cases in each quarter cannot be viewed as being linked to the change in President. None of the independent variables is significant; the adjusted r^2 is only .02. The finding of no effect for this variable is the predicted finding (see Table

Table 15.1. Presidential Influence: Duration.

Parameter Estimates

Variable	*DF*	*Parameter Estimate*	*Standard Error*	*T for HO: Parameter = 0*	*Prob > |T|*
INTERCEPT	1	−3.1002	71.0958	−0.044	0.9654
TREND	1	36.5243	7.8195	4.671	0.0001
INCUM	1	−43.4928	8.2923	−5.245	0.0001
REPUB	1	707.7144	112.7453	6.277	0.0001

Analysis of Variance

F Value	Prob > *F*
17.419	0.0001

R-square	0.5604	Adj. *R*-square	0.5282

Durbin-Watson D	1.679
First-order autocorrelation	0.151

Figure 15.1. Predicted Value of DURATION
by TREND, Using Presidential-Influence Model.

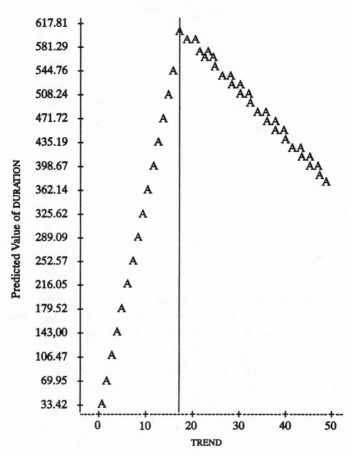

Note: The dashed line in the plot is set at the 16th quarter—the first quarter of 1980.

15.3). The number of cases filed varies significantly with the change in President. The adjusted r^2 of .3621, along with the significance of all three independent variables, indicates that some change took place in this variable at the same time the inauguration took place. This is *not* the hypothesized effect (see Table 15.4).

The results support the existence of a relationship between changes in budget and changes in duration of cases. All three independent variables were significant at $p < .01$. The strength of the interaction term was not expected, however, although the significance of that term was predicted (see Table 15.5).

As can be seen by these results, changes in the budget are not significantly related to changes in outcome. Nevertheless, the effect of facing a continually contracting budget can be seen in the negative signs found on all three of the independent variables (see Table 15.6).

Table 15.2. Presidential Influence: Outcome.

Parameter Estimates

Variable	DF	Parameter Estimate	Standard Error	T for HO: Parameter = 0	Prob > |T|
INTERCEPT	1	3.0693	0.4442	6.910	0.0001
REPUB	1	– 0.7749	0.7044	– 1.100	0.2777
TREND	1	– 0.0458	0.0489	– 0.938	0.3539
INCUM	1	0.0441	0.0518	0.851	0.3998

Analysis of Variance

F Value	Prob > F
1.358	0.2691

R-square   0.0904   Adj. R-square   0.0238

Durbin-Watson D   2.102
First-order autocorrelation   – 0.081

As was the case for this variable in the presidential-influence model, significance was found where it was not hypothesized. The strength of the budgetary influence was not as great (p = .0419) as presidential influence (p = .0003). It is interesting to note that TREND and INTER are the two independent variables that are significant; INDEX plays only an indirect role in influencing CASEFILE. The adjusted r^2 is very low for this model (adjusted r^2 = .1129).

Table 15.3. Presidential Influence: Casefile.

Parameter Estimates

Variable	DF	Parameter Estimate	Standard Error	T for HO: Parameter = 0	Prob > |T|
INTERCEPT	1	2.0762	1.9818	1.048	0.3009
TREND	1	0.6571	0.2179	3.015	0.0044
INCUM	1	– 0.8992	0.2311	– 3.890	0.0004
REPUB	1	14.9729	3.1428	4.764	0.0001

Analysis of Variance

F Value	Prob > F
7.693	0.0003

R-square   0.3602   Adj. R-square   0.3134

Durbin-Watson D   2.482
First-order autocorrelation   – 0.247

Table 15.4. Budgetary Influence: Duration.

| | | Parameter Estimates | | | |
Variable	DF	Parameter Estimate	Standard Error	T for HO: Parameter = 0	Prob > |T|
INTERCEPT	1	626.7317	168.1879	3.726	0.0006
TREND	1	− 51.0488	13.7409	− 3.715	0.0006
INDEX	1	− 0.0465	0.0167	− 2.777	0.0082
INTER	1	0.0060	0.0014	4.245	0.0001

Analysis of Variance

F Value	Prob > F
11.714	0.0001

R-square	0.4615	Adj. R-square	0.4221

Durbin-Watson D	1.581
First-order autocorrelation	0.192

Discussion

It is clear from these results that the change in presidential policy that occurred between 1976 and 1987 has affected antitrust enforcement. These effects can be seen in the significance of the models just reported, as well as in the differences between the models proposed for the three dependent variables.

Generally, the results can be summarized as no change in OUTCOME under either influence; significant change in CASEFILE, using the presidential-influence factors (less significant change, using the budgetary-influence factors);

Table 15.5. Budgetary Influence: Outcome.

| | | Parameter Estimates | | | |
Variable	DF	Parameter Estimate	Standard Error	T for HO: Parameter = 0	Prob > |T|
INTERCEPT	1	3.4393	0.9429	3.648	0.0007
TREND	1	− 0.0187	0.0770	− 0.242	0.8099
INDEX	1	− 0.0000504	0.0001	− 0.536	0.5946
INTER	1	− 0.0000002	0.0001	− 0.020	0.9844

Analysis of Variance

F Value	Prob > F
1.568	0.2116

R-square	0.1029	Adj. R-square	0.0373

Durbin-Watson D	2.049
First-order autocorrelation	− 0.059

Table 15.6. Budgetary Influence: Casefile.

Parameter Estimates

Variable	DF	Parameter Estimate	Standard Error	T for HO: Parameter = 0	Prob > |T|
INTERCEPT	1	13.0881	4.7971	2.728	0.0093
TREND	1	−0.8889	0.3919	−2.268	0.0287
INDEX	1	−0.0007	0.0005	−1.491	0.1436
INTER	1	0.0000979	0.0001	2.414	0.0203

Analysis of Variance

F Value	Prob > F
2.990	0.0419

R-square	0.1795	Adj. R-square	0.1195

Durbin-Watson D	1.994
First-order autocorrelation	−0.007

and significant change in DURATION, using both presidential- and budgetary-influence factors. Whenever significance was found with the budgetary-influence factors, higher levels of significance were found with the presidential-influence factors. This is to be expected, since the presidential-influence analysis incorporates all of the methods of change available to the President, while the budgetary influence analysis focuses on just one method of change.

OUTCOME

The finding of no effect for OUTCOME is the predicted finding. There does not appear to have been any way in which the Reagan policy change systematically altered final disposition of the cases pursued by the Division of Antitrust. This is one bureaucratic output that, from the results of this study, appears immune to manipulation. Although it would be naïve to suggest that no effect was felt in this area, it is obvious that so little was felt that the effect could not be captured in this analysis. The source of the resistance to manipulation is not clear. Eisner and Meier (1990) would argue that internal agency forces protect this type of enforcement effort from political manipulation. Another argument worth exploring concerns the judicial nature of this measure. The bureaucratic autonomy of the Division of Antitrust is reinforced by the results of the analysis on OUTCOME.

CASEFILE

CASEFILE was not as resistant to political change as hypothesized. Part of the failure of the hypothesis may be traced to an incomplete understanding of the massive job cuts that President Reagan imposed at the beginning of his tenure. As Eisner and Meier (1990) note, these cuts fell predominantly on the legal staff of the division. Even with the primary effects of budget cutbacks falling on the attorneys, it is difficult to believe that the legal professionals within the Division of Antitrust did not persist in filing cases, as a low-cost method of rejecting political control. It may be that the changes documented by Eisner and Meier (1990), coupled with the presence of fewer staff attorneys, form the basis for these results. If that is the case, then two competing forces within the organization — the economists and the attorneys — helped President Reagan achieve his desired goal of lower enforcement.

DURATION

The influence on DURATION was very much what was hypothesized. There was change based on President Reagan's inauguration and change based on budget cuts. It is feasible that the division began to change its behavior as President Reagan began his term, to avoid censure from the President. An alternative explanation is advanced by Eisner and Meier (1990): all the change that has been traced to the influence of the President was stimulated by internal agency changes. The pure hypothesis of bureaucratic autonomy is limited by the effects of budget changes, as is shown clearly in this analysis. This is an area worthy of study, since the ability of the President to create change in the bureaucracy has been shown, yet the links between the different methods of inducing change are still unclear.

16

WHAT IS WRONG
WITH THE REVOLVING DOOR?

Steven Kelman

Current legislation establishes several restrictions on the jobs that government employees may take upon leaving government service. These are known collectively under the rubric *revolving-door restrictions*. Although the first federal restrictions on the postemployment activities of government officials date back to 1872, such restrictions in their current form date from the passage of the Bribery, Graft and Conflicts of Interest Act of 1962. The current restrictions are based on the Ethics in Government Act of 1978 and on amendments to that act, passed in 1979 and 1989. Specific postemployment restrictions for Department of Defense officials also exist in other statutes.

Very broadly speaking, the current postemployment restrictions do place limitations, sometimes major limitations, on activities that public officials may undertake upon leaving government (Morgan, 1980; Potts, 1990). According to the level of the officials involved, such restrictions run the gamut from prohibitions against representing a private client on a matter with which one personally dealt while in government to a one-year blanket prohibition against representing any client at one's former agency at all, or even at any agency anywhere else in government. The impact of these restrictions, however, is significantly limited by the narrow definition (in the case of junior officials) of what kinds of matters are included in the ban and (for all officials) by the fact that the prohibition against representing a client applies only to direct appearances before government agencies, and not

Helpful comments on earlier drafts of this chapter were provided by an anonymous reviewer, as well as by Joel Feinberg, Mark Kleiman, Fred Schauer, Andrew Stark, Dennis Thompson, Alan Wertheimer, and participants in the University of Toronto Faculty of Law's Law and Economics/Public Policy Workshop; the Conference on Public Management Research at the Maxwell School of Citizenship and Public Affairs, University of Syracuse; and the Policy Values Seminar at the John F. Kennedy School of Government, Harvard University. Leslie Wilcox of the Office of Government Ethics helped me clarify some points on the nature of the revolving-door restrictions. Helpful research assistance was provided by Brad Setser, and funding was provided by the UNISYS Corporation.

to behind-the-scenes "aiding and advising" of clients on how to deal with an agency. Furthermore, except in some very narrow situations, no ban extends to taking a job with a private organization with which one previously dealt while in government, in an area that does not involve the private organization's dealings with the government. (That is, one may leave the government and take a job as vice president for Latin American marketing with a company that one had previously regulated while in government.) The current restrictions, then, neither give a public official complete liberty in choosing postgovernment employment nor forbid all postgovernment employment relationships with private employers with whom an official may have interacted while in government.

Specifically, the basic postemployment restrictions are the following:

1. A *permanent ban* on representing a party before the government, where the person while in government "participated personally and substantially" in the question. This ban applies only to questions involving "a specific party or specific parties" and therefore does not prohibit a former official from representing a party in a broad public policy dispute, even where the official was personally and substantially involved. For example, an Environmental Protection Agency official acting as project manager in a rule-making proceeding on pollution from oil refineries could leave government and immediately go to work for the American Petroleum Institute because the rule making involves many parties in general. Nor does the ban include what is called "aiding and advising" on otherwise prohibited matters — that is, providing behind-the-scenes advice to an organization about how the organization should deal with the official's former agency, as long as the former official does not himself appear personally before current officials of the agency.

2. A *two-year ban* on similar types of representation on matters that were under the official's "official responsibility" during the last year of the official's tenure in government, even though the official was not personally and substantially involved in those matters. The exceptions to this two-year ban are similar to those for the lifetime ban discussed above. And, although middle or senior officials may have had a large number of matters under their official responsibility and may thus be prohibited from dealing with them for two years, it should be noted that nothing in the ban prevents an ex-official from helping an organization on a matter that arises *after* the official has left his agency.

3. A *one-year ban* (often called a "cooling-off period") for top government officials only (those at grade level GS-17 or above) on similar representation on *any* matter before one's former agency at all. This ban does not extend to aiding and advising, but it does include broad policy matters, as well as those involving specific parties, and it applies to new matters that arise after the official has left the agency.

4. A *one-year ban* for the most senior government officials (those at Executive

Schedule grades) on similar types of representation to any similarly senior official anywhere in the federal government. This ban does not extend to aiding or advising.

In addition to these general provisions, there are a number of additional bans, introduced during the last few years, for trade negotiators and procurement officials. These additional restrictions put additional limitations on what kinds of work an ex-employee may perform for an organization outside government. They are as follows:

1. A *one-year ban* for officials who personally and substantially participated in trade negotiations from doing any work for a foreign organization or government regarding those negotiations, including aiding and advising, as well as a *one-year ban* on senior officials aiding or advising a foreign government on any matters.
2. A *two-year ban* for midlevel or senior Department of Defense officials (those at grade level GS-13 or above) who have had significant dealings with a contractor on a major weapons system (such as by being stationed at the contractor's plant or working more than half-time on that contract) from taking any employment at all with that contractor, no matter what the job is.

Two arguments might be made against legislating any revolving-door restrictions at all. One argument could involve the individual rights of the jobholder; the other could involve social utility. Normally, the right to liberty implies a person's right to seek any job he wishes and to sell his services to anyone willing to pay for them. Revolving-door restrictions impinge on such liberty by limiting the kinds of jobs people may accept after government employment. These restrictions on the liberty to choose occupations may also be argued to reduce net social welfare if we believe that such free occupational choice over a career lifetime maximizes the total social produce an individual produces.

A different kind of utilitarian argument can also be made, to the effect that government officials with knowledge of the private as well as the public sector make, on the average, better decisions than do those who spend their entire lives in government service—or, indeed, that private organizations make, on the average, better decisions in areas where a dimension of social responsibility should be involved when former government officials, with a more public perspective than those who have made their entire careers in the private sector, are involved in them. (The word *utilitarian* is used somewhat metaphorically here, since the better decisions argued to be produced may be public decisions that respect individual rights or do justice, rather than maximizing utility. The term is merely designed to contrast the argument with one that ignores the larger public implications of a policy that puts no postemployment restrictions on officeholders, on the grounds of those officeholders' own individual liberty.) According to this view, anything that discourages moves in and out of government service also hurts the average quality of government decisions by putting decisions in the hands of people less likely to have appropriate knowledge, judgments, or attitudes. It might also be argued that arrangements that make shifts out of government service more difficult make it harder for government officials to engage in whistle-blowing, because they become more dependent on their government jobs.

Revolving-door restrictions may also hurt the quality of government decisions, not via their effect on the knowledge and judgment of public officials but via their effect on their average ability level. Revolving-door restrictions reduce the rewards of government service below what they otherwise would be. Standard economic theory predicts that reducing the rewards associated with a given job will decrease the supply of people seeking the job. To the extent that the people who are most attractive to postgovernment employers are also those who would be most attractive as postgovernment employees, revolving-door restrictions discourage government service the most among just those people whom the government would find the most attractive employees. Alternatively, attracting people of the same quality would require that government pay higher salaries to compensate for the loss of postgovernment positions, which would impose an economic burden on government. (The extent to which revolving-door legislation actually causes people to shun government service depends on how sensitive the behavior of such employees is to changes in relative rewards. This question has never been investigated empirically, although there have been many anecdotal suggestions that revolving-door legislation may inhibit some people from taking high government positions, and there are some entry-level government jobs, particularly for lawyers doing tax or securities law, that certainly would be much more difficult to fill with good people at government salaries without the availability of postgovernment employment for private tax or securities clients.)

As we shall see shortly, many of the arguments on behalf of revolving-door restrictions are based on negative effects the revolving door has on the overall quality of government decisions (although these counterarguments do not address the quality of the decisions of private organizations that may be affected by the presence of former public officials). Perhaps what can most appropriately be noted at this point is that the argument that the revolving door may encourage good decisions stands as a challenge to arguments on behalf of revolving-door restrictions that will be based on negative effects of the revolving door on the quality of government decisions.

Are there good arguments on behalf of revolving-door legislation that can be made to outweigh the force of these arguments against such restrictions? And might arguments on behalf of revolving-door restrictions in fact justify a regime considerably stricter than the one we have now? Three arguments support revolving-door restrictions.

The first argument is that the inside knowledge that public officials

develop while working at jobs in government, as well as the personal friend-
ships and contacts made there, give such individuals an unfair advantage
after leaving government in influencing government decisions on behalf of
the clients that hire them. The image here is of "influence peddling," of the
former government employee who "fixes" government decisions for whoever
pays him to do so. Revolving-door restrictions are then justified as preventing former officials from enjoying an "unfair advantage" in influencing the
decisions of those still in government. We will call this the argument from
inside knowledge and contacts.

The second argument is that the prospect of future employment after
government service will encourage public officials to make bad decisions while
they are still in government. The image here is of the regulatory or military
official who "goes soft" on the industry his agency is supposed to regulate, or on
the contractor from whom the military buys weapons, in the hope of getting a
job in that industry after leaving government. (I shall use the phrase *organizations
that officials regulate* in this chapter somewhat loosely and generically, to characterize the relationship between a government organization and a private party or
organization whose interests may not be congruent with the public good the
agency is designed to promote.) The revolving door makes government decisions worse than they otherwise would be, and this fact justifies revolving-door
restrictions. We will call this the argument from "going soft."

The third argument involves an ideal of public spirit in public service.
People should display public spirit in public life and not profit financially,
beyond the salaries they receive from their jobs, from government service.
The image here is of a public official who gains important skills and contacts
while on the job (just as in the case of the first argument). But while the first
argument puts the emphasis in the term *influence peddling* on the word *influence,*
the third argument puts the emphasis on the word *peddling.* We will call this
the argument from the unacceptability of personal profit out of public service.

This chapter will analyze these three arguments for revolving-door
restrictions. The jumping-off point for this chapter will be the actual revolving-
door restrictions that exist and the actual arguments made on their behalf
by participants in debates on revolving-door legislation during Congress's
consideration, in committee and on the floor, of the Ethics in Government
Act of 1978 and the various amendments to it considered since then. I shall
take existing provisions seriously as data that will help us understand which
arguments have been taken seriously enough to have survived into law. This
will be only a starting point, however. I will devote most of this chapter
to analyzing the arguments more deeply than is done in congressional debate, to see whether these arguments make sense and what revolving-door
provisions they may justify or fail to justify.

The First Argument

The argument from inside knowledge and contacts justifies revolving-door
legislation in order to prevent former government employees from taking

postgovernment jobs that allow them to use special inside knowledge and contacts within their former agencies to influence government decisions made by their successors. The argument from inside knowledge and contacts is probably the most common argument presented on behalf of revolving-door restrictions in congressional debate on the topic (Senate Committee on Governmental Affairs, 1977, p. 31). (In the report of the Senate Governmental Affairs Committee on what became the Ethics in Government Act of 1978, this argument was the major one mentioned, although other arguments to be discussed here also appeared, in passing. The report stated, "Former officials should not be permitted to exercise undue influence over former colleagues, still in office, in matters pending before the agencies; they should not be permitted to utilize information on specific cases gained during government service for their own benefit and that of private clients.") Since the former official has the ability to influence decisions only (or almost only) within the agency where he formerly worked and, *a fortiori*, on matters on which he formerly worked, this argument justifies restrictions on postemployment representation of clients on matters with which one dealt while at one's former agency or in front of one's former agency in general.

How strong is the argument? One way to see this argument is to conceive of it as a utilitarian worry that the revolving door can produce poorer government decisions. When a current government official makes a decision out of friendship for a former colleague representing a party to that decision, or when a party's representative is in a better position to make arguments that will appeal to an agency because of inside knowledge that a former official representing that party has, the content of the decision is blown off course by considerations irrelevant to the merits of the issue at hand.

In public debates regarding revolving-door legislation, however, the argument about former government officials exerting illegitimate influence on the process because of inside knowledge or contacts is frequently phrased in terms of "unfair advantage" going to organizations that can hire former government officials. One may believe that the "unfair advantage" argument is otiose, with any force that it may have collapsing into a utilitarian argument about bad government decisions that result from having former government officials representing one party in an issue before an agency. If this were so, it would be strange that the nonutilitarian language of "unfair advantage" has appeared so frequently in discussions of these phenomena. I am therefore inclined to think that the worry about unfair advantage has force, independent of its utilitarian effects on the content of decisions.

What, then, is the notion of unfair advantage trying to capture? In relation to whom does the organization hiring the former public official have an unfair advantage? Presumably, the answer is that the organization has such an advantage in relation to those advocates of other policies seeking to influence government decisions who do not hire former government officials. But this response itself raises questions. First, is there any relevant difference between the advantage that an organization has in being able to hire former officials and other advantages that organizations may derive from superior financial resources, or from an articulate massive membership, or from concentration in key congressional districts, and so forth? Second, is there any reason for government to regulate, through legislation, the possession of unfair advantages that groups have, compared with other groups in the political process, and why should this unfairness be a public concern?

The language of "unfair advantage" would seem to aim at a vision of the way that people ought to interact, with each other in general and in the political process in particular. The idea of fairness captures the view that people ought not to seek advantage over others on the basis of considerations extraneous to the merits of the questions to be decided. It is unfair for me, in private life, to take advantage of the fact that the person hiring a new accountant is my uncle, to get myself hired for a position for which I am only marginally qualified. An unfair advantage in a revolving-door situation seems quite similar. Such an advantage creates the forward-looking problem that it may well result in the wrong decision. But it also creates the backward-looking problem that it has treated some people unfairly by arbitrarily disadvantaging them. Such unfair treatment remains, even if those treating others unfairly do not succeed in actually getting the final decision that the government officials make biased in their favor. It is the backward-looking problem of arbitrarily disadvantaging those who do not have a former government official to represent them that would seem to capture the content of a notion of "unfair advantage" that is independent of any bias in the public policy decision resulting from such representation by the former official (Sher, 1987).

As for the question of whether, or why, hiring former public officials is any more unfair than other demonstrations of superior organizational resources, the easiest situations to dispose of are those where superior organizational resources involve numbers of members, or where an organization's financial resources arise from great intensity of feeling among its members. Such sources of organizational advantage are not irrelevant to the merits of the public decision the organization seeks to influence, since a utilitarian calculation by a public official of what good public policy demands would require knowledge of the numbers and of the intensity of feelings behind different views. And even nonutilitarians accept a utilitarian calculation as one feature of an appropriate public judgment. Advantages are not due to irrelevant considerations; hence, they are not unfair.

However, when an organization's financial resources serve as more than a source of information about intensity of feeling, influence based on such resources becomes more troubling because the availability of money loses any tie with factors relevant to how one should treat the claims that a group makes. In these cases, it must be asked what an organization is purchasing with its money. An organization that used its money to bribe public officials would indeed be unfairly taking advantage of its financial resources, and we do prohibit such use of money. By contrast, at least within the executive branch, the major use that a money-rich organization typically makes of its money is to buy well-articulated and well-researched arguments on behalf of its position. The moral evaluation of such behavior is far less clear. The arguments that the organization buys are themselves clearly relevant to the public decision; one should avoid the "genetic fallacy" of judging the truth of an argument by its pedigree (Trigg, 1980, pp. 127–131). What is unfair, if anything, is that the ability to get such arguments developed varies, given the arbitrary fact that one group has more money than another. But at this level it is hard to distinguish such arbitrariness from the arbitrariness of the advantage enjoyed by a group consisting mostly of highly articulate people (such as groups dominated by the well educated). It would appear that the way to deal with such a problem would not be to gag good arguments (which, at the individual level, runs counter to any plausible concept of developing human excellence and, at the social level, impoverishes public policy debate) but rather to subsidize those who would otherwise have difficulty developing good arguments.

The argument from inside knowledge and contacts also helps explain why revolving-door restrictions do not (with only some exceptions) extend to aiding and advising. Arguments against restrictions on aiding and advising can be made on detection-cost grounds. How, it may be asked, can one police what goes on behind the scenes? Yet such an objection may not be very strong. In the normal course of business, law firms and consulting firms keep records to which clients their employees' terms are billed, and such records would be a low-cost source of information about who has been aiding or advising. Similarly, trade associations normally have directories or organization charts available, listing the policy areas for which their employees are responsible. (It would be possible, of course, to falsify either kind of information to escape detection, but this is not more of a problem here than in many other areas of criminal law.) If one is merely aiding and advising, however, one is by hypothesis not making use of one's inside contacts to influence decisions. One might still use one's inside knowledge to help others influence the government, such as by assisting those directly representing a client about the government's strategy in a case, or about what arguments are likely to impress the government officials the client is dealing with. But at least part of the force of the argument from inside knowledge and contacts on behalf of revolving-door restrictions does disappear. And much of the force of the argument from inside knowledge and contacts lies in the "contacts" part of the argument, as the image of *influence* peddling (not *information* peddling) suggests.

Finally, for those worried about the dangers to liberty from revolving-door restrictions, the argument from inside knowledge and contacts has the added advantage of justifying a limited set of restrictions that still leaves many opportunities for government officials to go on to jobs involving contacts with their former agencies or to work for employers who interact with their former agencies.

Nevertheless, if the only argument that could be made on behalf of revolving-door restrictions were the argument from inside knowledge and contacts, one would be hard-pressed to understand certain features of the revolving-door restrictions we have, as well as many important strains in the revolving-door debate.

In some ways, the revolving-door restrictions that exist, or that have been advocated by many participants in the debate, are stronger than the argument from inside knowledge and contacts would justify. Many people have supported bans on aiding or assisting, as well as on representing. In fact, Congress passed such a ban in the Ethics in Government Act of 1978, as part of its two-year restriction for former public officials dealing with their agencies on matters under their official responsibility, although the decision was reversed one year later. And the 1989 amendments introduced prohibitions against officials involved in trade negotiations aiding or advising foreign governments on those negotiations.

In other ways, the revolving-door restrictions we have are *weaker* than the argument from inside knowledge and contacts would suggest. Revolving-door restrictions do not apply to former federal government officials representing state and local governments, universities, and hospitals or medical research institutions. If the only argument on behalf of revolving-door restrictions were the argument from inside knowledge and contacts, it would be hard to see why such an exception should exist, since one may use one's inside knowledge or contacts to produce bad decisions or to give an organization an unfair advantage just as much if one works for a local government, a university, or a hospital as if one works for General Motors. Furthermore, legislation passed by Congress in 1988 would have applied revolving-door restrictions only to activities undertaken for compensation — again, an exception that does not make much sense on the basis of the argument from inside knowledge and contacts. (The 1988 legislation never went into effect because it was vetoed by President Reagan, but the veto was not based on an objection to this provision.)

The Second Argument

While the argument from inside knowledge and contacts focuses on the ability of ex–government officials to exert influence on decisions made by their successors, the argument from "going soft" focuses on decisions made by government officials while still in government, before they have proceeded to jobs with organizations that their agencies regulate. Again, it appears — initially, at any rate — that the force of this argument is the claim that the revolving door lowers social utility by producing bad government decisions.

The argument from "going soft," it should be noted, is less prevalent in public debates than the argument from inside knowledge and contacts. (In the report of the Senate Government Affairs Committee on the Ethics in Government Act of 1978, the committee went only so far as to note in passing that "there is a sense that . . . federal officials 'go easy' while in office in order to reap personal gain afterward"; see Senate Committee on Governmental Affairs, 1977, p. 32.) One reason for this, perhaps, is that the argument, if accepted, implies revolving-door restrictions considerably stronger than the ones currently in force. In particular, they could justify prohibitions against taking *any* kind of employment with an organization that one's agency has regulated. Almost all existing revolving-door legislation regulates the kind of work an individual may do, not the identity of the employer per se. But if an individual's decisions are biased toward a firm because of the prospects of postgovernment employment at that firm, such bias should occur equally whether the individual gets a job as the firm's vice president for government relations or as head of the firm's marketing operations in Latin America. What should matter, in terms of inducing improper influence, is the postgovernment job's salary, perks, and working conditions, not whether the job involves any contact with the public official's former agency or even with the government at all.

Although the argument from "going soft" is not the most prominent argument on behalf of revolving-door restrictions in public debate, it is perhaps the most common argument regarding the revolving door among those academic political scientists and economists who have thought and written about revolving-door issues. Scholars who have worried about "captured" regulatory agencies have often seen the postgovernment career paths of officials of regulatory agencies as part of the dynamic of capture (Bernstein, 1955; Peltzman, 1976).

The argument from "going soft" has been challenged on its own terms. The hope for postgovernment employment in a regulated industry need not, it has been suggested, push the public official toward being soft on the industry. A private firm wants people who are skilled, committed, and aggressively dedicated to their jobs. A feckless official who will abandon the goals of his government organization in order to curry favor on the outside may, the argument goes, be just as feckless when it comes to working on behalf of the goals of the private firm that is considering hiring him (Quirk, 1981). Indeed, private employers may especially seek to hire skilled and aggressively committed public officials in order to get those officials "off their backs," a situation that would create an incentive for displaying such commitment in one's government job as to generate such private job offers. (I am grateful to Andrew Stark for calling my attention to this argument in the version made by supporters of revolving-door restrictions.) The suggestion that private employers may seek to hire away aggressive public officials is typically raised as an argument *on behalf of* revolving-door restrictions, the suggestion being that such a drain should be dammed (Hammersmith, 1981). But when the incentive effects are considered, the argument may actually count against revolving-door restrictions.

The little empirical evidence that exists regarding the in-office behavior of public officials who go on to the industries they now regulate is mixed (Cohen, 1988; Quirk, 1981; Weaver, 1977, pp. 154–63). In the most careful existing empirical study, commissioners at the Federal Communications Commission who went to work for the broadcasting industry after working in government were found to be no more likely to cast votes in favor of the industry over the course of their government tenure than those who had not; but, in their last year in government, commissioners who went to work in the broadcasting industry did become somewhat more likely to cast proindustry votes than those who did not go on to such work.

The dispute over whether the revolving door influences the behavior of officials while they are in government does highlight an important feature of the argument from "going soft." The contention cannot be that *all* public officials who seek postgovernment employment in organizations that their agencies regulate *will* make decisions while in government that are biased by that fact; the claim must be a much weaker one — namely, that this situation *creates a risk* for biased decisions.

In terms of how great the risk of misbehavior is, one should imagine a continuum of situations that make bad behavior more probable. The continuum begins with bribery. The next step in the continuum is what is generally called "conflict of interest," where financial interests that a public official *already has* may lead that official to make decisions biased by such interest. That such decisions actually will be so influenced is not certain, however; it is possible to conceive of the conscientious public official who does not allow himself to be influenced by a conflict of interest. The third step in the continuum is a revolving-door situation, where the prospect of *future* employment may bias the official. If we control for the amount of the interest at stake, we can say that the *certainty* of a *current* interest could be expected to influence a decision more than the *prospect* of a *future* interest would. However, if one's current financial interest amounts to $100, and the value of the future prospect amounts to $100,000, the future prospect may have a greater likelihood of influencing a decision than a present certainty would.

Once we realize that we are talking about legislation that prohibits behavior that would otherwise be within one's rights (say, selling one's services to whoever is willing to pay for them), and that it does so because some people *will* allow such employment to influence their decisions illegitimately while in government, the problematic nature of the argument from "going soft" becomes apparent. It is one thing to punish a public official for taking a bribe or for actually allowing his decisions to be influenced by a conflict of interest or by the prospect of postgovernment employment. But what about the upright employee whose behavior in government is in no way influenced by his postemployment prospects? Doesn't revolving-door legislation constitute an injustice against such people, penalizing them (not, to be sure, through imprisonment or fines, but via restrictions on their right to accept employment) for offenses they did not commit? (I use the term *penalize* in a broad sense, one not restricted to criminal liability.) Justice would seem to require that rewards and punishments be allocated on the basis of the public official's own behavior (Feinberg, 1973). To put this another way, when we establish general rules restricting postgovernment employment, rules that apply to the upright as well as to the derelict, these rules, like rules in general, are applied willy-nilly to people whose behavior makes them appropriate targets of the rule and to those whose behavior does not. (Very similar arguments can be made with regard to restrictions on campaign contributions to candidates for elective office; see Thompson, 1987, pp. 111–116. The discussion that follows applies equally, I think, to that question.)

The problem of inappropriate rule-boundedness is a major topic of discussion in the literature on organizational theory and management that concerns the use of rules to guide the behavior of an organization's members (Bardach and Kagan, 1982; Kelman, 1990; Mintzberg, 1979b). It is a commonplace of this literature that the application of rules to specific situations, with no consideration of the special features of those situations, frequently results in inappropriate organizational behavior. Such problems, as discussed in the organizational theory and management literature, are seldom conceived in moral terms, however. Indeed, in this literature, the major way in which ethical issues (particularly as regards public organizations) are explicitly raised is typically in connection with the suggestion that the demand that government treat citizens "equitably" constitutes a reason *for* rule-based organizational behavior, rather than against it (Kaufman, 1977). Rules generally lead public organizations to treat all citizens in the same ways, and such treatment is seen as a virtue and as ensuring that, say, one citizen does not have a license application treated more favorably because he is a friend of the official in charge of granting the license. The organizational theory literature thus focuses on one part of the Aristotelian requirement for just treatment—namely, treating cases that are alike on relevant dimensions that are alike. But that literature ignores the other part of the dictum—that justice requires treating relevantly dissimilar cases dissimilarly. The organizational theory literature thus tends to miss situations where individuals are dissimilar in a relevant respect (one employee has let his decisions be biased by the prospect of future employment, while another has not), and rules treat the two similarly.

Having noted that rules restricting postgovernment employment appear to raise questions about whether individuals are being penalized whether or not they undertake the behavior that the rules are designed to inhibit, we may also note that revolving-door legislation is hardly the only example of a legal rule that exhibits such properties (Feinberg, 1970, 1990; Fletcher, 1978; Hart, 1968; Nagel, 1979; Schauer, 1991; Wertheimer, 1983; Williams, 1981; Zimmerman, 1987). We use speed limits and red lights to reduce unsafe driving, and we punish infractions, even by skilled drivers who create lower accident risks at high speeds, or who use their judgment more intelligently at flashing yellow lights, than do many others driving within the speed limit or stopping at red lights. We establish the minimum voting age as eighteen and the minimum drinking age as twenty-one, even though some people under those ages could vote (or drink) intelligently, and others over those ages can do neither. An individual who shoots a bullet at the heart of a person wearing a bulletproof vest — or who places poison in the coffee cup of an intended victim, who then spills the coffee before it can be drunk — will not be punished for murder, but if the individual had fired the identical shot and the intended victim not been protected by the vest, or if the other intended victim had not spilled the coffee, he would have been punished for murder. A person with a bad character who had volunteered as a guard in Auschwitz would have been punished very severely, while a person of equally bad character living today in Boston will suffer no such punishment, since there are no concentration camps for him to work in. We adopt rules of strict liability in some areas of tort law, including automobile accident law in many jurisdictions, even though such rules treat the blameless and the blameworthy the same.

Can such rules be justified? As we move from the level of a single individual deciding how to treat another specific individual to the level of a social institution treating large numbers of people, a number of utilitarian arguments for such rules appear. The most obvious such argument involves detection costs. It is much less costly to detect violations of a rule stated in terms of specific, easily observable behavior ("Don't drive faster than fifty-five miles per hour," "Don't work for an industry you regulated") than to detect the underlying behavior that the rule is designed to prevent (Schauer, 1991, pp. 43–52, 145–149). If one tried to determine whether the actual behavior of public officials was influenced by postgovernment employment, there would be huge numbers of decisions by huge numbers of officials to monitor, and no existing data source (such as the stock exchanges' computer systems, which the Securities and Exchange Commission uses to monitor suspicious stock trade) to monitor them. One would need to look at the in-office behavior not only of officials who later departed for suspicious post-government jobs but also of those who never did, since the latter may also have let the prospect of postgovernment employment influence their behavior, even though such employment never materialized.

Furthermore, it would be very hard to prove that an individual's decisions while in government were influenced by the prospect of postgovernment employment. To prove a criminal offense, one would surely need more than some simple correlation between a decision, or even a pattern of decisions, and the job a person took after leaving government. A witness who, the day before an important decision was to be made, saw an official eating lunch with an executive at the corporation affected by the decision, and where the official eventually took a job, might help persuade a jury. The evidence might be even more persuasive if the witness overheard the executive making the official a lucrative job offer. A prosecutor might also get phone records showing large numbers of telephone calls by the official to the corporation and to its personnel department. But proof "beyond a reasonable doubt" remains tough, and the high standard of proof encourages the guilty to invent excuses and evade punishment. Given detection costs, the *failure* to establish a rule might be argued as unjust because it would allow the guilty to go free, through the practical inability to detect and then punish their wrong-doing.

Rules that establish postgovernment employment restrictions, rather than simply penalizing biased decisions, may also deter biased decisions more than a narrowly drawn standard would. The difficulty of proving that decisions were influenced by postgovernment employment prospects will encourage some officials to behave illicitly and hope they can get away with it. Moreover, an individual sometimes may not know, even in his own mind, exactly what reasons he had for a policy decision he made; many people might subtly be influenced by postgovernment employment prospects without even fully realizing this themselves. By removing this factor from the life of the government official, we automatically decrease the influence of such job prospects on decision making.

With regard to each of these utilitarian arguments, however, the upright individual whose postgovernment behavior is restricted might still complain that he is being asked to pay a cost because of problems caused for the system by the behavior of others who are less virtuous. There are, however, arguments that might have force even for the upright person. If the upright person agrees that government decisions improperly influenced by postgovernment employment prospects should be penalized, he must be willing to accept enforcement activities to uncover such behavior. But such enforcement activities could involve significant interference with the privacy of government officials in general, including upright ones, if the prosecuting authorities are to have any chance of uncovering any significant numbers of violations at all. (I am grateful to Dennis Thompson for suggesting this point to me.) Fletcher (1978, especially pp. 88–89) argues that *attempts* should not be punished as severely as completed crimes, because inquiries into the mental states of people violate privacy unacceptably. And the role that the subjective state of mind of the government official plays in such a crime would increase the risk of prosecutions motivated by political or other vendettas. Therefore, when the upright individual contemplates the appropriate design of an *institution* to deal with policy decisions biased by postgovernment employment considerations, he may prefer clear rules to trusting his fate to imperfect human prosecutors (Schauer, 1991). If an individual is afraid that the prospects of lucrative postgovernment employment might be so attractive as to tempt him to abandon his ethical standards, then that individual may want there to be a rule that, by foreclosing certain postgovernment employment options, forecloses such unwanted temptations as well (Elster, 1979).

Even with all this, however, I believe that considerable uneasiness should remain over the treatment of upright individuals under revolving-door restrictions. The utilitarian arguments have considerable force, but they do ultimately penalize the innocent for problems created by the sins of the guilty. Were it not for the guilty, the upright individual would not need to worry about interference with his privacy or about prosecutorial vendettas, since there would be no need for prosecutorial activity in this area at all.

In most of the problematic instances discussed earlier — the person who can drive safely at high speeds, the person who shoots at the heart of somebody wearing a bulletproof vest, and so forth — the potential injustice existed only in rare and unusual cases. Such is not the situation for injustices brought about by revolving-door restrictions, however. Plausible accounts of "going soft" suggest that it may be a problem for some number of public officials; but existing empirical evidence, already discussed, suggests that there may be at least as many officials, or perhaps even more, who are not so influenced. Add to this the normal situations of people who seek to shift jobs — because, say, they are unhappy at their present jobs, or must move together with a spouse — and normal facts (such as that one is likely to seek work in an area where one has already been trained, and that contacts one makes at one job are often a source of leads for other jobs), and the likely extensiveness of the injustice of penalizing people who have done nothing wrong themselves becomes increasingly clear. Although high detection costs may indeed imply that a world without revolving-door restrictions would unjustly allow some people to go free, our legal system normally attaches greater weight to avoiding punishment of the innocent than to ensuring punishment of all the guilty.

One might well, on balance, be able to justify revolving-door legislation despite the restrictions such legislation imposes on the upright officials whose decisions would not have been so influenced. But the case is a close one, and the worry about the unjust treatment of the upright should occasion unease.

A different question raised by the argument from "going soft" is the exact nature of the impropriety to which objection is made when decisions are so influenced. A quick reaction might be that the impropriety is a departure from official impartiality. A public official whose decisions are influenced by the prospect of postgovernment employment does not, in this view, approach issues with an open mind. Such bias moves the content of government decisions away from the official's impartial judgment of what the public good requires, in the direction of responsiveness to the interests of future employers.

This reaction comes close to being right, I think, but in an important way it is not quite right. That it is not quite right is suggested by the very permissive stance taken toward public officials with clear *ideological* views regarding policies within the domain of the agencies for which they work. Occasionally, efforts are made to have public officials formally disqualified from making decisions regarding matters on which they have almost certainly made up their minds before having heard the arguments in the particular case, on the grounds that they have an ideological conflict of interest. (A court suit was brought in 1977, for example, seeking to bar Michael Pertschuk, chairman of the Federal Trade Commission, from participating in the agency's rule-making proceedings on children's television advertising, on the grounds that he had already given several speeches stating that he thought such advertising constituted unfair exploitation of children. The suit against Pertschuk was dismissed. Such efforts, when made, have rarely been successful, and many people regard the presence of firm convictions in public officials as something that can at least be healthy, rather than necessarily a problem. Certainly, nobody would propose legislation to prevent a Republican president from appointing probusiness commissioners to the National Labor Relations Board (NLRB) or a Democratic president from appointing activists in environmental organizations to high positions in the Environmental Protection Agency (EPA).

If we do not find the prospect of probusiness NLRB commissioners or environmentalist EPA administrators unacceptable in principle, then we must at least specify more clearly what notion of impartiality justifies revolving-door legislation to reduce decisions biased on behalf of future employers. It cannot be impartiality in the sense of a fully open mind. We must be drawing a distinction between prejudgment based on one's *ideas* and prejudgment based on *financial or other personal considerations* (such as a desire to help a friend or relative). Such a distinction could in turn be justified on the basis of the observation that one's ideology is (or at least may well be) founded on a conception of what the public good requires, while decisions driven by personal financial considerations are unlikely to be so determined. A decision driven by postemployment prospects, then, would not be based on prejudgment but rather on lack of public spirit. This is an issue to which I will return.

The Third Argument

There remains the argument from profiting out of public service, which expresses an ideal of public spirit in public service. (In endorsing the Ethics in Government Act of 1978, President Carter stated that the legislation sought to "curb the revolving door practice that has too often permitted former officials to exploit their government contacts for private gain" (House Committee on the Judiciary, 1978, p. 86). In the Senate report accompanying the bill, the legislation is justified as counteracting the impression that "federal officials use public office for personal gain." When public officials "reap personal gain" after government service, the report continues, this "leads to suspicion that personal profit was the motivation for the appointment in the first instance. All of this is repulsive to universally held principles of public service"; see Senate Committee on Governmental Affairs, 1977, p. 32.)

This argument explains some features of existing revolving-door legislation that appear anomalous from the standpoint of the first two arguments. It will be remembered that, from the perspective of improper influence on a public official's decisions while in government, it appears anomalous to worry about bias due to financial considerations, but not about bias due to ideological considerations. That anomaly disappears when the argument for revolving-door restrictions gets recast in terms of personal profit from public service. Similarly, there may be no distinction in terms of unfair advantage, whether an individual works for a nonprofit organization or whether he works without pay, but there is a distinction from the point of view of the ideal of public spirit in public service. (This was indeed the major argument made for the university and medical exemption when it was adopted in 1979. Secretary of Health, Education and Welfare Califano, who provided the major testimony on behalf of the change, argued that "these are not people who work for money. They don't make any more or less money" outside of government than inside it. "If we were talking about people that are going to go out and make money on some revolving door, that would be one thing; but we're not talking about people like that in this change" (Califano, 1979, pp. 40–41).

There is also an important feature in the debate over revolving-door restrictions that would be mysterious to anyone looking only at the argument from inside knowledge and contacts or the argument from "going soft." Supporters of revolving-door restrictions often present the example of a person who goes to work doing trade negotiations straight out of graduate school, essentially unformed prior to government service, but who becomes rich in knowledge and contacts while in government and then goes off to a lucrative private job, using that knowledge and those contacts. Opponents of revolving-door restrictions, by contrast, serve up a different example, that of an individual who is already rich in knowledge and experience before his government service (say, a securities lawyer who becomes head of the Securities and Exchange Commission, or an executive in an oil company who becomes a senior executive in the Department of Energy) and who merely wishes to go back and pursue his former job, or something like it, after leaving government. From the standpoint of the argument from inside knowledge and contacts (or of the argument from "going soft"), it is hard to see why the question of whether one is returning to a preexisting profession should make any difference. The struggle over these examples makes sense only if one sees that they have very different implications for whether one has profited from government service.

Likewise, I would suggest that a considerable part of the force of the argument from inside knowledge and contacts or from "going soft" really derives from associating them with the argument from profiting out of public service. The example of the official who has abused inside contacts or "gone soft," is invariably of a person who has done such a thing either (in the first case) in a lucrative postgovernment job or (in the second case) in the hope of obtaining one. It is hard to summon up indignation over the government official who uses his inside contacts as the Department of Housing and Urban Development to help him work more successfully on behalf of the homeless at a postgovernment job with a homeless advocacy group, or whose decisions while in government were biased on behalf of the homeless in the hope of his landing such a job after leaving government. Indeed, almost all the examples presented to illustrate the arguments from inside knowledge and contacts or from "going soft" tie these phenomena to concern about profiting out of public service.

One view of the argument from profiting out of public service is that it is a version of the utilitarian argument over the quality of the decisions that government officials make. If public spirit prompts government officials to make good decisions, then we should want public officials who are public-spirited. This viewpoint may underlie the rejoinder that the advocates of revolving-door legislation often make to those who worry that revolving-door legislation will discourage talented people from entering government service: people who wish to use a government career as a springboard to financial gain are not the kind of people we should want in government, anyway; their lack of public spirit provides evidence that they will make poor decisions while in government (see Wolpe, 1986, p. 52). At the level of institutional design, one may also argue that improvement in the management of government organizations frequently requires that public officials be given greater discretion and judgment than is currently the case (Kelman, 1990). If high levels of public spirit within government organizations encourage overseers to put greater trust in public officials, then public spirit among public officials is important for encouraging an appropriate institutional design for public management.

Other versions of this argument, however, are not simply restatements of the view that people who seek such profit are more likely to make bad decisions. The most important versions of this argument, I think, go beyond the question of the quality of decisions to include the qualities that people should have *as* people. One important reason for opposition to personal profit from public service would involve the moral value of good intentions by themselves, as independent of the quality of the decisions (or other results) that such good intentions might achieve. It has become almost a truism among those engaged in the scholarly study of public policy that good intentions are not enough. Unfortunately, this has often slid too easily into the suggestion that good intentions count for nothing. But surely there is a difference between somebody engaged in target practice on a legal shooting range, who accidentally kills another person who has strayed onto the range, and a person who wishes to murder another and succeeds against equally long odds (Fried, 1976, p. 170). Even a dog knows the difference between being stumbled over and being kicked (Holmes, 1881, p. 3).

Good intentions do have value, of course, partly because (despite the loving attention that unintended consequences have received from social scientists) they are generally correlated with good results. But good intentions have moral value in themselves, independently of whether they are ever translated into good consequences, because actions that grow out of good intentions display respect for the worth of human beings. We value a failed attempt to save a drowning swimmer more than we value sitting by the side of the pool sipping iced tea and watching the person drown, although the results are the same, and this is not just because the would-be rescuer is likely to succeed the next time he tries. In the classical formulation of Kant, even if a good will "by some special disfavor of destiny or by the niggardly endowment of step-motherly nature . . . is entirely lacking in power to carry out its intentions; if by its utmost effort it still accomplishes nothing, and only good will is left; even then it would still shine like a jewel for its own sake as something which has its full value in itself" (Kant, 1964, p. 62; see also Herman, 1981). In this view, revolving-door restrictions are in the realm of an ideal of public service that values public spirit not only for the decisions it produces but also for the intentions it represents.

Are we justified in giving an ideal of public service the coercive force of law, through revolving-door restrictions? Liberals generally worry about legislation that establishes one conception of how individuals should live their lives over other conceptions, yet these worries generally would not seem to apply here. First, insofar as the ideal of public spirit in public service improves, on balance, the decisions that government makes, efforts to encourage this ideal need not be justified simply as embodying an ideal of how to live one's private life but as an aid to achieving good government policies. Second, legislation on behalf of this idea may seek to encourage the general development of ethical behavior and ethical disposition on the part of citizens and hence improve the ethical quality of the decisions that citizens make in their everyday lives. Research by Tom R. Tyler and his colleagues, on the effects of evaluating the fairness of procedures used to resolve disputes, is relevant here (Lind and Tyler, 1988; Tyler, 1990; Casper and others, 1988; Tyler and others, 1989). Tyler has shown, in both laboratory and field settings, that people attribute importance to the fairness of the procedures that decision makers use to deal with disputes, independently of whether the disputes are substantively resolved in a particular person's favor. The most important consideration people use in judging is whether the decision makers try to be impartial (Tyler, 1990, pp. 135–140). Studies by Tyler and his colleagues also show that such evaluations have a significant impact on confidence in government in general, on acceptance of the obligation to obey the law, and on actual compliance with a number of laws (Tyler, 1990; Tyler and others, 1989). All three kinds of situations that are criticized by advocates of revolving-door restrictions—where former officials are able to exert special influence on their ex-colleagues, where officials bias their decisions in the hope of obtaining certain postgovernment jobs, and where ex-officials profit from public service—create the perception of lack of impartiality.

Presumably (although Tyler does not discuss this specifically), what is occurring is some form of social-climate effect, whereby citizens feel that if those in authority behave ethically, they as citizens should also behave ethically—and, conversely, that if even those in authority behave unethically, there is no reason for ordinary citizens to be ethical. Public life is so visible that it sets a good or bad example for ethical disposition and good intentions in the everyday lives of citizens. Hence, one has more reason to worry about unfair behavior in a public context (such as allowing ex-officials an unfair advantage in influencing public decisions because of inside knowledge and contacts) than one does in a private context (such as allowing an employer to hire his nephew over a more qualified candidate), where unfair behavior may be seen as within an employer's rights.

Taken together, these findings give some concrete content to the frequent contention in revolving-door debates that revolving-door legislation is necessary to promote citizens' confidence in government. If confidence is related to the tendency to obey the law, and if laws in turn generally embody moral obligations, then there can be a justification for coercive measures that encourage citizens' confidence in government. Ethical behavior on the part of citizens is not simply a private matter or a private conception of the good life; rather, this is a question of encouraging people to live up to moral obligations. Liberals should not object if such disposition and such behavior become objects of the coercive force of law.

The most problematic connection between a public-spirited ideal of public service and coercive legislation involves any argument for legislation based simply on the general worry, of a Rousseauian sort, about opulence. Stripped of any association with good decisions, good intentions, or the encouragement of ethical behavior in everyday life, such an argument would appear to involve a conception of how individuals should live their personal lives (and hardly a universally accepted one at that). Two points can be made here.

The first is that there is a distinction between coercive legislation that applies to citizens in general and legislation that regulates the behavior of the government's own employees. A significant part of the force of the liberal objection to endorsing, through legislation, one perfectionist ideal of the good life is that it stifles diversity and expresses intolerance toward other views of the good life. Legislation directed toward the government's own employees would appear to do this no more than the internal rules of the Roman Catholic Church, which require priests to take vows of poverty, or the rules of an academic "think tank," which require employees to devote themselves to scholarly pursuits. Revolving-door legislation does not eliminate social diversity, because it applies only to one occupational group.

The second point is that one purpose of the ideal of public service expressed in revolving-door legislation is to provide a visible example of public-spirited behavior that may encourage citizens outside government to choose to live their private lives in ways that emphasize things that life has to offer other than material acquisition. Such a visible public example hardly forces citizens to heed it, but it does display some government partiality to one view of the good life over others. Since this is a controversial ideal, why should this even be permissible? It is permissible, I would argue, because a *worry* about opulence and acquisitiveness is widely shared in our society (even as other currents drive many people, who in some sense share that worry, toward acquisitive behavior). Given the powerful psychological forces that encourage acquisitiveness among citizens (forces that hardly run the risk of being crushed by revolving-door restrictions), it is reasonable for citizens who share at least some nagging worries about opulence and acquisitiveness to wish to see established a repository for alternative values that will help keep those values alive and prevent them from being entirely overwhelmed by powerful acquisitive urges. The very visibility of government makes it an apt candidate to serve as such a repository. The type of encouragement that revolving-door restrictions give to one perfectionist ideal (nonmaterialism) over other possible ideals would seem mild enough to be justified if enough citizens shared enough worry about acquisitiveness to wish for such a repository.

The reach of revolving-door restrictions, based on the argument from profiting out of public service, is potentially extremely wide. It would certainly extend to aiding and advising and to total contact bans. It might extend to restrictions on what organizations one might work for after government employment. One might also ask why the argument from profiting out of public service could not be used to prohibit postgovernment-job book contracts and speaking engagements, or even to ban the use of general management skills acquired in government to obtain lucrative postgovernment jobs using those skills outside the substantive policy area or agency where one had worked. One might even criticize the fact that the military service advertise the salaries or on-the-job training that those who sign up to be soldiers will receive. (I owe these examples to Arthur Applbaum, who raised them as questions to me.)

Considerations of justice, however, put serious obstacles in the way of using the argument from profiting out of public service to make the reach of revolving-door restrictions so wide. Issues of justice arise because, as noted, there are public officials who learn about certain policy areas while in government, and there are those who interrupt careers involving certain areas in order to serve in government. This creates no problem of injustice regarding the existing revolving-door restrictions that are limited to where one was involved while in government or where one served as a high official. In a situation where an individual personally has been working on a certain matter while in government, even the person who was an expert in an area before entering government normally gains significant new knowledge and contacts through government service. Similarly, an agency head gains contacts and "clout" from his position as an agency head even if he was an expert in the agency's area of jurisdiction before taking the government job. Even the previously knowledgeable individual would therefore be able to profit financially from public service, without revolving-door restrictions. If restrictions are limited to situations in which even former securities lawyers or energy company executives would be profiting from government service in jobs they received after leaving government, then no question of penalization without fault exists.

The broader restrictions on foreign-trade negotiators and on officials working on major weapons systems are also not subject to the objection from injustice. (Officials working on weapons systems, however, are banned from aiding, advising, and working for certain employers at all.) As an empirical matter, very few of the people involved in trade negotiations or in major weapons-system procurement developed their knowledge about such matters prior to their government service. The worry about the injustice of penalizing people who simply wish to return to their prior professions after service in government seldom would apply to the people in these particular jobs. The situation is different, however, for the more general restrictions on aiding and advising than the argument from profiting out of public service might otherwise support. It was argued earlier that simple presence in government does not inevitably give an ex-official a significant unfair advantage when his or her work for an organization regulated by the government consists only of aiding or advising. If an unfair advantage does not arise inevitably in such aiding and advising, then a rule that extended a ban on aiding and advising, based on the argument from profiting out of public service, would indeed raise issues of injustice. People who have interrupted existing careers in policy areas to serve in government would be prohibited from using their knowledge or contacts that they gained before entering government to aid and advise in their policy areas after leaving government. In many cases, they might be prohibited from resuming activities identical to those they had performed before entering government. One might try to draw distinctions, on a case-by-case basis, between officials who learned policy areas while in government and those who interrupted existing careers. But this would have the result of producing more onerous restrictions on junior people, whose first jobs are in government, than on senior agency officials coming from lucrative and prestigious jobs in the private sector. Such vertical inequity would create a public impression of letting "big fish" off easily, an impression hardly consistent with the argument that one purpose of revolving-door restrictions is to foster public confidence that public institutions treat the humble and the mighty fairly.

As for book contracts and speaking engagements, similar issues of injustice arise, since people may write or speak about their areas of prior expertise. Such bans might also easily be rejected for exacting too great a cost in terms of the right to liberty, especially if one believes that free speech about public matters should, for various reasons, enjoy special protection. At the same time, the force of the argument from profiting out of public service suggests why it is that there was widespread criticism concerning the large sum of money that former President Reagan received from a Japanese newspaper executive for a small number of public appearances, and why there exists similar public uneasiness about lucrative book contracts for ex-officials. As for taking lucrative jobs after acquiring general management skills in government, the suggestion that such behavior specifically constitutes profiting from government service seems hard to sustain. This would seem to be a case of "profiting," so to speak, from the experiences of one's life in general. Nobody expects people to work for government without learning anything or being paid, and so the fact that the armed services offer recruits jobs that pay them something, or train them for relatively modest postgovernment jobs, should not be seen as a problem.

If the ideal of public spirit in public service is to encourage ethical behavior and disposition in the everyday lives of citizens, then the ideal must achieve wide enough acceptance among public officials for citizens to see that it is indeed present as a moral standard. Statutory revolving-door restrictions do not themselves create public spirit; they simply regulate behavior. Nevertheless, such restrictions do promote the development of public-spirited disposition in government. First, as noted earlier, they may discourage people who seek financial gain from taking government jobs in the first place. Second, they send a signal to public officials about the ideal of public spirit in public service and hence promote the spread of public spirit among those sensitive to signals from the environment. Third, because attitudes often grow out of behavior, rather than simply causing behavior, limits on any actions that do not display public spirit may produce actual growth in real public spirit (Kelman, 1974). Fourth, by making defections from public spirit more difficult, restrictions also protect a collective good (the norm of public spirit) from the danger of cascading defections (as individuals seeking to uphold the norm regard themselves as "chumps" if others defect). Finally, citizens have a hard time reading the hearts of public officials, but an easier time reading their behavior. A selfish individual who does not, because of revolving-door restrictions, profit financially from government service can still uphold the norm of public spirit in public service, even if his heart is sullied.

From the standpoint of the argument from profiting out of government service, there is thus one serious problem with the fact that considerations of justice make it very difficult to justify blanket restrictions on taking postgovernment jobs with organizations that one regulated while in government. Restrictions on profiting out of public service that improve the quality of government decisions create some value (that is, some better decisions), even if the restrictions are very incomplete. By contrast, the value that revolving-door restrictions create, through the public display of good intentions, public spirit and nonmaterialism, requires the creation of an overall impression that these character traits actually are prevalent among public officials. If revolving-door restrictions are so limited that many government officials are allowed to proceed from government into lucrative jobs, where they profit from skills and contacts they gained while in government, then the overall impression may be of profiteering, rather than of public spirit. It is unlikely that the public will discern fine distinctions between areas where restrictions are justified and those where they are not. If the conclusion of a process of reasoning about the justified scope of revolving-door restrictions should limit those restrictions severely, the result might be that much of the value of those restrictions, in terms of the argument from profiting out of government service, would be lost. This is an issue to which I shall return shortly, in drawing conclusions about the appropriate overall scope of revolving-door restrictions.

Conclusions

In this section, I will first consider what revisions of current revolving-door restrictions the arguments presented here might suggest (assuming one does not need to take account of competing considerations of liberty and utility). I shall then see whether the proposed menu of restrictions creates excessive burdens for liberty or utility.

As a general matter, consideration of the proper force and application of the arguments made on behalf of revolving-door restrictions appears to justify restrictions approximately as strong as the restrictions in place. There are some important areas, however, where the arguments on behalf of revolving-door restrictions would suggest tightening the current restrictions. The most obvious area concerns the current exclusion of rule-making or other policy-related activities from the limitations on the kinds of matters where people may represent the private parties involved. On the basis of any of the arguments on behalf of revolving-door restrictions, it is hard to see why leaving a job working on emissions from oil refineries for the Environmental Protection Agency, and going right to work for Exxon dealing with environmental policy on oil refinery emissions, is any less problematical than leaving a job working on a lawsuit that the EPA has brought against Exxon for oil refinery pollution, to go to work for Exxon on that lawsuit. Yet current restrictions, while prohibiting the latter, permit the former.

To deal with the problem of an overall impression of how easy it is to profit from government service, one might also create a presumption that the one-year bans for senior officials or agency heads on dealing with their previous agencies at all (or, in the case of agency heads, on dealing with agency heads in the rest of the government as well) include a ban on aiding or advising, as well as representing. The presumption could be overridden on a case-by-case basis by the Office of Government Ethics for individuals who wished to return to jobs or activities substantially similar to the jobs they held prior to government service, and thus for whom aiding or advising activities would create fewer ethical problems in terms of profiting out of service. (The Office of Government Ethics already makes rulings in individual cases about whether certain conduct is consistent with government ethics legislation.) Such an additional restriction is justified if there is a worry — as I believe there can reasonably be — that the limited nature of the current restrictions is likely to leave an overall impression among the public that it is easy, or common, to profit from government service through post-government jobs.

Finally, more difficult cases arise from other situations in government that are analogous to the examples of the trade negotiator and the weapons procurement official. These would involve organizations that become so dominated by people whose departure from government into previously regulated organizations represents profiting from public service that the objection from injustice no longer applies with such force against stronger restrictions (such as against aiding and advising, or even against contacts with the agency). An example of such a government agency is the Securities and Exchange Commission, from which attorneys leave to practice securities law in private law firms. On the basis of the argument from profiting out of public service, it might be justified to make agencies that typically give entry-level skills, later used for lucrative private employment, subject to restrictions similar to those imposed on trade negotiation or weapons procurement officials.

Does current revolving-door legislation (or the proposed menu of additional restrictions) constitute an unacceptable interference with the liberty of a government official to choose the employment he wishes? Except for trade negotiation and weapons procurement officials, it is very difficult to make any case that the present restrictions constitute any particularly burdensome interference with liberty, since they leave so many opportunities for postgovernment employment in roughly the area where one has previously worked in government. They are also unlikely to reduce the talent pool available to government significantly, or to prevent people from getting private as well as public experience (assuming such experience is felt to produce, on the average, better decisions).

The argument from liberty provides a very strong reason for time limitations on any revolving-door restrictions of significant breadth, particularly restrictions that include aiding or advising. If these restrictions were not time-bound, they would constitute an indefinite ban on an individual's practicing a profession he chooses. Similarly, the argument from liberty strengthens the case, already based on the argument from injustice, against bans on aiding or advising (that might otherwise grow out of the argument from profiting out of government service) and on taking any kind of employment in an organization one has previously regulated (that might otherwise grow out of the argument from "going soft").

The existing restrictions that raise the most serious problems, in terms of the argument from liberty, are those for trade officials, for very senior officials representing foreign governments, and for people involved in major weapons systems. In each of these cases, however, the existing restrictions fall far short of a prohibition against a person's practicing the profession for which he is trained. Trade officials may work on trade, just not on specific negotiations in which they were substantially involved. Very senior officials may aid and advise a range of organizations, just not foreign governments. Officials working on major weapons systems may work in the defense industry, just not for the contractors with whom they have just been dealing.

By contrast, the restrictions I have tentatively suggested for attorneys at the Securities and Exchange Commission would be considerably more onerous. They would be tantamount to preventing a person from using the skills developed in a government job in private employment, at least for a year.

This might be justified if one believed that public spirit in public service were being served, and as long as people knew about these restrictions when they took the jobs. There are many other contexts where individuals choose to waive exercise of the right to liberty, by signing employment contracts with "noncompete" provisions, or other limitations on their freedom to take certain kinds of jobs after leaving the jobs they have. And, of course, there is legislation (such as licensing requirements) that restricts the liberty of individuals to sell their services to willing buyers. If one voluntarily agrees, in an employment contract, to waive some specific exercise of the right to liberty, one is not committing an offense against the right to liberty, since the initial agreement is itself voluntary. This would become problematic only if one were to agree to waive *all* liberty that one might otherwise have (as in a contract to sell oneself into slavery), since, by giving up the right to liberty altogether, one would undercut the justification — namely, the right to liberty — that is made to argue for one's freedom to agree to the original contract. The courts have generally held that individuals may sign employment contracts that waive the exercise of the right to liberty, provided that the legitimate interest of the employer in requesting such a waiver is not overridden by some consideration of the public good, a problem that is presumably not at issue here. The Supreme Court upheld, for example, in the case of *Snepp* v. *United States,* a provision in CIA employment contracts prohibiting an ex-CIA employee from publishing anything related to his service in the organization without submitting it first for review and approval by the CIA.

Restrictions on trade negotiators and defense officials, as well as the suggested possible restrictions on Securities and Exchange Commission lawyers, are likely to create significant difficulties for the government in recruiting people of ability to work in these agencies, as well as making it significantly more difficult for private organizations to benefit from the skills these employees develop while in government. Again, it is only if the value of avoiding profit out of public service is taken seriously that such restrictions should be considered. If these values are taken seriously, then the government should be willing to pay something to attain them. We should raise the salaries of officials in agencies where postgovernment employment becomes further restricted, to a level where it is still possible to attract, for lifelong careers in government, at least those talented young people who are committed to public service (even if the salaries are not high enough to attract everybody). Without such pay increases, the talent loss and the resulting decline in the quality of government decisions might simply become so overwhelming that the ideal of public spirit in public service would, sadly, have to be sacrificed.

If salaries were raised, one might ask whether such officials were not "profiting from public service" through their government salaries, rather than through postgovernment employment, with lifetime expected income similar under the two arrangements. I would not accept this argument. The language of "profiting from" suggests somebody applying something from one sphere, where one is expected to take an ethical point of view, to gain a benefit in a different sphere that is governed more by self-interest. Thus one might accuse Mother Teresa of profiting from her work among the poor in Calcutta if she sold her life story to a Hollywood producer for several million dollars and pocketed the money; but if people around the world who admired her work raised the same amount of money for her, as a gesture of thanks for a lifetime of service, the accusation would probably not be raised. The language of "profiting from" is also more likely to be used if one actually *leaves* the sphere in which one has been active in order to get money. If one pays government officials higher salaries for their government work, the money does not come from a different sphere, governed by different norms, and officials need not leave for different spheres as a condition for receiving the benefits. Therefore, the problem of profiting from public service would appear not to arise.

I believe, however, that government salaries should be kept below salaries in the private sector. This means that government will attract less competent people, all other things being equal. But not everything else *is* equal: government will attract some talented people committed to public service; and some talented people, who will work for government only if salaries are fully competitive, may lack any commitment to public service and hence not be the kinds of people government wishes to attract. At some point in the private-public salary disparity, however, the competence loss starts to outweigh the public service gain. By relating government salaries to salaries in the marketplace, this proposal might be seen as violating the merit principle of compensation that is typically aimed for in government, which ties compensation to skills and responsibilities (since, say, two government lawyers with similar training, experience, and responsibilities might receive different salaries according to whether they worked for the NLRB or the EPA. Marketplace wages reflect demand as well as supply, and this may be seen as unjust. This is hardly the place to enter into a discussion of the complex philosophical issues surrounding the question of whether rewards that are demand-based as well as supply-based are just. It can be noted, however, that arguments can be made on both sides, and that most people, if asked to think about it, would be inclined to see elements of both arbitrariness and justice in demand-influenced compensation levels. The principle is not so clearly unjust as to suggest that government is not setting a good example. It might also be noted that existing practice directs government to look at market wages in the private sector as a benchmark for employee compensation in government.

One final observation is in order regarding this exercise in analysis of the arguments on behalf of revolving-door restrictions. Each of the three arguments on behalf of the restrictions involves the contention that the failure to restrict postgovernment employment would worsen the quality of the decisions that government makes. Arguments couched in such terms have a familiar, soothing ring to many of those who work on the academic analysis of public policies. A decision is something one can hold on to, something concrete.

By contrast, some of the other arguments that appear to lie behind the case for revolving-door restrictions do not involve decisions in any concrete case, but rather issues of how people should treat other people (the argument from unfair advantage) or issues concerning the appropriate character of government officials (the argument from good intentions and public spirit as a model for the everyday behavior of citizens). These arguments, because they are not so directly related to any individual public decision that does turn out worse, are the ones that most academic students of public policy are likely to find most difficult to appreciate. This does not mean that arguments of this sort are not important in public debate, but that academic students of public policy should learn to appreciate them more.

17

THE PORT OF NEW YORK AUTHORITY AS REGIONAL PLANNER AND TARGET OF OPPORTUNITY

Jameson W. Doig

> So when I think of the individual, I am always inclined to see him imprisoned within a destiny in which he himself has little hand, fixed in a landscape in which the infinite perspectives of the long term stretch into the distance both behind him and before. In historical analysis, as I see it . . . the long term always wins in the end.
>
> — Braudel, 1972, p. 1244

> Over and above the structure of politics, we must have a political history that is set out in narrative form — an account of adult human beings, taking a hand in their fates and fortunes, pulling at the story in the direction they want to carry it, and making decisions on their own.
>
> — Butterfield, 1957, p. 206

*I*n the volume of essays from which these quotations are drawn, Gertrude Himmelfarb praises Butterfield and criticizes the approach of Braudel and like-minded scholars. The Braudelian approach, which she argues is now dominant in the history profession, has "belittled individuals, ideas, and above all events," while stressing the impact of long-term geographic and demographic forces. What is needed, she argues, is a resurrection of traditional

I acknowledge with thanks comments on earlier drafts by Margot Ammann, Eugenie Birch, Barry Bozeman, Herbert Kaufman, and members of the Social Science Research Council's Conference on New York's Built Environment. My thanks as well for the assistance of Alexis Faust and Nancy Danch and for financial support from the Alfred Sloan Foundation. Portions of this chapter are also included in my chapter "Joining New York City to the Greater Metropolis," *The Landscape of Modernity,* edited by David Ward and Olivier Zunz (New York: Russell Sage Foundation, 1992).

historical study, with its emphasis on the "drama of events, the power of ideas, and the dignity of individuals." Only then, Himmelfarb concludes, can students and other citizens come to believe in the value of rational analysis, the possibility of individual choice and freedom, and the opportunity for social progress through rational thought and action—and so convert those possibilities into partial reality (Himmelfarb, 1987, pp. 11–12, 31–32).

Himmelfarb's critique extends to the other social sciences as well, where modern scholars seek to understand the evolution of government policies by focusing on long-term "administrative momentum," on the material interests and narrow prejudices of the populace, and on the maneuvering of politicians who play upon those narrow interests in order to enhance their personal power and "perquisites of office." These researchers—political scientists, sociologists, and social historians—bypass formal documents in order to look for private communications that will reveal "self-serving" motivations and in general select their evidence "as if interests are more real than ideas and passion more compelling than reason." Scholars would be far wiser and more constructive, Himmelfarb argues, if they would direct greater attention to laws, judicial decisions, and public debates—to those sources that will show that "political institutions are, at least in part, the product of a rational, conscious, deliberate attempt to organize public life so as to promote the public weal and the good life" (Himmelfarb, 1987, pp. 18–19).

This chapter offers some comfort to the aims of Butterfield and Himmelfarb; here we will see the power of ideas and the importance of individual choice and sustained effort in achieving important results. In our story these elements are married, however, to a rationality that is significantly "self-serving" and to passions that color reason even as they motivate action. But Braudel's deceptively landscaped prison is not absent; geography, long-term demographic patterns, and technological change open some gates of opportunity and close others, never allowing even the most enterprising social inmate to truly break free.

These extensive interconnections, when displayed through narrative and dramatic form, may provide a useful way to join historical analysis to the concerns of public administration, to the benefit of both.

The Story and Some Themes

This chapter first describes how the earliest "public authority" in the United States was created and the initial aspirations of the agency's founders, who hoped that the Port of New York Authority would be independent of politics, that it would be given extensive powers to control public and private development in the New York–New Jersey region according to a rational plan, and that it would create an efficient transport system, thereby providing a crucial building block in reconstructing the bi-state metropolis as an efficient, internationally dominant commercial enterprise. I then examine the obstacles that stripped away the Port Authority's proposed powers and blocked its early plans, the forces that led this railroad-oriented agency to embrace the motor vehicle, though reluctantly, while keeping one hand on the iron horse, and its evolution from passive target to active opportunist in the new automotive era. These developments took place in the fifteen years between 1916 and 1931.

In the final section of the chapter, I argue that the events of these years—particularly the striking culmination in 1926–1931—had a wide-ranging impact, shaping the pattern of suburban development in the New Jersey sector of the region, the future role of the Port Authority in the wider metropolis, the willingness of Franklin Roosevelt to champion the public-authority design for the Tennessee Valley and for federal-local housing activities across the nation, and the strategies of Robert Moses and other "public entrepreneurs" as they designed and employed public authorities from the 1930s into the 1990s.

Since the story is largely told following Butterfield's precept, let me note here some broader research themes and issues illustrated in the following pages of interest to students of public organizations and public administration. The first is the importance of taking historical context seriously. Students of organizations and public policy, like all of us perhaps, tend to look at the past in terms of the concerns and priorities of their own times. In the case of the Port of New York Authority, the agency's change in direction in the 1920s has sometimes been viewed by critics as irresponsible; the Authority abandoned the railroad-improvement plans that were part of its original mandate when it saw that it could grow wealthy by catering to automobiles and trucks. As a result, it helped to bankrupt the region's rail system and took a leading role in encouraging the inefficiencies of "suburban sprawl" (Condit, 1981, p. 131). As the discussion below suggests, the reality as perceived "inside" those years was complex and perhaps quite different.

The second point is the importance of specific individuals—their backgrounds, passions, reasoning ability, and strategies—in shaping public policies and in triggering significant changes in organizational patterns (Doig and Hargrove, 1987). The story of the creation and early years of the Port of New York Authority has frequently been told in the scholarly literature; it is recounted primarily as a tale of conflicts among large institutions—the railroads, the Interstate Commerce Commission (ICC), two state governments, and the New York State Chamber of Commerce—with an important role given also to Julius Henry Cohen, who drafted the Authority's charter and then served as its first general counsel (Bard, 1942; Walsh, 1978). Additional historical research suggests that the intellectual sources of the agency's origins have been misunderstood; they come out of Cohen's early experience with Louis Brandeis in labor disputes and in commercial arbitration work, as much as (or more than) they derive from the British experience with public authorities. Also, in analyzing the Port Authority's emergence as handmaiden of the automotive age, the critical early contribution of Othmar Ammann, then an unemployed engineer and political entrepreneur, has been neglected. Finally, Cohen's influence in shaping the design of the Tennessee Valley Authority, the Moses authorities, and other offspring has not been developed. The analysis below places these two men in crucial roles, as they employ imaginative ideas and strategic reasoning to achieve some portion of their preferred goals, in a complex environment of shifting popular sentiments and large bureaucracies.

Yet here the story does not entirely give comfort to Himmelfarb's hopes, when she urges the scholar to look for "a rationality and deliberation that were not self-serving, that were directed to the ends rather than the means of power, that embodied some conception of the national interest and public welfare" (Himmelfarb, 1987, p. 19). Did Ammann and Cohen not serve their own personal interests as they pressed forward under the banner of "the public interest"? Could one argue that—in this case and others—the combining of self-interest with broader goals generated just the passion and perseverance that were essential if any useful result was to be accomplished?

The third point worth noting is the relevance of the Port Authority's early history to what James March has called the garbage-can model of decision making. In the classic model of decision making in organizations, members identify problems that need attention, allocate resources to analyze those problems and identify possible solutions (with costs and benefits attached to each "solution package"), and then choose the solutions that have the highest benefit/cost ratio. In the garbage can model, members of an organization— and outsiders—continually generate an array of problems and of "solutions" (to as yet unidentified problems), often independently from each other and without the classical means-ends patterns of thinking. This array is tossed into the "garbage can." If a decision maker in the organization perceives a problem, he or she may latch on to a solution that is rolling about in the can; similarly, advocates of certain kinds of ideas or techniques may find solutions and actively look for problems to which the preferred solutions can be applied. In short, the garbage can includes "solutions looking for problems" as well as "problems looking for solutions." (As March and his colleagues comment, "A computer is not just a solution to a problem in payroll management, discovered when needed. It is an answer actively looking for a question. The creation of need is not a curiosity of the market in consumer products; it is a general phenomenon of processes of choice. Despite the dictum that you cannot find the answer until you have formulated the question well, you often do not know what the question is in organizational problem solving until you know the answer" (March, 1988, p. 297).)

Viewed in this way, the early years of the Port Authority (since 1972 titled the Port Authority of New York and New Jersey) illustrate both the classical and the garbage can models. Regional leaders identified a problem that needed attention, which led them to press for the creation of the Port Authority; its leaders then analyzed a range of options that might solve the problem and selected the solutions that appeared to have the best benefit/cost ratio. Alas, the costs were too high and the benefits were too low, from the narrow perspectives of the railroads, the ICC, and the state legislative majorities. So the detailed solution (a bi-state railroad and regional development plan) failed. In the course of the effort, however, the Port Authority had been created, it had been given the capacity to construct transport facilities and float bonds to pay for them, and now it sat, without a task to which its powers might be applied. So it became, one might say, a solution searching for a problem; commissioners and staff members — and some outsiders, too — looked for regional problems that might be used to show that this regional enterprise was worth the time and energy that had gone into creating it. The growing army of cars and trucks that congested the highways and ferries between New Jersey, Manhattan, and Staten Island provided a problem that the "solution" seemed to fit admirably.

Do these changes in the Port Authority's program illustrate the widely held view that survival is the highest goal of all or most organizations? Herbert Kaufman uses the Port Authority's early history, together with the story of the Polio Foundation, as preeminent cases to illustrate the "organizational survival" thesis (Kaufman, letter to the author, October 1990). I am not sure this is accurate as to the Port Authority or that it is the most useful route to understanding the twists and turns of the agency in the 1920s and beyond. If the basic goal of the agency's creators was to advance a "railroad plan," then abandoning that plan — and embracing a competing program — suggests that survival (of individual jobs and perhaps of a sense of useful purpose) might be assigned a dominant motive. However, if the basic goal was to encourage cooperation between two often antagonistic states on matters of mutual concern (transport, water pollution, economic development), then the shifts we see in the late 1920s deserve a more complex causal analysis. This is, I think, the situation as it was perceived by major players at the time. Perhaps the Port Authority case can be used to challenge the argument that organizational survival offers a persuasive way to explain why organizations, public and private, behave as they do.

These questions highlight the broad issue of how we can most usefully analyze the behavior of organizations and the factors that generate changes in organizations and in human society generally. The historian reminds us that we "need to be sure how things happened day by day before we can know *why* they happened." But we can hardly be so detailed; some analytical assumptions will shape our selection of facts and patterns. And here Butterfield's standard may again be of use, as Blair Worden suggests: "Good history requires not the separation of analysis from narrative but their interaction. The construction of narrative, an act of selection and therefore of interpretation, is always shaped by the analytical assumptions we bring to it, and the assumptions themselves are changed (or should be) when we submit them to the tests of narrative composition, for it is a test they *invariably fail*" (Worden, 1991, p. 39; emphasis added). In completing a coherent narrative account, then, the scholar finds the broader assumptions that have been used are under attack and are likely to need some rethinking — to the benefit of one's understanding, both historical and "scientific."

Finally, in any discussion of public authorities it is appropriate to call attention to the issue of democratic accountability. The first public authority in the United States was designed to insulate policy makers and staff officials from direct control by elected officials and the citizenry, principally by creating the authority's governing body as a multiheaded board, whose members have staggered multiyear terms (so that a newly elected governor or mayor cannot immediately bring in new leadership) and by permitting the agency to retain and use funds from its own revenue-producing facilities (airports, bridges, and so on), making it less subject to control via the legislative appropriation process. The Port Authority's offspring have generally been created with somewhat similar barriers to legislative and executive direction. Moreover, the leaders of these agencies often view their enterprises as profit-seeking businesses, though laced with a public purpose. In design and behavior, therefore, the public authority can be—and has been—criticized as violating essential norms of democratic government (Walsh, 1978; Mitchell, 1992). In evaluating the New York/New Jersey agency and its cousins from this perspective, it is essential to look also, in a comparative way, at the actual accountability of traditional line agencies of government. What standards of democratic accountability apply in reality, for example, to the U.S. Forest Service, the Federal Bureau of Investigation, the Defense Department, state departments of transportation, and state correction agencies? In what ways, and under what conditions, are the Port Authority of New York and New Jersey, Massport, the Meadowlands Authority, the Tennessee Valley Authority, and the Port of Oakland more or less accountable than some of these executive agencies?

And now we turn to the Port Authority story.

Creation of an Open Script:
J. H. Cohen and the Public Authority Idea

We begin in the first years of the twentieth century, for here—in the temper of the times and in the creative imaginings of one man—we find a crucial part of the explanation for the Port Authority's origins, its early limitations, and its later success. During the years 1900–1915, the "temper of the times" in the bi-state New York metropolis meant commercial rivalry and political conflict: between city and town, between machine politician and reformer, between those who identified with the world commercial center of Manhattan and the outlanders in New Jersey, where New York's dominance was associated with wrongful imperialism. The story of the Port Authority begins in this rivalry and contention, as it was played out in the search for strategies of economic development and for local advantage in using commercial trade as an engine of economic growth.

New York City's rise to the first rank of world cities, and much of the economic expansion that extended into the New Jersey and New York suburbs, were crucially linked to international and coastal trade. By 1915, nearly half of the nation's international commerce passed through the Port of New York, and a vast system of steamship companies and railroad lines converged on the Port. A complex array of rail and marine terminals in both states generated thousands of jobs directly tied to the transport system, along with thousands more in retail commerce, home and office construction, and industrial development.

The economic advantages linked to vigorous international, coastal, and intraregional trade were not evenly distributed across the cities and towns of the metropolis, and indeed there was a sharp contrast between the benefits provided to New Jersey and to her sister state. Manhattan was the dominant center for corporate decision making and office activities associated with maritime commerce, and most of the thriving marine terminals were located along the shores of Manhattan and Brooklyn. On the western side of the Hudson were hundreds of miles of railroad track, which brought freight from across the continent through New Jersey to large rail terminals on or near the Hudson shore in Jersey City, Hoboken, and smaller towns. The modest economic vitality generated by the railroads in New Jersey was far outstripped by the activity and impact on the New York side.

For some political and business leaders in Jersey City, Newark, and elsewhere in northern New Jersey, vigorous economic development in their part of the wider region seemed much more likely if marine cargo and railroad freight could be attracted from Manhattan and Brooklyn terminals to piers constructed along their own shores, and both public criticism and legal action were directed toward that goal. In 1916, New Jersey interests appealed to the Interstate Commerce Commission, arguing that the historic system of setting rates for freight delivery in the New York region was biased against New Jersey's economic rights. (The traditional system required that all pier delivery points in the region be subjected to the same railroad charge, regardless of actual cost of delivery to various local areas. However, the real cost to deliver transcontinental goods to New York City locations was much higher, for those goods had to be floated from the north Jersey rail terminals across the Hudson, or across New York Bay, to Manhattan and Brooklyn piers and inland locations.) If successful, the New Jersey suit would require the railroads to charge lower rates to deliver goods to north Jersey piers. A differential charge might encourage shippers to vastly increase their use of New Jersey marine terminals, thus fueling economic expansion across the cities and suburbs of that underdeveloped state.

New Jersey's suit was at once challenged by New York's political leaders and by some of its business interests, who wanted to maintain the rate advantage that had historically been theirs. They prepared to battle the upstart before the ICC and then in the courts.

Rivalry and conflict—but these were not the only tempers of the times. Some of New York's business leaders and their political allies resisted the view that competition among factions within the New York region was the best route to follow. They adopted a "wider" perspective, based on values often associated with the Progressive Era: the need for "efficiency" in economic relationships and for government action helpful in attaining a vigorous and efficient economy (Wiebe, 1967). In a complex, highly inter-dependent metropolis, one implication of these values is that rational, region-wide planning and action might be needed in order to provide transporta-tion facilities considered essential to a vital, expanding economy — and that this sort of regional action might require that public officials take a central role. However, another implication is that not any government will do: the common, everyday officials who occupied the political stage in New York City and across the River were objects of distrust, for those officials seemed uninterested in using government's powers to achieve broad regional effici-ency. Instead, they appeared to focus mainly on "what's in it for me" — what policies would most help their own local citizens and perhaps help line their personal larders too.

To these reformers, the New Jersey suit offered not only danger but opportunity, an opportunity to reach beyond the direct issue of rate differen-tials and to grapple with the large problems of inefficiency and congestion that had long burdened the Port and its bi-state region, which were in fact accurately portrayed in the New Jersey challenge. The initiative in think-ing about this broader possibility was taken by the Chamber of Commerce of the State of New York, which had a long history of campaigning for im-provements in docks, streets, and other transport facilities in New York City and for more centralized power to ensure that such advances were carried out (Hammack, 1982). Some of the Chamber's leaders saw the transport problem in regional terms, consistent with their own business interests. The Chamber turned to its counsel, Julius Henry Cohen, and asked him to ex-plore possible ways to meet the wider problem.

Before 1916, Cohen had given very little thought to port competition or freight rates — and perhaps even less to New Jersey. However, Cohen and other leaders of the Chamber soon visited the Port of London Authority, which had been created in 1908, and Cohen took that title, applied it to New York, and urged that a bi-state port authority be created to undertake the effort needed to rationalize the rail and port system in the region. Most discussions of the origins of the Port of New York Authority, as it came into Cohen's mind and from his pen, limit the evolution of his thinking largely to the experience in Great Britain (Bard, 1942; Tobin, 1953; Smith, 1974).

Cohen's thinking, and his ability to influence the shape of future de-velopments, had other and deeper roots as well. Cohen was born in 1873 and grew up in lower Manhattan, where his father, a tailor, was active in the local Tammany club. Julius Henry attended a night law school, and by 1900 he was active in reform politics on the West Side. In 1904 he was named chairman of the Legislative Committee of the reform-minded Citizens Union; in that post, which he held for more than ten years, Cohen became familiar with important issues and political figures in the city, including Alfred E. Smith, who evolved in 1911–1916 from machine politician to reformer (Cohen, 1916; Cohen, 1946; Doig, 1988).

Meanwhile, Cohen also served as counsel for the garment industry, and in 1910 he and Louis Brandeis (who represented the laborers) devised a treaty — called the Protocol of Peace — that brought an end to an acrimonious industrywide strike. Here we find an early model for the Port Authority; the protocol created several independent boards, which were charged with objectively reviewing differences between management and labor and proposing solutions. The protocol governed management-worker relations until 1915; during those years, an industry that had been riven by strikes and walkouts found some harmony. In these years, Cohen also had a major role in developing a program of arbitration to resolve business disputes, rather than relying on the courts.

By 1916 Cohen had developed a distinctive perspective on public policies and on ways to grapple with social conflict. He believed that government power should be used to address important social problems and that public programs should be developed and carried out mainly at local and state levels, rather than by the national government. Also, based on his experience with machine politics in New York City, he preferred that government programs be insulated from the vagaries and potential corruption of party politics. More generally, Cohen was a strong believer in resolving disagreements through cooperation, and he thought that the route to a healthy economy would often be found through cooperative planning, rather than by relying on vigorous competition in the marketplace.

The ICC suit landed on Cohen's desk in the summer of 1916, and as he reviewed the recent history of relationships between the two states, he found his inclination to seek a cooperative solution reinforced. New York and New Jersey had been trying to resolve problems of water pollution in the harbor and nearby bays for more than a decade, but during most of those years the two sides had been engaged in court battles over which side of the harbor deserved most of the blame. In 1916 no positive steps had yet been taken to solve the pollution problem, and the end of litigation was nowhere in sight.

Using his contacts in the reform movement (which included New York City mayor John Purroy Mitchel, the state's governor, Charles Whitman, and the Republican governor of New Jersey, Walter Edge, who shared the Progressive desire for "business efficiency" in government) Cohen persuaded the two states to take an initial step toward cooperation in the spring of 1917. A bi-state study commission was created and charged with finding some way of meeting the port development and related regional problems of the two contending partners.

The two governors appointed commissioners who were willing to work together, and they in turn named Cohen as counsel to the commission. Less than two years later, in December 1918, Cohen had written a draft proposal for a Port of New York Authority that was a regional planner's dream. A bi-state agency would be created and given the power to issue regulations governing construction by governmental bodies and by private industry in a large port district; it would also be given the power to block state actions that were inconsistent with plans (that it would devise) for the "comprehensive development" of the port area, a region that would embrace seventeen counties and more than one hundred communities in the two states. Moreover, if the two states could be persuaded to suspend litigation over water pollution, the Port Authority might then be given responsibility for regulating water quality as well as land development in the region. Through this agency, the growth potential of the metropolitan area could be shaped and controlled harmoniously (Doig, 1988).

Cohen's brainchild was a bi-state agency with commissioners appointed by the governors for six-year overlapping terms, its actions would not be subject to gubernatorial veto or other direct controls, and if it were able to generate its own revenues via self-supporting projects, the states could not use the traditional power of the purse to control its programs. In addition, if the Port Authority were unable to meet its total costs through its own revenues, it might be authorized to "borrow money upon the credit of the states."

With these safeguards to its independence, coupled with its substantial regulatory powers, the new agency would be an exemplar of the reformer's vision; insulated from intraregional jealousies and the many vagaries of politics, the Authority's skilled staff of engineers and planners would analyze, monitor, and shape the modernization of the Port and the economic growth of the surrounding region, guided only by principles of efficiency and the public interest (Cohen, 1920).

The problems of congestion and inefficiency in the Port of New York had reached intolerable levels in 1917. As the flow of goods bound for the European War increased sharply, the traditional system of transferring freight from the railroads to lighters and barges and floating them to freighters on the New York side of the harbor had been unable to handle the incoming traffic; loaded rail cars were backing up across New Jersey and as far west as Pittsburgh. Cohen's 1918 plan offered a way to end conflict between the states; moreover, the organization he proposed might be able to construct the regional rail system that now seemed essential to replace that ancient lighterage pattern. Therefore Cohen's proposal was greeted with enthusiasm by major business groups, the large metropolitan newspapers, and some political leaders on both sides of the Hudson.

However, once his initial draft was exposed to the light and heat of local and state political forces, many of its crucial provisions could not survive. Cohen's problems began early in 1919, when the governors and legislative leaders from both states met with Cohen and his colleagues in Albany. Most of the discussion was devoted not to the idea of creating a wide-ranging Port Authority, but to a narrow, separate question: would the two states agree to cooperate to build a tunnel under the Hudson River for motor vehicles? When discussion finally turned to Cohen's Port Authority treaty, he found that the legislative leaders were suspicious of his offspring. A legislative commission was appointed, and Cohen's text was submitted to its tender mercies.

In a series of public and private meetings over the next two years, state officials and their local counterparts raised the banner of "democracy" and urged that proper standards of "public accountability" be applied to the offending document (Doig, 1988). So the port authority idea was hammered through three successive drafts before it emerged, a much weakened animal, and was approved by the two states in the spring of 1921. All of its regulatory powers had been stripped away; the agency began life in 1921 with great regional scope — extending into seventeen counties in New Jersey and New York State — but with no capacity to use tax revenues and essentially no other powers. However, the formal political insulation provided in Cohen's early draft still survived; the Port Authority would be controlled by a six-member board, three chosen by each governor for six-year terms. And the bi-state compact did give the Port Authority the abstract ability to "purchase, construct, lease and/or operate any terminal or transportation facility" within the Port District and to "borrow money and secure the same by bonds." It was an open script, given to a toothless giant.

Uses of an Open Script: Regional Visions and Targets of Opportunity

That was the first step — the creation of an institution of metropolitan scope. In the complex political terrain of the New York area, however, there would be several missteps — and a dozen of serendipity — before the Port Authority would add any significant political and economic power to its banner of regionalism.

The compact provided the new agency with a wide field of potential action. The open character of the Authority's mandate was understood by the six commissioners appointed to the Port Authority in the spring of 1921, for almost all of them had been members of the bi-state study commission. They appointed Cohen as the Authority's counsel, which ensured that there would be at least one restless imagination at hand to think about political and legal strategies to advance the Port agency's cause. But there was also a specific regional task built into the agency's legislation and its legislative history. The Port Authority was required to turn its attention in its first months to the question of what physical plan should be undertaken in order to overcome the congestion and cost involved in handling rail and waterborne freight on both sides of the harbor. It was expected to consult extensively with the public and to negotiate with the railroads in the hope that its plan might gain widespread support.

In order to tap regional sentiment, the Port Authority created an advisory committee of business and civic associations in the summer of 1921, identified 114 organizations from all parts of the metropolis to be represented on the committee, and held meetings with the entire group and with subcommittees from various areas. The agency also met with local public officials across the region during the summer and fall of 1921, and it began discussions with the twelve rail corporations. In these meetings, the Port agency drew on the array of rail improvement ideas its staff had been developing since 1917, and it added more rail spurs wherever they were favored by substantial local sentiment.

In December 1921, the Port Authority announced its "Comprehensive Plan for the Development of the Port District." The plan called for an extensive system of railroad tracks throughout the bi-state region, including a rail freight tunnel from New Jersey under the Upper Bay to Brooklyn, together with unified marine terminals for railroad-to-ship transfers and an express freight tunnel that looped through Manhattan. The improved rail system would, the Port Authority announced, stimulate industrial and commercial growth not only in the central business district but in outlying areas as well.

To carry out any part of this plan would require active cooperation by the region's dozen rail lines, and during the fall of 1921 the Port Authority's staff began intensive consultations with representatives of the railroads. These negotiations continued sporadically into the early 1930s. But in the end, all these efforts were for naught. There were times in the early 1920s and again in the late 1920s when the Port Authority thought it might be able to persuade the railroads to join forces in cooperative action. But each railroad was unwilling to give up its own competitive advantage, and no significant agreements were ever reached. A decade after the Port Authority had been created, the rail freight system was as costly and as inefficient as it had been in 1921. The great hopes of Julius Henry Cohen and his colleagues for a vastly improved rail system that would stimulate economic growth across the region were but ashes (Bard, 1942; Doig, 1993).

However, the Port Authority was not an agency limited to reconstructing the railroad freight system of the metropolis. It was an enterprise with a formal mandate as wide as all "terminal, transportation, and other facilities of commerce." This meant that the Port Authority's leaders could look beyond the railroad problem and seek other projects, other ways to improve the "planning and development" of the extensive bi-state region around the Port of New York.

Julius Henry Cohen served as the Port agency's counsel, and when Al Smith was returned to Albany as governor in November 1922, Cohen also began working with him to develop legislation that would apply the "public authority concept" to water power and to public housing. It is likely, therefore, that in time Cohen would have pressed his Port Authority colleagues to shift their energies from the great railroad project and to send the bi-state agency into greener pastures. But in 1922 and 1923, most of his associates at the agency were "railroad men," and the prospects for agreement with the rail executives seemed promising. So neither Cohen nor his colleagues were fully alert to a political movement that was growing in the wilds of New Jersey—and that would soon envelop the Port Authority and turn it in a very different direction.

This new political movement had its roots in another project spawned in the railroad era. Ever since the 1880s, an Austrian-American bridge designer, Gustav Lindenthal, had been seeking support for his own scheme to improve the efficiency of regional transportation in the New York–New Jersey area. The centerpiece of Lindenthal's plan was an immense bridge that would span the Hudson River and land in mid-Manhattan; the span would carry twelve railroad tracks, funneling the region's rail lines from New Jersey over the River and then connecting them with rail-to-ship terminals along Manhattan's waterfront. In its early version, Lindenthal's railroad bridge entered Manhattan at 23rd Street. A revised plan, announced in 1921, moved the bridge uptown to 57th Street; in a modest bow to the growing use of motor vehicles, he added twenty automotive lanes to his dozen railroad tracks (Shanor, 1988).

Lindenthal was one of the world's great bridge engineers, and his striking proposal caught the imagination of New Yorkers who measured the eminence of their city by the size of its wondrous construction projects. But its cost was equally striking — $200 million or more — and neither the rairoads nor elected officials were eager to add that sum to their existing burdens. The city's leaders were also dismayed at the thought of massive freight trains and twenty lines of automotive traffic plowing into Manhattan's central business district.

The fledgling Port Authority studied Lindenthal's plan in 1921 and rejected it in favor of the rail freight system adopted in December of that year. That did not dissuade Lindenthal, who denounced the Port Authority as short-sighted and mounted a campaign to gain business and governmental support for his great project. And out of this effort, much to Lindenthal's distress, arose a campaign for a very different Hudson crossing, a bridge that would be built, that would shape the future of the Port Authority and of suburban development in the northwest sector of the region, and that would influence the thinking of Franklin Roosevelt as he completed his term as governor and prepared to go to Washington.

In designing his combined rail and vehicular bridge, Lindenthal had hired as his chief assistant Othmar Ammann, who had worked with him earlier on the Hell Gate railroad bridge (which spans the East River). As Lindenthal carried his campaign for the 57th Street bridge forward, through the fall and winter of 1921 and then into the summer and fall of 1922, Ammann reluctantly concluded that the political and financial obstacles confronting the proposal were too formidable, at least in the near term. He appealed to Lindenthal to reduce the size of the project and to move it north of the business district, but Lindenthal refused. Finally, reluctantly, Ammann left Lindenthal and struck out on his own (Doig, 1990a).

Ammann had been trained in Switzerland, and like Lindenthal, he had come to the United States in search of opportunities to build wide bridges over America's great rivers and bays. Arriving in New York in 1904 at the age of twenty-five, Ammann had worked on several bridges under the supervision of Lindenthal and other senior engineers, but he had never designed or supervised construction of a single span, large or small. Now, in the winter and spring of 1922–1923, Ammann began to devise a set of political and engineering strategies that would in time lead to the building of a great bridge over the Hudson River — the George Washington Bridge — with a center span twice as wide as any yet constructed (Doig, 1990a). And in the course of this effort, he would vault into the front ranks of bridge builders of the nineteenth and twentieth centuries.

Ammann's first and crucial step was to conceive of a very different kind of span across the Hudson, a bridge that would be oriented primarily to the new automotive age, serving only motor vehicles and light rail transit. A crossing of this kind, which would not be connected with the railroad system, could be built far north of congested mid-Manhattan and its dense system of railroad tracks. Ammann's preference was to cast the bridge across the River six miles north of 57th Street, between 179th Street in Manhattan and Fort Lee on the western shore. This decision had several beneficial effects:

- The span could be much lighter than a bridge designed to carry loaded freight cars, and the construction cost would therefore be a fraction of Lindenthal's total.
- A bridge at Fort Lee would rise atop the Palisades and cross to a high point on the Manhattan shore, far enough above the Hudson to clear all ship masts. Thus the burden that Lindenthal faced — building long approaches from the low shores at 57th Street and at Weehawken across the River so the bridge deck would be high enough for ship clearance — would be eliminated. With these two advantages, Ammann estimated that his bridge would cost only $25 million, compared with $200 million or more for the 57th Street span.
- Ammann's bridge would not face the fervent opposition of Manhattan business leaders, and he would not be compelled to persuade a dozen railroad corporations to use the bridge, an essential element to make Lindenthal's scheme financially viable.

Coupled with these advantages was one important problem: would there be enough automobile and truck traffic to justify (and pay tolls to finance) a crossing this far north? In the winter and spring of 1923, Ammann studied the patterns of ferry traffic, which at busy periods often required travelers to wait two or more hours to cross the River, and he consulted with the staff of the recently formed Committee on the Regional Plan. He also dug into earlier history, and he found a 1910 report that advocated a bridge at 179th Street as a crucial step in creating a regional park system and improving access for work, residences, and shopping.

Ammann's analysis indicated that a toll bridge at Fort Lee would be heavily used, both for travel to work and for recreation, by the 2.5 million people who lived near the bridge. In addition, it would serve as an important link between New England/Westchester traffic and western points, providing a northern bypass for autos and trucks around the congested Manhattan central business district. With these major flows of traffic, Ammann concluded that his bridge could be self-supporting.

The engineering and financial questions had been resolved, at least to Ammann's satisfaction. But two difficult issues still remained. First, who would be willing to undertake the project? Could a private corporation take responsibility? (A group of private investors had recently, in 1922, developed plans to construct a tunnel under the Hudson at 125th Street. Might they be persuaded to invest in a bridge instead?) Or should Ammann ask the two state Bridge and Tunnel Commissions, then struggling to make progress with the Holland Tunnel, to take on the task? Or could the Port Authority, despite its recent commitment to a "comprehensive plan" that focused almost entirely on railroad freight problems, be persuaded to throw its energies into a very different kind of enterprise?

Second, would the cities and towns in the region, and the leaders of the two contentious states, join together to support a cooperative plan to build a bridge across the Hudson? The recent experience of the tunnel commissions, whose efforts were often delayed by conflicts between Jersey City and New York factions, and the attempts to solve the region's water pollution problem, which were still mired in litigation, suggested that the political path to a bridge at Fort Lee would not be easy.

The central role in exploring these issues was taken by Ammann. Ammann was a political novice and a taciturn man, reluctant to engage in political campaigning. However, he knew George Silzer, a Democratic politician who was elected governor of New Jersey in the fall of 1922 and who was interested in developing a record of accomplishment as governor. The two men worked out a strategy to serve both their interests. Ammann would travel across Bergen and other northern New Jersey counties and into Westchester and the Bronx, explaining the engineering advances that at last made a bridge of such great size feasible and organizing local political support for his trans-Hudson crossing. Meanwhile, Silzer would speak publicly about the advantages of a bridge to connect Manhattan to the "high, healthy" suburbs of north Jersey.

The governor would also use his personal influence with the Port Authority's commissioners to persuade them that their goals need not be limited to solving the railroad freight problem; the Authority might take action to meet the growing problem of vehicular congestion in the bi-state region. The long lines of automobile and truck traffic, waiting for ferries between New Jersey and Manhattan, were notable examples of this congestion; a bridge at 179th Street, Silzer pointed out, would make a great contribution to solving this interstate problem. Silzer and Ammann also suggested the Port Authority make a more modest contribution to improving transport in the region by building two smaller bridges that would connect Staten Island to nearby New Jersey cities.

Ammann's political activities lasted more than two years. He met with business groups and civic associations on both sides of the Hudson and with state senators and newspaper editors, seeking support for his bridge at 179th Street, while he also fended off those who favored a tunnel at 110th Street or 125th Street. He continued to work with the Committee on the Regional Plan, analyzing traffic conditions and the advantages of a bridge that would bypass the congested center of the region. And he and Governor Silzer met with officials of the Port Authority, where they found a modicum of enthusiasm for adding motor vehicle projects to their other work, although some were reluctant to divert the agency's energies from the railroad issue, where success seemed elusive but almost at hand.

In the spring of 1924, the Authority's leaders took the first step into the automotive age, agreeing to build a pair of bridges to join Staten Island to New Jersey. However, they turned down Ammann's offer to design those spans (now the Goethals Bridge and the Outerbridge Crossing); since these would be the agency's first projects, they informed Ammann, they concluded that the contracts should be awarded to "an engineer of long established reputation" (Ammann, 1925). Finally, early in 1925, Ammann's extensive organizing effort bore fruit. The Fort Lee project now had wide support on both sides of the Hudson, and the Port Authority at last agreed to take responsibility for the project. In March, the two state legislatures authorized the bi-state agency to undertake the task of constructing the world's longest spanning bridge at Fort Lee and 179th Street. And Ammann, who had been unemployed since the spring of 1923, was asked to join the Port Authority as bridge engineer.

There, in the summer of 1925, he took charge of the bridge-building effort, organized a dedicated staff, brought the George Washington Bridge into existence well ahead of the target date and under budget, and so deserved a large measure of acclaim, as Governor Franklin D. Roosevelt noted in his dedication address in October 1931: "Behind this mighty structure, that seems almost superhuman in its perfection, there is an inspiring background of that high intelligence. It is only fitting that we should for a moment today pause to congratulate Mr. O. H. Ammann, the Chief Engineer, and indeed the entire staff of the Port of New York Authority who are responsible not only for the design of this bridge but for its speedy and successful execution" (Roosevelt, 1931).

For Ammann, then, the Port Authority served as opportunity. If that agency—a somewhat empty vessel of railroad hopes and plans and unrequited love—had not been at hand, it is not clear that he could have constructed a viable strategy to carry out his grand engineering project. We might instead have a series of tunnels through the Hudson mud and perhaps a Port Authority of quite different cast.

The Impact of the Bridge and Its Port Authority

What Julius Henry Cohen, Othmar Ammann, and their colleagues had wrought by 1931 was a great bridge—completed earlier than expected and at a lower cost — and an organization whose strong reputation derived largely from that striking accomplishment. The impact of the George Washington Bridge on the New York region and on the fortunes of the Port Authority was immense, and it flowed in several directions.

First, there was the influence of the span on suburban development in the vast open land extending out from Fort Lee and on traffic congestion in the central portion of the region. As soon as the state legislatures at Albany and Trenton authorized the Port Authority to construct the Fort Lee bridge, real estate developers and other civic boosters across north Jersey recognized what the giant span would mean for residential and commercial development in their area. The bridge would displace a set of ferries (which were then, within the New York region, the only way to cross the Hudson), sharply cutting travel time to Manhattan and points east. Although the Holland Tunnel would be completed earlier, in 1927, the Port Authority's bridge would be nine miles further north, away from the congested core and therefore attractive to residents and other travelers bound to and from Bergen, Morris, Rockland (New York) and other northwestern counties. The new bridge would also be of great value to truckers delivering goods into and out of New England, Westchester, and the Bronx, who would be glad to be able to reach the rest of the continent via a bridge well north of the congested center of the region — instead of threading their way down Manhattan's crowded thoroughfares to Canal Street, where the Holland Tunnel would carry them under the Hudson River, to emerge onto busy Jersey City streets.

The hopes of developers and local officials were fulfilled, and throughout the 1930s and 1940s, the George Washington Bridge had a profound effect, attracting those who worked in New York's business district to seek homes in the northwest suburbs and turning the rural valleys of Bergen and points north and west into suburban enclaves of the middle class. The bridge also improved the efficiency of truck travel from New York City, Westchester, and New England to locations west of the Hudson — the Trenton area, Philadelphia, Bethlehem, Pittsburgh, Chicago — and in that way strengthened the competitive advantage of truckers as they sought to attract freight traffic from the faltering railroads.

Second, by carrying out this complex project with striking effectiveness, the Port agency demonstrated that it was not only a group of planners; it could be used as an instrument of public action as well. Its success with this project placed the Port Authority's leaders in a strong position when they argued that the Holland Tunnel should be removed from the control of the Bridge and Tunnel Commissions and brought into their own domain (Doig, 1993, chap. 7). Indeed, the Port Authority's record appeared particularly impressive when compared to that of the Holland Tunnel builders, who had begun their project in 1919, found their early efforts marred by bickering and political conflict, and completed the task in 1927, years behind schedule and far over budget.

Even before the great bridge was completed, Julius Henry Cohen had grasped the significance of this comparison. In terms of effective action to meet regional problems, surely the Port Authority's record was superior. Moreover, to keep the two trans-Hudson crossings in separate hands would risk the possibility of destructive competition, as each tried to attract traffic by lowering tolls below its competitor's level. Also, if future tunnels and bridges were the responsibility of the Port Authority, the earnings from the Fort Lee bridge and the Holland Tunnel could be used for those crossings, rather than requiring legislative appropriations. So the Port Authority's counsel turned reasonable opportunist, urging that his agency be given jurisdiction over all trans-Hudson vehicular crossings. As the bridge moved toward completion, the governors and legislatures on both sides of the Hudson finally agreed with Cohen and his colleagues, and early in 1931, the two states permitted the Port Authority to take control of the Holland Tunnel and its growing toll revenues. They also agreed that the Authority would have monopoly power over all interstate crossings that might in the future be constructed between New Jersey and the Empire State.

This "merger," as it was called, provided the Port Authority with the toll revenues of the Holland Tunnel, which totaled millions of dollars a year, even in the Depression. In the short run, this ensured that the Port agency would not go into bankruptcy; without the tunnel revenue, that would have been a distinct possibility. The Authority found itself loaded down with debt from bonds issued to finance the Staten Island bridges, which produced little revenue, and the Fort Lee bridge, which would produce no revenue until late in 1931 and only a modest stream in 1932 and 1933 (Bard, 1942). The Holland tolls also permitted the Port Authority to begin a third Hudson crossing, the Lincoln Tunnel, in 1931, before the bi-state agency sunk into the doldrums of the deeper Depression years.

Looking still further ahead, the merger meant that the Port agency could, once the Depression and World War II had ended, apply the combined net revenues of the Holland and Lincoln tunnels and the George Washington Bridge to new opportunities in the wide field of "terminal and transportation facilities," opportunities that might be discovered or created anywhere along the shores or inland reaches of the one hundred cities and towns and the seventeen counties that comprised the Port District.

Moreover, in developing the Fort Lee project, the Port Authority established a pattern of cooperative relations with the Committee on the Regional Plan that would be of value to both organizations in the short run and in later years, as the committee evolved into the permanent Regional Plan Association (RPA). As noted earlier, Ammann had begun to consult with the committee's planners in 1923, and throughout the 1920s, he and other Port Authority staff members worked with that group on the development of regional highway and rail systems. The Port Authority benefited, since its proposals were endorsed by an "objective" group of planners; the Regional Plan staff, in turn, was able to indicate that its efforts were influential in shaping the Port Authority's thinking and its important projects

(Fishman, 1992). Later, when the Port Authority cast an admiring gaze on the region's airports, it again turned to the RPA staff for support. Their endorsement of the Port Authority's argument—that the three major airports should be controlled by a single regional agency—helped wrest those air terminals from Newark's city commissioners and from Robert Moses and his City Airport Authority (Doig, 1990b).

It does not stretch our understanding of causal connections too far, perhaps, to argue that the Port Authority's successful effort in devising and carrying out the George Washington Bridge was crucial to all that followed: to its ability to escape bankruptcy and failure in the 1930s, to its capacity to attract "entrepreneurial" planners and project developers to its staff in the 1940s and beyond, and to its later successes in redeveloping old airports and piers at Newark, Hoboken, and LaGuardia and in developing gigantic new projects at Idlewild (now Kennedy Airport) and Elizabeth (home of the largest containerport on the East Coast). Even the World Trade Center, with its 110-story boxes that grace lower Manhattan, owes much to its more graceful metal cousin that spans the Hudson upriver. And so do the thousands of jobs that early and continuing investment has generated at these many facilities, especially at Kennedy Airport (the largest employment center in Queens) and the Newark/Elizabeth seaport and airport facilities (the largest employment generator in that section of north Jersey).

The impact of the George Washington Bridge can be extended still further. It helped, for example, to shape the thinking of Franklin Roosevelt. In his dedication address, Roosevelt argued that the immense project demonstrated the impact that "skill and scientific planning" could have in surmounting large obstacles, as well as the benefit of "constructive cooperation" across state lines and the great value of leadership by citizens who approached public projects with "high and unselfish devotion." Because of this distinctive combination, the George Washington Bridge had been completed "six months ahead of schedule and at a cost well below the original estimate." Roosevelt then drew from this experience a lesson he would soon apply at Albany and in the nation's capital: "To my mind, this type of disinterested and capable service is a model for government agencies throughout the land. Their methods are charting the course toward the more able and honorable administration of affairs of government—a course they have proved can be safely steered through political waters with intelligence and integrity at the helm" (Roosevelt, 1931).

In that same year, Roosevelt built on a proposal devised by Al Smith and Cohen and won legislative approval for the creation of a Power Authority, would would develop the state's hydroelectric potential. Traveling to Washington, Roosevelt used some of the Port Authority's distinctive elements—its multiheaded board, its "business-like" ethos, and its loosely defined, open-ended mandate—in setting forth plans in 1933 for a Tennessee Valley Authority. A few years later, his proposal that cities create local housing authorities also built on the Port Authority's model (Walsh, 1978; Doig, 1983).

Meanwhile, one of Governor Smith's aides, Robert Moses, had watched throughout the 1920s as the governor and Julius Henry Cohen devised ways to expand the Port Authority's reach and to create state agencies for housing and water power that were based on the Port Authority design. Moses had seen how the struggling infant had grown in ten years to a healthy cub, using its vague mandate and its potential toll revenue to reach out for new opportunities. By the early 1930s, Moses was prepared to use what he had learned, and during the next several decades, he employed the authority model as a crucial vehicle in shaping highways and recreation and other activities throughout New York City and across much of New York State (Kaufman, 1952; Caro, 1974, pp. 627–630).

In retrospect, it can be argued that the Port Authority's decision to go forward with the George Washington Bridge and the Staten Island spans set it on a trajectory that would exacerbate the problems of planning and development in the city and its region. The Authority's bridges and tunnels would encourage travelers from the western suburbs to enter Manhattan by automobile, and thousands who worked in the center city would, in the coming decades, search for housing in the thinly developed reaches of the metropolis, away from the network of commuter rail lines. The result, in time, would be suburban sprawl, greater use of automobiles for transport into the region's core, deterioration of rail services, and increased traffic congestion in and near the central business district (Wood, 1961; Danielson and Doig, 1982).

In the 1920s, however, the George Washington and the array of other regional highway improvements were viewed more positively. The number of automobiles and trucks traveling in the bi-state region expanded sharply throughout the decade, and to the Regional Plan staff and others, that expansion was seen as beneficial in stimulating economic growth across the metropolis. In facilitating this favorable pattern, the Hudson River crossings were essential projects. (As the Regional Plan's leaders argued in 1923, "There can be no questioning the urgency of the need for more bridges and tunnels across the Hudson. . . . The prosperity of five counties in New Jersey should be immensely promoted, and their prosperity should react more helpfully on Manhattan Island — and also on the Bronx, lower Westchester County, and Queens County — if the improvement of [motor vehicle] circulation across the river is combined with the comprehensive planning of the undeveloped areas in New Jersey that would thereby by brought into close and direct physical connection with Manhattan" (Adams, 1923, pp. 10, 17).) Indeed, the bridge at Fort Lee would be especially helpful, since it would encourage suburban growth in the undeveloped northwestern counties while providing a bypass for trucks and automobiles with destinations outside the congested center.

To Ammann and the Port Authority planners, and to the Regional Plan experts, the future would not arrive on rubber tires alone; rather, it seemed likely to hold a harmonious mix of rail and road facilities, which would stimulate and serve an expanding and efficient regional economy.

Thus the George Washington span was designed so that a light rail track could be added on a lower deck; if local authorities then agreed, rail service on the bridge could be connected with the north Jersey trolley system and with New York's subway system. Meanwhile, the Port Authority continued its campaign to improve the efficiency of rail freight operations, and it took a major role during 1927–1931 in a regional effort to improve suburban rail transit operations (Bard, 1942).

Those rail plans foundered on the rocks of the Great Depression, railroad intransigence, and the American love for the automobile. So the Port Authority was left with half a loaf: its "skill and scientific planning" yoked to the demands of the automotive age. During the 1930s and beyond, that partial loaf seemed far better than none, however; not only did it permit the agency itself to thrive but the George Washington span and its other bridges and tunnels appeared certain to aid transportation efficiency and economic growth in the vast bi-state metropolis. That was, at least, the expectation of the region's planners, and the general public, in those early years of the automotive revolution.

Narrative and Causal Understanding

In the slice of history and organizational experimentation considered in this chapter, Gertrude Himmelfarb's hopes appear to have been realized: as political institutions were created and their purposes revised and reconstructed, individuals took on crucial roles, behaving rationally and deliberatively, seeking to make a difference despite Braudelian forces. And those individuals were motivated by some image of the good life as well as by narrower concerns. In the New York region of those years, as in other parts of the world in which public agencies make a difference, a first interpretation will often suggest an historical inevitability in the rise and fall of technique, structure, and program, or at least the impact of a faceless crowd of institutional officials. But a closer look, using the "old history," will frequently show the impact of individual leaders with their distinctive priorities. If, as Dwight Waldo (1980, p. 17) argues, "public administration is a powerful, creative force," a fair portion of that creativity may depend on the ideas and strategic skills of crucially placed leaders. Narrative history is a helpful tool in separating that causal element from bureaucratic tradition, from the desire of organizations to survive, and from Braudel's Mediterranean Sea.

Part Six

INNOVATION AND
TECHNOLOGY MANAGEMENT

*F*ittingly, the only section of this book with just two chapters is the one providing quantitative studies of public management. Admittedly, an objective of this book is to include broader pieces, and most quantitative studies are somewhat narrower in focus; but the proportion of quantitative studies included in this volume is a reasonably accurate reflection of the proportion in the public management literature.

The topics addressed in the two chapters of this section — computers, technology, and innovation — seem to invite quantitative analysis, but there is no necessary relation between topic and method. Daniel T. Bugler and Stuart Bretschneider seek to understand the determinants of public managers' adoption of new information technology. They reason that an interest in information technology, or in innovation, precedes adoption, and so they focus on factors related to that interest. Like many other quantitative studies of public management, their study is based on survey responses — in this case, responses from a questionnaire mailed to more than one thousand data-processing managers and nearly three thousand program managers in state government. The authors assumed that management information system (MIS) managers would be more interested than program managers in new information technologies, but this assumption proved incorrect. The search for new technical solutions is often driven by program managers' need to solve problems, and this need-driven approach increases program managers' interest in being early adopters of technology. By contrast, more experienced (and perhaps more jaded) MIS managers — the ones who have to address the technological problems created by new systems — tend to prefer proved technologies and are therefore less likely to be proponents of early adoption.

James L. Perry, Kenneth L. Kraemer, Debora E. Dunkle, and John Leslie King also concern themselves with managers and users of information systems; and, similarly, they focus on the motivations surrounding innovation. Using "social judgment analysis," the authors seek to determine managers' underlying criteria for decisions about computer applications. They hypothesized that managers' approaches and criteria would differ as a result of varying roles in organizational hierarchies and differences in professional

orientation. The authors provided twenty-five hypothetical software packages, along with criteria for assessing the software, to participants who were
asked to rate their own likelihood of purchasing the software, according to
relative weights assigned to the criteria. The managers rated productivity
and service enhancement as important criteria, but innovativeness and enhancement of professional recognition were not often rated as important.
It is especially interesting that top managers' patterns of ratings varied little
from those of other managers.

18

TECHNOLOGY PUSH OR PROGRAM PULL: INTEREST IN NEW INFORMATION TECHNOLOGIES WITHIN PUBLIC ORGANIZATIONS

Daniel T. Bugler,
Stuart Bretschneider

Government agencies are spending increasingly large amounts of public money for new information technology, seeking to enhance communications, coordination, and control capabilities (Huber, 1990). Since these are core management functions, the adoption and control of new information technology has great implications for organizational operations and power structures. Organizations may seek to adopt these technologies to improve performance, but the adoption of new information technologies serves to fuel political questions of control and access as well (King, 1982). Different groups within an organization may therefore be expected to have different levels of interest in acquiring new information technology. Technology managers might view acquisition of new technologies as a means to maintaining power and authority within an organization, while program managers might view the value of such innovations only in terms of potential programmatic benefits. Recognizing that both power and programmatic performance might influence interest in new information technologies, a central question of this paper is, Are information technology managers more likely than program managers to initiate the acquisition process?

To look at the influence of organizational role or position, it is necessary to shift the traditional focus on the adoption decision to the process that

This research was supported by Bell South, Bell Worldwide Information Systems, Digital Equipment Corporation, Electronic Data Systems, IBM Corporation, NCR Corporation, NYNEX Corporation, Plexus Computers and U.S. West Communications. The research was also partially supported by the School of Information Studies and the Technology and Information Policy Program of Syracuse University, along with the National Association for State Information Systems.

precedes the action decision. This chapter focuses on a prior question, by looking at the factors that affect decisions that precede the adoption decision. The purpose of this chapter is to develop a *theory of initiation* for the innovation-adoption process, based on the theory of reasoned action (Fishbein and Ajzen, 1975; Ajzen and Fishbein, 1977; Ajzen and Fishbein, 1980; Davis, Bagozzi, and Warshaw, 1989). This model is then used to develop testable hypotheses surrounding factors affecting interest in new information technologies. The hypotheses are tested empirically with survey data from state-level program managers and information systems managers. The final sections of the chapter discuss the results and offer some conclusions.

Initiation of the Innovation-Adoption Process

An innovation is defined as the adoption of a "device, system, policy, program, process, product or service that is new to the adopting organization" (Damanpour, 1991). The innovation-adoption process is often defined in terms of "stages" of adoption (Tornatzky and Fleischer, 1990). From the perspective of the user of an innovation, these "stages" are awareness, matching, adoption, implementation, and routinization (Tornatzky and Fleischer, 1990). While stage models suggest that innovation consists of naturally ordered events, the actual process of adoption is nonlinear and iterative, full of feedback loops, and marked by complexity and delays (Tornatzky and Fleischer, 1990). It is better to think of the models as describing core aspects of behavior leading to innovation adoption.

Rather than attempting to define specific steps in the innovation-adoption process, Damanpour (1991) refers to two broad stages; initiation and implementation. The initiation stage consists of all the activities leading up to the actual decision to adopt, including problem perception, information gathering, attitude formation, and evaluation, and the implementation stage consists of the initial and continued use of an innovation, including modifications necessary to deploy the innovation (Damanpour, 1991).

Two stages are defined because different organizational attributes affect the outcome of each stage (Damanpour, 1991). Damanpour has analyzed the results of twenty-three empirical studies of innovation adoption. Of these, only three are concerned with the initiation of innovation (Aiken, Bacharach, and French, 1980; Hull and Haige, 1982; Zmud, 1982). This chapter seeks to add to our knowledge base about the initiation of the innovation-adoption process.

The initiation of innovation adoption is not necessarily a rational process whereby the problem is defined, solutions are sought, and the best choice among alternatives is selected (Tornatzky and Fleisher, 1991; Feldman and March, 1981). Agencies decide to adopt innovative processes and technologies for a variety of reasons (Bingham, 1976; Bozeman and Loveless, 1983; Baldridge and Burnham, 1975; Danziger and Dutton, 1977; Feller, 1980; Lambright, Teich, and Carroll, 1977; Perry and Danziger, 1980; Perry and Kraemer, 1978; Yin, 1977). Whether one has a solution in search of a problem, or a problem in search of a solution, a successful information search leads to interest in one or many innovations. The level of interest in a new technology or process among organizational actors affects the intention to adopt that innnovation. Thus interest in an innovation precedes the intention to adopt it, and the intention to adopt precedes the actual decision to adopt an innovation. This interest-intention-adoption model restates Fishbein and Ajzen's theory (1975) of reasoned action and Davis, Bagozzi, and Warshaw's technology acceptance model (1989) and extends it to the process of initiating innovation adoption.

Ajzen and Fishbein's social psychological theory of behavior (1975) suggests that attitudes about a behavior precede the intention to engage in the behavior. Intention to perform a behavior is in turn a predictor of actual performance. The theory of reasoned action provides a basis for modeling innovative adoption. In brief, the mode posits that attitudes about a particular behavior are influenced by beliefs about the probable outcome of that behavior. Attitudes, tempered by the concern for normative values, in turn affect the intention to perform (or not to perform) the action. Mathieson (1991) has found ample evidence to support a link between intention and behavior.

Davis, Bagozzi, and Warshaw (1989) have applied the theory of reasoned action in the computer setting, to develop a technology acceptance model. Attitudes about using a new computer technology are influenced by the perceived usefulness and the perceived ease of use of the new system. Potential users of a new technology were found to have more positive attitudes about using that technology when it appeared to be useful and relatively easy to use. Positive attitudes in turn were associated with stronger intention to use the technology and with higher actual use. In both models, attitudes affect intentions, which affect actual behavior. Moore and Benbasat (1991) support the findings of Davis, Bagozzi, and Warshaw and find that attitudes toward using a technology are also affected by voluntariness of use, compatibility of existing systems, effect of use on image, demonstrability of the results of use, visibility of the technology, and trialability of the technology.

These models, applied to the innovation process, yield a slightly more complex model. For organizational actors to make judgments about the perceived usefulness and ease of use of a new technology, and to assess the probable outcomes of adopting that technology, they need to make predictions about the use of the technology, their organization, and the environment in which they operate.

In the early stage of innovation adoption, organizational actors seek information about problems and potential solutions (Bozeman and Loveless, 1983). Decisions about new technologies will be considered in light of existing organizational and environmental concerns, as well as perceived attributes of the technology itself. Interest in that technology fuels efforts to obtain more information about it and to begin evaluating the probable outcome for adopting the technology as an organizational innovation.

Figure 18.1. Theory of Innovation Adoption.

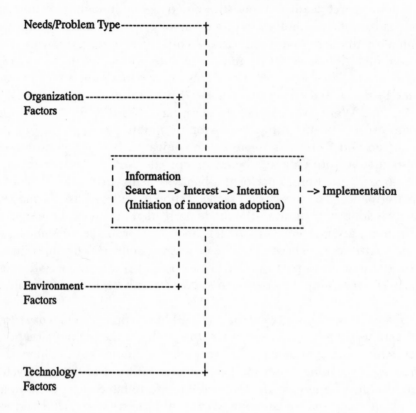

Figure 18.1 presents a model of innovation-adoption decision making that highlights the initiation stages of the innovation process. The process is contingent on the interplay of technology, organization, and environmental factors. For simplicity's sake, the model is drawn in a linear fashion, but the entire process is messy, iterative, and full of feedback loops (Tornatzky and Fleischer, 1990). The important point is that organizational needs and/or problems lead to an information search (Feldman and March, 1981). As potential solutions and opportunities are found, interest precedes the intention to adopt, which in turn must precede actual adoption of an innovation, if it occurs.

Interest in New Information Technology Among Public Organizations

Current management information systems (MIS) literature seeks to understand effects on organizations after they adopt computing technology (Danzinger and Kraemer, 1986; Kraemer, King, Dunkle, and Lane, 1989). Much literature about the use of computers in organizations stresses the political nature of the technology. Downs (1967a), Laudon (1974), and others suggest that information technologies shift power to higher-level managers. For others, computing is seen to reinforce existing power structures and may be adopted as much for potential gains in productivity as for the increase in power that goes to those who control resources (Attewell and Rule, 1984; Kraemer and King, 1986; Yin, 1977; Feller, 1980; Kraemer, King, Dunkle, and Lane, 1989).

One theory that attempts to differentiate among types of managers was put forth by Kraemer, King, Dunkle, and Lane (1989). The theory of management states presents a political model of computing organizations, based on the locus of control of the computing organization and the interest served by the organization. Knowing who controls the computing resources and who benefits from those resources has predictive power for how the system is used. Thus an MIS manager in charge of the computing resources of an organization is more likely to emphasize technical needs when considering new information technologies. A program manager or senior manager with authority over an agency's computing resources is more likely to consider service or strategic goals when considering new technologies. The computing system becomes a means to enhance the power and prestige of the manager's primary area of responsibility.

Baldridge and Burnham (1975) have found that individual characteristics are poor predictors of innovative behavior within organizations, but administrative roles or positions are predictors of participation in innovative efforts. Innovation studies also suggest the importance of contact with those external to the organization in becoming aware of and implementing an innovation (Tornatzky and Fleischer, 1990; Bozeman, 1982; Bozeman and Loveless, 1983). Gatekeepers span the boundaries of the organization to bring in new information. Administrators serve as gatekeepers, transferring information from sources external to the organization to internal users, and their interest in an innovation is important to bring about change (Damanpour, 1991; Tornatzky and Fleischer, 1990).

From this discussion, and from our model of initiation of the innovation-adoption process, we expect certain factors to influence the level of interest in new information technologies. Figure 18.2 presents a model of those factors. In this model, interest in new information technologies is affected by the organizational roles assigned to managers who make decisions about technology purchases. Interest is also affected by the organization's interactions with external groups, and by barriers to those interactions. Finally, we expect interest in new information technologies to be affected by characteristics of the organization and its environment.

Given the MIS manager's advantage in knowledge about the technical aspects of new information technology, it is likely that the role of gatekeeper and product champion will be held by the MIS manager (Tornatzky and Fleischer, 1990). Thus the MIS manager's interest in new information technologies is likely to be stronger than a program manager's level of interest because the MIS manager has greater access to technical information,

Figure 18.2. Factors Affecting Interest in New Information Technology.

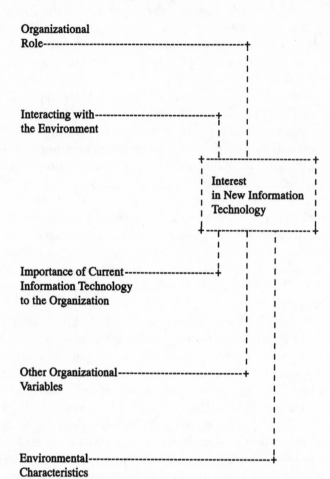

greater knowledge of and appreciation for the capabilities of new technologies, and a greater interest in maintaining control over the MIS function.

This is not a trivial concern, from the managerial perspective. Concern over technological elites replacing programmatic leaders are common, despite strong empirical evidence to the contrary. If technical expertise controls interest in new technologies, it follows that such expertise influences the technology and structure of the organizational information system. This is particularly relevant in government, where many core functions (such as regulation and oversight) are of necessity information-intensive. From this discussion arises the main hypothesis of this chapter:

H1: MIS managers are likely to place greater importance on new information technologies than are program managers.

While a particular manager acting in an organizational role may act as gatekeeper of knowledge, organizations often have many communication routes with external organizations. Communication with external groups increases the possibility that an organization will gain awareness of potential innovations. This is important because the adoptability of an innovation has been found to increase with its visibility (Perry and Danziger, 1980; Moore and Benbasat, 1991). The need to communicate with external organizations in turn increases the need to find better, cheaper, and faster ways of communicating and transmitting information. Thus external communication will lead to higher levels of interest in new information technologies by increasing awareness of innovations and by increasing the demand for better communication tools:

> H2: Agencies that have higher levels of information sharing with outside groups are likely to place greater emphasis on the importance of new information technologies than are agencies with lower levels of external communications.

Managers often seek innovations in response to perceived problems (Huber, 1990; Bozeman and Loveless, 1983). The growing use and the high popularity of management tools in government are testament to managers' seeking of solutions (Poister and Streib, 1989). Problems engender normal search processes aimed at solution development. Different types of problems will require different types of solutions. A manager seeks to match the two to produce the best result. A manager is likely to show interest in a particular technology or process when it is "matched" to the problem at hand. Thus a manager with financial difficulties may seek new methods of financial control. A manager facing barriers in processing information, or in transmitting information is likely to seek new information technology to overcome the obstacles.

> H3: Agencies reporting higher levels of barriers to sharing information with external groups are more likely to place greater emphasis on the importance of new information technologies than are agencies with lower reported levels of barriers to information sharing.

Kraemer and King (1986) and Northrop, Dutton and Kraemer (1982) have found that the most important variable in determining the success of computing implementation is the agency's commitment to advanced technology. Such a commitment would show itself by the level of importance an agency places on data processing (DP) and data-base administration and by top management's involvement in the coordination of MIS and DP activities.

H4: Agencies that place a high level of importance on data processing and data-base administration are more likely to place
greater emphasis on the importance of new information technologies than are agencies with lower levels of importance
attached to these activities.

This last hypothesis also reflects the structure of the organization. MIS organizations more closely linked to top management are also more likely to
have higher organizational status and influence than those farther down the
chain of command.

Data Collection

Data for this study were obtained from a stratified survey sampling design.
The surveys were part of the National Study of Information Resources Management in State Government done at Syracuse University in cooperation
with the National Association of State Information Systems (NASIS; see
Caudle and others, 1989). Data were collected from public managers in MIS
units and in program units. The unit of analysis is the program department
or data-processing organization.

With the NASIS data bases and other published directories, separate
lists of program and data-processing managers were compiled, representing forty states and a total of 1,361 data-processing managers and 2,988
program managers. Separate surveys were developed for the two popula-
tions following extensive reviews of the literature.

Multiple drafts of the surveys were developed and refined by a committee at Syracuse University. The instruments were pretested, using a random sample of 100 managers from both mailing lists. "Alert" letters were
sent one week before the pretest survey, with follow-up letters and surveys
sent three weeks later to nonrespondents. Results of the pretest were included
in the final survey design. The same procedure of "alert" and follow-up mail-
ings was used for the final survey.

In all, 2,259 surveys were sent back, for a response rate of 51.9 percent. Of those, 622 were from MIS managers, for a response rate of 44.5
percent, and 1,637 were from program managers, for a response rate of 54.8
percent. The samples were found to differ geographically from the sampling
frame. This could be a problem, if innovations and interest in innovations
were spatially related (innovative states tend to cluster). To control for differences in geographical distribution, a variable for the state of the respondent
is included in the analysis that follows.

Measurement Data and a Formal Model

Dependent Variables

The dependent variables rate the importance of new technologies by the subject agency. Survey respondents were asked to indicate how important they

believed each of a group of new information-related technologies would be in the agency's operations over the next three years. A Likert scale (1 = very important; 5 = not important) was used to measure eight information technologies. The new information technologies included input technology (optical scanners), output devices (laser printers), end-user technology (desktop publishing, facsimile, portable personal computers), communications services (teleconferencing, video text, electronic mail), telecommunication technology (cellular mobile phones, satellite, fiberoptics), voice technology (PBX, paging, call handling), information systems configuration (distributed processing and departmental systems), and geographical information systems.

The eight Likert scores were summed, to yield an aggregate measure of the overall importance of new information and communications technologies to the agency (SUMTECH). Since communications and telecommunications are often organizationally independent of data processing, separate aggregate scales were constructed, including only the communications-related technologies (SUMCOMM) and another for the traditional data-processing technologies (SUMDP). Analyses were then performed on the three composite dependent variables, as well as on each of the eight individual measures of interest in information technologies.

Control Variables

This group of variables reflects factors expected to influence interest in new information technologies that derive from factors other than those identified in the major hypotheses. Two variables reflect differences in the background of the managers that may represent role requirements, while the rest focus on obvious organizational differences.

A manager's level in the hierarchy of an agency can have a significant impact on interest in new information technologies (Bretschneider, 1990). Level in the organization determines the importance of one's role in the organization. For example, a data-processing unit that serves only a staff function will play a different role in an agency from one with line management status (Kraemer, King, Dunkle, and Lane, 1989). Such organizations may lack decision authority, limiting their level of interest, given lack of control over final decisions. Thus the number of levels between an organization's manager and the highest executive levels of management must be considered as a surrogate for internal organizational importance and authority. The variable LEVEL counts the number of levels between top management and the individual respondent.

Managers with scientific or technical backgrounds may be more interested in new technologies because they understand them better than managers with nonscience backgrounds and are more likely to occupy organizational roles requiring technical expertise. Given the same educational requirements, managers occupying MIS roles are expected to have a higher interest in new technologies. Thus this variable is included as a control variable. FIELD is a categorical variable that differentiates educational background, a surrogate for differences in personal technical capacities among respondents.

A number of organizational attributes also affect the hypotheses. The size of an agency can affect many aspects of agency operation as related to the hypotheses (Bozeman and Bretschneider, 1986; Gooding and Wagner, 1985; Tornatzky and Fleischer, 1990; Baldridge and Burnham, 1975). Larger organizations may have greater resource slack to devote to new technologies, while smaller ones may not have the resources to consider new technologies. To control for size effects, the log of the total number of employees was taken (LSIZE), since size is expected to have decreasing effects.

The central task or function of an agency affects the degree to which it relies on technology to perform its mission. A transportation agency involved in routing hazardous wastes or controlling the movement of large numbers of vehicles may require sophisticated computers to model transportation routes. A license bureau may only need to keep a small data base of clients. The variable FUNCTION is included to control for different effects of organizational mission for computing and information technology. It is a categorical variable listing the primary activity of the agency. (See Tables 18.1 and 18.2 for a summary of this variable.)

Agencies that experience higher levels of external control may have less discretion over decisions to innovate and may not exhibit high levels of interest in new information technologies relative to agencies with low levels of external control. External control is also related to formalization among public organizations (Damanpour, 1991). Respondents were asked how much control over a number of decision areas was subject to external influence. For each item, respondents indicated a score on a 5-point scale running from mostly internal control to mostly external control. The composite variable SUMEFFCT sums ten scores: control over program policies, administrative procedures, organizational structure, client qualification, service delivery, supplier selection, personnel, data processing, planning procedures, and reporting requirements.

A final control variable used was the STATE in which an agency is located. Controlling for location ensures that agencies' interest in new technologies will not be subject to regional variations. It also controls for differences in geographical distribution between the survey respondents and the original sampling frame.

Treatment Variables

The term *treatment variable* indicates those explanatory variables that are directly related to our hypotheses. The first treatment variable is ROLE. This variable identifies the respondent as occupying the role of either MIS manager or program manager in an organization. One difficulty with using a simple dichotomy is that the mix of technologies within MIS is not accounted for completely. To enhance the power of ROLE to discriminate between

Table 18.1. Descriptive Statistics for Relevant Categorical Variables, Based on the Subset of the Data for Which All Model Variables are Consistently Measured.

Sampling Distribution for the Variable SUMTECH

	Frequency	Percentage
MIS managers	413	27
Program managers	1119	73

Sampling Distribution of MIS Managers by Area of Responsibility[a]

	Frequency	Percentage
Voice communications	270	65
Telecommunications	371	90
E-mail	82	20
Office systems	23	06
Printing and output	215	52

Sampling Distribution by Function

	Frequency	Percentage[b]
Commerce	239	16
Education	64	4
Employment	119	8
Environment	273	18
Health	106	7
Human/social	257	17
Safety/crime	269	18
Transportation	144	9
Other	61	4

Sampling Distribution for Levels Between Director and Respondent

	Frequency	Percentage
0	476	31
1	674	44
2	270	18
3	77	5
4	22	1
5	8	1
6	3	—
More than 6	2	—

[a]Adds up to more than 100 percent, since individuals may have multiple responsibilities
[b]Adds to more than 100 percent due to rounding

programmatic and technical managers, additional distinctions were made by further differentiating MIS managers. Specifically, a series of additional binary variables was developed, to indicate extended levels of responsibility for MIS managers. If an MIS manager had responsibility for voice communications systems (such as telephone and voice mail), then the variable VOICEC took on the value 1; otherwise, this variable was valued at 0. In a similar fashion, responsibility for telecommunications systems was included through the binary variable TELECOMC, responsibility for electronic mail was captured by EMAILC, office automation services by OFFICEC, and responsibility for printing and graphic services by PRINTC.

Table 18.2. Means and Standard Deviations for Relevant Quantitative Variables.

Variable	N	Mean	Standard Deviation	Minimum	Maximum
LSIZE	2196	5.29	2.01	—	11.06
INOUT	2166	19.38	5.15	8.00	40.00
INFBAR	2155	23.08	6.34	6.00	42.00
SUMEFFCT	1888	24.48	6.93	10.00	50.00
PHILOS	2106	18.47	5.29	4.00	28.00
SUMTECH	2051	19.12	5.60	8.00	40.00
SUMCOMM	2169	8.12	2.76	3.00	15.00
SUMDP	2160	8.34	2.78	4.00	20.00

These five additional binary variables control for existing levels of responsibility within MIS for some of these areas. For example, in comparing two MIS managers—one with responsibility for printing and graphic services, and one without such functions—it seems reasonable that the one with these additional responsibilities would, other things being equal, be more interested in output devices than the counterpart without such responsibilities. The inclusion of ROLE and the additional five binary variables controls comparisons for role, as well as for level of technical responsibility within the MIS department.

A second treatment variable attempts to measure the level of information sharing between the responding agency and external organizations. Respondents were asked to indicate how often they shared information with the state legislature, other area agencies, other agencies, local government, the media, federal government, private business, and agency clients. A Likert scale was used (1 = very often; 5 = never). The eight answers were summed to obtain a measure of the intensity of external information sharing, called INOUT.

The third treatment variable measures the level of perceived barriers to information sharing with external agencies—that is, problems with information management. Respondents indicated level of agreement (with 1 indicating "strongly disagree" and 7 "strongly agree") that each barrier was a problem. High levels of agreement suggest that the agency faces significant barriers to information sharing with external agencies. The independent variable INFBAR is a composite of ratings of seven statements on barriers faced by the agency in sharing information with external agencies. The seven barriers consisted of the high cost of providing information, lack of authority, privacy requirements, loss of data integrity, technical barriers, problems with data definitions, and an "others" category.

The final treatment variable measures the level of importance attached to data and data-processing activities. Respondents rated their agreement or disagreement on a 7-point Likert scale with four statements on agency data and data-processing policy: "Data processing responds to new applications," "Data processing standards are vigorously enforced," "Data bases are maintained by data-processing management," and "Agency and data-processing management set policies." The variable PHILOS is an aggregate measure of the scores for these four statements. A high level of agreement suggests that data and data-processing are perceived as being very important to the agency, and that data-processing managers are actively involved in computing and information policy. Table 18.2 provides summaries of the major categorical variables, and Table 18.3 summarizes the quantitative variables just described.

Formal Model

Analysis of covariance was used to estimate the formal model (Neter, Wasserman, and Kutner, 1989). The independent variables are a mix of categorical and continuous variables. Tables 18.3 and 18.4 provide results of estimating this model from survey data in terms of individual regression coefficients for quantitative and binary independent variables, as well as F-statistics for the categorical variables with multiple qualitative levels. Those tables also provide statistics on the overall model fit with the data. Although

Table 18.3. Results of Model Estimation for Overall Interest in New Technologies, Interest in Communications Technology, and Interest in New Data-Processing Technologies.

Source	DF	Sum of All		Sum of Communications		Sum of Technical	
		Coefficient	$Pr > |T|$	Coefficient	$Pr > |T|$	Coefficient	$Pr > |T|$
INTERCEPT	1	19.496	0.0001	8.020	0.0001	9.444	0.0001
ROLE	1	4.090	0.0002	2.066	0.0001	1.208	0.0247
VOICEC	1	− 0.353	0.5181	− 0.441	0.1028	−	−
TELECOMC	1	− 2.025	0.0151	− 1.075	0.0093	−	−
EMAILC	1	− 3.067	0.0001	− 1.881	0.0001	−	−
OFFICEC	1	− 1.015	0.3735	−	−	− 1.153	0.0323
PRINTC	1	0.301	0.5440	−	−	− 0.224	0.3707
LSIZE	1	− 0.555	0.0001	− 0.221	0.0001	− 0.312	0.0001
LEVEL	1	0.162	0.1982	0.077	0.2198	0.019	0.7622
INOUT	1	0.253	0.0001	0.103	0.0001	0.097	0.0001
INFBAR	1	− 0.074	0.0004	− 0.034	0.0009	− 0.031	0.0039
SUMEFECT	1	0.012	0.5219	0.008	0.4007	0.005	0.6007
PHILOS	1	− 0.070	0.0050	− 0.030	0.0174	− 0.036	0.0046

Source	DF	F Value	$Pr > F$	Value	$Pr > F$	Value	$Pr > F$
FUNCTION	8	4.92	0.0001	9.08	0.0001	1.42	0.1827
FIELD	7	2.98	0.0042	2.18	0.0334	1.66	0.1147
STATE	55	1.47	0.0148	1.58	0.0046	1.38	0.0351
RMSE		4.81		2.45		2.50	
R-square		0.2522		0.2295		0.1841	
Adjusted R-square		0.2099		0.1887		0.1412	
F-statistic		5.96		5.62		4.30	
Cases		1532		1588		1583	

Table 18.4. Results of Model Estimation
for Interest in Individual New Technologies.

Source	DF	Input Technology		Communications Technology		System Configuration	
		Coefficient	Pr > |T|	Coefficient	Pr > |T|	Coefficient	Pr > |T|
INTERCEPT	1	2.717	0.0001	2.191	0.0001	2.699	0.0001
ROLE	1	0.302	0.0008	0.666	0.0001	0.113	0.5926
VOICEC	1	—	—	—	—	—	—
TELECOMC	1	—	—	—	—	—	—
EMAILC	1	—	—	−0.770	0.0001	—	—
OFFICEC	1	—	—	—	—	−0.197	0.3458
PRINTC	1	—	—	—	—	—	—
LSIZE	1	−0.127	0.0001	−0.063	0.0001	−0.136	0.0001
LEVEL	1	0.053	0.0822	−0.013	0.5762	−0.044	0.0827
INOUT	1	0.026	0.0001	0.024	0.0001	0.027	0.0001
INFBAR	1	−0.014	0.0047	−0.003	0.4286	−0.010	0.0200
SUMEFECT	1	0.003	0.5182	−0.001	0.7851	0.006	0.1154
PHILOS	1	−0.007	0.2649	−0.006	0.2429	−0.007	0.1384

Source	DF	F Value	Pr > F	F Value	Pr > F	F Value	Pr > F
FUNCTION	8	1.22	0.2840	1.80	0.0736	1.67	0.1019
FIELD	7	0.84	0.5541	1.12	0.3460	0.58	0.7748
STATE	55	0.90	0.6863	1.87	0.0001	1.27	0.0891

RMSE		1.21		0.93		0.99	
R-square		0.1189		0.1570		0.1635	
Adjusted R-square		0.0734		0.1137		0.1204	
F-statistic		2.64		3.62		3.79	
Cases		1594		1595		1592	

Source	DF	Telecommunications Technology		Voice Communications		End-User Technology	
		Coefficient	Pr > |T|	Coefficient	Pr > |T|	Coefficient	Pr > |T|
INTERCEPT	1	3.008	0.0001	2.983	0.0001	1.896	0.0001
ROLE	1	0.092	0.3058	0.395	0.0001	−0.114	0.0356
VOICEC	1	—	—	−0.563	0.0001	—	—
TELECOMC	1	−0.646	0.0007	—	—	—	—
EMAILC	1	—	—	—	—	—	—
OFFICEC	1	—	—	—	—	—	—
PRINTC	1	—	—	—	—	—	—
LSIZE	1	−0.110	0.0001	−0.076	0.0001	−0.034	0.0011
LEVEL	1	0.045	0.1352	0.050	0.0651	−0.015	0.4131
INOUT	1	0.043	0.0001	0.036	0.0001	0.023	0.0001
INFBAR	1	−0.017	0.0007	−0.014	0.0021	−0.001	0.7628
SUMEFECT	1	0.002	0.6061	0.007	0.0961	−0.003	0.3678
PHILOS	1	−0.014	0.0234	0.011	0.0513	−0.013	0.0006

Source	DF	F Value	Pr > F	F Value	Pr > F	F Value	Pr > F
FUNCTION	8	13.82	0.0001	5.08	0.0001	2.18	0.0264
FIELD	7	2.38	0.0203	1.62	0.1265	1.96	0.0578
STATE	55	1.63	0.0028	1.55	0.0063	1.29	0.0799

Table 18.4. Results of Model Estimation
for Interest in Individual New Technologies, Cont'd.

Source	DF	F Value	Pr > F	F Value	Pr > F	F Value	Pr > F
RMSE		1.18		1.07		0.73	
R-square		0.2006		0.1663		0.1129	
Adjusted R-square		0.1594		0.1233		0.0678	
F-statistic		4.87		3.87		2.51	
Cases		1593		1590		1593	

		Output Technology		GIS Technology	
Source	DF	Coefficient	Pr > |T|	Coefficient	Pr > |T|
INTERCEPT	1	2.115	0.0001	2.050	0.0001
ROLE	1	− 0.048	0.4867	0.116	0.1872
VOICEC	1	−	−	−	−
TELECOMC	1	−	−	−	−
EMAILC	1	−	−	−	−
OFFICEC	1	−	−	−	−
PRINTC	1	− 0.146	0.0562	−	−
LSIZE	1	− 0.020	0.0708	− 0.046	0.0075
LEVEL	1	0.020	0.3189	0.035	0.2466
INOUT	1	0.023	0.0001	0.050	0.0001
INFBAR	1	− 0.005	0.1158	− 0.011	0.0335
SUMEFECT	1	− 0.000	0.9806	0.001	0.8085
PHILOS	1	− 0.011	0.0059	− 0.000	0.9732

Source	DF	F Value	Pr > F	F Value	Pr > F
FUNCTION	8	1.85	0.0635	13.21	0.0001
FIELD	7	3.14	0.0027	3.25	0.0020
STATE	55	1.48	0.0137	1.24	0.1147
RMSE		0.78		1.16	
R-square		0.114		0.2059	
Adjusted R-square		0.0685		0.1643	
F-statistic		2.50		4.95	
Cases		1591		1548	

2,259 surveys were received, only a subset of these data had consistent measurements for the numerous variables used in this model. Approximately 68 percent to 71 percent of the survey responses were used in the estimation process, depending on the particular model. No significant problems in selection bias emerged in comparisons between those surveys used in the estimation and the overall sample of cases.

Discussion

Table 18.5 summarizes the somewhat complex results obtained from estimating the model with regard to the first hypothesis. In all *undifferentiated* comparisons between the MIS technical managers and their programmatic counter-

Table 18.5. Summary of Who Has Higher Levels
of Interest in New Information Technology.

	Program Managers	No Difference	MIS Managers
Sum of all	XX[a] ⟶[g] TT[c]	EE[d]	
Sum of communications	XX ⟶ TT	EE	
Sum of technical	XX ⟶ OO[e]	PP[f]	
Input technology	XX		
Communications technology	XX ⟶	EE	
System configurations		XX	
Telecommunications technology		XX ⟶ TT	
Voice communication	XX ⟶ VV[b]		
End-user technology	XX		
Output technology		XX ⟶ PP	
GIS technology		XX	

[a]Base-level results of model estimation (at .05 level of significance)

Adjusted results, after controlling for additional MIS responsibilities:

[b]Voice communications technology
[c]Telecommunications technology
[d]E-mail
[e]Office systems
[f]Printers and output technology
[g]Indicates shift in effect after estimation with controls

parts, the program managers, after controlling for all other model variables, typically indicated a higher level of interest in new information technology. This was true in all three aggregate measures and in four of the eight individual technologies. The remaining four individual technologies experienced essentially no difference in interest level between MIS and program managers.

For MIS managers with a wider range of responsibilities (such as communications, office automation, and outout display), the levels of interest shifted. MIS managers with responsibilities for telecommunications and electronic mail exhibited levels of interest comparable to the typical program manager when looking at all new technologies, the aggregate measure of communications technologies, and each of the communications technologies by itself. Similar results emerge for voice communications and the aggregate measure of more traditional MIS technical systems. When all the corrections are accounted for, two technologies — telecommunications and output devices — are of more interest to the technical managers, while input approaches and end-use techniques are relevant to program managers.

These results are somewhat complex, but a general outcome is that program managers typically have higher levels of interest in new information technologies than traditional MIS managers. In most cases, the expansion of an MIS manager's responsibilities into such fields as voice mail, radio systems, and office automation is new. As new areas of responsibility are assigned, these managers must quickly begin to build basic understanding of these technologies. This recent shift in the core technology acts as a short-term stimulus to interest in the technologies.

These findings also offer support to Kraemer, King, Dunkle, and Lane's theory of management states (1989). Both MIS and program managers are interested in technologies that support their control over their areas of responsibility. Thus new technologies are sought to reinforce or extend traditional areas of responsibility. The undifferentiated results also reflect a shift in the control of computing as an organizational resource, away from centralized technicians and toward general management. Program managers are more interested in new technologies because they seek to gain greater control over computing resources.

There are other explanations of program managers' interest in new technologies. Kraemer, King, Dunkle, and Lane (1989) suggest that MIS managers are more skeptical of new technologies. While they will keep track of innovations, they tend to wait and see how they perform. Perhaps MIS managers are also more aware of the problems associated with new technologies and their maintenance (Edwards, 1984). Lederer and Mendelow (1990) have found that MIS managers like to stay behind the leading edge of technology, to avoid the problems associated with early (or premature) implementation.

Program managers, by contrast, could be responding to reports of successful use of computers and seeking similar returns (Northrop, Dutton, and Kraemer, 1982; Northrop, Kraemer, Dunkle, and King, 1990). They may be responding to research that suggests that computer users are perceived as being smarter, more dynamic, and of higher status (Safayeni, Purdy, and Higgins, 1989; Kraemer and King, 1986). A more likely explanation is that program managers are attempting to find innovative solutions to real problems (Huber, 1990; Bozeman and Loveless, 1983). The technologies they are interested in — input technology, and end-user technologies — are systems that provide direct support for program services. Thus the interest in new information technologies reflects an interest in getting the job done.

The second hypothesis was significant in every model. It confirms previous research: greater information flows, into and out of the organization, are likely to generate increasing interest in new information technologies (Bozeman, 1982; Bozeman and Loveless, 1983; Perry and Danziger, 1980; Tornatzky and Fleischer, 1990). Increases in the number of groups with which an agency shares information are associated with increased emphasis on new information technologies. Increased contacts with outside agencies will increase the need for better information technology and awareness of information innovations in other organizations.

The third hypothesis, that interest in new technology is driven in part by perceptions of higher barriers to information sharing, is found to be significant for two types of technologies — those that enhance communications, and those that enhance reporting capabilities. Thus perceptions of higher barriers to information sharing were found to be associated with higher levels of interest in all communications technologies, voice technologies, and telecommunication technologies; and they were found to be associated with higher levels of interest in data-processing technologies, input technologies, and geographical information systems.

These findings suggest that public organizations seek new communication technologies to overcome technical barriers that make communications slow, expensive, or difficult. At the same time, they seek new technologies to improve their reporting capabilities to external agencies. Thus the desire to lower costs motivates the search for new technologies associated with data collection, to improve data integrity and privacy and to improve the ability to provide accurate analysis. Public organizations are matching interest in new technologies (potential solutions) to current perceptions of problems with information sharing.

The results for the fourth hypothesis were not as expected. All three of the aggregate measures and four of the individual models contain significant effects at the .10 level or better. When public organizations place high levels of importance on data processing and data-base management, they become *less* interested in new telecommunications, voice communications systems, end-user technologies, and output systems.

A possible explanation of this is that the variable PHILOS is not tapping agency commitment to advanced technology but is actually a measure of agency commitment to data integrity. Public organizations that enforce policies designed to maintain accurate data, and where upper management is concerned with data-processing policies, are more likely to look to better policies and data-management practices to improve data integrity. New technology alone cannot ensure better, more accurate data if sound policies on data handling and storage are not in place.

Another interpretation is that the variable PHILOS is measuring the degree to which data processing is centralized. This would suggest that, in more centralized settings, information about new information technologies and their early assessments are handled centrally. Thus the level of interest in new information technologies is shifted downward, particularly for program managers.

This analysis controls for a number of variables at the organization level, including size, function, external control, and location. With the exception of level of external control, these variables were found to be significant in the overall model and in many of the individual technology models. Size of the agency was significant in every model, confirming the need to include it in the model. This is not surprising. Larger agencies may have more slack resources to devote to innovation.

The level of external control over an agency was not found to be a significant factor (beyond the .05 level) in any of the models. This suggests that an agency's interest in new technologies is not a function of who controls the agency; rather, it is a function of agency needs.

Conclusions

The results of the hypothesis tests show that the initiation of the innovation process for new information technologies among public organizations can be partially explained by organizational roles, communications, communication barriers, and commitment to data integrity. When the technology appears to meet the needs (whether politically motivated or performance-related) of a public manager, interest in that technology increases. When the organizational tasks require high levels of contact with external agencies, interest in new information technology increases. If there are high levels of perceived barriers to external communications, interest in new technologies that overcome the problem increases. If the government agency places high levels of importance on data integrity and shared MIS decision making, it will place less importance on new information technologies.

For a given manager, the type of need influences interest in the type of information technology. Thus program managers are more interested in input and end-use technology; MIS managers are more interested in output and communications technology. These results compare favorably with other empirical work, which suggests that computing tends to reflect existing relationships and influence in public organizations, as opposed to shifting them (Kraemer, King, Dunkle, and Lane, 1989). Computers are a powerful and expensive new investment. Control of this resource augments the power of any self-interested manager in an agency.

Thus management role has predictive power for determining interest in new information technologies. A manager's area of responsibility suggests the programmatic problems the manager will likely face, and it suggests the type of information technology the manager is most likely to control. At the same time, the results of the hypothesis tests on information sharing, barriers to that sharing, and agency philosophy show that managers are reacting to needs, opportunities, and internal strategies when they seek new information technologies. This suggests that managers are reacting to conditions with a search for new solutions to match existing problems. A public manager's interest in new information technology is driven by organizational needs and by the manager's area of responsibility.

These findings serve to support, in part, the technology acceptance model (Davis, Bagozzi, and Warshaw, 1989). In that model, a manager's interest in using a new information technology is influenced by the perceived usefulness and perceived ease of use of the new system. Technology that is directly related to a manager's area of responsibility should appear to be most useful to that manager. Thus a manager will show early interest in technologies that address an area of concern for the manager.

19

MOTIVATIONS TO INNOVATE
IN PUBLIC ORGANIZATIONS

James L. Perry, Kenneth L. Kraemer,
Debora E. Dunkle, John Leslie King

*M*otivation is a central issue in many theories of the behavior of public officials (see, for example, Downs, 1967b; Ostrom and Ostrom, 1971; Perry and Wise, 1990; Miller, 1991). A key controversy surrounding efforts to model the motivations of public officials is the extent to which their behavior is driven by self-interest, in contrast to altruism (Mansbridge, 1990). Some theories argue that the behavior of public officials can be understood as narrowly self-interested; others contend that much of observed behavior in the public realm can be understood only if citizens and policy makers are motivated by altruistic considerations.

This chapter investigates, empirically, the motivations of public officials in a particular decisional context—the decision to innovate. Although the motivations of public officials appear to be important for understanding the choices that are made about innovation (Nelson and Winter, 1977, 1982), researchers have been content to infer motives from innovation decisions, rather than measure them more directly. This study examines a number of motives that have been identified as important in the innovation-adoption process, and that have been associated with varying degrees of self-interest. It uses a policy-capturing methodology to identify the underlying structure of these motives and to discover how these motives differ among local government officials making decisions about computer applications.

Literature Review

Research on innovation has occupied the attention of large numbers of social scientists in many disciplines. Rogers (1983, p. xv) aptly notes that

This is a revised version of a paper presented at the National Public Management Research Conference, September 1991. The authors would like to thank David Anderson and John Rohrbaugh for their helpful comments on an earlier draft.

"there is almost no other field of behavior science that represents more effort by more scholars in more nations." The focus of this study is on one important dimension of the innovation literature: the *motivation to innovate*. Nelson and Winter (1977, 1982) suggest that the motivation to innovate is an important component of the innovation process. They argue that innovation is purposive but inherently stochastic. They use the concept of the *selection environment* to organize the different factors that determine how the relative use of different technologies changes over time. In nonmarket settings, the selection environment essentially consists of three primary elements: the motivations of organizations in the sector; the ways in which consumers (usually voters) and financiers (usually legislators) constrain agencies' behavior; and the mechanisms for information and value sharing among organizations in the investment and imitation process.

According to Nelson and Winter (1977), the selection environment in nonmarket settings is quite different from that found in market settings, and one reason is that the separation of interests between firms and customers is not as sharply defined. This, in turn, reduces both the applicability of competition among providers as a control mechanism, on the one hand, and the utility of profit as a motivator, on the other. If profit does not motivate organizations in the nonmarket sector, then what does?

Feller (1980, 1981) distinguishes between two potential motivations. One involves the extent to which an innovation increases production efficiency (that is, reduces the cost of producing a given level of output). The other, contrasting motivation is service efficiency, whereby an innovation is adopted because, without reducing costs, it augments or enhances services and potentially increases them. The latter motivation is grounded in Niskanen's model of bureaucratic behavior (1971) and Yin and others' bureaucratic self-interest model (1976). Feller's contention is that bureaucrats prefer service-augmenting innovations: these increase agency budgets (to which bureaucratic emoluments are positively correlated), expand the clientele served by an agency, and obscure an agency's production costs by simultaneously altering input mixes and services provided. Feller concludes that while public bureaucracies may be more risk-averse, the innovations they adopt may improve service rather than efficiency.

Others have implied that some innovations involve trade-offs between citizens' interests and bureaucratic control. Summarizing the research on computing in the federal, state, and local governments, Kraemer and Kling (1985) identify two models for the adoption of computer systems. In the rationalist model, computer technology serves citizens by providing more services, more equitably. In the reinforcement-politics model, computers are tools for the most powerful interests. According to this model, computerized systems are used primarily for routine operations and overhead control. Thus, another dimension of the motivation to innovate is decision making and control. Kraemer and Kling agree with Feller that the adoption of technologies is not primarily driven by efficiency considerations, but they suggest that service efficiency is less important than the reinforcement of existing power arrangements.

Hannaway's research on bureaucratic growth (1987), which examines central office managers in a large school district, provides further support for the contention that production efficiency is secondary and control is primary as a motivation to innovate. Hannaway contends that growth is more the result of managers' attention to immediate concerns than of any maximizing of utility. She argues that the manager is "trying to get a nearly boundless job done without understanding clearly either the means-end relationships involved or the meaning of much of the feedback received, and without incurring much personal risk" (p. 129).

Mohr (1969) identifies yet a fourth potential motivation to innovate in public organizations: professional status. In a study of health organizations, Mohr argues that large departments chose to adopt a large number of programs, rather than the smaller number of programs supported at higher levels. He infers that this choice reflects status-motivated innovation, and he reasons that this pattern of adoption reflects "innovation motivated largely by a desire for prestige and professional status on the part of the health officer and other health department staff members" (p. 122).

A fifth motivation to innovate, which may reside in the newness of a process or a product, is the symbolism of innovation. Individuals may favor a new product or process simply because it *is* new and represents a new way of doing things. An innovation may appeal to the preference for "things modern" or "change for the sake of change."

Hypotheses

Because of their different roles in the hierarchy and their different professional orientations, we expected different managers to select applications that reflected different mixes of values. Although all managers may hold certain values in common, we expected top managers to be more interested in applications that would enhance decision making and control, since they are concerned with the overall direction of the organization. Similarly, we expected department managers to be especially concerned with applications that would promote productivity and service enhancement, because of their responsibility for the day-to-day operations of government and for delivery of services to citizens. Finally, we expected information systems managers to be the most interested in applications that seemed to be innovative or to enhance professionalism, because their own professional status would be enhanced by cutting-edge computer applications.

Methods

Social judgment analysis (Hammond, McClelland, and Mumpower, 1980; Milter and Rohrbaugh, 1988; Whorton, Feldt, and Dunn, 1988–89) was applied, to determine the underlying criteria used by managers in decisions about computer applications. In social judgment analysis, a decision (referred to as a *judgment*) is a function of (1) the relative *weight* that an individual assigns to the dimensions of the issue under consideration, (2) the *form* of the relationship of the dimensions (referred to as *cues*) to the final decision, and (3) the method used to *organize* these relationships. The measurement of decisions involves three tasks: identification of the decision to be made, identification of the relevant dimensions for making the decision, and creation of decision profiles in which the dimensions are varied (that is, different mixes — presence, absence; positive, negative — of the dimensions are presented). In this research, the task set for managers was to provide an overall assessment of the likelihood that a specific software application would be selected for use, given a summary of the effects that using five criteria would have if the application were implemented. The five criteria, based on our review of the literature, were *productivity, service enhancement, decision making and control, professionalism,* and *innovation.* The description of each criterion (dimension) in the survey instrument was preceded by the following statement:

> We are interested in the kinds of criteria managers use to make assessments of investments in computing. Assume that your department reviewed twenty-six packages and scored each on the five criteria often used in evaluating computer applications — their contributions to productivity, service enhancement, professionalism, decision making and control, and innovation. The cost of these packages is essentially the same, so cost is not a consideration.

The criteria were described to the respondents in the following ways:

> *Productivity,* that is, the extent to which an application reduces the resources required to perform a service or increases the services that can be provided with the same resources. An application that reduces staff or reduces cost would receive a high value on this criterion. In contrast, an application that requires additional staff or increases cost would receive a low value.
>
> *Service enhancement,* that is, the extent to which an application improves an operating department's ability to meet the needs of its clients. An application that makes it possible for departments to speed up service delivery, better target services to clients' needs, or ease interaction with clients would receive a high value on this criterion. In contrast, an application that increases the complexity of service delivery or increases the difficulty of interaction with clients would receive a low value on this criterion.

Decision making and control, that is, the extent to which an application aids decision making and control over government operations. An application that provides relevant information for decision making and monitors operational performance would receive a high score. An application that produces no information for decision making or performance monitoring would receive a low score.

Professionalism, that is, the extent to which an application enhances professional recognition for you or your organization. An application that brings substantial publicity and prestige at the local, regional, or national level would receive a high score. An application that does not generate any publicity or prestige would receive a low score.

Innovation, that is, the extent to which an application promises a new and better way of doing things but involves some risk. A highly promising but risky application would receive a high value. A less promising, low-risk application would receive a low value.

A total of twenty-five hypothetical software packages was provided to each respondent, with the five criteria varying for each software package. The respondent was asked to provide an overall assessment of making a purchase, given the relative importance he or she assigned to each of the criteria. For example, for one software profile, the respondent was asked to rate, on a scale from 1 (low probability of purchase) to 10 (high probability of purchase), whether the application would be selected for use if it were high on productivity (10) and innovation (9), low on professionalism (1) and decision making and control (2), and neutral on service enhancement (5). Each respondent made a total of twenty-five decisions regarding applications, with a total of twenty-five weights for each of the five criteria.

Multiple linear regression analysis was used to obtain the judgment descriptions. It was assumed that the form of the judgment was an additive, linear function. The overall assessment of the likelihood of purchase of the software (decision) is the dependent variable, and the preassigned weighting scores (cues) for the criteria are the independent variables. The beta weights obtained from the regression analysis reflect the relative weighting applied to each of the five cues. The multiple R provides an indication of how well the regression model can predict the observed decisions.

This analysis uses data obtained during an intensive study of computer use in forty-six cities and one county during 1988. The investigators spent one to two person-weeks conducting field research in each location, gathering data about local conditions, political and administrative systems, and information systems. Data-collection methods included semistructured interviews with top managers, information system (IS) professionals, and department personnel. In addition, user surveys were distributed to approximately five thousand employees. The user survey focused on questions about the twenty-five profiles of applications and the uses and impacts of computerization. This chapter uses only the responses of the 464 top managers (mayors or deputy mayors, city managers, or assistant city managers), department heads, and IS managers who responded to the values section of the user questionnaire. Response rates to the values section of the questionnaire varied by role type: 75 percent of top managers, 68 percent of department heads, and 85 percent of IS managers responded.

Because it was expected that not all respondents would be consistent in their judgments or would understand the task, multiple linear regression analysis of the twenty-five judgments was performed for each respondent. For the subsequent analyses, we accepted a multiple R of .80 or better as sufficient evidence of consistency of response at the individual level. By this criterion, 43 of the 464 respondents were considered to be too inconsistent in responding to the twenty-five profiles and were dropped from further analysis. Our sample, therefore, consists of 421 respondents — or, more precisely, 10,525 judgments.

An inspection of the beta weights produced for each respondent indicated that it was highly probable that distinct groups of individuals (sharing similar function forms) could be identified. Three steps were involved in identifying the subgroups. First, a principal-components factor analysis, with varimax rotation, was performed on the twenty-five judgments. The result was a six-factor solution (eigenvalue 1.0 or greater), which accounted for 65.5 percent of the variance in the twenty-five judgments). Factor scores were generated. Second, cluster analysis of the six factor scores, using Ward's minimum-variance method, was performed to identify the subgroups. The cluster analysis was performed using SAS. A pseudo-t^2 statistic was used to evaluate the optimal number of clusters. The results indicated that a four-cluster solution was optimal. Finally, multiple linear regression analysis of the individual judgments was performed for each of the four clusters, to obtain the relative weights and organization of the group's decisions.

Results

Regression analyses of the individual judgments were performed for (1) all managers, (2) top managers, (3) department and division heads (excluding IS managers), and (4) information system managers. These results are shown in Table 19.1.

All Managers

The results indicate that, across the entire sample, productivity and service enhancement were weighted fairly equally as criteria used for selection of applications. Innovation and professionalism were not used as selection criteria: the near-zero beta weights indicate that these two criteria had no

Table 19.1. Relative Weights of Five Criteria.

Criteria	All Managers (N = 421)		Top Managers (N = 41)		IS Managers (N = 76)		Department Heads (N = 304)	
	Beta	Standardized Beta[a]	Beta	Standardized Beta[a]	Beta	Standardized Beta[a]	Beta	Standardized Beta[a]
Productivity	.51	36%	.55	38%	.55	41%	.49	34%
Service enhancement	.45	32%	.44	30%	.44	32%	.46	32%
Decision making and control	.28	20%	.30	21%	.27	20%	.28	19%
Innovation	.10	7%	.12	8%	.06	4%	.11	8%
Professionalism	.09	5%	.04	3%	.04	3%	.10	7%
Mulitple R (agreement measure)	.75		.79		.76		.70	
Total judgments in set	10,525		1,025		1,900		7,600	

[a]Standardized beta calculated as (beta/sum of betas) × 100

impact on the decision-making process. The extent to which an application might aid decision making and control was not entirely discounted but was weighted substantially less in final decisions than were productivity and service enhancement.

Top Managers. This group did not evidence a pattern different from that of all managers. Productivity and service enhancement were heavily weighted, with productivity of moderately greater importance than service enhancement.

Information System (IS) Managers. This group also placed heavy emphasis on productivity considerations. A greater proportion of IS managers were influenced by productivity considerations than were top managers, and they placed less emphasis on innovation.

Other Department and Division Heads. These managers showed a somewhat different pattern from those of top managers and IS managers. They assigned almost equal weight to productivity and service enhancement.

Subgroups

The preceding analysis indicates that judgment patterns were very consistent across role types. Any variations in patterns of decision making cut across roles in local governments. To identify variations, cluster analysis was performed.

The cluster analysis, presented in Table 19.2, indicates that there were four subgroups among the managers. Group 1, which we call the *productivity and service-enhancement dominants,* was motivated equally by considerations of efficiency and effectiveness; other values, including bureaucratic control, were given a low level of importance. Group 2, the *organization controllers,* was as concerned about implications for organizational control as they were about consequences related to efficiency and effectiveness; this cluster of managers was the largest in the sample. Group 3, the *efficiency dominants,* was driven by productivity implications above all other factors; only a relatively small proportion of the sample fell into this group. Group 4, the *risk avoiders,* sought not only to maximize efficiency, effectiveness, and control but also to avoid innovations that might be construed as new and risky.

An assessment of differences among members of the four groups is shown in Tables 19.3 and 19.4. Analyses of variance were computed for a series of characteristics and factors on which the groups might be expected to differ: government environment, characteristics of information services, individual characteristics, and attitudes toward computing. As Table 19.3 indicates, none of the group means were significantly different at the .05 level for the first three of these. Table 19.4, by contrast, shows that significant differences among the groups were found on each of the measures of attitudes toward computing. In general, group 1 individuals tended to be

Table 19.2. Relative Weights of Five Criteria: Four Subgroups[a].

Criteria	Beta	Standardized Beta
GROUP 1 (N = 231) Productivity and service-enhancement dominants		
Service enhancement	**.51**	33%
Productivity	**.49**	32%
Decision making and control	.22	14%
Innovation	.18	12%
Professionalism	.12	8%
Multiple R = .78 (agreement measure)		
GROUP 2 (N = 75) Organization controllers		
Service enhancement	**.55**	37%
Productivity	**.46**	31%
Decision making and control	**.35**	24%
Innovation	.08	6%
Professionalism	.03	2%
Multiple R = .80 (agreement measure)		
GROUP 3 (N = 74) Efficiency dominants		
Productivity	**.66**	46%
Service enhancement	.33	23%
Decision making and control	.29	20%
Innovation	.07	5%
Professionalism	.07	5%
Multiple R = .80 (agreement measure)		
GROUP 4 (N = 40) Risk avoiders		
Productivity	**.53**	35%
Service enhancement	**.43**	29%
Decision making and control	**.30**	20%
Innovation	**−.18**	12%
Professionalism	.04	3%
Multiple R = .76 (agreement measure)		

[a]Clusters based on Ward's minimum variance method (squared Euclidean distances)

the most experienced with computing and to have the strongest belief in the potential of the technology to alter both productivity and service delivery in positive ways. The group 2 and group 3 managers tended to be in the middle on these measures, while group 4 managers—the risk avoiders— generally had less understanding of what computers can do and considerably less confidence in positive results of their use. The differences across attitudes reported in Table 19.4 could be ascribed to a common-methods problem; but the different ways in which the social judgments and attitudes toward computing were derived—by means of ratings of hypothetical packages

Table 19.3. Analysis of Variance for Groups on Environment, Information Services Characteristics, and Individual Variables.

	Group 1	Group 2	Group 3	Group 4	F-ratio	F-significance
Government environment						
Population of city, 1980	314,547	246,971	395,239	294,174	2.43	.065
Total operating expenditures (in millions)	$394.7	$263.0	$450.4	$364.7	1.95	.121
Total employees in city	5,300	3,897	6,434	5,652	1.50	.214
Proportion in council-manager cities	.67	.53	.64	.61	1.58	.193
Proportion in cities using written objectives for services	.57	.52	.72	.56	2.33	.074
Proportion in cities using measures of performance to meet objectives	.46	.41	.55	.46	1.06	.367
Proportion in cities using cost-accounting procedures	.56	.49	.55	.41	1.24	.293
Proportion in cities using team management strategy	.48	.51	.51	.63	1.02	.384
Characteristics of information services						
Total applications operational in city	133.46	128.16	142.05	123.78	2.24	.083
Total functions automated in city	16.37	15.85	17.07	14.90	2.22	.085
Number of employees per terminal in city	8.41	9.01	8.64	8.18	0.29	.832
Individual Characteristics						
Proportion male	.88	.81	.87	.82	0.84	.472
Proportion with graduate/professional degree	.53	.53	.42	.36	1.94	.123
Proportion who attend professional meetings	.83	.83	.78	.65	2.52	.058
Mean age	46.07	47.03	45.21	44.04	1.103	.380
Years of computer experience	10.94	9.89	11.03	10.54	0.45	.715
Proportion with programming skill	.24	.17	.28	.14	2.24	.084
Proportion with coursework in computers	.81	.75	.80	.75	0.48	.696
Frequency of using computer-based information in reports[a]	5.10	5.11	4.93	0.63	.595	
Frequency of direct use of computing in job[b]						

[a] Scores on index: 1 = never, 2 = at least once a year, 3 = several times a year, 4 = a few times a month, 5 = a few times a week, and 6 = daily. Index was calculated by taking the maximum (most frequently done) of the following activities: requesting others to get information from computerized files or receive reports that contain data from computer files.

[b] Scores on index: 1 = never, 2 = at least once a year, 3 = several times a year, 4 = a few times a month, 5 = a few times a week, and 6 = daily. Index was calculated by taking the maximum (most frequently done) of the following activities: using a microcomputer, using a microcomputer as a terminal to a larger computer, using a microcomputer on a local-area network, or using a computer terminal.

Table 19.4. Analysis of Variance of Group Attitudes Toward Computing.

	Group 1	Group 2	Group 3	Group 4	F-ratio	F-significance
Attitudes toward computing						
Computers allow departments to handle a greater volume of service without corresponding increases in cost.[a]	**3.42**	3.18	3.20	**2.93**	4.91	.002
I lack a good understanding of what computers can do.[a]	**1.79**	2.25	**1.70**	1.97	4.61	.004
Within the next five years, computers will greatly improve the way my job is done.[a]	**3.38**	3.34	**3.00**	3.14	3.58	.014
Quality of department's service to clients[b]	4.54	4.29	4.53	4.26	3.66	.013
Computers save me time in looking for information.[c]	3.09	2.90	2.75	2.67	3.80	.011
Overall, computers have enabled me to be more effective in performing my work.[c]	3.09	2.84	2.72	2.59	4.16	.007

[a] 4-point scale (1 = disagree; 4 = agree)
[b] 5-point scale (1 = decreased; 5 = increased)
[c] 4-point scale (1 = almost never true; 4 = nearly always true)
Note: Boldface type means statistically significant differences between groups.

and through the use of Likert scales, respectively — make it unlikely that the use of common methods can account for this result.

Discussion

Analysis revealed that production efficiency and service enhancement were the dominant factors influencing choices about computer applications. The weightings of criteria in the cluster analysis indicated, however, that few of the public managers were motivated solely by productivity considerations. Instead, most managers were motivated about equally by productivity *and* service enhancement. If judgments driven by considerations of service enhancement are construed as self-interested, then the results indicate that most managers act with decidedly mixed motives.

We expected different managers to select applications on the basis of different mixes of values. In particular, we expected top managers to select applications for reasons of decision making and control, department managers to select applications for productivity and service enhancement, and information systems managers to select applications for innovation and professionalism. Only the results for the department managers turned out as expected. The broad agreement on criteria across organizational roles indicated that the values associated with computing innovations were widely shared among managers at all levels.

It was also clear that innovation and professionalism were not important factors in the managers' decisions about computing, at any level. Indeed, among the risk avoiders, there was even an aversion to newness as a consideration in the selection of computing packages.

What factors accounted for differences in the values that the managers employed in choosing innovations? We identified four distinctive clusters associated with the decision criteria, but many of the background factors that might account for such differences were not significant. The only variables that could account for differences among the groups were those related to attitudes toward computing. Our results suggest that the most powerful determinant of an individual's motivation in this context may be his or her technology-related experiences. For instance, the results clearly indicate that most of the managers were not risk-averse, but a small subset of the population was likely to reject risky innovations. The aversion to risk of this subset of managers, as in the other subsets responding to different criteria (such as productivity or control), may have been a product of social learning, so that responses to particular cues may have been a function of past experiences in similar situations. The lack of significance of such variables as organizational role and context suggests that motivation is not determined purely or even primarily by environmental factors; instead, it may be the result of more complex interactions among environment, experience, and personality. These relationships merit further research, using methodologies capable of identifying such interactions.

If the motivation to innovate is a product of a social learning process, would we find similar motivational patterns for other technologies? Quite possibly not. Computing is a relatively well-known managerial technology, which has grown incrementally in most public organizations. If motivation is a function of social learning, we would expect variations across different technologies. A new, discrete, service-specific technology might possibly reveal radically different motivational patterns, and this conjecture also deserves further research.

Part Seven

POLICY DESIGN
AND PUBLIC MANAGEMENT

The three chapters in this final section each provoke reflection about big issues in public management. From the "hollowing out" of the state to designs for sharing power to speculation about public management in the next century, these chapters cover tradition-shattering developments in public management.

H. Brinton Milward, Keith G. Provan, and Barbara A. Else examine the implications of subcontracting and "government by proxy." The authors attempt to determine the workings of the "hollowing" process by focusing in depth on a community mental health system and then contrasting a public sector "hollowing" to what occurs in a private sector organization, Nike, which has undergone similar transformation. The authors identify a set of variables apparently associated with "hollowing" and suggest that future studies measuring those variables might tell us how "hollowing" varies across policy arenas, states, nations, and levels of government.

John M. Bryson and Barbara C. Crosby present a framework designed to help planners and policy analysts operate more effectively in "shared-power, no-one-in-charge situations." To illustrate their framework, they draw from a case study of the creation of the Twin Cities Metropolitan Council and its subsequent effects on coordination and planning of regional policies.

Finally, Mark A. Emmert, Michael M. Crow, and R. F. Shangraw, Jr., use the futures-studies literature as "secondary data" to arrive at conclusions about the likely future environment of public management and some prescriptions about effective public management responses to likely future trends. This approach is important because, as the authors point out, public management theory is based on dated technology and concepts. The themes examined by the authors include social and organizational complexity, privatization and public sector–private sector interaction, technological change, workforce diversity, scarcity, individualism, environmentalism, and processes of transition. As in the other two chapters in this section, the authors center their analysis on a case study — here, the U.S. Department of Energy's Environmental Restoration and Waste Program. The authors' hopeful prescription involves organizational design. They argue that organization designers seeking to cope with the future and to incorporate likely future trends in their designs may significantly enhance the quality of public management.

20

WHAT DOES THE "HOLLOW STATE" LOOK LIKE?

H. Brinton Milward,
Keith G. Provan,
Barbara A. Else

Several years ago, *Business Week* ran a cover story on "the Hollow corporation" ("Special Report," 1986). The editors believed that a new organizational form had emerged and that Nike, the athletic-shoe company, was the template for this new type of organization. The hollow corporation consisted of a lean headquarters operation that had only four departments — research and development, design, marketing, and financial control. What was unique about Nike was that it had no production capability of its own. Nike shoes were made all over the world, under contract with various manufacturing firms.

An even more extreme type of hollow corporation has been introduced by management guru Tom Peters. In a recent article, he advocates subcontracting anything and everything: "Subcontracting is hardly new. What's new is that major firms [MCI, Apple, and Boeing] are looking at subcontracting as a way of life; they conceive of themselves, in fact as 'nothing more' than a web of subcontractors (they retain 'systems integration skills,' to use Boeing's term)" (Peters, 1990, p. 13). Whether this type of organization is effective is a matter of debate. Peters clearly believes that it is; Bettis, Bradley, and Hamel (1992) believe that the evidence is mixed for the firm, and harmful for the economy.

The "hollow corporation" seems to us to be the analogue of the "hollow state," a concept that captures many of the recent structural developments in the local delivery of health and human services in the United

The research reported in this chapter was funded by grant R01MH43783 from the National Institute of Mental Health.

States. Specifically, in many communities, even though health and human services are funded by public agencies, the distribution of these funds is controlled and monitored by nongovernmental third parties, who themselves determine which agencies to subcontract with for the actual provision of services. Thus involvement by the state is indirect and extremely limited. The "hollow state" is the result of several different trends. The federal government has always relied on state and local government to deliver services that the federal government has paid for. Government funding of nonprofit agencies increased during the grant-in-aid explosion of the 1960s and 1970s and continued during the Reagan and Bush administrations, under the banner of "privatization." In addition, contracting for such services as public works and defense has been with us for a very long time. In recent years, organizational scholars have attempted to describe, operationalize, and model the resulting new organizational forms — often called *network organizations* or *service implementation networks* — in the public, nonprofit, and private sectors (Chisholm, 1989; Landau, 1991; Lawless and Moore, 1989; Miles and Snow, 1986; Provan and Milward, 1991; Wise, 1990). Nevertheless, the funding of such network-based systems, and its impact on the provision of services, has generally not been examined in detail. The "hollow state" concept is particularly useful in making sense of the specific case we investigated for this chapter: the redesign of a metropolitan area's community mental health network to deal with the multiple problems faced by the growing number of seriously mentally ill adults.

We can take no intellectual copyright on the "hollow state," because it is similar to a set of related concepts that have been used to describe the same phenomenon. Wolch (1990) uses the phrase "shadow state" to refer to the increased role that nonprofits play in the delivery of human services to clients. Kettl (1988) and Smith (1990), respectively, describe government contracting to third parties as "government by proxy" and "the contracting regime." Mosher (1980) calls our attention to the growing phenomenon of "third-party government," and Salamon (1981) attempts to classify and predict the impact of the "tools" that govern the implementation of public policy by third parties. All these authors have either set forth general descriptions of the scope of the problem or provided sets of examples of the characteristics of the metaphor used to describe the problem. What we propose to do is to attempt to tie the "hollow state" concept to a more general organizational model, and to develop a set of dimensions of "hollowness" that vary and thus have the potential to be used in empirical research. We attempt to do this in the context of a detailed study of the redesign of a community mental health system that is largely run by third parties.

Implementation by Nongovernmental Entities

Control of agents in a federal system like the United States is always difficult, which is one of the virtues of James Madison's "compound republic." Different levels of government share authority for the implementation of health, welfare, education, and many other policy areas. The traditional problem of control in a federal system is how to implement and control policy effectively when relations between levels of government are based on bargaining, rather than on hierarchy (Ingram, 1977).

A different problem is the implementation of public policy by nonpublic entities. Whether nonprofits or for-profit organizations are involved, the problem is how to control the behavior of people who are not public servants and whose loyalty, in addition to serving their clients, is either to the prosperity of their own firms or to their nonprofit callings.

Brudney (1990) has found evidence to support the hollowing out of the state. Specifically, less than 15 percent of the federal government's budget is spent on programs that it administers itself; some federal departments support four indirect workers for every one on departments' payrolls. The "hollow state" is not simply the federal government turning over the delivery of services to states and cities; state and city governments, too, are creating "hollow" service systems as they turn over hospitals and mental health centers, parks, water treatment, prisons, and transportation facilities to nonprofit or for-profit entities.

Since the taxpayer revolt of the late 1970s, there have been major limitations on governmental spending at all levels. In addition, an antigovernment zeitgeist, reflected in the two terms of President Ronald Reagan, has significantly changed the way in which policy can be implemented. With respect to privatization, most policy analysts would recommend that government rationally weigh the costs and benefits of direct provision of a service by government versus provision of the same service by a firm or firms under contract with the government. Given the limitations on resources and capacity faced by many governments today, the choice often has little to do with the merits of the case for or against privatization. It is simply a question of finding some scheme to do the job, without direct costs to the taxpayer.

Barriers to revenue increases are so stringent, and the privatization ethos is so strong, that government is turning over the delivery of services to third parties, and sometimes financial control and eligibility-determination functions as well, for the simple reason that there are few other options: "The goal is survival" ("Cash-Strapped Cities . . . ," 1991, p. A8).

In the case of EPA's Superfund program, for instance, contractors have actually performed the basic work of the agency. Because of severe manpower and technical constraints, contractors "were involved in literally every phase of the program, for virtually no important task within EPA was not contracted out. Contractors researched Freedom of Information Act requests received by the agency. They drafted memos for top EPA officials. They prepared congressional testimony. They wrote regulations and drafted international agreements on behalf of EPA. They trained and wrote statements of work for other contractors and then evaluated their performance. They even wrote the Superfund program's annual report to Congress" (Kettl, 1991,

p. 12). What the effect of the nongovernmental provision of public services will be, in the long run, we do not yet know, but the implications of such a system raise serious questions about whether services are being provided adequately and whether the spending of taxpayers' dollars is being monitored and controlled effectively.

To better understand the efficacy of the "hollow state" and how such a system works, we decided to explore one community mental health system in depth. We make no claim that it is representative of all such systems. In light of the underdeveloped state of theory in this area, however, a case study seemed highly appropriate. We needed first to know much more about the new landscape of nongovernmental provision of public services, we reasoned, before we could attempt to generalize about the effects of the "hollow state" on the delivery of public goods and services.

A "Hollow" Community Mental Health System

This case explores the restructuring of a community mental health system in a city in the western United States with a 1990 population of slightly over 600,000. (Information describing this system comes from an analysis of public documents, personal interviews, newspaper accounts, and participants' observations.) The case demonstrates how local providers attempted to restructure a loose collection of mostly nonprofit agencies serving, among other clienteles, seriously mentally ill adults. (The seriously mentally ill are persons who, as a result of mental disorders, exhibit emotional or behavioral functioning that is so impaired as to interfere substantially with their capacity to remain in the community without supportive treatment or services of a long-term or indefinite duration. In these persons, mental disability is severe and persistent, resulting in long-term limitation of their functioning capacities for the primary activities of daily living.) Patient care is important in any such system, but the agencies that deliver these services have interests and agendas of their own.

In an earlier attempt to coordinate community mental health care, the state government had created regional administrative "entities" to funnel state money to providers of services to seriously mentally ill adults. In this community, an existing nonprofit agency was designated by the state as the comptroller for most mental health spending in the community. Nonprofit "entities" like this one control the flow and distribution of mental health dollars at the community level in this state.

One characteristic of a public organization is that it is publicly funded (Perry and Rainey, 1988; Wamsley and Zald, 1973). In this community mental health system, the funds were largely public, but there was little attempt to coordinate the services that these various agencies provided. The local service agency received funds from the "entity," which received money from the state. Each agency, in consultation with the entity, largely determined what services it would provide to its clients. A key feature of this system was that, although the provider agencies were publicly funded, there was little attempt by the state or by its agent, the entity, to control how the funds were spent or to account for whether the funds were used effectively. It is often assumed that organizations that receive most of their funds from one source will be highly responsive to that source. This is the essence of exchange (Emerson, 1962) and resource-dependence theories (Pfeffer and Salancik, 1978). Dependence is, however, a two-way street. Organizations that are highly dependent on funding from one source may receive that funding because they perform critical functions for the funding agency, or it may reflect the fact that there are no alternative providers of a critical service. One explanation for why the state attempted to exercise so little control over the entity — and, through it, the local nonprofit provider — is that there were no other options for providing services to the seriously mentally ill population. There were no barriers to entry to the mental health market. If any new organizations wished to enter the field, they certainly could have done so and competed for contracts with the existing providers. The state also lacked the ability to determine whether the system was performing well. In response to a state audit of the system, the department of health services, which funds the entities, stated that it was unable to exercise effective oversight of the entities because of lack of administrative capacity. Thus an additional effect of hollowing may be loss of the capacity to evaluate the performance of contractors.

The system, at this time, had a fairly complex structure. The state department of health services contracted with the nonprofit entity to provide mental health services for the community. The entity then contracted with local providers. Two of the local providers operated pilot programs, to test the efficacy of case managed care. These were both directly funded by the state, rather than through the entity. In addition, the state directly funded a community mental health agency, which provided a range of services but played no direct role in coordination of the system. The county government also provided funds to operate and staff a psychiatric component at the county-owned hospital. The county paid for these services, but the hospital was operated by a for-profit health care chain, and the mental health component was run by a nonprofit provider.

Coordination was a problem in this largely privatized system, just as it has been in publicly run systems. There were coordination problems of patient care and coordination problems between agencies. The level of dissatisfaction with the performance of the system increased over the years, as families of seriously mentally ill clients saw how their sons and daughters slipped through the cracks of an uncoordinated system. The families organized a very effective chapter of the National Alliance for the Mentally Ill. Together with one of the providers, they began to push the other local providers and the state in the direction of creating a coordinated and case-managed community mental health system. This effort was aided by the fact that one of the leaders of the local chapter of the alliance was elected to the state house of representatives. Widespread dissatisfaction with the system was heightened by the state's ranking at or near the bottom in several surveys of the quality of state mental health care, and by a lawsuit that challenged the entire system of care in the state's largest county. There were many reasons for wanting to change the system. A major facilitating factor was the county government's decision to transfer its responsibilities and resources for services to the indigent mentally ill to the state department of health services. This was accomplished by intergovernmental agreement. The state became the only funding source in the system. This began a period of intense planning and bargaining over ways to restructure the community mental health system.

This effort led to a redesigned system of mental health care. The entity still contracted with local providers, but a new agency had also been created. It was a nonprofit, but it was created by the state to provide capitated, case-managed care that would allow the purchase of needed services from the existing set of mental health providers. Capitated and case-managed systems control funding through a prospective payment scheme, whereby a defined pool of funds is available on a per-capita basis to a fixed set of clients. Case management means that a client is assigned to a team that includes a clinical case manager, a doctor, a nurse, and a social worker. Services are purchased by the team according to the client's specific needs. Services under case management include the full continuum of care — medications, day treatment, crisis stabilization, transportation, residential services, outreach, mobile crisis services, and therapy.

With the creation of the case-management agency, there were two state-sponsored nonprofits. The entity was to provide overall guidance and control both in patient utilization of services and in purchase of services with public funds. The case-management agency was to determine exactly what services a client needed from local providers. This was a system with little public accountability built in. The entity was responsible to a division of the state department of health services. The case-management agency was responsible to the entity. The state-"owned" community mental health center was now responsible to the entity, as were all the other local providers. Thus all control over who got what services, what clients were served, and exactly how taxpayers' dollars were spent rested in the hands of an agency that was not directly responsive or responsible to public authority. This is the essence of the "hollow state."

The idea for a case-management agency to help coordinate services to the seriously mentally ill was developed by a cluster of key community mental health professionals and advocates, none of whom worked in state government. In fact, few worked for the state at all. State systems are typically redesigned when those who fund services are trying to "correct" the behavior of those who provide the services. Here, the situation was quite different: a group of service providers and advocates mobilized to redesign a system funded by the state.

All the local providers and the entity accepted the need for change, but various parties stalled and tried to use their influence with the state to moderate the extent of the changes. There was conflict over whether the system needed both an entity and a case-management agency. The original plan called for only one agency to do both case management and funding. This plan was abandoned, even though that action added to the administrative complexity of the system. There was opposition to case management from the local providers, given the uncertainty about how many services would be purchased by the teams from the case-management agency. In the past, the providers had been given contracts by the entity, to provide a certain amount of service to clients. The notion of the "retail" purchase of services by a case manager, as opposed to the "wholesale" purchase of a fixed number of units of service at the beginning of the fiscal year, created a great deal of uncertainty for the providers. The state budget contained funds specifically allocated for the purchase of services that the entity controlled, and the providers had little influence over the dissemination and administration of those funds. The entity, responsible for assessing, monitoring, and implementing, controlled the allocation of funds to provider agencies. It assumed all fiscal responsibility, as well as oversight of quality and utilization activities among the agencies it funded. The entity behaved much as a quasi-state or public organization would, but without public accountability. Other agencies in the system viewed it as risk-averse and were very worried about how its actions would be perceived by the press. Both the press and some legislators had made the lack of public accountability an issue.)

Entrepreneurship, Advocacy, and Evolution of the System

The need for case management of the seriously mentally ill population was the central issue in the redesign of the community mental health system. This issue did not just emerge, however. Case management emerged because of the activity of an entrepreneur, who focused attention on it as a mechanism for creating a more effective and responsive system of services. Policy entrepreneurs play key roles in decentralized service systems. They often forge informal links that bind the system (or at least parts of it) together, or they provide the energy and ideas to get the system to adopt innovations (Hull and Hjern, 1987; Milward and Laird, forthcoming; Roberts and King, 1991). The vocal and committed policy entrepreneur in this system had labored long and hard for a capitated and case-managed system while he was head of the mental health component of the county hospital. He worked with others in the system to get the state to fund two pilot programs, to test whether a case-managed system produced more beneficial outcomes than the existing system. He was a man of great energy who had standing in national mental health circles and with the state legislature. Through his formal and his informal connections, he was in a position to influence the implementation of a more humane and efficient mental health system in a state that had a tradition of neither. In so doing, he attempted to influence the reform of a fragmented system. One of his major achievements, for instance, was to play a key role in the founding of the local chapter of the National Alliance for the Mentally Ill. By acting as a vocal advocate for the mentally ill, however, he alienated many local providers, who sometimes took his criticisms of the system as personal attacks on their agencies.

This policy entrepreneur and the local chapter of the National Alliance for the Mentally Ill were the forces behind the creation of the new case-management agency. It was formed as a private nonprofit organization responsible for providing case-management services to the community's seriously mentally ill population. Unanswered questions about its funding, however, repeatedly altered the agency's scope of services.

The new agency had a stormy beginning. Several months after the agency was formed, the executive director resigned, followed two weeks later by the policy entrepreneur, who had left the county hospital to become the new agency's medical director. Both resignations ostensibly resulted from disagreements between the agency and its funders—the entity and, ultimately, the state department of health services.

The key question was whether a fully capitated model of funding would be utilized. The case-management agency argued that the system could realize this goal only if funding was directly linked to number of clients served. On the other side, the state submitted that the approximately $13 million budgeted for case-managed services was simply all that was available. Underlying this dispute was a disagreement over how many seriously mentally ill clients resided in the community. The state's estimate placed this population at roughly 1,600, while the case management agency's preliminary projections put this figure at between 2,200 and 3,500 (depending on the definition of serious mental illness). While state officials did revise their estimate of the population up to 1,800, they still maintained that the budget was set and could not be increased.

The agency "accepted" the state's estimate of 1,800 by limiting enrollment to that cap: the idea was to eventually take on all the local seriously mentally ill adults and place the onus on the state to come up with more funding. This forced the professional community to face the reality of who would be served by the case-management agency and who would not be served. At this point, the task became one of deciding which 1,800 clients the agency would initially serve. At the time when this list of clients was published, the other local providers were informed that the residual population was not slated to join the agency's list and thus would remain outside the case-managed, capitated system until the state provided more funding. This decision sent shock waves through the mental health community: the local providers, comparing their lists of clients with the case-management agency's list, realized that many of their clients were not "on the boat."

Since virtually all local mental health officials seemed to agree that the case-management agency's proper role was to provide and oversee services, and since it was generally agreed that bouncing individual clients from agency to agency was less than optimal, a major strategic decision on client load was made. In negotiations between the entity and the case-management agency, the agency agreed to take responsibility for the roughly 1,800 clients formally designated as seriously mentally ill while continuing to serve a substantially larger number.

Discussion

Our original question was "What does the 'hollow state' look like?" From our examination of this community mental health system, we can define hollowness as the degree to which government agencies are separated from their output. Aspects of hollowness involve the degree to which a government agency's work is contracted out to third parties, the degree of competition among the third parties for contracts, the degree of control exercised over third parties, the degree to which third parties are given power to run the system, the degree of coordination among the third parties, and the degree to which the performance of the third parties is evaluated.

Contracting

In the community mental health system explored in this chapter, the degree of contracting was very high. All treatment dollars came from the state to the entity, which then subcontracted with the providers and the case-management agency. The community mental health center's staff were state employees, and the center was "owned" by the state. In terms of treatment, however, all reimbursement came either from contracts with the entity or reimbursement for services provided to clients.

Competition for Contracts

Competition among likely contractors is central to the argument for privatization. Competition is the hidden hand that creates efficient allocation of resources in marketlike arrangements. In the market for mental health services in the community we examined, competition simply did not exist. The original contract with the entity was negotiated in 1985. Contracts between the local providers and the entity were negotiated every year. During the two years we observed the system, no contracts were terminated. The case-management agency was added to the list of contractors, and several other providers merged. The degree of competition over services among the local providers was difficult to determine. At the beginning of the case, there was some competition among the providers, since several offered similar services. The competition may have been less than it seemed, since the large size of the area and its ethnic diversity may have led to specialization by geography or ethnicity. In the redesign of the community mental health system, there seemed to be an attempt to keep the level of competition low by carving out specific niches for each of the local providers. This was true in regard to client intake, outpatient treatment, and the rest of the continuum of care. While the level of competition among the providers was eventually low, there was a great deal of conflict among the providers during the redesign of the system. That level of conflict decreased as the new system became operational.

Control

The degree of control exercised by the state department of health services was quite low. Since 1985, when the entity won the contract to provide mental health services to the county, there has still been no rebidding of the state's business. There was no attempt by the state department of health services to control the behavior of either the entity or the local providers except in the most general way. Control resided in no governmental hierarchy. There was indeterminate control in terms of both accountability and performance regarding the system's relationship to the state government. Cooperation and a weak form of control depended on a sense of professional norms, flowing from the fact that the providers dominated the system and wanted the system to work better than it had in the past (Provan and Milward, 1991; Weiss, 1990). The state and the nonprofit entity used their control of funds to influence the behavior of the local providers and the case-management agency, but the dependence was reciprocal. Neither the state nor the entity had the capacity to deliver either case management or treatment services.

Delegation

The degree of delegation of power to third parties was very high in this community mental health system. Elected and appointed public officials were simply absent from the system. It was a provider-dominated system. With public authority weak, there was a great deal of power in the hands of professionals in mental health. With no hierarchy, there was little general accountability to elected officials. Clients were represented in the system through the local chapter of the National Alliance for the Mentally Ill, and there were "public advocate" positions funded by the entity, but this representation also served the provider's interest in having an articulate group of advocates for increasing the level of funding for the system.

Coordination

The degree of coordination in the system was reasonably high. After the restructuring of the community mental health system, and with the addition of the case-management agency, the degree of coordination among the local providers increased as case management and capitation created incentives for coordination. Since the local providers were increasingly reimbursed for treatment provided to clients, this focused their attention on the range of services clients needed. The directors of the local agencies and the entity worked to develop differentiated roles for each of the providers. This served to decrease competition among the providers who had offered similar services.

Coordination of services is desired by most officials in mental health; this is the way in which the full continuum of care can be delivered to clients by multiple agencies, each of which provides some part of the service continuum. Those who observe professionally dominated service systems often notice another type of coordination: coordination among providers, against attempts by funders to cut their budgets. The one thing that tends to unite contentious groups in a policy domain is an external threat to their continued existence (Warren, Rose, and Bergunder, 1974).

In this system, there was a concerted attempt on the part of the entity, the case-management agency, and all the local providers to work together and present a united front in opposition to the state's attempt to cut the budget for mental health services or further redesign the system. The agencies now meet several times a month, and they have joined with local providers of drug, alcohol, and children's services and with general mental health care providers to create a coalition that lobbies for their needs with the state legislature.

Coordination is the touchstone of service provision in mental health, as in other human services areas. Since the 1960s, coordination has been sought by human services professionals because human services have always been delivered by multiple providers at the local level, whether local government agencies, nonprofits, or for-profit firms. The shared belief has been that efficiency and effectiveness flow from a coordinated system of services. Coordination appears inconsistent with the promotion of competition in contracting. Organizations that compete fiercely for contracts may find it difficult to lay that reality aside and cooperate. Whether coordination and competition are antithetical or not, the desire for both exists among advocates of privatization and nonprofit provision of human services.

Evaluation of Third Parties

The degree of performance evaluation was very low, close to nonexistent. There was no attempt by the state department of health services to monitor the performance of the local providers. The department of health services stated that it did not have the administrative capacity to engage in performance evaluation.

Hollow State and Hollow Corporation

We have presented an extended description of a community mental health system that, we believe, is similar to many other service delivery systems in a variety of different policy areas. The lack of service delivery capacity on the part of federal, state, or local government led us to label this type of system the "hollow state." The "hollow corporation" lacks production capacity — indeed, this is its chief design feature — but it retains responsibility for financial control, research and development, design, and marketing. The question we turn to now is to what extent the "hollow state" exhibits the same functions.

Financial Control

In this case, the state did exercise some control over finance of the system, through a series of contracts issued to the entity and then to the local providers. The state used persuasion and, on occasion, threats to try to influence the design of the system or the behavior of the agencies that comprised the system. The state could exert this influence through its control of most of the financing for the system. By contrast with the situation in the "hollow corporation," this financial control did not come from the specificity of the contracts with the provider agencies. To the extent that the state could exercise control, it came from informal intervention in the system, through control over scarce resources.

Government funding of nonprofit agencies shifts control from voluntary community boards to salaried employees. Government funding is often much greater than what a nonprofit has received in the past, and thus the nonprofit has a much greater need for professional management than before. The role of volunteers and community boards often decreases after government funding. Nonprofits also become tied to the state budget cycle and to legislative and bureaucratic politics. What emerges, over time, are organizations that are likely to be more tied to state politics than to the communities they serve (Lipsky and Smith, 1989–90; Smith, 1990). The result is that systems of this nature become "producer"-dominated. The network of directors, staff, and state officials come to see one another as the "principals" of the system.

In this case, the local chapter of the National Alliance for the Mentally Ill attempted to keep the system focused on the needs of the clients. This advocacy organization was necessary because government funding of nonprofits dampens the traditional mediating and advocacy role between client and government that nonprofits traditionally have played (Smith, 1990). The fact that the entity funded "advocate" positions is also evidence of this tendency.

Research and Development

A second function of "hollow" corporations is research and development. There was a functional equivalent here in the pilot programs that the policy entrepreneur persuaded the state to fund, to test the viability of the case-management approach. While the results were not clear, these pilot programs did provide the model and part of the justification for the adoption of the case-management approach by the system and the creation of the state-sponsored case-management agency. Research and development were different here than at Nike, where it is a corporate function; here, it was initiated and carried out at the local, not the state, level.

Marketing

Marketing is centrally controlled by "hollow" corporations, but this is not something that government does in usual circumstances. Government public affairs offices are very efficient at churning out justifications for actions and for increased funding, but marketing is foreign to government-funded service delivery systems. The reason is clear: these systems typically have inadequate funding. This was certainly true in this state, which ranked at or near the bottom in per-capita funding of mental health (Torrey, Wolfe and Flynn, 1988). In a poorly funded system, the incentive is not to market. The more the client load increases, the more services deteriorate. Here, the "discovery" of clients in excess of the expected number almost led to the collapse of the new system. Thus marketing is one area that differs greatly between sectors.

Design

In the "hollow" corporation, design is critical. If the corporation has no production capabilities, it must be very careful in devising specifications for what it wants to produce. This is precisely the problem confronting managers of the "hollow" state. In this case, the difference could not have been more striking. In the redesign of the system we examined, design came from the producers themselves. Case management was already a well-accepted method of mental health delivery nationally, but in the system we studied it was not the state but rather an entrepreneur within the system who was its champion (along with the group advocating for the rights and needs of the clients and their families). The entity system originally had been created to funnel money to the providers. The fact that the system had to be redesigned only five years later is an example of how top-down system design often fails to achieve its purposes.

The quality and quantity of services that the system was to produce were poorly specified. One feature that was missing in the state system of mental health care was the capacity to produce information that would allow the system to increase its level of performance. This lack may have been due to turnover in government, bureaucratic rigidity, or years of budget cuts that simply eroded the ability of governmental agencies to be effective. The state information system was useless to the community mental health system for purposes of management or evaluation, and so the entity, the case-management agency, and the local providers attempted to create a management information system for their own use.

What is so interesting about this case is that the state did not have the capacity to bring about system redesign, but the third parties did. Local learning did occur, and an interdependent set of providers, with the aid of an entrepreneur and local advocates, was able to bring significant change to the system. The case also raises a number of normative issues related to the impact of "hollow" service systems on citizens' capacity to influence public policy. The use of nonprofits to deliver taxpayer-provided public services loosens the connection between the citizen and the state, since nonprofits may be less responsive to public demands. From the perspective of the service provider, that is indeed one of a "hollow" system's virtues. The long-run effects on citizenship and on the willingness of taxpayers to support these systems are unclear. State funding and the state sponsoring of nonprofits may damage the mediating role that nonprofits play in buffering the citizen from the state. This is certainly true if the nonprofits begin behaving as if they were government agencies — risk-averse, bound by red tape, and more concerned with those who provide their funding than with their clients. Both issues — the effects of state funding, and insulation from citizen control — are important and will need both normative and empirical attention if we continue to use the "hollow state" to deliver publicly provided services.

Conclusions

What does the hollow state look like? We have tried to contrast it with the "hollow corporation." Much of the literature on public organizations concerns the differences between public and private organizations, and we have contrasted a community mental health system with Nike, which we took as the model for the "hollow corporation." Financial control, research and development, marketing, and design were the dimensions on which we compared the community mental health system to Nike.

If the variables that we identified as being associated with "hollowness" can be operationalized and measured, we can begin to determine how this quality varies across policy arenas, states, and nations and between levels of government. If this can be done, we can construct a model that relates the characteristics of "hollowness" to the set of dependent variables (efficiency, effectiveness, responsiveness, accountability, and equity) that are used to judge governmental performance. The payoff would be quite high, since we could move the debate over public or private provision of publicly funded services onto much more solid ground.

21

POLICY PLANNING AND THE DESIGN AND USE OF FORUMS, ARENAS, AND COURTS

John M. Bryson,
Barbara C. Crosby

*I*n today's shared-power, no-one-in-charge, interdependent world, public problems and issues spill over organizational and institutional boundaries. Many people are affected by problems like global warming, AIDS, homelessness, drug abuse, crime, growing poverty among children, and teen pregnancy, but no one person, group, or organization has the necessary power or authority to solve these problems. Instead, organizations and institutions must share objectives, resources, activities, power, or some of their authority in order to achieve collective gains or minimize losses (Bryson and Einsweiler, 1991).

Historically, the public administration, planning theory, and policy analysis literatures have paid particular attention to procedural approaches to formulating problems, developing policies, plans, or recommendations for addressing those problems, and overseeing implementation of approved solutions. In recent years, attention has focused directly on the various institutional contexts and settings within which procedural aspects of policy planning occur (Mandelbaum, 1985; Friend and Hickling, 1987; Lynn, 1987; Bryson, 1988; Healey, McNamara, Elson, and Doak, 1988; Brandl, 1988; Forester, 1989; Alexander, 1990; Eden and Radford, 1990; Krumholz and Forester, 1990). Our desire in this chapter is to build on these efforts so that we can all help planners and policy analysts more effectively address important public problems and issues that bridge organizational and institutional boundaries.

This chapter was originally a paper prepared for the National Public Management Research Conference sponsored by the Maxwell School at Syracuse University. An earlier version was presented at the Joint International Congress of the Association of Collegiate Schools of Planning and the Association of European Schools of Planning, Oxford, England, July 1991.

We present a descriptive framework that we think can help planners and policy analysts be more effective in shared-power, no-one-in-charge situations. The chapter is divided into several sections. We begin with an illustrative case example that we will draw on and elaborate throughout the chapter, to indicate how the framework might be used to understand and improve policy planning.

Next, we discuss public action and the three "dimensions" of power. We also identify three basic kinds of public policy–related actions.

After that, we show how policy-related action and underlying social structures are intimately linked. Then, combining the dimensions of power with the three basic kinds of public policy–related action, we develop a triply three-dimensional — and wholistic — conception of power. This wholistic conception of power allows us, in the three sections that follow, to describe in detail the principal settings and social practices associated with each type of policy-related action — namely, the design and use of forums, arenas, and courts. These settings form the structural basis for public policy–related action, and their design and use provide the principal ways in which planners and policy analysts can affect public policies or plans and their implementation.

In shared-power situations, public leaders, planners, and policy analysts rely on forums for discussion, arenas for policy making and implementation, and courts to manage residual disputes and enforce the underlying norms in the system. The design and use of these settings will have profound effects on how public issues are raised and resolved, as well as profound implications for how policy planning can most usefully be viewed. Indeed, for the purposes of this chapter, we define *policy planning* as the intentional design and use of forums, arenas, and courts to formulate and achieve desired policy outcomes.

The chapter's final section presents several conclusions. The framework helps make the point that in shared-power, no-one-in-charge settings, planners and policy analysts can have their biggest impact by paying attention indirectly and focusing on the ideas, rules, modes, media, and methods that link action and structure in forums, arenas, and courts. Fortunately, because the design and use of forums, arenas, and courts can be extremely complex, planners have innumerable opportunities to exert beneficial influence over both stability and change in social systems.

Creating the Twin Cities Metropolitan Council

The case we use throughout the chapter to illustrate our framework is the creation of the Twin Cities Metropolitan Council and its subsequent impact on the planning and coordination of regionally significant activities.

In the post–World War II era, the area surrounding the twin cities of Minneapolis and St. Paul underwent the same kind of rapid growth characteristic of many other U.S. urban centers at the time. An expanding population found employment in expanding commercial and industrial enterprises. New housing proliferated in the suburbs surrounding the two central cities, as burgeoning highway construction made formerly rural areas accessible to commuters.

By the 1960s, the growth had begun to tax the abilities of suburban officials to provide the services and amenities their constituents demanded. Lacking adequate sewer systems, many communities were plagued with overflowing septic tanks that polluted wells and waterways. Prime farmland and potential parkland were being gobbled up by subdivisions, while school districts complained of crowded classrooms and strained budgets.

Central-city officials, meanwhile, were trying to cope with another, related, set of problems. As the suburbs became attractive places to live, the central cities began to lose middle-income and upper-income families. Like other U.S. cities, Minneapolis and St. Paul increasingly became home to the poor, the elderly, and unskilled and semiskilled workers. The cities' property-tax bases were eroding, but demand for their services was growing.

In the mid 1960s, several leaders in the Minneapolis–St. Paul area were suggesting that some form of metropolitan government might be needed to handle the problems plaguing the Twin Cities area. Among them was Verne Johnson, director of the Citizens League, a "good government" group of business and civic leaders initially organized to focus on Minneapolis. Under his direction, the league moved increasingly to a metropolitan focus and began comprehensive studies of metropolitan problems. Another early advocate of the regional perspective was Ann Duff, an activist in the League of Women Voters and a resident of a western Minneapolis suburb. She believed something had to be done to ensure that metropolitan communities had enough tax revenues to educate their young people and provide other basic services, like health care and housing, to people in need.

Yet another early leader was Robert Einsweiler, head of planning for the Twin Cities Metropolitan Planning Commission (MPC). He realized that MPC, which had merely advisory status, should be superseded by an entity with more real authority over area development.

It was clear to these and other leaders and planners that each of the problems affecting the suburbs or inner cities was really a regional problem, and that the problems were all interrelated. Johnson, Duff, Einsweiler, and many others concluded that a new set of institutional arrangements was needed in the region. These leaders seemed to act implicitly in accord with the dynamics of our forums-arenas-courts framework as they sought to bring about those changes. In particular, they focused on how to use various forums, arenas, and courts in order to create the Metropolitan Council, which is itself a new set of forums, arenas, and courts designed to affect the planning and coordination of regionally significant development.

Public Action and the Dimensions of Power

Partly on the basis of work by Giddens (1979, 1984), we identify three basic kinds of public policy–related action: communication; decision making, particularly as it relates to policy adoption and implementation; and adjudication, or, more broadly, the management of residual conflicts and the enforcement of the underlying norms in the system. Each of these kinds of action is shaped—and biased—by three different dimensions of power (see Lukes, 1974; Clegg, 1989).

The first dimension of power is emphasized by the pluralists (Dahl, 1961), who argue that the power of public actors in the United States varies with issues, that there are several bases of power (such as wealth, status, knowledge, and skill), and that there is some substitutability among power bases. In other words, winners and losers vary by issue, and society is therefore pluralist rather than elitist. The pluralists focus on observable behavior (in our terms, communication, decision making, and adjudication), key issues, and interests (defined as policy preferences revealed by political participation).

In the second dimension, power is exercised more subtly, through manipulation of what comes up for decision and action. As Bachrach and Baratz (1962, 1963, 1971) note, people have power to the extent that they reinforce, consciously or unconsciously, barriers to the public airing of policy conflicts. Various ideas, rules, modes, media and methods are the principal barriers that bias attention toward some matters and away from others (Forester, 1989; Healey, McNamara, Elson, and Doak, 1988).

Bias in all organizations (Schattschneider, 1960) is due to asymmetrically distributed rules and resources (such as control over agendas) that create decision and "nondecision" categories, and "live" issues as opposed to what must remain, at least for a time, "potential" issues. In other words, bias has the effect of creating rules (broadly conceived) in power's second dimension, which "rule out" certain behaviors, which therefore will not be observed (Bryson and Crosby, 1989; Crenson, 1971; Gaventa, 1980; Bromiley, 1981).

The third dimension reveals an even subtler exercise of power: the shaping of felt needs, or even consciousness itself (Gaventa, 1980). Felt needs are deeply rooted in "bedrock" social, political, and economic structures. These structures provide the "generative" rules, resources, and transformation relations that allow human relations, organizations, and coalitions within and among organizations to exist in the first place (Giddens, 1979). The bedrock (or "deep") social, political, and economic structures of a society furnish the basis for a potential set of issues, conflicts, policy preferences, and decisions, all rooted in consciously or unconsciously felt needs, that public actors *may* address. In turn, the ideas, rules, modes, media, and methods of the second dimension influence the transformation of that potential set into *actual* issues, conflicts, policy preferences, and decisions addressed in the first dimension and into those items that remain in the second dimension as potential issues, covert conflicts, grievances, or "nondecisions" (Bryson and Crosby, 1989).

This three-dimensional view of power reveals how the biases embedded in "layered" structures of rules, resources, and transformation relations (in the second and third dimensions of power) may severely distort communication, policy making, policy implementation, and adjudication, so that some matters of importance are considered while others are not (Clegg, 1981). In particular, action carries with it the conscious and unconscious production and reproduction of these biases.

The Structural Base for Public Action

Within and among organizations, action is linked to rules, resources, and transformation relations (or the dimensions of power) primarily through the design and use of forums, arenas, and courts. Forums, arenas, and courts are the basic *social settings* that humans use in shared-power situations for communication, decision making, and adjudication, respectively. In these settings, human beings interactively draw on social structures or relationships (organizational and interorganizational rules, resources, and transformation relations) to *produce* instrumental effects (such as discussion papers, policy statements, or action plans) at the same time that they *reproduce* organizational and interorganizational social relations and structures. Reproduction, in this case implies "ongoing strengthening, altering, or weakening of those social relations without which the production of desired results (e.g., plans, reports, recommendations) would not be possible" (Forester, 1989, p. 71; see also Giddens, 1979). In other words, actors draw on rules, resources, and transformation relations, including social relations, to *create* action, which subsequently *recreates* the structures (rules, resources, and transformation relations) that permitted the action in the first place. Structures are therefore rules, resources, and transformation relations, organized as properties of social systems, and are characterized by "the absence of the subject" (Giddens, 1979). Our view of forums, arenas, and courts highlights the central role played by ideas, rules, modes, media, and methods in governing both the continuity and transformation of structures, and therefore the production and reproduction — or *structuration* — of social systems (Giddens, 1979).

An appreciation of structuration implies that planners can have their greatest influence over action and outcomes by focusing on the second dimension of power — that is, by strengthening, weakening, or altering the ideas, rules, modes, media, and methods that divide what is theoretically possible into what is actually possible and what is not.

In a shared-power world, planners are rarely able to prescribe actions and dictate terms to other actors. Similarly, planners are unlikely to be able to make significant changes in underlying "bedrock" social structures. Nevertheless, planners may be able to have a significant impact on the ideas, rules, modes, media, and methods used to link action with bedrock social structure — perhaps in part simply because other people may not pay as much attention to these matters. Influence over ideas, rules, modes, media, and methods in turn will have a major impact on what is up for discussion, decision, and control — and on what will remain in a sort of public policy "never-never land." In other words, to raise and resolve public problems constructively, planners must attend to human interaction that is empowered and influenced by rules, resources, and transformation relations; to institutional arrangements of rules, resources, and transformation relations; and to how human interaction and social structures are linked through ideas, rules, modes, media, and methods.

A Wholistic Approach to Power

A wholistic conception of power requires an understanding of how the three basic types of public policy–related action — communication, decision making and implementation, and adjudication — are connected to the three dimensions of power and how the types interact as part of recurrent social practices. In general, we agree with Giddens's view (1979, 1984), in which social practices are seen as the regular dynamics produced by the patterned interaction of human actors empowered and influenced by rules, resources, and transformation relations in specific situations. Social practices may be seen, then, as systems of interaction that have structural properties but are not themselves structures.

All social practices involve communication, decision making, and the sanctioning of conduct, at least to some extent, but that extent depends on the practice (see Healey, McNamara, Elson, and Doak, 1988). This leads us, in later sections of this chapter, to a more detailed discussion of the design and use of forums, arenas, and courts, practices that differentially emphasize the different kinds of policy-related action.

In order to apply the approach to actual situations, it is necessary to identify and examine those social practices principally associated with each type of policy-related action. We call the social practice that results principally in the creation and communication of meaning the *design and use of forums;* the social practice that results principally in policy or plan adoption and implementation the *design and use of arenas;* and the social practice that results principally in the normative regulation of conduct the *design and use of courts* (see Figure 21.1).

In other words, human beings engage in the creation and communication of meaning chiefly through a social practice — the design and use of forums. This process is shaped by what Giddens (1979, 1984) calls principles of "signification" — bedrock principles of language use, and basic ways of looking at the world. Human beings communicate in various settings by using interpretive schemes that draw on these principles.

Decision making for policy or plan adoption and implementation is shaped by aspects and principles of domination embodied in (or rationalized by) unequal distribution of generative rules, resources, and transformation relations (for example, social position, skills, intelligence, status, or money). Unequal distribution of rules and resources in turn generates individual or group capacities to make and implement policies. Human beings adopt and implement policies through the use of a particular social practice — the design and use of arenas.

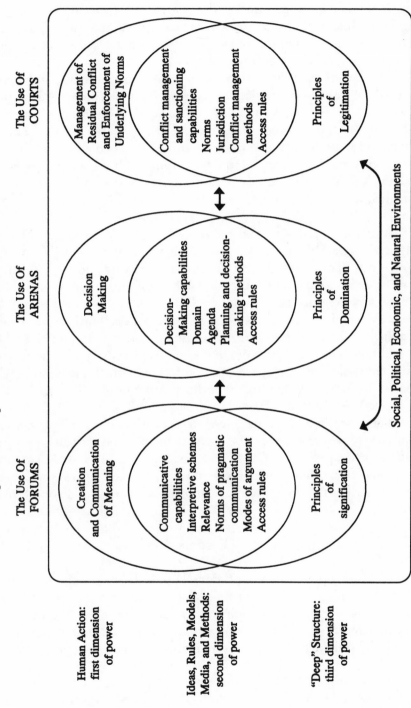

Figure 21.1. Triple Three-Dimensional View of Power.

The Use Of
FORUMS

The Use Of
ARENAS

The Use Of
COURTS

Creation
and Communication
of Meaning

Decision
Making

Management of
Residual Conflict
and Enforcement of
Underlying Norms

Communicative
capabilities
Interpretive schemes
Relevance
Norms of pragmatic
communication
Modes of argument
Access rules

Decision-
Making capabilities
Domain
Agenda
Planning and decision-
making methods
Access rules

Conflict management
and sanctioning
capabilities
Norms
Jurisdiction
Conflict management
methods
Access rules

Principles
of
signification

Principles
of
Domination

Principles
of
Legitimation

Social, Political, Economic, and Natural Environments

Human Action:
first dimension
of power

Ideas, Rules, Models,
Media, and Methods:
second dimension
of power

"Deep" Structure:
third dimension
of power

Finally, human beings engage in the normative regulation of conduct through another social practice—the design and use of courts. This process is made possible by the social principles of legitimation—that is, by bedrock moral or evaluative standards or logics. These standards or logics then generate the norms that people use to sanction conduct.

We have chosen the design and use of forums, arenas, and courts as labels for the three major social practices because the commonsense generic meanings of *forum, arena,* and *court* make them apt descriptors in singling out and understanding these practices in real-world situations. They also draw attention to the settings where meaning is created and communicated, where policies and plans are adopted and implemented, and where conduct is sanctioned. When these practices are referred to as the design and use of forums, arenas, and courts, one can more readily identify and analyze them.

Although the design and the use of forums, arenas, and courts are analytically separable, in reality these basic principles are in constant interaction. Thus, if one is to understand decision making and implementation, one must also understand the creation and communication of meaning and the normative regulation of conduct. Indeed, it is the interaction of these three basic practices that splits a society's potential decisions, issues, conflicts, and policy preferences into two sets—those that will be considered, and those that will not. The emphasis, of course, on each activity may vary greatly in different situations—indeed, to the point where it makes sense to use different labels for practices that highlight different kinds of policy-related action (see Healey, McNamara, Elson, and Doak, 1988).

Therefore, to summarize, in order to arrive at a triply three-dimensional view of power—that is, the capacity to *affect* and *effect* change—in real situations where power must be shared, one must locate the pertinent forums, arenas, and courts and understand and explain their operation. The next section describes the design and use of forums, arenas, and courts in more detail.

Forums

In today's society, forums abound. For example, there are discussion groups and brainstorming sessions; formal debates, public hearings, task forces, and conferences; newspapers, television, and radio; plays and other forms of dramatization; and popular and professional journals. Forums may be place-bound (public hearings) or non–place-bound (newspapers, television, radio).

In the case of the Twin Cities Metropolitan Council, Verne Johnson, Ann Duff, Robert Einsweiler, and others organized multiple forums in the mid 1960s, to understand and delineate the problems affecting the metropolitan area and to develop solutions to the problems. Johnson's Citizens League organized task forces that produced study after study. Duff chaired the newly created Council of Metropolitan Leagues of Women Voters, which studied and discussed problems like water pollution.

Beginning in 1962, the Metropolitan Planning Commission undertook the Joint Program for Land Use and Transportation, funded in part by the federal government. The initial forums, organized by Einsweiler and his staff, brought together representatives of Minneapolis and St. Paul; state, local, and federal highway officials; housing officials; and MPC staff, to discuss public problems resulting from urban growth in the Twin Cities area. Those discussions led to several reports demonstrating that the essentials of high-quality urban living — affordable housing and reliable transportation — would be in short supply if current development patterns and practices continued.

By late 1965, Joint Program participants were focusing on recommendations for minimizing the problems they had identified. At this stage, the program participants worked with the Elected Officials Review Committee (consisting of about three hundred elected officials from throughout the metropolitan area) and the citizen advisory committee (comprising about one hundred people).

Other groups sponsoring forums on metropolitan problems were the Upper Midwest Research and Development Council, chambers of commerce, and organizations of local officials. The forums facilitated networking because of their overlapping membership; that is, many participants in one group's forums were often invited to the other groups' forums. Eventually, most of the groups sponsoring the forums effectively became a coalition that advocated specific actions in the legislative arena.

Another important forum was the evening daily newspaper in Minneapolis. In the fall of 1965, Ted Kolderie, an editorial writer for the paper, wrote a series of articles emphasizing the inability of local governments to cope with the problems of rapid growth. He also reported a growing consensus in the Twin Cities area that some kind of areawide agency should be established to handle genuinely areawide problems — sewage disposal, water supply, roads and transit, and other issues (Kolderie, 1965).

What forums do is link speakers and audiences — through discussion, debate, and deliberation — to create and communicate meaning. Forums distribute and redistribute access to the creation and communication of meaning and thereby help maintain or change symbolic orders and modes of discourse.

How this happens becomes clearer when we apply the three-dimensional view of human action to the use of forums. In the first dimension (action), people use symbols to discuss, debate, and deliberate various issues. Their ostensible goal (desired outcome) is to advance their views and create shared meaning (and perhaps shared values) in the minds of the relevant publics around a policy issue. In the third dimension are the basic signification principles ("bedrock" signification structures) — the requirement of a speaker and an audience (of at least one), plus an at least partly shared set of linguistic rules and resources, as well as one or more basic world views.

The second dimension consists of the ideas, rules, modes, media, and methods used to link the other two dimensions. The most important ideas, rules, modes, media, and methods involve communicative capability, interpretive schemes, relevance, norms of pragmatic communication, modes of argument, and access rules. Each will now be discussed in turn.

Communicative capability is simply the capacity to create and communicate meaning. That capability may include, for example, rhetorical skill, the ability to use various print and electronic media, or the potential to pull together a supportive, chanting crowd on a moment's notice.

Organizers of the forums that laid the foundation for establishing the Metropolitan Council clearly had strong communicative capacity. Johnson, Duff, Einsweiler, and others had long experience in organizing task forces and committees and producing and publicizing reports at critical junctures. Their positional status also gave them increased access to the mass media.

Interpretive schemes (Schutz, 1967) are intersubjective organizing frameworks that we humans use to structure the cognition, interpretation, or understanding of events in ways that are meaningful and that allow us to articulate and evaluate elements of those schemes as the desired values or interests behind our practical communication (Bolan, 1980; Bartunek, 1988; Wildavsky, 1987). These schemes include the beliefs, expectations, and rules through which we interpret our personal experience and the social knowledge we receive. Interpretation is thus based on our own experience and on our knowledge of the experiences of others. An individual's set of interpretive schemes is structured by a set of "relevances" determined by his or her concerns (Schutz, 1967; Bernstein, 1976).

Inside a forum, competing, conflicting, or contradictory interpretive schemes must be at least partly mediated, as a necessary condition for the emergence of some sort of concerted action. Norms of relevance and of pragmatic communication, as well as modes of argumentation and access rules, play crucial roles in mediating among incompatible interpretive schemes.

As we have already noted, there is a personal aspect to relevance, but there is also a clearly social aspect, since particular forums are usually not open to the discussion of every topic. Instead, discussion must be germane to the occasion prompting the use of the forum.

In the forums leading to creation of the Metropolitan Council, a number of interpretive schemes dominated the discussion:

1. *"One community."* The believers in this interpretive scheme argued that the major problems of any one Twin Cities community could not be solved without attention to all communities in the seven-county region, understood as constituting an economic unit.
2. *"Accountability."* In a democracy, government must be accountable to "the people" or to some elected body. Many advocates of forming the Metropolitan Council pointed out that the Twin Cities area already had regional government in the form of its various single-purpose districts,

agencies and compacts. The problem was that these entities were largely independent, and their policy making was hidden from public view.

3. *"More government is not the answer."* This scheme was adopted by suburban mayors who feared that the state legislature would respond to regional problems by creating more independent service districts like the one already in charge of airports and sewage disposal. The people who promoted this scheme tended to promote county cooperation, or a slightly strengthened MPC, as the solution to areawide problems.

4. *"Local government is best."* Government should be kept as close to "the people" as possible: the bigger and more removed government becomes, the more it endangers citizens' rights and infringes on their freedom. In keeping with this theme, those who wanted a stronger regional governance mechanism promoted their proposals as a way of strengthening local government and protecting it from the whims of state and national government.

5. *"Government and market failures."* The adherents of this scheme emphasized that market-driven growth in the Twin Cities after World War II had brought some undesirable side effects. Most of these people were not against the market or against growth but rather against disorderly, disruptive growth that excessively burdened public services and threatened the quality of the Twin Cities environment. It was also clear to these people that local governments, separately or together, were unable to deal with regional problems, especially sewage disposal.

In addition to relying on interpretive schemes, people presume that norms of pragmatic communication will be met in communicative interactions (Habermas, 1979; Forester, 1989). Forester, drawing on the work of Habermas, suggests that these norms lead to four practical criteria for judging speech aimed at influencing subsequent action: "In every interaction, speakers may be expected to speak more or less (1) comprehensibly, (2) sincerely, (3) appropriately or legitimately in the context at hand, and (4) accurately. In every interaction, too, a listener's subsequent action depends in part on how these same four criteria are satisfied" (p. 36). Social action is therefore predicated on communication that is comprehensible, sincere, legitimate and accurate. When these criteria are violated, listeners feel confusion, distrust, lack of consent and disbelief or, alternatively, "puzzlement, mistrust, anger and disbelief" (Forester, 1989, p. 280).

Generally, the spokespeople for groups advocating new governance arrangements for the Twin Cities were likely to be viewed as having legitimate and sincere concerns about metropolitan problems, by virtue of their organizational affiliations and status. Moreover, their descriptions of these problems probably matched the experiences of their listeners, who were living with the problems.

Argumentation is another important aspect of the mediation of differing interpretive schemes aimed at the creation of at least partially shared meaning and values in forums. Dunn (1981, pp. 40-43), drawing on the work of Toulmin (1958) and Freeley (1976), contends that policy arguments (arguments related to decisions, issues, conflicts, or policy preferences) have several elements:

- Policy-relevant information
- A policy claim, which is the conclusion of a policy argument
- A warrant, which is an assumption permitting the move from information to claim
- The backing for a warrant, which consists of additional assumptions or arguments in support of the warrant (often based on scientific laws, the authority of experts, or ethical or moral principles)
- A rebuttal, or a second conclusion, assumption, or argument, that indicates the conditions under which the original claim is unacceptable or in need of modification
- A qualifier, which expresses the degree to which the arguer is certain about the policy claim

The design and use of forums will influence which information is offered, which claims (along with which rebuttals) will be accepted on the basis of which warrants and backing, and how much weight will be given to the qualifiers (see also Bozeman, 1986; Bozeman and Landsbergen, 1989).

Perhaps the most important mode of forum-based argumentation leading to creation of the Metropolitan Council was the plethora of reports issued by the organizations that sponsored the forums. These reports contained a wealth of policy-relevant information supporting policy claims. The reports often included alternative ways of viewing the problems and solutions under discussion; but, cumulatively, they steered policy makers and interested citizens toward consensus and decision.

Finally, rules governing access to participation in forums strongly influence who says what, where, when, why, and how, and who listens. In so doing, they strongly influence which decisions, conflicts, issues, and policy preferences are discussed and which are not. For example, having the more senior people in a meeting talk first may inhibit discussion by junior people, or forcing people to talk only about "the issue at hand" may make it difficult to redefine the issue. But the most powerful rules are those that cause people to be absent from the discussion. For example, holding meetings in places or at times or at a cost that make attendance by interested parties difficult or impossible can be expected to alter the resulting discussions, debates, or deliberation by altering the set of persons among whom communication will develop.

In the forums debating the need for new governance mechanisms in the Twin Cities, access was by invitation. A relatively elite group of people (business leaders, planners, Citizens League members, and local officials) was invited to attend the organized forums and informal strategy sessions in which creation of the Metropolitan Council was discussed. The forum organizers also involved legislators, either by inviting them to the forums or by sending them copies of the reports prepared in conjunction with the forums. The debate about regional governance was carried on essentially by people whose jobs compelled them to spend time on regional issues, or whose jobs left them time for civic activities. One result was that the forum participants probably reached consensus on their general direction more easily than they would have done if more diverse groups had been included.

In sum, the design and use of forums in particular circumstances does two things. First, it establishes the structural (collective) basis of a potential list of decisions, issues, conflicts, and policy preferences that may be discussed, debated, or deliberated. Second, it mediates the transformation of that list into a list of the actual decisions, issues, conflicts, and policy preferences that will be addressed and a list of those that will not be discussed.

In the case of the Metropolitan Council, the potential list of decisions, issues, conflicts, and policy preferences resulting from the design and use of forums excluded any consideration of assigning sole responsibility for resolving area problems to state government. Also excluded was the possibility of doing nothing. The actual decisions, issues, conflicts, and policy preferences discussed all included some role for federal, state, and local government, as well as for nongovernment groups.

Arenas

In 1967, the partisans in the debate over metropolitan government focused their energies on the legislative arena—in this case, the Minnesota state legislature. They urged the legislature to create an elected metropolitan council that would guide regional development and oversee regional services.

Arenas distribute and redistribute access to participation in policy making and implementation and thereby help maintain or change political and economic relations (see Friend, Laffin, and Norris, 1981; Mintzberg, 1985). Examples of arenas are legislatures; city councils; corporate executive committees and boards of directors; the decision-making mechanisms of public bureaucracies, nonprofit organizations, and interorganizational networks; and various markets. Arenas may be place-bound (legislatures), or non–place-bound (mail-order markets).

There are arenas that are primarily political and those that are principally economic. The market is the basic form of economic arena. Deciding what to leave inside and outside of markets is a basic determinant of what happens subsequently in most societies (Lindblom, 1977; Wildavsky, 1979; Bryson, 1984; Giddens, 1984; Williamson, 1985).

In the first dimension of an arena, actors interact as they use their capabilities to obtain desired outcomes—that is, preferred policies and their implementation. Policy making in arenas characteristically involves the establishment of rules, laws, norms, principles, policies, standards, or prices that apply generally to a specified population or category of actions. In addition, plans, programs, budgets, or particular recommended actions may be adopted.

The basic structure, or third dimension, of an arena is a policy maker and at least one other participant. The policy maker must be able to affect a shared resource base that makes policy making necessary and possible. The ideas, rules, modes, media, and methods (second dimension) used to link action with the basic structure include decision-making capabilities; domains; agendas; planning, budgeting, decision making, and implementation methods; and rules governing access to participation in the arenas.

The decision-making capabilities that an actor has available to influence a sequence of policy-related interactions depend on the rules and resources that the actor can use and mobilize. These capabilities may range from verbal skill to the ability to hire and fire to the capacity to use a computer to the threat of physical violence. *Capability* refers, in other words, to an actor's potential to affect outcomes by drawing on rules, resources, and transformation relations that offer any kind of advantage. Decision making refers to the actual application of some or all of these advantages in interaction. Different capabilities held by differing actors will strongly influence which decisions, issues, conflicts, and policy preferences "count" in particular arenas and which ones do not.

In the legislative arena, legislators themselves have the greatest potential to directly affect outcomes. Some legislators, however, by virtue of personal skills or position, have considerably more capability than others to affect outcomes. In the 1967 Minnesota state legislature, an extremely powerful rural senator was able to thwart fellow legislators whose stance on metropolitan governance reflected the consensus developed in the forums sponsored by the Citizens League, MPC, the League of Women Voters, and others. While two legislators sponsored legislation that would establish an elected council with operating control over regional services, the rural senator introduced a bill that would create an appointed council that merely coordinated regional services. He controlled the committee to which the council legislation was assigned, and so his bill became the heart of the law that eventually was passed.

Domains, agendas, planning, budgeting, and decision-making and implementation methods help account for how differing, contesting, or conflicting capabilities in arenas are at least partially mediated. Further, rules governing access to participation in arenas strongly influence which persons, groups, organizations, and capabilities are admitted to an arena and thus influence which conflicts, issues, and policy preferences will be considered in the process of policy making and implementation and which ones will not.

The term *domain* refers to the spatial and substantive extent of an arena's policy-making and implementation authority. Planning, budgeting, and decision-making and implementation methods are the rules used to govern the process of putting together policies and plans, making decisions, and implementing them. Selection of methods constitutes, therefore, some of the most important action in any arena, since different methods favor different actors' capabilities and purposes (see Friend, Laffin, and Norris, 1981).

In the case of the Metropolitan Council, the legislature's domain included the Twin Cities area and the establishment of governing structures for that area. Perhaps the most important legislative method resorted to in the case was the use of the committee system to debate and vote on policy proposals. The committee system allowed a powerful senator to exert considerable control over the substance of the act establishing the Metropolitan Council.

Because time is a limited resource, agendas are a crucial mediator among competing capabilities. Agendas consist of general and recurring problems (the systemic or public agenda), as well as those currently under serious consideration by authoritative decision makers (the formal agenda) (see Cobb and Elder, 1972). Only capabilities applicable to dealing with agenda items become relevant. Furthermore, the kind of agenda item, and its order on the agenda, will differentially favor the relevant capabilities of competing actors or coalitions (Riker, 1986). Agendas are composed of issues. An issue is a public problem with at least one solution attached that has pros and cons from the standpoints of various stakeholders. In other words, an issue represents a point of controversy between two or more actors over procedural or substantive matters involving the distribution of resources (Cobb and Elder, 1972). The way an issue is framed—and here arenas are clearly linked to forums—will dramatically affect coalition formation (Riker, 1986).

To claim a place on the legislative agenda, the advocates of metropolitan governance developed a compelling, integrated picture of public problems and proposed solutions backed by considerable consensus among interested groups. The advocates emphasized the urgency of the problems and highlighted the likelihood that the federal government would impose its own partial solutions if state government failed to act. Rules permitting testimony and lobbying by outside groups allowed the advocates of regional governance access to legislative deliberations. Especially influential were the business leaders who testified and lobbied on behalf of creating the Metropolitan Council.

The rules governing access to participation in arenas strongly influence who decides what, where, when, why, and how. Access may be based on formal rules, position, precedent, reputation, financial resources, rhetorical skill, or other criteria. Regardless of the particular rules, the inclusion of some actors and the exclusion of others can be expected to affect what gets on the formal agenda and, later, which decisions are made on which issues, conflicts, and policy preferences.

In 1966, legislative reapportionment changed the legislative actors, ensuring that the advocates of metropolitan governance would get at least some of what they wanted. In the early 1960s, when rural legislators were

firmly in charge, the legislature went into gridlock over every proposed solution to metropolitan problems. The 1966 reapportionment aligned representation more closely with population, thus increasing the number of metro-
politan-area legislators and loosening the domination of rural politicians.

Most societies use rules to govern access and establish hierarchies within
arenas, reserving more global decision making for those nearer the top. Procedures for appealing decisions to higher-level arenas are also usually established. The rules of access and of appeal are basic methods of hierarchical
political management, allowing those farther up the hierarchy to exercise
greater power than those below. In the case of the Metropolitan Council,
local governments on their own could not establish regional agencies or binding cooperative arrangements; the state legislature had to authorize such
structures.

To summarize, the design and use of arenas in concrete situations
does two things. First, it establishes the structural, or collective, basis for
a set of potential policies, plans, programs, decisions, budgets, and implementation actions. Second, it transforms that list into the list of actual policies,
plans, programs, decisions, budgets, and implementation actions that will
be dealt with and the list of those that will not.

In this case, the state legislature considered basically two sets of potential policies, plans, programs, decisions, budgets, and implementation actions. Both sets would result in new institutional arrangements for governing metropolitan development. One set would create an elected council with
operating control over regional services. The other would create an appointed
council that would coordinate metropolitan services. The actual policies, programs, decisions, budgets, and implementation actions were contained in
legislation that combined elements of both sets and that built in opportunities for future strengthening of the council. The final bill also gave the council
limited taxing power.

The council was authorized to review long-term comprehensive plans
of the various governmental units in the Twin Cities area if the plans had
areawide effects, multicommunity effects, or substantial effects on metropolitan development. The new council could also suspend the plans of metropolitan agencies if the plans were inconsistent with the council's development
policies. Moreover, the legislature directed the council to prepare reports
(including legislative recommendations) on air and water pollution, parks
and open space, sewage disposal, taxation, assessment practices, storm
drainage, and consolidation of local services.

By creating the Metropolitan Council and assigning it these tasks, the
legislative arena, in effect, established a new forum for discussing metropolitan
issues, a new arena for making some decisions about metropolitan development, and a new court for resolving conflicts among local governments,
among metropolitan service agencies, and between metropolitan and local
interests.

Courts

Courts are used to judge or evaluate conduct or decisions in relation to laws or norms, usually in order to settle disputes. Courts are associated with the organization of laws (or norms, principles, policies, rules, standards, criteria, or decisions) and modes of sanctioning (that is, ways of allowing some kinds of conduct but not others). Courts distribute and redistribute access to legitimacy and therefore help maintain or change laws or other modes of sanctioning conduct.

Courts may be formal or informal. Formal courts include the Supreme Court, military tribunals, and local traffic courts. The most important informal court is the "court of public opinion." Courts that fall between the formal courts and the informal court of public opinion include regulatory bodies hearing differing views before issuing or changing regulations; professional licensing bodies involved in disciplinary hearings; deans' offices resolving disputes between college departments or individual professors; binding arbitration; special court-appointed masters dealing with individual cases as part of a class-action settlement; and the host of various alternative dispute-resolution mechanisms that are now receiving serious attention (where these alternatives, such as third-party mediation of differences, are seen as preferable to the use of formal courts). In each example, the emphasis is on conflict resolution through judging or evaluating decisions or conduct in relation to laws or norms, not on the basis of communication or policy making (although each of these is present). The use of courts may or may not be confined to particular places. The "court of public opinion," for example, is not a place-bound construct.

The principal activity (first dimension) in courts is moral evaluation and sanctioning of conduct, especially through conflict management. The disputes that are settled are typically "residual"—that is, they are left over after arenas have established policies and made decisions, or they cannot be handled, for some reason, by regular political or economic arenas. The activity of courts either affirms or modifies policies and/or the underlying norms in the system. The basic structure (third dimension) of courts is two disputants plus a third party to help them resolve their dispute, along with at least partially shared norms to govern resolution of the dispute.

Action and structure are linked through the mediation of conflict management and sanctioning capabilities, norms, jurisdiction, methods of conflict management, and access rules (second dimension). Each will be discussed in turn, with examples from the Metropolitan Council case.

The phrase *conflict resolution and sanctioning capabilities* refers to the capacities that actors bring to courts to engage in conflict resolution or the sanctioning of conduct. For example, the Metropolitan Council was assigned responsibility for regional governance in the Minneapolis–St. Paul area, yet many other governing units within the region exercise authority over limited areas. Partly because the council's domain overlaps with that of so many other policy-making bodies, it has been necessary for some public body or official to resolve conflicts over whose policies or decisions will prevail. In some cases, the council itself has played the role of court. In others, the formal court system, the legislature, or the state attorney general has handled the conflict. In other words, differing actors have had differing capabilities to resolve conflicts over domain.

Norms, in the broadest sense, are the standards against which, or with which, conflicts are resolved. These norms may be formal (legal due-process rules) or informal (typical norms of etiquette or fairness). For example, Minnesota courts have reconciled the conflict between personal property rights and government authority over regional development by permitting local governments to enact reasonable development controls as long as due process is observed.

The term *jurisdiction* denotes the spatial and substantive extent of a court's authority to interpret and apply norms in resolving conflicts. For example, the Metropolitan Council was given review power over federal grant applications from local governments in the council's region. The council then used this jurisdiction to resolve conflicts between local government authority and metropolitan authority.

Methods of conflict management govern the process of conflict management in specific cases. The methods significantly affect the outcomes of the process, since they sanction some conduct and decisions and rule out others (see Filley, 1975; Fisher and Ury, 1981; Susskind and Cruikshank, 1987; Fisher and Brown, 1988; Gray, 1989). Furthermore, since methods of conflict management differ in the manner and extent to which they invoke or refer to specific norms, they also differ in their efficacy as methods of social control. The selection of methods, therefore, is one of the more important actions in any court setting, since different methods will favor different actors' objectives.

Standard methods of conflict resolution include use of a go-between, mediation, arbitration, and substitution of law and office for consent, which has become the conventional courtroom method in the United States. The methods differ in the extent to which they rely on consent or coercion, on the one hand, and on nondichotomous or dichotomous solutions, on the other. In nondichotomous solutions, each party gets something; in dichotomous solutions, the "winner takes all" (Shapiro, 1975, 1981).

Formal courts try in several ways to avoid the instabilities and difficulties of coercive, dichotomous solutions. The first way is simply to avoid dichotomous solutions, principally by converting disputes over something that is indivisible (such as injury, trespass, or breach of contract) into something that is divisible (chiefly money), and by converting disputes over legal right or wrong into disputes over the "balancing of equities" (Shapiro, 1975, p. 228). Courts can also channel the bulk of conflict in legal cases into negotiations between the disputants, who are threatened with eventual formal court action if the negotiations fail. The instruments for such negotiations (mediation or arbitration procedures) are often built in to legally binding contracts between the parties (Williamson, 1985). Another solution is to give the losing party several channels of appeal. The Metropolitan Council, for example, had the authority to overrule local land-use plans that conflicted with council policies, but local governments could appeal the council's decision to the state courts. Finally, courts usually rely on the parties themselves to enforce the terms of the settlement. Courts typically have limited capabilities to monitor compliance with their rulings, and they reintervene to ensure compliance only at the request of one of the parties (Shapiro, 1975).

Finally, rules governing access to participation in courts strongly influence which residual conflicts will be resolved according to which norms, and therefore which actions—and especially which decisions and policy preferences—will be allowed and which will not. Access may be based on evidence of rule violation or demonstrated injury; on formal rules (including rules of appeal); on position, precedent, custom, and financial resources; or on some other criterion. Regardless of the particular rules, the inclusion of some actors and the exclusion of others will strongly influence which disputes get raised and resolved, and who will benefit from the process and who will not.

When the Metropolitan Council acts as a court, resolving conflicts between its own authority and local authority, the local officials and citizens advocating the triumph of local authority do have access to the court, but it is naturally outweighed by the access of the council members themselves and their staff members. A similar imbalance of access occurs when the council acts as a court resolving conflicts between its own authority and that of other regional agencies.

In sum, as with forums and arenas, the design and use of courts in particular circumstances does two things. First, it creates a potential list of residual conflicts that may be raised and resolved and actions that may be condoned. Secondly, it transforms that list into the list of actual conflicts that are addressed and actions that are morally sanctioned and the list of those that are not.

In the Metropolitan Council case, state courts resolved conflicts among metropolitan authority, the state legislature's authority, local government authority, and individual rights. The state courts also sanctioned and thereby legitimized the council's actions.

Before leaving our discussion of courts, we must say more about their role as general mechanisms of social control. We must discuss the role of the courts *beyond* resolution of particular residual disputes. The courts serve as general mechanisms of social control principally because conflict management almost invariably relies on the norms generally held by society at large (or, in the case of intraorganizational conflict resolution, by particular organizations within society). The use of such norms to govern disputes reproduces social control on the basis of those norms. The link between courts and general social control becomes even clearer with the substitution of law and office for consent, since judging is an extension of sovereignty, and since the judge is responsible for enforcing constitutions, legislation, or precedents, instead of the norms originated by the disputants (Shapiro, 1975).

Social control is also a product of the use of more formal courts, because these courts make supplementary laws, typically in accord with more general rules. Judges thereby become agents of social control for more distant authorities. Judging in all societies thus tends to be associated with sovereignty because of its potential for social control and lawmaking. In other words, no sovereign power is likely to tolerate a fully independent judiciary.

Appeal procedures are also a method of hierarchical social control. The availability of appeal helps stabilize the system by not straining the logic and structure of any single court. In other words, the possibility of appeal tells the loser that he or she may always try another court and thus need not contemplate changing the system. Procedures for moving through the appeals hierarchy also allow judicial and political authorities time to explore the implications of basic legal changes that may be mandated by "final" rulings of the highest courts. The use of appeal procedures thus allows central political authorities to do two things: monitor the operations of lower courts, to enforce compliance and uniformity throughout the system of laws; and prepare for changes as cases work their way through the system. Since the chain of appeal typically ends with the chief political authorities, appeal can be seen as a means of centralized political control and change.

Conclusions

The design and use of forums, arenas, and courts is the principal social practice that planners (broadly conceived) can use to raise and resolve public issues in a shared-power world. Forums are used for discussion, arenas for decision making, and courts for the management of residual conflicts and enforcement of the underlying norms of the system.

In working to establish the Metropolitan Council, leaders and planners demonstrated shrewd understanding of how to design and use forums, arenas, and courts effectively. They used forums to develop a regional consensus on important problems and desired solutions, so that when they moved to the legislative arena some form of regional government was a foregone conclusion; the only real debate was over what form that government would take. The legislature crafted new institutional arrangements—that is, forums, arenas, and courts—that would withstand court challenges and provide both stability and opportunities for change through the years. Those arrangements and the council's developmental framework (its basic-policies plan) have been used to guide and coordinate regionally significant development in the Twin Cities area ever since. Further, Metropolitan Council leaders and planners have continuously advised the legislature on proposed alterations to the design and use of council forums, arenas, and courts, to promote achievement of particular desired outcomes.

Several conclusions can be drawn from our discussion of power and the design and use of forums, arenas, and courts. The first, and perhaps most distressing, conclusion is that social life can be quite complicated. An awful lot is going on, particularly in complex, shared-power situations. Furthermore, what one sees on the surface is not the only thing going on — and very well may not be the most important thing. Underlying ideas, rules, modes, media, methods, and "bedrock" social structures strongly influence what becomes observable action.

Second, the very complicatedness of social life — and of forums, arenas, and courts in particular — makes change quite possible. Forums, arenas, and courts are almost always at least partially amenable to design, and the design elements are numerous. Therefore, planners can and must pay attention to these elements, because they are the basic levers of change in situations where no one is fully in charge. In addition to the design of individual forums, arenas, and courts, planners should also pay attention to separations among (and sequencing of) forums, arenas, and courts. Different outcomes are likely to emerge from different separations and sequences. For example, planners often bemoan their lack of access to decision-making arenas, but the Metropolitan Council case indicates that planners should not underestimate the power that flows from the ability to *design* and *use* forums. Indeed, to carry the argument farther, planners usually gain leverage through their ability to organize forums that no *one* group can dominate. The possibilities are thereby enhanced for the emergence of a collective interest or a vision that transcends narrow partisan interests. Once a collective vision emerges, it can have a profound impact on subsequent decision making in arenas, or on conflict management in courts (Bryson and Crosby, 1989).

Third, planners can have their greatest influence over action and outcomes by strengthening, weakening, or altering the ideas, rules, modes, media, and methods that divide what is theoretically possible into what is actually done and what is not. Figuring out what to do in particular circumstances involves attention to social interactions and to institutional arrangements, as well as to how they are linked through the design and use of forums, arenas, and courts. Essentially, this means that planning in shared-power situations involves influencing action and outcomes indirectly. Planning by indirection, however, certainly does not mean that planning and planners are without influence. For example, the work of Friend and Hickling (1987), Bryson (1988), Eden and Radford (1990), and Nutt and Backoff (1992) indicates that enormous power can be derived from creative and wise use of planning-process methods, a traditional focus of planning theory. Further, planning by indirection does not mean planning *without* direction. Indeed, the emergence of a shared-power world — in which what is acceptable to all, rather than to just the few, may prevail — holds considerable promise for pursuit of the values that public planners typically hold dear, such as efficiency, equity, liberty, and justice. We hope so, and we also believe that there are existing or imaginable forums, arenas, and courts that will favor those values, and that planners can help design and use those settings in such a way that virtuous outcomes emerge (Stone, 1988; Krumholz and Forester, 1990; Bryson and Ring, 1990; Bryson and Crosby, 1989).

Fourth, planners should search for forum, arena, and court designs that result in the continuous production of desirable outcomes, at the same time that the designs are amenable to desirable changes in their constituting elements. This will be no easy task, but the world is crying out for new sets of forums, arenas, and courts that can help us address the serious public problems that afflict us. The renewed emphasis on institutions in economics (Williamson, 1985; Ostrom, 1990), political science (Wildavsky, 1979, 1987; Kaufman, 1990), sociology (Sarason, 1972; Giddens, 1984), public policy (Lynn, 1987; Brandl, 1988; Bryson and Ring, 1990) and planning itself (Healey, McNamara, Elson, and Doak, 1988; Alexander, 1990; Bolan, 1991) offers considerable promise for improving our understanding of how to design better forums, arenas, and courts. We hope that the framework offered in this chapter is a useful contribution to that effort.

22

PUBLIC MANAGEMENT
IN THE FUTURE:
POST-ORTHODOXY AND
ORGANIZATION DESIGN

Mark A. Emmert,
Michael Crow,
R. F. Shangraw, Jr.

Of all the theories and explanations of behavior in the public sector, few have proved so robust and accurate as the notion of incrementalism. Change in public policy, budgets, and organizations comes through incremental reaction to the politics or economics of the moment. We have not mastered the art of anticipating the future and making large-scale adjustments accordingly. Rather, we tend to look at the past and accept it as prelude to the future. Our organization structures and theories of public management reflect marginal adjustments made to existing formulations. Efforts at organizational learning notwithstanding (Etheridge, 1985), rarely do either practitioners or scholars look to projections about the future for guidance in building theories or organizations. The rationale and virtues of "thoughtful incrementalism" are well established and not under debate here. Our general inability to adapt to the times, however, is a severe constraint on forming theories and organizations that meet the needs of the public sector.

An underlying premise of this chapter is that public management theory is built around "old technology" and dated conceptualizations of public organizations and the environments in which they operate. At least two generations of scholars have criticized and attacked the "old orthodoxy" of early public administration that posited "principles" of management and structure as the guiding force of public administration practice. But, despite this critique, the basic structures and practices espoused by the old orthodoxy remain largely intact. Organizations are still assembled with very conventional building blocks of lateral and horizontal specialization and occasional experiments in matrix structures. Personnel systems continue to be predicated upon views first articulated in the 1883 Pendleton Act. Mechanisms for facilitating interorganizational relations are still an afterthought, an appendage grafted on after organizational boundaries and domains are established. Assumptions and attitudes toward clients and employees remain largely unchanged from the days of the "doctrine of privilege." Despite all the arguments to the contrary, practitioners, and even many academics, continue to construct organizations and management theories by rearranging the same building blocks and the same assumptions again and again.

Moreover, the changes in the environments and missions of public organizations that have occurred since the establishment of the old orthodoxy are enormous. The transformations that have occurred in the public sector are both dramatic and swift. Just a few examples point to the new context of public management. The role of government in launching and nurturing quasi-private organizations, the greatly increased litigiousness of society (even to the point of allowing interagency lawsuits), the realities of the new federalism and the resulting shifts in responsibility and authority, the continuing rise of privatization as a policy tool of choice, the changing demographics of the work force and clientele, the flood of information technologies — all these and much more have transformed the context within which public organizations must be structured and managed. Organizational environments and the broader society are not bound by the shackles of incrementalism, nor should organization and management theory be, if we are to gain a better understanding of our subject and develop relevant, applicable theories.

Despite all that is new and changing, public organizations, with some notable exceptions, continue to do business as they have for decades. Revisions, when made at all, are made incrementally and always in reaction to the past. For examples, one need only look to the public school systems, where scant organizational modifications have occurred, despite overwhelming evidence of organizational failure, a dramatically different environment, and nearly universal calls for "restructuring." Instead, incremental revisions are made to organizational, managerial, and personnel systems built for another time. The realities of the current environment and the prospects for the near future call for entirely new approaches to the organization and management of schools, but the response is a reapplication of old constructs. The practices and theories of the past are deployed in response to the challenges of today, with predictable results.

Rather than look to the past as prelude, we should look to the present and anticipate the future. Theories of management must be established while the new realities of the public sector are considered. This is not a call for a reckless rejection of history or the old orthodoxy. Rather, it is an invitation to consider where we are going and what effective "post-orthodoxy" organizations and management systems will look like. The balance of this chapter is devoted to exploring this approach. We turn first to the futurist literature, to obtain a better grasp on the present, since those are the data on which futurists expand, and to seek some insights into the future, building on the work of others (Porter, 1987). We will then discuss an example of a "post-orthodoxy" organization, pointing to the coping mechanisms it has established and to how it differs from conventional organizational and managerial systems. Finally, we offer an argument for the use of a design-science approach to public management and organization theory as an adaptive tool in this complex and dynamic age.

The Future Public Managers Will Face

The art of the futurist is to know the inherently unknowable—a challenging task. Nevertheless, it is a challenge to which many good minds have risen (as well as no small number of crackpots). Fallible though futures studies may be, they do provide some hints of what is to come. And, when well reasoned and researched, futurists' prognostications often serve as a compass, pointing us in the right general direction. We can therefore turn to futurists to help us identify broad trends, if not detailed predictions.

For our purposes, futures studies offer trend data and extrapolations that help identify the prospective environments within which public managers will operate. By turning to futurists, we can gain a sense of the forces that will shape organizations in the next century. Moreover, since the best futures studies are premised on current events and conditions, they can present a clearer picture of what is actually occurring today, not just ten or twenty years hence. Conversely, managerial practices and organizational structures are typically established with an eye on the past, not on the present, and certainly not on the future. Thus, the futurists can bring us up-to-date, at the very least, and, at their best, move us ahead a decade or two.

To avoid reliance on a single perspective, a number of futures studies were consulted, including some compilations of a number of views. The trends identified in these studies take a variety of perspectives and could be grouped under any number of rubrics, as one would expect. For this chapter, we sought to identify trends that were directly relevant to public organizations and management and then to reclassify them within a more readily interpreted framework.

Common Themes Among Futurists

A review of the futures literature reveals an assortment of predictions that are directly related to public organizations and management. We selected only those trends around which substantial consensus existed. This conservative approach probably leads to more accurate near-term projections while missing some important but less predictable developments in the longer term. It also increases the face validity of the predictions. We relied heavily on the summaries provided by other futurists, notably the work of Coates and Jarratt (1989), Coates, Jarratt, and Mahaffie (1991) and the United Way Strategic Institute (1989, 1990). Our grouping of eight future trends follows.

Social and Organizational Complexity. Not surprisingly, most futurists believe that organizational and social structures and processes will become
increasingly complex. This complexity is driven by a number of forces, including rising interdependencies among organizations and sectors, technological change, increased demands on organizations, and globalization of
interactions. Increased interdependencies among levels of government, different agencies, public and private sectors, and even nation-states will add an
expansive level of complexity to public organizations. Technical and social
innovations are complicating rather than simplifying the nature of governmental work. Michael Marien believes that the outstanding world problem
is the integration of the many pieces of our now complex physical, environmental, governmental, and social systems (Marien and Jennings, 1987). This
new complexity is expected to be widespread. Large and small units of government will be forced into more complex and dynamic internal and external
environments.

Moreover, futurists find current organizations, particularly governmental organizations, out of date and unable to adjust to the coming complexity. Summarizing the views of seventeen leading futurists, Coates and
Jarratt write, "Almost all human endeavors, institutions and systems are
becoming more complex because new layers of technology and bureaucracy
are being incorporated . . . . Our current institutional structures, such as
government, are not the answer to managing complexity. Most are out of
date, bureaucratic, sluggish, with short time frames and attention spans and
lacking a world view" (1989, p. 20). These views are best exemplified by
King (1986), who notes that the issues facing government are increasingly
complex and that government structures are simply anachronistic, having
been built to satisfy the needs of a far simpler society.

Privatization and Public Sector–Private Sector Interaction. Futurists find
generally that the trend toward increased interaction between the public and
the private sector and the increased reliance on private sector solutions to
public problems will continue. The privatization movement begun in the
1980s will likely expand, although not for ideological and political reasons.
Privatization will likely expand as a result of limited resources and greater
involvement of corporations in social issues. Naisbitt and Aburdene (1990)
expect a movement away from traditional governmental agencies, toward
"competitive" public services, citing the selling off of government-run industries in Great Britain and the U.S. Postal Service's efforts in competitive
markets.

Most futurists we reviewed believe that the rise of large-scale corporations, particularly global multinational corporations, will diminish the importance and power of governmental bodies. Indeed, Ogilvy (1987) sees economic institutions taking over governmental functions, much as the nation-
state usurped the role of the church centuries ago. This transition will place
demands on public organizations both to be more responsive to market forces

and to learn to interact more effectively with private sector partners. In short, the blurring of public and private sectors will continue.

Continuation of Technological Change. There is a clear consensus among futurists that the rate of technological change will increase and that technical innovations will have significant effects for organizations. Indeed, most futurists see technology as the primary driver of change (but that social innovations in management are likely to be at least as important as technical innovations; see Drucker, 1986). Futurists see technological innovation placing many demands on organizations. Technological change will require greater technical skills for the work force, the ability to incorporate changes into organizational structures, and a capacity to redeploy resources, both to take advantage of technologies and to respond to issues arising from the new technologies. It is also likely that different technological skills will be folded into new positions, challenging existing personnel structures and concepts about the nature of work.

Many futurists have expressed concern about information overload and information integrity (Inose and Pierce, 1984). Future organizations will be confronted by ever-growing masses of data. Their ability to determine which data deserve attention and which do not will become as important as their ability to organize and interpret data. Moreover, distributed computing power will put greater analytical and data-processing power in the hands of individuals. Governmental agencies are likely to be confronted with their own data and requests from those outside government for access to data bases. Government, as *the* information-based enterprise, may lose its claims to expertise to other organizations and even to citizens with analytical skills. Many futurists expect issues of individual privacy to continue to frustrate both individuals and organizations. As access to data increases, so will concerns about its use.

Limited Public Sector Resources and Growth. None of the futurist literature we consulted predicts more than modest growth in the size of government and the resources available to it. Even those who expect economic booms (Naisbitt and Aburdene, 1990) do not expect government to grow significantly. Indeed, many predict a relative decline in the size and role of government (Coates and Jarratt, 1989). Government, it would seem, must continue to do more with less—a well-established trend. The tendency of private organizations to "shop" for tax incentives will likely lead to "tax competition" at the local, state, regional, and even international levels (Naisbitt and Aburdene, 1990). This process will add to the inherent resistance to increasing taxes and other sources of public revenue.

As a result of limited resources, efforts to increase productivity should expand in both the public and the private sector, according to Drucker (1986). Public managers will be asked to find more effective ways to deliver services and address public issues. Government agencies will be required to innovate and develop new means of organizing their resources, including the use of external contractors and partnerships. The labor-intensity of public organizations may be challenged as inefficient, leading to reductions in work-force size, but an increase in the skills required of employees will give new meaning to the expression "lean and mean." There will also be more emphasis on private solutions to public problems.

Diversity of Work Force and Clientele. All futurists agree that the American work force and citizenry will continue to grow more diverse in composition. This diversity will take many forms, including racial, ethnic, and cultural. The United Way Strategic Institute (1989, 1990) has labeled this diverse mix the "mosaic society." Toffler (1971) has referred to this process as the "demassification" of American society. Futurists see American society forming a larger number of small, distinct units with their own interests and needs. This differentiation will complicate service delivery and demands on public organizations, requiring solutions tailored to local conditions, rather than universal solutions.

Naisbitt and Aburdene (1990) see the changing role of women in organizations as especially significant; the distinctive leadership styles women bring to the workplace will change the nature of management, and this style change will be well suited to the new principles of organizing: "The dominant principle of organization has shifted, from management in order to control an enterprise to leadership in order to bring out the best in people and to respond quickly to change" (p. 218). The "mosaic society" will be reflected in the composition of the work force. It will become increasingly multicultural and multilingual, including larger proportions of recent immigrants, and will include fewer traditional households. This diversity will challenge organizations to make accommodations to employees' various needs, such as flexible hours, child-care benefits, and training.

Individualism and Personal Responsibility. Most futurists see a shift away from reliance on large institutions, particularly governmental institutions, and toward self-reliance and the acceptance of greater personal responsibility. There will be a general redefinition of the roles of individuals and society, with an emphasis on individual distinctions rather than on homogeneity. Individuals will take on a larger role in their own lives, such as the maintenance of health and the acquisition of education, relying less on public agencies to provide these services for them (United Way Strategic Institute, 1990). Naisbitt and Aburdene go so far as to state that the "great unifying theme" in our day is "the triumph of the individual."

This trend will accelerate the movement toward privatization and voluntarism (President Bush's "thousand points of light"). It is also likely to change the expectations of individuals in their dealings with governmental agencies. The movement should tend to empower individuals. As public sector employees, they will expect greater autonomy at lower levels in organizations. Similarly, public sector clients will be less tolerant of non–service-oriented agencies. The movement toward organizational accountability will continue, and the increasing decentralization of power to individuals will facilitate power shifts from the federal government to state and local governments. Bell (1976a, 1976b, 1987) sees human capital appreciating while the sense of *civitas*, or community-oriented values, declines.

Quality of Life and Environmentalism. There is a strong consensus among futurists that interest in the quality of life will increase, and that this movement will include an expanded concern for environmental quality. Some futurists see the quality-of-life issue resulting in a reduction in the importance of work as a central life interest and leading to shifts in worker attitudes. Concerns over personal health and physical work environments will also rise (Coates and Jarratt, 1989). The quality and cost of health care will continue to be a major concern of individuals and organizations alike (United Way Strategic Institute, 1990). Others see the rising influence of women in the workplace and in policy processes promoting initiatives to support families and children (Naisbitt and Aburdene, 1990).

The emphasis on quality of life and on environmentalism is likely to spark innovations in the workplace to accommodate employees' interests other than work. These innovations will include flexible work schedules, on-site day care, access to health facilities and programs, and any number of self-development activities. Individuals may also be less willing to relocate and will consider quality-of-life issues before accepting positions, transfers, or promotions. Moreover, quality-of-life concerns will place greater burdens on governmental agencies to ensure that their activities are "environmentally neutral." They will also further stimulate the growing environmental cleanup industry. Finally, some futurists believe that environmental and quality-of-life issues will inhibit growth and economic development, thereby limiting government resources but perhaps saving the planet (Meadows, 1980).

Transitions with Continuity, Not Revolution. The futurists all see significant, even dramatic changes on the horizon. Nearly all, however, see these transformations occurring within the general frameworks of our social, political and institutional structures. None of the futurists we reviewed foresee revolutionary changes in the United States. In this regard, Coates and Jarratt (1989) write, "This is not to say conflicts and flareups will not occur, but these are part of the world's continuity and are not expected to disable the day-to-day life of most people. Here and there, increasing complexity may outrun our ability to manage a system, but for the most part we can muddle through" (p. 23).

The encouraging news is that radical transformations of our systems and institutions may not be necessary. The bad news is that there may not be sufficient stimulus for change until problems have reached the point of no return. History suggests that when "muddling through" will suffice, that is the road chosen. The transitions-within-continuity scenario suggests that we have the opportunity to improve institutions to enhance their effectiveness. It also indicates that structural change will be difficult to stimulate in the absence of crises.

Summary of Trends

The trends identified by the futurists allow us to envision an organizational context that is substantially different from that of the traditional public bureaucracy. It is a context of great complexity and ambiguity, with large numbers of interactions outside the vertical relations of formal organizational structures and reliance on interdependency among levels and units within organizations, and among any number of public and private organizations. The old boundaries between sectors and levels of government are further obfuscated with interactions occurring in virtually any direction and at any level. Ogilvy (1987), describing complex future organizations such as these, labels them "heterarchies," public organizations in which "A may be over B, B over C, and C over A. Heterarchies include 'strange loops' of [organizational relationships]" (p. 15).

Within this context, a premium will be placed on the ability to integrate complex and ever-changing organizational "partners." Public organizations must be both more responsive to markets and sensitive to their private sector partners. At the same time, public organizational and managerial systems must absorb and incorporate technological change, particularly information-based technologies. Technological shifts will also create new demands, to which organizations will need to respond quickly. This will require structural flexibility, a capacity to redeploy resources on an as-needed basis, and a keen organizational sense of the external environment.

Organizations must also be able to respond to increasingly sophisticated clients who have a sound understanding of complex public policy issues. These clients, rather than being homogeneous masses, will be organized around clusters of shared interests. Organizations will need to be flexible in the delivery of services, rather than applying cookie-cutter approaches. Simultaneously, managerial systems will have to maximize the return on scarce resources through creative application of resources or contracting out to nongovernmental bodies and the private sector. Human resource systems must be suited to the recruitment, retention, and constant retraining of a highly diverse work force that will be required to incorporate new technologies. These systems will need to respond to the personal needs of employees and to provide mechanisms for workers to coordinate their private and professional lives. Finally, the post-orthodoxy public organization must incorporate these developments into the existing institutional framework. They will be evolutionary, not revolutionary.

A Post-Orthodoxy Agency Today

One of the most instructive approaches to understanding organizations of the future is to look at the most current organizational designs. They may not be of the future, but at least they may provide insights into the most recent practices and offer a sense of how organizations will adapt to the futurists' visions. An excellent example of an organization built to suit the current context, with consideration given to the future, is the Environmental Restoration and Waste Management program (or EM program) of the U.S. Department of Energy (DOE). The EM program is a new multibillion-dollar organization responsible for cleaning up the nuclear-weapons production complex in the U.S. Its purpose, design, and mode of operation reflect a post-orthodoxy perspective. Rather than building solely on traditional organizational-design concepts, the EM program has been structured to accommodate many of the environmental characteristics identified by the futurists.

The EM program is one of the most recent examples of organizational design in action, having been designed in 1990 and being still under construction. It is a public sector enterprise designed to fulfill the mission of environmental cleanup at sites around the nation. To accomplish this mission, EM has been organized around a small headquarters staff (less than five hundred persons). This staff has been given the traditional staff functions of planning, budgeting and coordination. In addition, and as a reflection of new design concepts, the EM headquarters has adopted a variety of other functions, blurring the distinctions between line and staff and headquarters and field functions. Although the jury is still out on the performance of the EM program design, we can still benefit from an assessment of its constituent parts and the manner in which they are assembled. Rather than dwell on details of the structure, we need only look to the broader characteristics to gain a sense of what this 1990s design looks like and how it is intended to function. Along with its functions have come uncommon characteristics.

One of the distinctive characteristics of the EM program is the manner by which it interacts with the world outside its organizational walls. An interesting trait is the incorporation of an open, accountability-oriented management posture. In an effort to respond to external demands and longstanding criticism of the Department of Energy and the Atomic Energy Commission before it, the organization's policies, procedures, and structure have been premised on increased input and oversight from Congress, the administration, and external constituency groups. Previously, DOE addressed environmental issues as much through obfuscation and confrontation as through integration and forthrightness. By assimilating a permeable structure that provides greater accountability, the new organization will be able to integrate a variety of actors into the solution of environmental problems. In particular, all units within EM headquarters are expected to involve public groups in contributing to planning and evaluation. This results in high levels of exposure to media attention and interest groups, both at headquarters and in the field. Similarly, the EM program has accepted the realities of external oversight. The principal regulatory authority in this case is the U.S. Environmental Protection Agency (EPA), which serves as the EM watchdog. The EM program has designed its interactions with EPA by means of a corporate model, with informal technical communications mixed with formal interorganizational communications.

The EM program also relies extensively on external support and assistance as part of its primary labor force and technology base. While the use of outside contractors is hardly novel, the extent to which they are assimilated into all stages of the agency's operations is. Contractors are actively engaged in program planning, management, and implementation. Management support through external contractors is one of the distinctive design characteristics of the EM program. The EM headquarters structure is mirrored by contractors, so as to provide EM staff access to high-quality personnel and the latest technologies and knowledge without expanding the size of EM on a permanent basis. In some case, outside contractors have also taken over government sites for the management of cleanup efforts and restoration, generating a high degree of interdependence. Indeed, the boundaries of the organization are ambiguous, making it difficult to draw a distinction between who is "inside" and who is "outside" the agency itself. These relationships did not evolve as the need to capture new technologies arose, or as a result of some mandate to "privatize." Rather, they were designed into the structure and procedures of the EM program from the start, as one of the operating premises.

Intergovernmental cooperation, as is true in many other federal agencies, will be a key to EM's success. Within the organization, it is assumed that significant coordination with other federal agencies, state governments, and Native American tribes will be required, since the cleanup sites are in various states, and many are on reservations. EM seeks to treat intergovernmental partners as equals and to integrate them into planning, implementation, and evaluation.

This integration and interdependence with "external" actors also manifests itself in the acquisition of technologies. One emphasis within the agency is acquisition of the best available technology, regardless of organizational and national borders. The agency engages in technology development at the global level, "growing its own" as appropriate and contracting out when such solutions are better suited to the issue at hand. It eschews artificial barriers that detract from accumulating the information, skills, or technologies it needs. Technology development is assumed to be an integral part of the program's mission. Technology is acquired from any appropriate source, developed or purchased from either the public or the private sector. The EM program is also expected to engage in technology transfer and serve as a catalyst to the development of new businesses within the environmental cleanup industry. It is thus required to interact with yet another set of external actors.

Internal managerial processes share the integrative tendencies of the external structures. Policy making and implementation are integrated, from planning through actual application. Strategic efforts and program planning bring together the ideas and experiences of the headquarters and field staffs. This forces the incorporation of site-specific information into broad-based strategies. Integrative strategic planning is designed to link program planning and budgeting with the policy environment of the whole Department of Energy and the external environment of the EM program. Within this structure, integrative strategic planning is a precursor to program planning and budgeting. Formal program integration is required as part of the effort to coordinate activities among the various units within EM headquarters operations. No single program unit can operate separately and independently. It is assumed that all program activities will involve some level of interdependence. This relationship is also found in the budgeting process. The EM program now has an elaborate program planning and budgeting system that involves bottom-up planning and top-down strategic direction, in the common tradition of such systems, but the EM program may also develop and install a risk-based budgeting system, which would require the rank-ordering of projects according to their relative calculated risks to human health. Allocation decisions would then be based, at least in part, on the risk factors established for each project.

Internal management processes are supported by a complex, aggressive decision-support system. Data bases are to be established for all current and planned projects from 1989 to 2019. These data bases are being designed for strategic and program-level analytical manipulations, including scenario building and analysis, cost assessments, and decision analysis. The data are then to be made widely available within the organization, to promote data-driven decisions and policies.

The EM program appears also to have adopted something akin to a client-centered approach to its activities. Serious attention is given to various constituencies, with an emphasis on equity of treatment. The agency seeks to integrate Native American tribes, rural states, and local governments into the planning and program processes. At the same time, efforts are made to differentiate the distinct concerns of these disparate groups, acknowledging their diversity rather than assuming homogeneity of clientele.

To summarize, the characteristics found in the structure and processes of the EM program are as follows:

1. Extensive involvement of the public at large
2. Structured external oversight
3. Management support through external contractors
4. Intergovernmental coordination central to mission

5. Implementation through contractors
6. In-house technology development and acquisition
7. Technology transfer and business support
8. Integrative strategic planning
9. Formal program integration
10. Complex, integrated budgeting processes

None of these characteristics is unique to this organization, but the inclusion of all of them in a structure intended to meet the needs of the 1990s does offer at least one portrait of a post-orthodoxy design. By comparing the futurists' projections with the example of the EM program, we can begin to understand what might be required of organizations in the future.

Post-Orthodoxy Design Principles

Two of us have argued elsewhere that the most constructive model for public administration as a disciplinary field is that of design science (Shangraw and Crow, 1989). The perspective of design science emphasizes the application of knowledge as one means of testing hypotheses and broader theories (Argyris, 1991). Application and iterative learning become an epistemology for acquiring and assessing knowledge and theories. In fact, a design-science perspective, in which knowledge is converted into design "factors" or "principles" and then applied to real-world settings, imposes very harsh validity tests on one's theories. As Argyris writes, "A theory must be robust in order not to be disconfirmed in the world of practice, where variables not taken into account during research will operate. Moreover, the conceptual structure and the operational definitions will have to be rigorous so that ways to act can be derived and tested in the context of practice" (1991, p. 338).

The design-science approach calls on researchers to establish "theories of action" that serve as explanations for both the academic and the practitioner and that allow organizational learning and scholarly understanding to advance coincidentally (Schön, 1983). This chapter is an attempt to identify some potential "theories of action" by considering the design principles or parameters that appear well suited to organizational futures, as embodied in the EM program, and that respond to the future already described. There is no pretense that these principles are much more than speculations, but they are informed speculations, based on descriptions of future environments and on the real example of the EM program.

Design principles, as described here, are not intended to provide universal rules or algorithms for the construction of public organizations or the solution of management problems. Indeed, they are far from the "principles" of scientific management. Rather, they are more analogous to schools of thought and the attendant guidelines one might find in industrial design or architecture, such as in a Prairie School or postmodern approach, as others have suggested (Hummel, 1990a). The principles establish the underlying themes, while the actual design of an organization or management system must be tailored to the specific circumstances and needs "on the ground." Given this orientation, we wondered what a "post-orthodoxy" school of organizational design would include. What principles would flow from a general model? Returning to our futurists' projections, and to the example of the EM program, we offer the following as some prospective post-orthodoxy design principles.

1. *Incorporate external oversight and accountability as a premise, not as an afterthought.* Organization designs of the future should accept external review and oversight as an integral function and establish structures and processes accordingly. In the past, this accommodation has meant grafting oversight committees or policy-review boards onto hierarchical agencies built within the tradition of the orthodoxy. Citizen review boards have often had little effect and resulted in a loss of credibility by the agency. The failures of the inclusiveness of the "new public administration" in the 1960s and 1970s may have resulted, in part, from the addition of new functions to old designs. Accountability mechanisms should be designed into mission statements, operating procedures, and the structure of organizational units from the beginning. This may mean bringing clients and constituencies into organizational processes at a variety of stages, rather than after the fact.

2. *Design organizational borders and structures to resemble an amoeba, rather than a pyramid.* The shape of a formal organizational chart for a post-orthodoxy agency may not fit with the traditional hierarchical model, with its clear lines of authority and fixed shape. Indeed, the movement toward matrix structures has already taken organizations a good way toward flexible designs. Organizational designers should not begin with rigid parameters as a premise but should consider the needs for integration and intraorganizational linkages, as well as the command and control functions of authority lines. Thus the outer shell of an organization (or some portion of the shell) may well be pyramidal, but segments of the structure may be much less hierarchical, adopting the "strange loops" that Ogilvy (1987) describes. Similarly, it should not be assumed that organizational boundaries are fixed and impermeable. On the contrary, the role of management is shifting away from protecting the technological core against external perturbations and toward integrating the technological core with external actors (Thompson, 1967). While circular, or even spherical, organizational models begin to capture the nonpyramidal nature of these designs, post-orthodoxy approaches may be more fluid, with organizational boundaries shifting and moving, adding a temporal nature to organizations' shapes (see Hummel, 1990a). This will require a malleable and permeable organizational border, not unlike that of an amoeba.

3. *Integrate external "partners" at the design phase.* External partners, in the form of other agencies, other branches and units of government, and private sector contractors, must be integrated into future organizations as

essential resources. Thus integration, like accountability functions, cannot be spliced onto conventional structures. Current contracting rules and relationships seek to maintain a boundary with external partners, rather than integrate them. Interdependencies should be identified at the design stage, and structures and policies should be established that bring external actors into all appropriate phases of the operation. It should be assumed, not discovered after the fact, that an agency will need partners. Incorporation of key participants in the planning, design, and implementation stages will enhance program delivery in a complex environment.

4. *Make a commitment to solving problems and learning, not to implementing solutions.* Given the rate at which problems and issues change, as well as the speed with which we accumulate new knowledge and technologies to apply to problems, agencies need to be able to shift gears and apply new approaches to policy questions. The ability to redeploy human, financial, and intellectual resources requires a commitment to solving problems, rather than a commitment to the implementation of given solutions. Current organizational structures and budgeting, personnel, and management systems focus on specific programs. There is too much at stake in any one program to abandon or modify it as issues and information change. Future organizations must be designed to keep the agency focused on problem resolutions, not on program delivery. Organizational units, and personnel and budget commitments, need to be problem-based, not program-based. Planning, evaluation, and decision processes need to focus on resolution of issues.

5. *Bring strategic planning and implementation processes together.* Organizations based on the orthodoxy differentiate clearly between line and staff functions. Most strategic planning is conducted by staff personnel, while most implementation is performed by line personnel, resulting in an intellectual mismatch. As the need for increased effectiveness and innovation increases, the integration of planning and implementation must be greater. Designs need to consider structures and processes that force the interdependence of line and staff responsibilities. Indeed, the differentiation of line and staff may be artificial and harmful to organizational performance. Instead of being a permanent distinction, perhaps it should be a temporal one, with personnel performing staff duties at one point and line duties at another. The current tendency to organize around specializations establishes barriers that must be eliminated.

6. *Make the acquisition, analysis, and distribution of strategic information a central activity.* In keeping with the notion that staff and line functions may be blurred or integrated, the collection and dissemination of information essential to the organization's success must be integral to agency operations. Decision-support systems should be considered part of the backbone of the organizational design, not an appendage. Timely and accurate information, presented in an intelligible fashion, is an essential resource for organizations in complex, turbulent environments. Organizational response time and flexibility are direct functions of the quality of information and its applica-

tion to organizational problems. Information needs to be widely distributed in the organization, as well as to external actors. Access to data bases and distributed computing power will relocate analytical functions to dispersed units in the organization. This will increase the review of key information and enhance its application to immediate organizational problems. Moreover, data should pass through a variety of points in the organization, not into a single staff unit. The number of organizational eyes should not be limited to those in a planning or institutional research department.

7. *Couple strategic planning and budgeting in a meaningful way.* The integration of planning and budgeting has been the shining goal of budgeting theorists and practitioners for at least a quarter of a century, and post-orthodoxy designs will need to develop mechanisms to achieve this union at least partially. The need to bring these two functions together will not diminish in the future. The principle of problem-centered organizational systems may offer the hope of doing so. By focusing organizational efforts on problem resolution instead of on program delivery, the organization, in effect, must constantly monitor the results of an ongoing series of experiments and redeploy resources for the next iteration of experiments. This process involves planning, assessment, and budget decisions. It provides the basis for a marriage of strategic planning, operational planning, and budgetary processes. Systems that can distinguish accounting and oversight functions from problem-resolution functions will need to be established.

8. *Make organization designs client-centered.* As people increasingly compare the performance of public and private organizations and raise their expectations, designs must reflect the needs of clients and the impact that structures and systems will have on meeting their needs. The design process should first identify clearly who the organization's clients are. Clients may be individual citizens, other agencies, private sector or nongovernmental organizations, or, most probably, some combination of these. Moreover, clients, once identified, should be brought into organizational processes in an appropriate fashion. This incorporation could go well beyond traditional stakeholder analysis in strategic planning. If future organizations apply the problem-centered, experimenting perspective, there will be ubiquitous opportunities for including clients and for considering their needs in the redesign of programs and program delivery. The future organization will also need to build a client-centered culture and create reward mechanisms that provide incentives for employee responsiveness to client needs, as advocated in the total quality management (TQM) movement.

9. *Make personnel systems respond to employee and organizational needs.* The diverse work force of the future will strain personnel systems premised on the "old orthodoxy," beyond their ability to adapt. Future personnel systems must respond to the needs of employees with very divergent backgrounds and life experiences. The organizational systems and culture will need to be inclusive, providing flexibility of career paths, work schedules, and entry requirements. Such notions as flexible hours and stop-out career ladders

should no longer be novel. They should be commonplace, basic design tools. Training and retraining should be considered to be as routine as maintenance of computers. Future organizations will also need to tap the distinctive resources of minority groups and women. Management systems must look more to the individual incumbent and determine what contributions he or she can make now and in the future, instead of focusing myopically on a job description and force-fitting an individual into a predesigned pattern.

Summary and Conclusions

It has been our contention throughout this chapter that current managerial and organizational theory and practice are out of step with the emerging dynamics in our society, and that they are very poorly suited to the future. The prevailing thoughts and practices are derived from the old orthodoxies of public administration. Those principles served well within a stable, benevolent environment, but many have lost their utility. These shortcomings have been described by others (Argyris, 1990; Drucker, 1986; Schön, 1983) and need not be enumerated here. Instead, we have made a first attempt at establishing some design principles for the post-orthodoxy public organization. We developed these design principles by looking first to the future, as described by leading futurists, that public organizations will probably face. Having consolidated their views into some key assumptions, we turned to one of the most recent real-world examples of organizational design, the EM program within the Department of Energy, to gain some sense of how one organization plans to adjust to the future environment. The frailties of case studies notwithstanding, we believe that the EM program offers clues to what post-orthodoxy structures and management systems will look like. We went on to offer nine post-orthodoxy design principles.

An underlying notion here is the centrality of a design-science approach to public management and organization theory. Within this framework, design principles shape questions rather more than answers. They force the scholar and practitioner to ask how a design will address one factor or another. Our first suggested principle, for example, introduces the idea that external oversight will be such a prominent characteristic of public management in the future that any design should consider how to incorporate it as a basic premise. The more orthodox practice is to shape management systems around service delivery needs and then, as an afterthought, splice on a review board. The design approach that we support moves these factors to the front end of the design process.

CONCLUSION:
SEARCHING FOR THE CORE
OF PUBLIC MANAGEMENT

Barry Bozeman

*E*ach of the chapters in this book underscores that public management theory is an exciting place to be these days. The individual chapters demonstrate the vitality, range, and diversity of public management research and theory. Sometimes the notion of diversity is just more upbeat than fragmentation or disarray. The question is, Does the excitement generated by individual bits and pieces of public management theory really amount to much? Is there anything more here other than a group of interesting people indulging themselves? Is there a nascent discipline? Is there a school (or are there schools) of thought? Is there even a field of study? Or (to borrow from Doig's borrowing from Cohen and March) is public management scholarship simply a "garbage can" of theory, with solutions chasing problems?

To be sure, there are some "garbage can" elements. One staggers under the intellectual weight of pet theories, explanations, ideas, and concepts imported to shape up public management theory. Consider Lynn's chapter and his prologue statement in Part One. He suggests that we draw from agency theory, coalition theory, and a variety of theoretical approaches. In his chapter, commendably, he follows his own advice. Other chapters draw from bits and pieces of legal theory (O'Leary and Straussman), historiography (Doig), and even futures studies (Emmert and colleagues). There seems no reason whatsoever to hold down the number or variety of epistemologies, theories, and concepts brought to bear on public management problems. After a point, however, one begins to wonder whether public management, with so much that is attractive at its periphery, is entirely hollow at its core. Do all roads lead nowhere?

The easy, glib response is that public management theory is better for its diversity. But that optimistic balm, however appealing, suffers under the reality that there is essentially *no* public management theory (not, at least, if one excludes theories grafted on from economics, political science, history, and other fields). While there is certainly nothing wrong with applying functionalism, agency theory, or the *I Ching* to public management problems, it is nevertheless relevant to ask what is at the core.

There *is* something at the core, and it can be identified through reflection on the chapters included here. There is, I think, little that is unique to public management theory itself, but its distinctive elements do add up to a unique field of study. These elements, few of which pertain directly to theoretical knowledge, are more related to the structure and objectives of knowledge. Taken as a whole, the chapters included in this book seem to reflect (1) a concern with prescription and, often, prescriptive theory; (2) a focus on the distinctive nature of *public* management and *public* organizations and, particularly, the effects of politics; (3) a problem focus more than a process focus; (4) a strong emphasis on contextual and experiential knowledge (as compared to empirically based theoretical knowledge); and (5) a focus on strategy and multiorganizational problems. I think that in these chapters one can find considerable evidence of each of these characteristics. Further, when one adds them up, one obtains a sum that is a bit different from sociology, political science, economics, and even public administration. Therefore, what is at the core is a distinctive *approach to knowledge,* rather than a distinctive *body of theory.*

One characteristic of public management inquiry deserves more than mere enumeration: prescription should be public management's chief contribution to theory and practice. But, all too often, the characteristic approach to prescription is flawed. If one examines the structure of argumentation in the various chapters (and I am not suggesting a deconstruction of the chapters, but only a look at their basic premises and styles of presentation), one finds a wealth of "should" statements. If there is not exactly a paucity of "because" statements, neither is there an abundance of them. Public management theorists — as compared, say, to economists or political scientists — are rarely content to examine causal issues and then rely on others to apply, refashion, or ignore their scholarly efforts. Public management scholars more often jump right into the fray and deduce their own "shoulds" from the "becauses"; indeed, they very often deduce "shoulds" from very little attention to "becauses." Public management, while its concern with prescriptive theory is laudable, falters chiefly when it evinces too much concern with prescription and too little with theory. It is all too easy for public management scholars to lapse into armchair pontificating. Thousands of harried public managers are always looking for a better way, and for reasoned advice. In my view, public management scholarship is at its best when it concerns itself with theoretically informed, experience-based prescription. It is at its worst when it races to the public manager's rescue armed with nothing more than reflection on one allegedly relevant case or, worse, one scholar's idiosyncratic experience. Public management scholarship's major liabilities are its impatience with deeper causal questions and its lack of concern for the type of theoretical structure that might support deeper analysis of causal questions.

If we public management scholars do little more than report, vicariously, the ideas and experiences of able public managers, we will surely find that, no matter how we hone our reportorial skills, our "value added" will remain modest. If we "go native," we will discover that public managers themselves are better than we are at being public managers. But, by encouraging the development and use of theory (especially prescriptive theory, although virtually any generalization-seeking theory will do), public management scholars may be able to offer a sort of knowledge that public managers themselves are not already doing a better job of offering.

REFERENCES

Adams, T. Testimony at hearing on future vehicular crossings of the Hudson River, convened by the Port Authority of New York, Dec. 5, 1923.

Aiken, M., Bacharach, S. B., and French, J. L. "Organizational Structure, Work Process, and Proposal Making in Administrative Bureaucracies." *Academy of Management Journal,* 1980, *23,* 631–652.

Ajzen, I., and Fishbein, I. "Attitude-Behavior Relations: A Theoretical Analysis and Review of Empirical Research." *Psychological Bulletin,* 1977, *84*(5), 888–918.

Ajzen, I., and Fishbein, M. *Understanding Attitudes and Predicting Social Behavior.* Englewood Cliffs, N.J.: Prentice-Hall, 1980.

Alchian, A. A., and Demsetz, H. "The Property Rights Paradigm." *Journal of Economic History,* 1973, *33,* 16–27.

Alexander, E. "A Transaction-Cost Theory of Planning." Paper presented at the annual conference of the Association of Collegiate Schools of Planning, Austin, Tex., Nov. 1990.

Allerton, W. S. "An Administrator Responds." In V. Bradley and G. Clark (eds.), *Paper Victories and Hard Realities.* Washington, D.C.: Georgetown University Health Policy Center, 1976.

Allison, G. T., Jr. "Public and Private Management: Are They Fundamentally Alike in All Unimportant Respects?" Paper presented at the Public Management Research Conference, Brookings Institution, Washington, D.C., Nov. 1979.

Allison, G. T., Jr. "Public and Private Management: Are They Fundamentally Alike in All Unimportant Respects?" In J. L. Perry and K. L. Kraemer (eds.), *Public Management: Public and Private Perspectives.* Palo Alto, Calif.: Mayfield, 1983.

Ammann, O. H. "Study of a Highway Bridge Across the Hudson River." Unpublished manuscript, papers of Governor George S. Silzer, New Jersey State Archives, 1923.

Anderson, J. "The Reagan Administration, Antitrust Action, and Policy

Change." Paper presented at the annual meeting of the Midwest Political Science Association, Chicago, 1986.

Ansoff, H. I. *Implanting Strategic Management.* Englewood Cliffs, N.J.: Prentice-Hall, 1984.

Anspach, R. R. "Everyday Methods for Assessing Organizational Effectiveness." *Social Problems,* 1991, *38*(1), 1–19.

Anthony, R. N., and Young, D. *Management Control of Nonprofit Organizations.* Homewood, Ill.: Irwin, 1988.

"Antitrust Lawyer Rises to Stardom on Combination of Caution and Zeal." *New York Times,* Nov. 6, 1990, p. A18.

Appleby, P. H. *Policy and Administration.* University: University of Alabama Press, 1949.

Argyris, C. *Overcoming Organizational Defenses: Facilitating Organizational Learning.* Needham Heights, Mass.: Allyn & Bacon, 1990.

Argyris, C. "The Use of Knowledge as a Test for Theory." *Journal of Public Administration Research and Theory,* 1991, *1*(3), 337–354.

Argyris, C., Putnam, R., and Smith, D. M. *Action Science.* San Francisco: Jossey-Bass, 1985.

Arrow, K. J. "The Economics of Agency." In J. W. Pratt and R. J. Zeckhauser (eds.), *Principals and Agents: The Structure of Business.* Boston: Harvard Business School, 1985.

Astley, W. G., and Van de Ven, A. H. "Central Perspectives and Two Debates in Organization Theory." *Administrative Science Quarterly,* 1983, *28,* 245–273.

Attewell, P., and Gerstein, D. R. "Government Policy and Local Practice." *American Sociological Review,* 1979, *44,* 311–327.

Attewell, P., and Rule, J. "Computing and Organizations: What We Know and What We Don't Know." *Communications of the ACM,* 1984, *27,* 1184–1192.

Axelrod, R. *The Evolution of Cooperation.* New York: Basic Books, 1984.

Babbage, C. *On the Economy of Machinery and Manufactures.* London: 1832.

Bachrach, P., and Baratz, M. S. "Two Faces of Power." *American Political Science Review,* 1962, *56,* 947–952.

Bachrach, P., and Baratz, M. S. "Decisions and Nondecisions: An Analytical Framework." *American Political Science Review,* 1963, *57,* 632–642.

Bachrach, P., and Baratz, M. S. *Power and Poverty.* Oxford, England: Oxford University Press, 1971.

Backoff, R. W., and Nutt, P. C. "Organizational Publicness and Its Implications for Strategic Management." Paper presented at the annual meeting of the Academy of Management, Public Sector Division, San Francisco, Aug. 1990.

Backoff, R. W., and Nutt, P. C. "The Study of Strategy in Public Organizations." Paper presented at the annual meeting of the Academy of Management, Public Sector Division, Miami Beach, Aug. 1991.

Backoff, R. W., and Nutt, P. C. *Strategic Management of Public and Third Sector Organizations: A Handbook for Leaders.* San Francisco: Jossey-Bass, 1992.

Backoff, R., and Nutt, P. "Organizational Publicness and Its Implications for Strategic Management." *Journal of Public Administration Research and Theory,* forthcoming.

Baker, R. "Organization Theory and the Public Sector." *Journal of Management Studies,* 1969, 15–32.

Baldridge, J. V., and Burnham, R. A. "Organizational Innovation: Individual, Organizational, and Environmental Impacts." *Administrative Science Quarterly,* 1975, *20,* 165–176.

Baldwin, J. N. "Public Versus Private: Not That Different, Not That Consequential." Public Personnel Management, 1987, *16,* 181–193.

Bard, E. W. *The Port of New York Authority.* New York: Columbia University Press, 1942.

Bardach, E. *The Implementation Game.* Cambridge, Mass.: MIT Press, 1977.

Bardach, E., and Kagan, R. A. *Going by the Book: The Problem of Regulatory Unreasonableness.* Philadelphia: Temple University Press, 1982.

Barley, S., Meyer, G., and Gash, D. "Cultures of Culture: Academics and Practitioners and the Pragmatics of Normative Control." *Administrative Science Quarterly,* 1988, *33,* 24–60.

Barnard, C. I. *The Functions of the Executive.* Cambridge, Mass.: Harvard University Press, 1938.

Bartunek, J. "The Dynamics of Personal and Organizational Reframing." In R. Quinn and K. Cameron (eds.), *Paradox and Transformation.* New York: Ballinger, 1988.

Barzelay, M. *Breaking Through Bureaucracy: A New Vision for Managing in Government.* Berkeley: University of California Press, 1992.

Barzelay, M., and Armajani, B. J. "Managing State Government Operations: Changing Visions of Staff Agencies." *Journal of Policy Analysis and Management,* 1990, *9*(3), 307–338.

Bazelon, D. "The Impact of Courts on Public Administration." *Indiana Law Journal,* 1976, *52,* 101–110.

Behn, R. D. "The Nature of Knowledge About Public Management: Lessons for Research and Teaching from Our Knowledge About Chess and Warfare." *Journal of Policy Analysis and Management,* 1987, *7,* 200–212.

Behn, R. D. "Management by Groping Along." *Journal of Policy Analysis and Management,* 1988, *7*(4), 643–663.

Behn, R. D. *Leadership Counts: Lessons for Public Managers from the Massachusetts Welfare, Training, and Employment Program.* Cambridge, Mass.: Harvard University Press, 1991a.

Behn, R. D. "Memo to Nancy Hempstead: An Analysis of 'Assignment Collections.' " Paper presented at annual research conference of the Association for Public Policy Analysis and Management, Bethesda, Md., Oct. 1991b.

Behn, R. D. *Homestead Air Force Base.* Teaching case and sequel. Institute of Policy Studies, Duke University, 1992a.

Behn, R. D. "Management and the Neutrino: The Search for Meaningful Metaphors." *Public Administration Review,* 1992b, *52,* 404–419.

Behn, R. D. "Gordon Chase's Management Reporting System." Unpublished manuscript, n.d.

Bell, D. *The Coming of the Post-Industrial Society.* New York: Basic Books, 1976a.

Bell, D. *The Cultural Contradictions of Capitalism.* New York: Basic Books, 1976b.

Bell, D. "The World and the United States in 2013." *Daedalus,* 1987, *116* (3), 1–32.

Bellavita, C. "The Public Administrator as 'Hero'." *Administration and Society,* 1991, *23,* 155–185.

Bendor, J. "Review Article: Formal Models of Bureaucracy." *British Journal of Political Science,* 1988, *18,* 353–395.

Bendor, J. "Formal Models of Bureaucracy: A Review." In N. B. Lynn and A. Wildavsky (eds.), *Public Administration: The State of the Discipline.* Chatham, N.J.: Chatham House, 1990.

Bendor, J., and Moe, T. "An Adaptive Model of Bureaucratic Politics." *American Political Science Review,* 1985, *79,* 755–774.

Bendor, J., and Mookherjee, D. "Institutional Structure and the Logic of Ongoing Collective Action." *American Political Science Review,* 1987, *81*(1), 129–154.

Benn, S. I., and Gaus, G. F. *Public and Private in Social Life.* New York: St. Martin's Press, 1983.

Bernstein, M. *Regulating Business by Independent Commission.* Princeton, N.J.: Princeton University Press, 1955.

Bernstein, R. J. *The Restructuring of Social and Political Theory.* Philadelphia: University of Pennsylvania Press, 1976.

Bettis, R. A., Bradley, S. P., and Hamel, G. "Outsourcing and Industrial Decline." *The Executive,* 1992, *6*(1), 7–22.

Bingham, R. D. *Technological Innovation in Local Government.* Lexington, Mass.: Heath, 1976.

Bisno, H. *Managing Conflict.* Newbury Park, Calif.: Sage, 1988.

Blume, S. *Toward a Political Sociology of Science.* New York: Free Press, 1974.

Blumenthal, J. M. "Candid Reflections of a Businessman in Washington." In J. L. Perry and K. L. Kraemer (eds.), *Public Management: Public and Private Perspectives.* Palo Alto, Calif.: Mayfield, 1983.

Boje, D. M. "The Storytelling Organization: A Study of Story Performance in an Office-Supply Firm." *Administrative Science Quarterly,* 1991, *36,* 106–126.

Bolan, R. S. "The Practitioner as Theorist: The Phenomenology of the Professional Episode." *Journal of the American Planning Association,* 1980, *46,* 261–274.

Bolan, R. S. "Planning and Institutional Design." Paper presented at the Joint International Congress of the Association of Collegiate Schools of

Planning and the Association of European Schools of Planning, Oxford, England, July 1991.

Bolling, R. *House Out of Order.* New York: Dutton, 1965.

Bolman, L. G., and Deal, T. E. *Reframing Organizations: Artistry, Choice, and Leadership.* San Francisco: Jossey-Bass, 1991.

Borchelt, R. "Alternative Practices Boost Long-Term Farm Productivity." *News Report,* 1989, *39*(9), 2–5. (Published by National Research Council.)

Boss, R. W. "Trust and Managerial Problem Solving Revisited." *Group and Organization Studies,* 1978, *3,* 331–342.

Bower, J. L. *Two Faces of Management.* New York: New American Library, 1983.

Box, G., and Tiao, G. "Intervention Analysis with Applications to Economic and Environmental Problems." *Journal of the American Statistical Association,* 1975, *70,* 70–79.

Boyatzis, R. E. *The Competent Manager: A Model for Effective Performance.* New York: Wiley, 1982.

Bozeman, B. "Scientific and Technical Information in Public Management: The Role of Gatekeeping and Channel Preference." *Administration and Society,* 1982, *13,* 479–493.

Bozeman, B. "Retrospective Technology Assessment: Method and Approach." Unpublished paper, 1985.

Bozeman, B. "The Credibility of Policy Analysis: Between Method and Use." *Policy Studies Journal,* 1986, *14,* 419–439.

Bozeman, B. *All Organizations Are Public: Bridging Public and Private Organizational Theories.* San Francisco: Jossey-Bass, 1987.

Bozeman, B. "Exploring the Limits of Public and Private Sectors: Sector Boundaries as Maginot Line." *Public Administration Review,* 1988, *48,* 672–674.

Bozeman, B., and Bretschneider, S. "Public Management Information Systems: Theory and Prescription." *Public Administration Review,* 1986, *46,* 475–487.

Bozeman, B., and Landsbergen, D. "Truth and Credibility in 'Sincere' Policy Analysis: Alternative Approaches for the Production of Policy-Relevant Knowledge." *Evaluation Review,* 1989, *13,* 355–379.

Bozeman, B., and Loveless, S. "Innovation and the Public Manager." In W. Eddy (ed.), *Public Organization Management.* New York: Marcel Dekker, 1983.

Bozeman, B., and Loveless, S. "Sector Context and Performance: A Comparison of Industrial and Governmental Research Units." *Administration and Society,* 1987, *19*(2), 197–235.

Bozeman, B., and Straussman, J. D. "Publicness and Resource Management Strategies." In R. Hall and R. Quinn (eds.), *Organization Theory and Public Policy.* Newbury Park, Calif.: Sage, 1983.

Bozeman, B., and Straussman, J. D. *Public Management Strategies: Guidelines for Managerial Effectiveness.* San Francisco: Jossey-Bass, 1990.

Bradley, R. T. *Charisma and Social Structure: A Study of Love and Power, Wholeness and Transformation.* New York: Paragon House, 1987.

Bragaw, L. K. *Managing a Federal Agency: The Hidden Stimulus.* Baltimore: Johns Hopkins University Press, 1980.

Brandl, J. "On Politics and Policy Analysis as the Design and Assessment of Institutions." *Journal of Policy Analysis and Management,* 1988, *7,* 419–424.

Braudel, F. *The Mediterranean and the Mediterranean World in the Age of Philip II.* Trans. S. Reynolds. New York: HarperCollins, 1972.

Braybrooke, D., and Lindblom, C. E. *A Strategy of Decision: Policy Evaluation as a Social Process.* New York: Free Press, 1963.

Brenneman, D. S., and Kittredge, L. D. "Matching Management Systems to Organizational Realities of Large State Agencies." *Public Productivity Review,* 1983, *7,* 354–377.

Bretschneider, S. "Management Information Systems in Public and Private Organizations: An Empirical Test." *Public Administration Review,* 1990, *50,* 536–545.

Bromiley, P., "Task Environments and Budgetary Decision Making." *Academy of Management Review,* 1981, *6,* 277–288.

Bromiley, P. "Planning Systems in Large Organizations: A Garbage Can Approach with Application to Defense PPBS." In J. G. March and R. Wessinger-Baylon (eds.), *Ambiguity and Command: Organizational Perspectives on Military Decision Making.* Marshfield, Mass.: Pitman, 1986.

Brown, D. S. *Managing the Large Organization: Issues, Ideas, Precepts, Innovations.* Mt. Airy, Md.: Lomond Books, 1982.

Brown, H. *Thinking About National Security: Defense and Foreign Policy in a Dangerous World.* Boulder, Colo.: Westview Press, 1983.

Brown, H. (ed.). *Toward Consensus in Foreign and Defense Policy.* Lanham, Md.: University Press of America, 1989.

Brown, R. D., Braskamp, L., and Newman, D. "Evaluator Credibility as a Function of Report Style: Do Jargon and Data Make a Difference?" *Evaluation Review,* 1978, *2,* 331–341.

Brudney, J. L. "Expanding the Government-by-Proxy Construct." *Nonprofit and Voluntary Sector Quarterly,* 1990, *19*(4), 62–73.

Bryson, J. M. "The Policy Process and Organizational Form." *Policy Studies Journal,* 1984, *12,* 445–463.

Bryson, J. M. *Strategic Planning for Public and Nonprofit Organizations.* San Francisco: Jossey-Bass, 1988.

Bryson, J. M. *Public Leadership: How to Tackle Public Problems When No One's in Charge.* San Francisco: Jossey-Bass, 1992.

Bryson, J. M., Bromiley, P. and Jung, Y. S. "Influences of Context and Process on Project Planning and Success." *Journal of Planning Education and Research,* 1990, *9,* 183–195.

Bryson, J. M., and Crosby, B. C. "The Design and Use of Strategic Planning Arenas." *Planning Outlook,* 1989, *32,* 5–13.

Bryson, J. M., and Einsweiler, R. C. *Shared Power: What Is It? How Does*

It Work? How Can We Make It Work Better? Lanham, Md.: University Press of America, 1991.

Bryson, J. M., and Ring, P. S. "A Transaction-Based Approach to Policy Intervention." *Policy Sciences,* 1990, *23,* 205–229.

Buckholdt, D. R., and Gubrium, J. F. "The Underlife of Behavior Modification." *American Journal of Orthopsychiatry,* 1980, *50*(2), 279–290.

Bullock, C. S., and Lamb, C. M. *Implementation of Civil Rights Policy.* Pacific Grove, Calif.: Brooks/Cole, 1984.

Butterfield, H. *George III and the Historians.* London: Collins, 1957.

Califano, J. A. "Restrictions on Postemployment Activity of Former Federal Officers and Employees." In U.S. House of Representatives Committee on the Judiciary, *Hearings Before the Subcommittee on Administrative Law and Governmental Relations.* 96th Congress, 1st session. Washington, D.C.: U.S. Government Printing Office, 1979.

Calvert, R., McCubbin, M., and Weingast, B. "A Theory of Political Control and Agency Discretion." *American Journal of Political Science,* 1989, *33*(3), 588–613.

Campbell, D. T. "Degrees of Freedom and the Case Study." *Comparative Political Studies,* 1975, *8,* 178–193.

Cantelon, P. L., and Williams, R. C. *Crisis Contained: The Department of Energy at Three Mile Island.* Carbondale: Southern Illinois University Press, 1982.

Caputo, R. K. *Management and Information Systems in the Human Services.* New York: Haworth, 1988.

Caro, R. A. *The Power Broker: Robert Moses and the Fall of New York.* New York: Knopf, 1974.

Caro, R. A. *The Power Broker: Robert Moses and the Fall of New York.* (Rev. ed.) New York: Vintage Books, 1975.

"Cash-Strapped Cities Turn to Companies to Do What Government Once Did." *New York Times,* May 14, 1991, p. A8.

Casper, J. D., and others. "Procedural Justice in Felony Cases." *Law and Society Review,* 1988, *22,* 483–507.

Caudle, S. L., and others. *Managing Information Resources: New Directions in State Government—A National Study of State Government Information Resources Management.* School of Information Studies, Syracuse University, 1989.

Chandler, A. D., Jr. *Strategy and Structure: Chapters in the History of the American Industrial Enterprise.* Cambridge, Mass.: MIT Press, 1962.

Chapman, N. J., and Pancoast, D. L. "Working with the Informal Helping Networks of the Elderly and the Experiences of Three Programs." *Journal of Social Issues,* 1985, *41*(1), 61–62.

Chase, G., and Reveal, E. C. *How to Manage in the Public Sector.* Reading, Mass.: Addison-Wesley, 1983.

Chayes, A. "The Role of Judge in Public Law Litigation." *Harvard Law Review,* 1976, *89,* 1281–1316.

Cheney, D. *Defense Management: Report to the President.* Washington, D.C.: U.S. Government Printing Office, 1989.

Chilton, B. S., and Talarico, S. M. "Politics and Constitutional Interpretation in Prison Reform Litigation: The Case of *Guthrie* v. *Evans*." In J. J.
DiLulio, Jr. (ed.), *Courts, Corrections, and the Constitution*. New York: Oxford University Press, 1990.

Chisholm, D. *Coordination Without Hierarchy: Informal Structures in Multiorganizational Systems*. Berkeley: University of California Press, 1989.

Chubb, J. E., and Moe, T. M. "Politics, Markets, and the Organization
of Schools." *American Political Science Review*, 1985, *82*, 1065–1088.

Chubb, J. E., and Moe, T. M. *Politics, Markets, and America's Schools*. Washington, D.C.: Brookings Institution, 1990.

Cigler, B. A. *Intermunicipal Organizations: The Untapped Potential for Rural Pennsylvania*. Technical Paper no. 10. Harrisburg: Center for Rural Pennsylvania, 1991.

Clegg, S. R. "Organization and Control." *Administrative Science Quarterly*, 1981,
26, 545–562.

Clegg, S. R. *Frameworks of Power*. Newbury Park, Calif.: Sage, 1989.

Clotfelter, C. T., and Cook, P. J. "Redefining 'Success' in the State Lottery
Business." *Journal of Policy Analysis and Management*, 1990, *9*(1), 99–104.

Coates, J. F., and Jarratt, J. *What Futurists Believe*. Mt. Airy, Md.: Lomond,
1989.

Coates, J. F., Jarratt, J., and Mahaffie, J. B. "Future Work." *The Futurist*,
May–June 1991, pp. 9–19.

Cobb, R. W., and Elder, C. D. *Participation in American Politics: The Dynamics
of Agenda Building*. Boston: Allyn & Bacon, 1972.

Cohen, J. E. "The Dynamics of the 'Revolving Door' at the FCC." *American
Journal of Political Science*, 1988, *30*, 689–708.

Cohen, J. H. *Law and Order in Industry*. New York: Macmillan, 1916.

Cohen, J. H. "The New York Harbor Problem and Its Legal Aspects." *Cornell Law Quarterly*, 1920, *5*, 373–408.

Cohen, J. H. *They Builded Better Than They Knew*. New York: Julian Mess-
ner, 1946.

Cohen, M., March, J., and Olsen, J. "A Garbage Can Model of Organizational Choice." *Administrative Science Quarterly*, 1972, *17*, 1–25.

Collins, J. M. *U.S. Defense Planning: A Critique*. Boulder, Colo.: Westview
Press, 1982.

Committee on the Judiciary, U.S. House of Representatives. *Ethics in Government Act of 1978*. Report to the 95th Congress, 2nd session. Washington,
D.C.: U.S. Government Printing Office, 1978.

Committee on Science and Technology, U.S. House of Representatives.
Investigation of the Challenger *Accident*. Report to the 99th Congress, 2nd
session. Washington, D.C.: U.S. Government Printing Office, 1986.

Condit, C. W. *The Port of New York*. Chicago: University of Chicago Press,
1981.

Conlan, T. *New Federalism: Intergovernmental Reform from Nixon to Reagan*. Washington, D.C.: Brookings Institution, 1988.

Cooke, M. L. *Our Cities Awake.* New York: Doubleday, 1918.

Cooper, P. J. *Hard Judicial Choices: Federal District Court Judges and State and Local Officials.* New York: Oxford University Press, 1988.

Coursey, D. "Credibility Logic and Decision Making: An Experiment Developing Measurement Instruments and Evaluating Their Influence on Optimal Choice." Unpublished Ph.D. dissertation, Syracuse University, 1990.

Coursey, D. "Information Credibility in Choosing Policy Alternatives: An Experimental Test of Cognitive Response Theory." *Journal of Public Administration Research and Theory,* 1992, *2*(3), 315–332.

Coursey, D., and Bozeman, B. "Decision Making in Public and Private Organizations." *Public Administration Review,* 1990, *50,* 525–535.

Cover, R. M., and Fiss, O. M. *The Science of Procedure.* Mineola, N. Y.: Foundation Press, 1979.

Cox, G. H., Jr., Brogan, D. R., and Dandridge, M. A. "The Effectiveness of Home Visitation in Reducing AFDC Case Payment Errors." *Social Service Review,* 1986, *60*(4), 603–618.

Cramton, R. "Judicial Lawmaking and Administration in the Leviathan State." *Public Administration Review,* 1976, *36*(5), 551–555.

Crane, D. "Fashion in Science." *Social Problems,* 1969, *16,* 433–440.

Crecine, J. P. "Defense Resource Allocation: Garbage Can Analysis of C3 Procurement." In J. G. March and R. Wessinger-Baylon (eds.), *Ambiguity and Command: Organizational Perspectives on Military Decision Making.* Marshfield, Mass.: Pitman, 1986.

Crenson, M. *The Unpolitics of Air Pollution.* Baltimore: Johns Hopkins University Press, 1971.

Crozier, M. *The Bureaucratic Phenomenon.* Chicago: University of Chicago Press, 1964.

Crozier, M., and Friedberg, E. *Actors and Systems: The Politics of Collective Action.* Chicago: University of Chicago Press, 1980.

Cunningham, R. B. "Perspectives on Public-Sector Strategic Management." In J. Rabin, G. M. Miller, and W. B. Hildreth (eds.), *Handbook of Strategic Management.* New York: Marcel Dekker, 1989.

Cutchin, D. "Municipal Executive Productivity: Lessons from New Jersey." *Public Productivity Review,* 1990, *13,* 245–270.

Dahl, R. A. "The Science of Public Administration: Three Problems." *Public Administration Review,* 1947, *7,* 1–11.

Dahl, R. A. *Who Governs?* New Haven, Conn.: Yale University Press, 1961.

Dahl, R. A., and Lindblom, C. E. *Politics, Economics, and Welfare.* New York: HarperCollins, 1953.

Damanpour, F. "Organizational Innovation: A Meta-Analysis of Effects of Determinants and Moderators." *Academy of Management Journal,* 1991, *34*(3), 555–590.

Dandridge, T. "Organizational Stories and Rituals." In R. Tannebaum, N. Margulies, and F. Massarck (eds.), *Human Systems Management.* San Francisco: Jossey-Bass, 1985.

Daneke, G. A. "Strategic Management of Chaotic Environments: An Advanced Systems Perspective." Paper presented at the annual meeting of the Academy of Management, San Francisco, Aug. 1990.

Danielson, M. N., and Doig, J. W. *New York: The Politics of Urban Regional Development.* Berkeley: University of California Press, 1982.

Danziger, J. N., and Dutton, W. H. "Technological Innovation in Local Government: The Case of Computers." *Policy and Politics,* 1977, *6,* 27–49.

Danziger, J. N., and Kraemer, K. L. *People and Computers: The Impacts of Computing on End Users.* New York: Columbia University Press, 1986.

Davies, D. G. "The Efficiency of Public Versus Private Firms: The Case of Australia's Two Airlines." *Journal of Law and Economics,* 1971, *13,* 149–165.

Davies, D. G. "Property Rights and Economic Efficiency: The Australian Airlines Revisited." *Journal of Law and Economics,* 1977, *20,* 223–226.

Davis, F. R., Bagozzi, R. P., and Warshaw, P. R. "User Acceptance of Computer Technology: A Comparison of Two Theoretical Models." *Management Science,* 1989, *35*(8), 982–1,003.

Davis, L. V., and Hagen, J. L. "Services for Battered Women: The Public Policy Response." *Social Service Review,* 1988, *62*(4), 649–667.

De Alessi, L. "Implications of Property Rights for Government Investment Choices." *American Economic Review,* 1969, *59,* 13–24.

De Alessi, L. "The Economics of Property Rights: A Review of the Evidence." In R. Zerbe (ed.), *Research in Law and Economics.* Greenwich, Conn.: JAI Press, 1980.

De Greene, K. B. *The Adaptive Organization: Anticipation and Management of Crisis.* New York: Wiley, 1982.

Deming, W. E. *Out of the Crisis.* Cambridge, Mass.: MIT Press, 1982a.

Deming, W. E. *Quality, Productivity, and Competitive Position.* Cambridge, Mass.: Center for Advanced Engineering Study, Massachusetts Institute of Technology, 1982b.

Demsetz, H. "Toward a Theory of Property Rights." *American Economic Review,* 1967, *57,* 347–359.

Denhardt, R. B. *Theories of Public Organization.* Belmont, Calif.: Brooks/Cole, 1984.

Dennison, H. S. *Organization Engineering.* New York: McGraw-Hill, 1931.

Derthick, M. *New Towns In-Town.* Washington, D.C.: Urban Institute, 1972.

Derthick, M. *Agency Under Stress: The Social Security Administration in American Government.* Washington, D.C.: Brookings Institution, 1990.

Digman, L. A. *Strategic Management.* Homewood, Ill.: Irwin, 1990.

DiLulio, J. J., Jr. *Governing Prisons: A Comparative Study of Correctional Management.* New York: Free Press, 1987.

DiLulio, J. J., Jr. "Recovering the Public Management Variable: Lessons from Schools, Prisons, and Armies." *Public Administration Review,* 1989, *49,* 127–133.

DiLulio, J. J., Jr. *Courts, Corrections, and the Constitution.* New York: Oxford University Press, 1990.

Dimond, P. R. *Beyond Busing: Inside the Challenge to Urban Segregation.* Ann Arbor: University of Michigan Press, 1985.

Diver, C. S. *Park Plaza.* Three-part case sequence. School of Management, Boston University, 1975.

Diver, C. S. "The Judge as Political Powerbroker: Superintending Structural Change in Public Institutions." *Virginia Law Review,* 1979, *65,* 43–106.

Doig, J. W. " 'If I See a Murderous Fellow Sharpening a Knife Cleverly . . . ' ": The Wilsonian Dichotomy and the Public Authority Tradition." *Public Administration Review,* 1983, *43,* 292–304.

Doig, J. W. "Entrepreneurship in Government Research: Historical Roots in the Progressive Era." Paper presented at the annual meeting of the American Political Science Association, Washington, D.C., Sept. 1988.

Doig, J. W. "Politics and the Engineering Mind: O. H. Ammann and the Hidden Story of the George Washington Bridge." *Yearbook of German-American Studies,* 1990a, *25,* 151–199.

Doig, J. W. "Regional Conflict in the New York Metropolis: The Legend of Robert Moses and the Power of the Port Authority." *Urban Studies,* 1990b, *27,* 201–232.

Doig, J. W. "Joining New York City to the Greater Metropolis." In D. Ward and O. Zunz (eds.), *The Landscape of Modernity.* New York: Russell Sage Foundation, 1992.

Doig, J. W. *Empire on the Hudson.* New York: Columbia University Press, forthcoming.

Doig, J. W., and Hargove, E. C. (eds.). *Leadership and Innovation.* Baltimore: Johns Hopkins University Press, 1987.

Dolbeare, K., and Hammond, P. *The School Prayer Decisions: From Court Policy to Local Practice.* Chicago: University of Chicago Press, 1971.

Donahue, J. D. *The Privatization Decision: Public Ends, Private Means.* New York: Basic Books, 1989.

Downs, A. "A Realistic Look at the Final Payoffs from Urban Data Systems." *Public Administration Review,* 1967a, *27,* 204–210.

Downs, A. *Inside Bureaucracy.* Boston: Little, Brown, 1967b.

Drucker, P. F. *The Practice of Management.* New York: HarperCollins, 1954.

Drucker, P. F. *The Frontiers of Management.* New York: Dutton, 1986.

Drucker, P. F. "The Coming of the New Organization." *Harvard Business Review,* 1988, *66,* 45–53.

Duncan, W. J. *The Great Ideas in Management.* San Francisco: Jossey-Bass, 1989.

Duncan, W. J., Ginter, P. M., and Capper, S. A. "Excellence in Public Administration: Four Transferable Lessons from the Private Sector." *Public Productivity Review,* 1991, *14,* 227–236.

Dunleavy, P. "Bureaucrats, Budgets, and the Growth of the State: Reconstructing an Instrumental Model." *British Journal of Political Science,* 1985, *15,* 299–328.

Dunn, W. N. *Public Policy Analysis: An Introduction.* Englewood Cliffs, N.J.: Prentice-Hall, 1981.

Eden, C., and Radford, J. *Tackling Strategic Problems*. Newbury Park, Calif.: Sage, 1990.

Eder, D., and Enke, J. L. "The Structure of Gossip: Opportunities and Constraints on Collective Expression Among Adolescents." *American Sociological Review*, 1991, *56*, 494–508.

Edwards, C. "Information Systems Maintenance: An Integrated Perspective." *MIS Quarterly*, 1984, *8*, 237–256.

Edwards, G. *The Presidency and Public Policy Making*. Pittsburgh, Pa.: University of Pittsburgh Press, 1985.

Einhorn, H., and Hogarth, R. "Behavioral Decision Theory: Processes of Judgment and Choice." *Annual Review of Psychology*, 1981, *32*, 6–39.

Eisenhardt, K. M. "Agency Theory: An Assessment and Review." *Academy of Management Review*, 1989, *14*(1), 57–74.

Eisner, M., and Meier, K. "Presidential Control Versus Bureaucratic Power: Explaining the Reagan Revolution in Antitrust." *American Journal of Political Science*, 1990, *34*, 269–287.

Ekland-Olson, S., and Martin, S. J. "Organizational Compliance with Court-Ordered Reform." *Law and Society Review*, 1988, *22*(2), 359–385.

Ekland-Olson, S., and Martin, S. J. "*Ruiz:* A Struggle Over Legitimacy." In J. J. Dilulio, Jr. (ed.), *Courts, Corrections, and the Constitution*. New York: Oxford University Press, 1990.

Elmore, R. F. "Backward Mapping: Implementation Research and Policy Decisions." In W. Williams (ed.), *Studying Implementation: Methodological and Administrative Issues*. Chatham, N.J.: Chatham House, 1982.

Elmore, R. F. "Forward and Backward Mapping: Reversible Logic in the Analysis of Public Policy." In K. Hanf and T.A.J. Toonen (eds.), *Policy Implementation in Federal and Unitary Systems: Questions of Analysis and Design*. Dordrecht, The Netherlands: Martinus Nijhoff, 1985.

Elster, J. *Ulysses and the Sirens: Studies in Rationality and Irrationality*. Cambridge, England: Cambridge University Press, 1979.

Emerson, R. E. "Power-Dependence Relations." *American Sociological Review*, 1962, *27*, 31–40.

Etheridge, L. S. *Can Governments Learn?* Elmsford, N.Y.: Pergamon Press, 1985.

Evered, R. "So What Is Strategy?" *Long-Range Planning*, 1983, *16*, 57–72.

Fayol, H. *General and Industrial Management*. London: Pitman, 1949. (Originally published 1916.)

Feigenbaum, A. V. *Total Quality Control*. New York: McGraw-Hill, 1954.

Feinberg, J. *Doing and Deserving*. Princeton, N.J.: Princeton University Press, 1970.

Feinberg, J. *Social Philosophy*. Englewood Cliffs, N.J.: Prentice-Hall, 1973.

Feinberg, J. "Overlooking the Merits of the Individual Case: An Unpromising Approach to the Right to Die." Unpublished manuscript, 1990.

Feldman, M. A., and March, J. G. "Information in Organizations as Signal and Symbol." *Administrative Science Quarterly*, 1981, *26*, 171–186.

Feldman, M. S. *Order Without Design: Information Production and Policy Making.* Stanford, Calif.: Stanford University Press, 1989.

Feller, I. "Managerial Response to Technological Innovations in Public Sector Organizations." *Management Science,* 1980, *26,* 1021–1030.

Feller, I. "Public Sector Innovation as Conspicuous Production." *Policy Analysis,* 1981, *7,* 1–21.

Ferejohn, J. "Incumbent Performance and Electoral Control." *Public Choice,* 1986, *50,* 5–25.

Fiedler, F. E. *A Theory of Leadership Effectiveness.* New York: McGraw-Hill, 1967.

Fiedler, F. E. "The Contingency Model — New Directions for Leadership Utilization." *Journal of Contemporary Business,* 1974, *3,* 65–80.

Filley, A. *Interpersonal Conflict Resolution.* Glenview, Ill.: Scott, Foresman, 1975.

Finn, P. "Coordinating Services for the Mentally Ill Misdemeanor Offender." *Social Service Review,* 1989, *63*(1), 127–141.

Fiol, C. M. "A Semiotic Analysis of Corporate Language: Organizational Boundaries and Joint Venturing." *Administrative Science Quarterly,* 1989, *34,* 277–303.

Fishbein, M., and Ajzen, I. *Belief, Attitude, Intention, and Behavior: An Introduction to Theory and Research.* Reading, Mass.: Addison-Wesley, 1975.

Fisher, L. *Presidential Spending Power.* Princeton, N.J.: Princeton University Press, 1975.

Fisher, R., and Brown, S. *Getting Together: Building a Relationship That Gets to Yes.* Boston: Houghton Mifflin, 1988.

Fisher, R., and Ury, W. *Getting to Yes: Negotiating Agreement Without Giving In.* New York: Viking Penguin, 1981.

Fishman, R. "The Regional Plan and the Transformation of the Industrial Metropolis." In D. Ward and O. Zunz (eds.), *The Landscape of Modernity.* New York: Russell Sage Foundation, 1992.

Fiss, O. M. *The Civil Rights Injunction.* Bloomington: Indiana University Press, 1978.

Fletcher, G. P. *Rethinking Criminal Law.* Boston: Little, Brown, 1978.

Forester, J. *Planning in the Face of Power.* Berkeley: University of California Press, 1989.

Foster, J. L. "Bureaucratic Rigidity Revisited." *Social Science Quarterly,* 1990, *71*(2), 223–238.

Fottler, M. O. "Management: Is It Really Generic?" *Academy of Management Review,* 1981, *6,* 1–12.

Fox, R. J. *The Defense Management Challenge.* Boston: Harvard Business School Press, 1988.

Fredrickson, J. W. "Strategic Process Research: Questions and Recommendations." *Academy of Management Review,* 1983, *8*(4), 565–575.

Freeley, A. J. *Argumentation and Debate: Rational Decision Making.* (4th ed.) Belmont, Calif.: Wadsworth, 1976.

Fried, C. "Right and Wrong: Preliminary Considerations." *Journal of Legal Studies,* 1976, *5,* 165–200.

Friedrich, C. J. "Public Policy and the Nature of Administrative Responsibility." In C. J. Friedrich and E. Mason, *Public Policy 1940*. Cambridge, Mass.: Harvard University Press, 1940.

Friedson, E. "Dominant Professions, Bureaucracy, and Client Services." In W. R. Rosen and M. Leston (eds.), *Organization and Clients: Essays in the Sociology of Service*. Columbus, Ohio: Merrill, 1970.

Friend, J., and Hickling, A. *Planning Under Pressure*. Elmsford, N.Y.: Pergamon Press, 1987.

Friend, J., Laffin, M. J., and Norris, M. E. "Competition in Public Policy: The Structure Plan as Arena." *Public Administration*, 1981, *59*, 441–463.

Frost-Kumpf, L., and Ishiyama, H. "Transformation Strategies in General-Purpose Government Agencies: A Case Study of Strategic Management in the Ohio Department of Mental Health." Paper presented at the annual meeting of the Academy of Management, Public Sector Division, Miami Beach, Aug. 1991.

Frug, G. E. "The Judicial Power of the Purse." *University of Pennsylvania Law Review*, 1978, *126*, 715–794.

Gabarro, J. J. *Robert F. Kennedy High School*. Teaching case. Graduate School of Business Administration, Harvard University, 1974.

Gansler, J. *Affording Defense*. Cambridge, Mass.: MIT Press, 1989.

Gauthier, B. *Hierarchies and Delegation: Sequential Production and Process in an Organizational Setting*. Political Economy Working Paper no. 138. St. Louis: Washington University, 1990.

Gaventa, J. *Power and Powerlessness: Quiescence and Rebellion in an Appalachian Valley*. Urbana: University of Illinois Press, 1980.

Geertz, C. *Interpretation of Culture*. New York: Basic Books, 1973.

Gemmill, G., and Smith, C. "A Dissipative-Structure Model of Organization Transformation." *Human Relations*, 1985, *38*(8), 751–766.

Gerth, H. H., and Mills, C. W. (eds.). *From Max Weber: Essays in Sociology*. London: Oxford University Press, 1946.

Gibb, J. "TORI Theory." *Journal of Contemporary Theory*, 1972, *1*, 33–42.

Giddens, A. *A Central Problem in Social Theory: Action, Structure, and Contradiction in Social Analysis*. Berkeley: University of California Press, 1979.

Giddens, A. *The Constitution of Society*. Berkeley: University of California Press, 1984.

Gilbreth, F. B. *Motion Study*. New York: Van Nostrand Reinhold, 1912.

Gilder, G. *Microcosm: The Quantum Revolution in Economics and Technology*. New York: Simon & Schuster, 1989.

Gitlow, H. S., and Gitlow, S. J. *The Deming Guide to Quality and Competitive Position*. Englewoods Cliffs, N.J.: Prentice-Hall, 1987.

Glazer, M. P., and Glazer, P. M. *The Whistleblowers*. New York: Basic Books, 1989.

Glazer, N. "The Imperial Judiciary." *Publius: The Journal of Federalism*, 1975.

Glazer, N. "Should Judges Administer Social Services?" *The Public Interest*, 1978, *50*, 64–80.

Glick, H. R. "Policy Making and State Supreme Courts: The Judiciary as an Interest Group." *Law and Society Review,* 1970, *5*(2), 271–291.

Glisson, C., and Durick, M. "Predictors of Job Satisfaction and Organizational Commitment in Human Service Organizations." *Administrative Sciences Quarterly,* 1988, *33,* 61–81.

Golembiewski, R. T. *Public Administration as a Developing Discipline.* New York: M. Dekker, 1977.

Golembiewski, R. T. *Approaches to Planned Change.* New York: M. Dekker, 1979.

Golembiewski, R. T. *Humanizing Public Organizations.* Mt. Airy, Md.: Lomond Books, 1985.

Golembiewski, R. T. "Public Sector Management Today: Advanced Differentiation and Early Institutionalization." *Journal of Management,* 1987, *13,* 323–338.

Golembiewski, R. T. "Toward a Positive and Practical Public Management." *Administration and Society,* 1989, *21,* 200–227.

Golembiewski, R. T. "More on 'A Positive and Practical Public Management.'" *Administration and Society,* 1990, *21,* 493–500.

Golembiewski, R. T., and Kiepper, A. *High Performance and Human Costs.* New York: Praeger, 1989.

Golembiewski, R. T., Proehl, C. W., Jr., and Sink, D. "Success of OD Applications in the Public Sector." *Public Administration Review,* 1981, *41,* 679–682.

Golembiewski, R. T., and Sun, B.-C. "Positive-Findings Bias in QWL Research: A Comparison of Public and Business Sectors." *Public Productivity and Management Review,* 1989, *13,* 145–155.

Golembiewski, R. T., and Sun, B.-C. "Positive-Findings Bias in QWL Studies." *Journal of Management,* 1990, *16,* 665–674.

Gooding, R. Z., and Wagner, J. A., III. "A Meta-Analytic Review of the Relationship Between Size and Performance: The Productivity and Efficiency of Organizations and Their Subunits." *Administrative Science Quarterly,* 1985, *30,* 462–481.

Goodnow, F. J. *Politics and Administration.* New York: Macmillan, 1900.

Goodsell, C. *The Case for Bureaucracy.* Chatham, N.J.: Chatham House, 1983.

Gray, B. *Collaborating.* San Francisco: Jossey-Bass, 1989.

Graziano, J., and Rehfuss, J. "Twenty-five Years of PAR Research: A Study of Professional Change." *Public Administration Review,* 1974, *34,* 268–273.

Greenwood, R. G. "Management by Objectives: As Developed by Peter Drucker, Assisted by Harold Smiddy." *Academy of Management Review,* 1981, *6,* 225–230.

Greising, D., and Morse, L. *Brokers, Bagmen, and Moles: Fraud and Corruption in the Chicago Futures Markets.* New York: Wiley, 1991.

Groves, L. R. *Now It Can Be Told: The Story of the Manhattan Project.* New York: HarperCollins, 1962.

Gruber, J. E. *Controlling Bureaucracy: Dilemmas in Bureaucratic Governance.* Berkeley: University of California Press, 1987.

Grumet, B. R. "The Changing Role of the Federal and State Courts in Safeguarding the Rights of the Mentally Disabled." *Publius: The Journal of Federalism,* 1985, *15,* 67–80.

Habermas, J. *Communication and the Evolution of Society.* Boston: Beacon Press, 1979.

Haire, M. *Modern Organization Theory.* New York: Wiley, 1959.

Halachmi, A. "Dealing with the Conflict of Loyalties: The Continuing Seminar and Action Research." *Journal of Health and Human Resources Administration,* 1980, *2*(4), 505–531.

Halachmi, A. "Ad Hocracy and the Future of the Civil Service." *International Journal of Public Administration,* 1989, *12*(4), 617–650.

Hale, G. E. "Federal Courts and State Budgetary Process." *Administration and Society,* 1979, *11*(3), 357–386.

Hamburger, H. *Games as Models of Social Phenomena.* New York: W. H. Freeman, 1979.

Hammack, D. *Power and Society: Greater New York at the Turn of the Century.* New York: Russell Sage Foundation, 1982.

Hammersmith, S. M. "Firm Disqualification and the Former Government Attorney." *Ohio State Law Journal,* 1981, *42,* 579–602.

Hammond, K. R., McClelland, G. H., and Mumpower, J. *Human Judgment and Decision Making.* New York: Praeger, 1980.

Hammond, P. Y. "Disincentives for the Development of National Strategy: The Executive Branch." Paper presented to a symposium sponsored by the National Defense University, Washington, D.C., Dec. 1988.

Hannan, T. H. "The Benefits and Costs of Methadone Maintenance." *Public Policy,* 1976, *24,* 197–226.

Hannaway, J. "Supply Creates Demand: An Organizational Process View of Administrative Expansion." *Journal of Policy Analysis and Management,* 1987, *7,* 118–134.

Hanushek, E., and Jackson, J. *Statistical Methods for Social Scientists.* San Diego, Calif.: Academic Press, 1977.

Hardin, R. *Collective Action.* Baltimore: Johns Hopkins University Press, 1982.

Hardin, R. "Trusting Persons, Trusting Institutions." In R. J. Zeckhauser (ed.), *Strategy and Choice.* Cambridge, Mass.: MIT Press, 1991.

Hargrove, E. C., and Glidewell, J. C. *Impossible Jobs in Public Management.* Lawrence: University Press of Kansas, 1990.

Harmon, M. M. *Action Theory for Public Administration.* New York: Longman, 1981.

Harmon, M. M., and Mayer, R. T. *Organization Theory for Public Administration.* Boston: Little, Brown, 1986.

Harriman, L., and Straussman, J. D. "Do Judges Determine Budget Decisions? Federal Court Decisions in Prison Reform and State Spending for Corrections." *Public Administration Review,* 1983, *43,* 343–351.

Hart, H.L.A. *Punishment and Responsibility.* Oxford, England: Oxford University Press, 1968.

t'Hart, P. "Groupthink in Government: A Study of Small Groups and Policy Failure." Unpublished doctoral dissertation, Leiden University, 1990.

Hasenfeld, Y. *Human Service Organizations.* Englewood Cliffs, N.J.: Prentice-Hall, 1983.

Healey, P., McNamara, P., Elson, M., and Doak, A. *Land-use Planning and the Mediation of Urban Change.* Cambridge, England: Cambridge University Press, 1988.

Heckathorn, D. D., and Maser, S. M. "The Contractual Architecture of Public Policy: A Critical Reconstruction of Lowi's Typology." *Journal of Politics,* 1990, *52*(4), 1101–1123.

Heclo, H. *A Government of Strangers: Executive Politics in Washington.* Washington, D.C.: Brookings Institution, 1977.

Heclo, H. "Issue Networks and the Executive Establishment." In A. King, (ed.), *The New Political System.* Washington, D.C.: American Enterprise Institute, 1978.

Heise, D. R. *ETHNO, Version 2.* Software package. Dubuque, Ia.: William C. Brown, 1988a.

Heise, D. R. "Modeling Event Structures." *Journal of Mathematical Sociology,* 1988b, *13,* 138–168.

Hempel, C. G. *Philosophy of Natural Science.* Englewood Cliffs, N.J.: Prentice-Hall, 1966.

Hendrickson, D. *Reforming Defense.* Baltimore: Johns Hopkins University Press, 1988.

Herman, B. "On the Value of Acting from the Motive of Duty." *Philosophical Review,* 1981, *90.*

Heymann, P. B. *The Politics of Public Management.* New Haven, Conn.: Yale University Press, 1987.

Higgs, J. "Identity and Cooperation: A Comment on Sen's Alternative Program." *Journal of Law, Economics, and Organization,* 1987, *3*(1), 140–142.

Himmelfarb, G. *The New History and the Old: Critical Essays and Reappraisals.* Cambridge, Mass.: Harvard University Press, 1987.

Hoch, C., and Hemmens, G. C. "Linking Informal and Formal Help: Conflict Along the Continuum of Care." *Social Service Review,* 1987, *61*(3), 432–446.

Hofer, C. W. "Some Preliminary Research on Patterns of Strategic Behavior." *Academy of Management Proceedings,* 1973, 46–59.

Hogan, J. C. *The Schools, the Courts, and the Public Interest.* (2nd ed.) Lexington, Mass.: Lexington Books, 1985.

Hogarth, R. "Beyond Discrete Biases: Functional and Dysfunctional Aspects of Judgmental Heuristics." *Psychological Bulletin,* 1981, *90,* 197–217.

Holmes, O. W. *The Common Law.* Boston: Little, Brown, 1881.

Holmstrom, B., and Milgrom, P. "Multitask Principal-Agent Analysis: Incentive Contracts, Asset Ownership, and Job Design." *Journal of Law, Economics, and Organization,* 1991, *7,* 24–52.

Hood, C. H. *The Tools of Government.* Chatham, N.J.: Chatham House, 1983.

Horn, M. J., and Shepsle, K. A. "Commentary on 'Administrative Arrangements and Political Control of Agencies': Administrative Process and Organizational Form as Legislative Responses to Agency Costs." *Virginia Law Review,* 1989, *75,* 499–508.

Horowitz, D. L. *The Courts and Social Policy.* Washington, D.C.: Brookings Institution, 1977.

Horowitz, D. L. "Decreeing Organizational Change: Judicial Supervision of Public Institutions." *Duke Law Journal,* 1983, 1265–1307.

Huber, G. P. "A Theory of the Effects of Advanced Information Technologies on Organizational Design, Intelligence, and Decision Making." *Academy of Management Review,* 1990, *15,* 47–70.

Hull, C. J., and Hjern, B. *Helping Small Firms Grow: An Implementation Approach.* London: Croom Helm, 1987.

Hull, F., and Haige, J. "Organizing for Innovation: Beyond Burns and Stalker's Organic Type." *Sociology,* 1982, *16,* 564–577.

Hummel, R. P. "Circle Managers and Pyramid Managers: Icons for the Postmodern Public Administrator." In H. D. Kass and B. Catgron (eds.), *Images and Identity in Public Administration.* Newbury Park, Calif.: Sage, 1990a.

Hummel, R. P. "Uncovering Validity Criteria for Stories Managers Hear and Tell." *American Review of Public Administration,* 1990b, *20*(4).

Hummel, R. P. "Stories Managers Tell: Why They Are as Valid as Science." *Public Administration Review,* 1991, *51*(1), 31–41.

Ingraham, P. W., and Ban, C. R. "Models of Public Management: Are They Useful to Federal Managers in the 1980s?" *Public Administration Review,* 1986, *46*(2), 152–160.

Ingraham, P. W., and Kettl, D. F. *Agenda for Excellence: Public Service in America.* Chatham, N.J.: Chatham House, 1992.

Ingram, H. "Policy Implementation Through Bargaining: The Case of Federal Grants in Aid." *Public Policy,* 1977, *25*(4), 499–526.

Ingram, H., and Schneider, A. "Improving Implementation Through Smarter Statutes." *Journal of Public Policy,* 1990, *10*(1), 67–88.

Inose, H., and Pierce, J. R. *Information Technology and Civilization.* New York: Freeman, 1984.

Janis, I. L. *Victims of Groupthink: A Psychological Study of Foreign Policy Decisions and Fiascoes.* Boston: Houghton Mifflin, 1972.

Janis, I. L. *Groupthink: Psychological Studies of Policy Decisions and Fiascoes.* (2nd ed.) Boston: Houghton Mifflin, 1982.

Jantsch, E. *Design for Evolution: Self-Organization and Planning in the Life of Human Systems.* New York: Braziller, 1975.

Jantsch, E. *The Self-Organizing Universe.* Elmsford, N.Y.: Pergamon Press, 1980.

Jelinek, M., Litterer, J. A., and Miles, R. E. "The Future of Organization Design." In M. Jellinek, J. A. Literer, and R. E. Miles (eds.), *Organizations by Design: Theory and Practice.* (2nd ed.) Plano, Tex.: Busines Publications, 1986.

Johnson, C. A. "Judicial Decisions and Organizational Change: A Theory." *Administration and Society,* 1979a, *11*(1), 27–51.

Johnson, C. A. "Judicial Decisions and Organizational Change: Some Theoretical and Empirical Notes on State Court Decisions and State Administrative Agencies." *Law and Society Review,* 1979b, *14*(1), 27–56.

Johnson, C. A., and Canon, B. C. *Judicial Policies: Implementation and Impact.* Washington, D.C.: Congressional Quarterly Press, 1984.

Johnson, R. *The Dynamics of Compliance.* Evanston, Ill.: Northwestern University Press, 1967.

Jones, L. R., and Doyle, R. B. "Public Policy and Management Issues in Budgeting for Defense." Paper presented to the Association of Public Policy and Management, Washington, D.C., Nov. 1989.

Jones, V. C. *Manhattan, the Army, and the Atomic Bomb.* Washington, D.C.: Center for Military History, U.S. Army, 1985.

Kahneman, P., and Tversky, A. (eds.). *Judgment Under Uncertainty: Heuristics and Biases.* Cambridge, England: Cambridge University Press, 1982.

Kane, E. J. *The S&L Insurance Mess: How Did It Happen?* Washington, D.C.: Urban Institute Press, 1989.

Kane, T. J. "Giving Back Control: Long-Term Poverty and Motivation." *Social Service Review,* 1987, *61*(3), 405–419.

Kane, T. J. "The Crunch Underfoot." *Association for Preservation Technology Bulletin,* 1989, *2,* 4–5.

Kant, I. *Groundwork of the Metaphysic of Morals.* New York: HarperCollins, 1964.

Kanter, A. *Defense Politics: A Budgetary Perspective.* Chicago: University of Chicago Press, 1983.

Kanter, R. M. *The Change Masters.* New York: Simon & Schuster, 1983.

Kates, N., and Roberts, M. *Pam Hyde and Ohio Mental Health: Shifting Control of Inpatient Care.* Cambridge, Mass.: President and Fellows of Harvard College, 1987.

Kaufman, H. "Gotham in the Air Age." In H. Stein (ed.), *Public Administration and Policy Development.* Orlando, Fla.: Harcourt Brace Jovanovich, 1952.

Kaufman, H. *The Forest Ranger.* Baltimore: Johns Hopkins University Press, 1960.

Kaufman, H. *Red Tape: Its Origins, Uses, and Abuses.* Washington, D.C.: Brookings Institution, 1977.

Kaufman, H. *The Administrative Behavior of Federal Bureau Chiefs.* Washington, D.C.: Brookings Institution, 1981.

Kaufman, H. *Time, Chance, and Organizations: Natural Selection in a Perilous Environment.* (2nd ed.) Chatham, N.J.: Chatham House, 1990.

Kaufmann, W. W. *A Reasonable Defense.* Washington, D.C.: Brookings Institution, 1986.

Kelly, G. *The Psychology of Personal Constructs.* (2 vols.) New York: Norton, 1955.

Kelman, H. C. "Attitudes Are Alive and Well and Gainfully Employed in the Sphere of Action." *American Psychologist,* 1974, *29.*

Kelman, S. *Procurement and Public Management: The Fear of Discretion and the Quality of Government Performance.* Washington, D.C.: American Enterprise Institute, 1990.

Kemeny Commission (President's Commission on the Accident at Three Mile Island). *The Need for Change: The Legacy of TMI.* Washington, D.C.: U.S. Government Printing Office, 1979.

Kennedy, M. "Working Knowledge." *Knowledge: Creation, Diffusion, Utilization,* 1983, *5,* 193–211.

Kettl, D. F. *Government by Proxy: (Mis?)Managing Federal Programs.* Washington, D.C.: Congressional Quarterly Press, 1988.

Kettl, D. F. "The Perils—and Prospects—of Public Administration." *Public Administration Review,* 1990, *50*(4), 411–419.

Kettl, D. F. "Who's Minding the Store? The Decline of Competence in American Administration." Paper presented at the annual meeting of the American Political Science Association, Washington, D.C., Mar. 1991.

King, A. "The Club of Rome: Reaffirmation of a Mission." *Interdisciplinary Science Reviews,* 1986, *11*(1), 13.

King, J. L. "Local Government Use of Information Technology: The Next Decade." *Public Administration Review,* 1982, *42,* 25–36.

Kingdon, J. W. *Agendas, Alternatives, and Public Policies.* Boston: Little, Brown, 1984.

Kirk, S. A., and Kutchins, H. "Deliberate Misdiagnosis in Mental Health Practice." *Social Service Review,* 1988, *62*(2), 225–237.

Knauft, E. B., Berger, R. A., and Gray, S. T. *Profiles of Excellence: Achieving Success in the Nonprofit Sector.* San Francisco: Jossey-Bass, 1991.

Knorr-Cetina, K. *The Manufacture of Knowledge.* Elmsford, N.Y.: Pergamon Press, 1981.

Knott, J. H., and Miller, G. J. *Reforming Bureaucracy: The Politics of Institutional Choice.* Englewood Cliffs, N.J.: Prentice-Hall, 1987.

Kolderie, T. "Agreement Has Almost Been Reached." *Minneapolis Star,* Oct. 10, 1965, p. 3–6.

Koteen, J. *Strategic Management in Public and Nonprofit Organizations.* New York: Praeger, 1989.

Kotter, J. *The General Managers.* New York: Free Press, 1982.

Kraemer, K. L., and King, J. L. "Computing and Public Organizations." *Public Administration Review,* 1986, *46,* 488–496.

Kraemer, K. L., King, J. L., Dunkle, D., and Lane, J. P. *Managing Information Systems: Change and Control in Organizational Computing.* San Francisco: Jossey-Bass, 1989.

Kraemer, K. L., and Kling, R. "The Political Character of Computerization in Service Organizations: Citizen Interests or Bureaucratic Control?" *Computers and the Social Sciences,* 1985, *1,* 77–89.

Kraemer, K. L., and Perry, J. "Institutional Requirements for Research in Public Administration." *Public Administration Review,* 1989, *49,* 9–16.

Krumholz, N., and Forester, J. *Making Equity Planning Work.* Philadelphia: Temple University Press, 1990.

Kuhn, T. *The Structure of Scientific Revolutions.* (2nd ed.) Chicago: University of Chicago Press, 1970.

Lambright, W. H., Teich, A., and Carroll, J. *Adoption and Utilization of Urban Technology: A Decision—Making Study.* Report to the National Science Foundation, grant no. RDA-75-19704. Syracuse, N.Y.: Syracuse Research Corporation, 1977.

Lan, Z., and Rainey, H. "Goals, Rules, and Effectiveness in Public, Private, and Hybrid Organizations." *Journal of Public Administration Research and Theory,* 1992, *2*(1), 5–28.

Landau, M. "On Multiorganizational Systems in Public Administration." *Journal of Public Administration Research and Theory,* 1991, *1*(1), 5–18.

Landsbergen, D., and Bozeman, B. "Credibility Logic and Policy Analysis." *Knowledge: Creation, Diffusion, Utilization,* 1987, *8*, 625–648.

Lau, A. W., Newman, A. R., and Broedling, I. A. "The Nature of Managerial Work in the Public Sector." *Public Administration Review,* 1980, *40*, 513–520.

Lau, A. W., and Pavett, C. M. "The Nature of Managerial Work: A Comparison of Public- and Private-Sector Managers." *Group and Organization Studies,* 1980, *5*(4), 453–466.

Laudan, L. *Progress and Its Problems: Towards a Theory of Scientific Growth.* Berkeley: University of California Press, 1977.

Laudon, K. C. *Computers and Bureaucratic Reform.* New York: Wiley, 1974.

Lauth, T. "Rehabilitation Agencies as Public Bureaucracies: Professionalism and Political Control." *Journal of Rehabilitation Administration,* 1978, *14*, 143–152.

Lawless, M. W., and Moore, R. A. "Interorganizational Systems in Public Service Delivery." *Human Relations,* 1989, *42*(12), 1167–1184.

Lawrence, P., and Lorsch, J. *Organization and Environment.* Boston: Harvard Business School, 1967.

Lederer, A. L., and Mendelow, A. L. "The Impact of the Environment on the Management of Information Systems." *Information Systems Research,* 1990, *1*(2), 205–222.

Lempert, R. "Strategies of Research Design in the Legal Impact Study: The Control of the Plausible Rival Hypotheses." *Law and Society Review,* 1970, *1*(1), 111–132.

Levine, C. H. "Organizational Decline and Cutback Management." *Public Administration Review,* 1978, *38*, 316–324.

Levine, C. H. "More on Cutback Management: Hard Questions for Hard Times." *Public Administration Review,* 1979, *39*, 179–183.

Levine, C. H., Backoff, R. W., Cahoon, A. R., and Siffin, W. J. "Organizational Design: A Post-Minnowbrook Perspective for the 'New' Public Administration." *Public Administration Review,* 1975, *35*, 425–435.

Levine, J. P. "Methodological Concerns in Studying Supreme Court Efficacy." *Law and Society Review,* 1970, *4*(4), 583–611.

Levinthal, D. "A Survey of Agency Models of Organizations." *Journal of Economic Behavior and Organization,* 1988, *9*, 153–185.

Lewis, E. *Public Entrepreneurship: Toward a Theory of Bureaucratic Political Power.* Bloomington: Indiana University Press, 1980.

Lewis, M. *Liar's Poker: Rising Through the Wreckage on Wall Street.* New York: W. W. Norton, 1989.

Liebman, C. "Teaching Public Administration: How Can We Teach What We Don't Know?" *Public Administration Review,* 1963, *23,* 167–169.

Light, P. *The President's Agenda: Domestic Policy from Kennedy to Carter (with Notes on Ronald Reagan).* Baltimore: Johns Hopkins University Press, 1982.

Lilienthal, D. E. *The Journals of David E. Lilienthal.* 5 vols. New York: HarperCollins, 1964–1971.

Lincoln, Y., and Guba, E. *Naturalistic Inquiry.* Newbury Park, Calif.: Sage, 1985.

Lind, A., and Tyler, T. R. *The Social Psychology of Procedural Justice.* New York: Plenum Press, 1988.

Lindblom, C. E. "The Science of 'Muddling Through.'" *Public Administration Review,* 1959, *19*(2), 79–88.

Lindblom, C. E. *Politics and Markets.* New York: Free Press, 1977.

Lipsky, M. *Street-Level Bureaucracy: Dilemmas of the Individual in Public Service.* New York: Russell Sage Foundation, 1980.

Lipsky, M., and Smith, S. R. "Nonprofit Organizations, Government, and the Welfare State." *Political Science Quarterly,* 1989–90, *104*(4), 625–648.

Lodahl, J., and Gordon, G. "The Structure of Scientific Fields and the Functioning of University Graduate Departments." *American Sociological Review,* 1972, *37,* 57–72.

Long, D. A., Mallar, C. D., and Thornton, C.V.D., "Evaluating the Benefits and Costs of the Job Corps." *Journal of Policy Analysis and Management,* 1981, *1,* 55–76.

Lukes, S. *Power: A Radical View.* New York: Macmillan, 1974.

Luttwak, E. N. *The Pentagon and the Art of War.* New York: Simon & Schuster, 1985.

Lynn, L. E., Jr. *Managing the Public's Business: The Job of the Government Executive.* New York: Basic Books, 1981.

Lynn, L. E., Jr. *Managing Public Policy.* Boston: Little, Brown, 1987.

Lynn, L. E., Jr. "Managing the Social Safety Net: The Job of the Social Welfare Executive." In E. C. Hargrove and J. C. Glidewell (eds.), *Impossible Jobs in Public Management.* Lawrence: University Press of Kansas, 1990.

Lynn, L. E., Jr. "The Budget-Maximizing Bureaucrat: Is There a Case?" In A. Blais and S. Dion (eds.), *The Budget-Maximizing Bureaucrat: Appraisals and Evidence.* Pittsburgh, Pa.: University of Pittsburgh Press, 1991.

McCubbin, M. D., Noll, R. G., and Weingast, B. R. "Administrative Procedures as Instruments of Political Control." *Journal of Law, Economics, and Organization,* 1987, *3*(2), 243–277.

McCubbin, M. D., Noll, R. G., and Weingast, B. R. "Structure and Process, Politics and Policy: Administrative Arrangements and the Political Control of Agencies." *Virginia Law Review,* 1989, *75,* 431–482.

McCubbin, M. D., and Schwartz, T. "Congress and Oversight Overlooked: Policy Controls Versus Fire Alarms." *American Journal of Political Science*, 1984, *28*, 165–179.

McCurdy, H. E. "Organizational Decline: NASA and the Life Cycle of Bureaus." *Public Administration Review*, 1991, *51*, 308–315.

McCurdy, H. E., and Cleary, R. "Why Can't We Resolve the Research Issue in Public Administration?" *Public Administration Review*, 1984, *44*, 49–55.

Macey, J. R. "Organizational Design and Political Control of Administrative Agencies." Unpublished manuscript, Law and Government Program, University of Chicago, 1991.

MacLeod, R. "The Social History of Science." In I. Spiegel-Rosing and D. de Solla Price (eds.), *Science, Technology, and Society*. Newbury Park, Calif.: Sage, 1977.

Mahler, J. "The Quest for Organizational Meaning: Identifying and Interpreting the Symbolism in Organizational Stories." *Administration and Society*, 1988, *20*, 344–368.

Mainzer, L. *Political Bureaucracy*. Glenview, Ill.: Scott, Foresman, 1973.

Mandelbaum, S. "The Institutional Focus of Planning Theory." *Journal of Planning Education and Research*, 1985, *5*, 3–9.

Mandell, M., and Sauter, V. "Approaches to the Study of Information Utilization in Public Agencies." *Knowledge: Creation, Diffusion, Utilization*, 1984, *6*, 145–164.

Mansbridge, J. (ed.). *Beyond Self-Interest*. Chicago: University of Chicago Press, 1990.

March, J. G. "How We Talk and How We Act: Administrative Theory and Administrative Life." In T. J. Sergiovanni and J. E. Corbally (eds.), *Leadership and Organizational Culture: New Perspectives on Administrative Theory and Practice*. Urbana: University of Illinois Press, 1984.

March, J. G. *Decisions and Organizations*. New York: Basil Blackwell, 1988.

March, J. G., and Olsen, J. P. *Rediscovering Institutions: The Organizational Basis of Politics*. New York: Free Press, 1989.

March, J. G., and Sevon, G. "Gossip, Information, and Decision Making." In L. S. Sproull and P. D. Larkey (eds.), *Advances in Information Processing in Organizations*. Vol. 1. Greenwich, Conn.: JAI Press, 1984.

Margolis, H. "Free Riding Versus Cooperation." In R. J. Zeckhauser (ed.), *Strategy and Choice*. Cambridge, Mass: MIT Press, 1991.

Marien, M., and Jennings, L. (eds.). *What I Have Learned: Thinking About the Future Then and Now*. New York: Greenwood Press, 1987.

Marini, F. (ed.) *Toward a New Public Administration: The Minnowbrook Perspective*. Scranton, Pa.: Chandler, 1971.

Martin, J., Feldman, M. S., Hatch, M. J., and Sitkin, S. B. "The Uniqueness Paradox in Organizational Stories." *Administrative Science Quarterly*, 1983, *28*, 438–453.

Mathieson, K. "Predicting User Intentions: Comparing the Technology-

Acceptance Model with the Theory of Planned Behavior." *Information Systems Research*, 1991, *2*(3), 173–191.

Mayo, G. E. *The Social Problems of an Industrial Society.* Boston: Harvard Business School, 1933.

Meadows, D. L. "Are There Limits to Growth?" *Wharton Magazine*, 1980, *4*(2), 16–18.

Mechling, J. E. "A Successful Innovation: Manpower Scheduling." *Urban Analysis*, 1974, *3*, 259–313.

Meier, K. J. "Bureaucratic Leadership in Public Organizations." In B. D. Jones (ed.), *Leadership and Politics: New Perspectives in Political Science.* Lawrence: University Press of Kansas, 1989.

Melnick, R. S. *Regulation and the Courts: The Case of the Clean Air Act.* Washington, D.C.: Brookings Institution, 1983.

Melnick, R. S. "The Politics of Partnership." *Public Administration Review*, 1985, *45*, 653–660.

Merton, R. "Behavior Patterns of Scientists." *American Scientist*, 1969, *57*, 1–23.

Merton, R. *The Sociology of Science.* Chicago: University of Chicago Press, 1973.

Metcalfe, L., and Richards, S. *Improving Public Management.* Newbury Park, Calif.: Sage, 1987.

Meyer, M. W., and Zucker, L. G. *Permanently Failing Organizations.* Newbury Park, Calif.: Sage, 1989.

Mezey, S. G. "Policymaking by the Federal Judiciary: The Effects of Judicial Review on the Social Security Disability Program." *Policy Studies Journal*, 1986, *14*(3), 343–361.

Miles, R. E., and Snow, C. C. "Organizations: New Concepts for New Forms." *California Management Review*, 1986, *28*(3), 62–73.

Milgrom, P., and Roberts, J. "An Economic Approach to Influence Activities in Organizations." *American Journal of Sociology*, 1988, *94*, S154–S179.

Miller, G. E., and Iscoe, I. "A State Mental Health Commissioner and the Politics of Mental Illness." In E. C. Hargrove and J. C. Glidewell (eds.), *Impossible Jobs in Public Management.* Lawrence: University Press of Kansas, 1990.

Miller, G. J. *Administrative Dilemmas: The Role of Political Leadership.* Political Economy Working Paper no. 118. St. Louis: Washington University, 1987.

Miller, T. "Political Design Science: A Synthesis of Traditional Political Values and Behavioralism." *Research in Public Administration*, 1991, *1*, 49–78.

Milner, N. "Comparative Analysis of Patterns of Compliance with Supreme Court Decisons: 'Miranda' and the Police in Four Comunities." *Law and Society Review*, 1970, *5*(1), 119–134.

Milter, R. G., and Rohrbaugh, J. "Judgment Analysis and Decision Conferencing for Administrative Review: A Case Study of Innovative Policy Making in Government." *Advances in Information Processing in Organizations*, 1988, *3*, 245–262.

Milward, H. B., and Laird, W. "Where Does Policy Come From?" In B. G. Peters and B. Rockman (eds.), *The Discipline of Public Administration.* Chatham, N.J.: Chatham House, forthcoming.

Mintzberg, H. *The Nature of Managerial Work.* New York: HarperCollins, 1973.

Mintzberg, H. "Strategy-Making in Three Modes." *California Management Review,* 1974, *16*(2), 44–53.

Mintzberg, H. "An Emerging Strategy of 'Direct' Research." *Administrative Science Quarterly,* 179a, *24.*

Mintzberg, H. *The Structuring of Organizations.* Englewood Cliffs, N.J.: Prentice-Hall, 1979b.

Mintzberg, H. "The Organization as Political Arena." *Journal of Management Studies,* 1985, *22,* 133–154.

Mintzberg, H. "The Design School: Reconsidering the Basic Premises of Strategic Management." *Strategic Management Journal,* 1990, *11,* 171–195.

Mitchell, J. (ed.). *Public Authorities and Public Policy: The Business Of Government.* New York: Greenwood Press, 1992.

Mitnick, B. "The Theory of Agency: The Policy Paradox and Regulatory Behavior." *Public Choice,* 1975, *2,* 27–47.

Mitnick, B. *The Political Economy of Regulation.* New York: Columbia University Press, 1980.

Mitnick, B., and Backoff, R. W. "The Incentive Relation in Implementation." In G. C. Edwards III (ed.), *Public Policy Implementation.* Greenwood, Conn.: JAI Press, 1984.

Mitroff, I. I. *The Subjective Side of Science: A Philosophical Inquiry into the Psychology of the Apollo Moon Scientists.* New York: Elsevier Science, 1974.

Mitroff, I. I., and Kilmann, R. H. "Stories Managers Tell: A New Tool for Organizational Problem Solving: *Management Review,* 1975, *64*(7), 18–28.

Mitroff, I. I., and Kilmann, R. H. "On Organizational Stories: An Approach to the Design and Analysis of Organizations Through Myths and Stories." In R. H. Kilmann, L. R. Pondy, and D. P. Slevin (eds.), *The Management of Organizational Design.* Vol. 1: *Strategies and Implementation.* New York: North Holland, 1976.

Mizuno, S. *Company-Wide Total Quality Control.* Tokyo: Asian Productivity Organization, 1988.

Moe, R. C. "Exploring the Limits of Privatization." *Public Administration Review,* 1987, *47*(6), 453–460.

Moe, R. C. " 'Law' Versus 'Performance' as Objective Standard." *Public Administration Review,* 1988a, *48,* 674–675.

Moe, R. C. "Liabilities of the Quasi Government." *Government Executive,* 1988b, *20,* 47–50.

Moe, R. C., and Stanton, T. H. "Government-Sponsored Enterprises as Federal Instrumentalities: Reconciling Private Management with Public Accountability." *Public Administration Review,* 1989, *49*(5), 321–329.

Moe, T. M. "Regulatory Performance and Presidential Administration." *American Journal of Political Science,* 1982, *26,* 197–224.

Moe, T. M. "The New Economics of Organization." *American Journal of Political Science,* 1984, *28,* 739–777.

Moe, T. M. "Control and Feedback in Economic Regulation: The Case of the NLBR." *American Political Science Review,* 1985, *79,* 1064–1116.

Mohr, L. B. "Determinants of Innovation in Organizations." *American Political Science Review,* 1969, *63,* 111–126.

Moore, G. C., and Benbasat, I. "Development of an Instrument to Measure the Perceptions of Adopting an Information Technology Innovation." *Information Systems Research,* 1991, *2*(3), 193–222.

Morgan, G. "Rethinking Corporate Strategy: A Cybernetic Perspective." *Human Relations,* 1983, *36*(4), 345–360.

Morgan, G. *Images of Organization.* Newbury Park, Calif.: Sage, 1986.

Morgan, T. D. "Appropriate Limits on Participation by a Former Agency Offical in Matters Before an Agency." *Duke Law Journal,* 1980, 1–63.

Mosher, F. C. *Democracy and the Public Service.* New York: Oxford University Press, 1968.

Mosher, F. C. "The Changing Responsibilities and Tactics of the Federal Government." *Public Administration Review,* 1980, *40*(4), 541–552.

Moss, K. "The Catalytic Effect of a Federal Court Decision on a State Legislature." *Law and Society Review,* 1983, *19*(1), 147–157.

Moynihan, D. P. *Maximum Feasible Misunderstanding.* New York: Free Press, 1969.

Mueller, W. "A New Attack on Antitrust: The Chicago Case." *Antitrust Law and Economics Review,* 1986, *18,* 29–66.

Muir, W. *Prayer in the Public Schools: Law and Attitude Change.* Chicago: University of Chicago Press, 1967.

Murphy, J. T. "Title I of ESEA: The Politics of Implementing Federal Education Reform." *Harvard Educational Review,* 1971, *41*(1).

Murray, M. A. "Comparing Public and Private Management: An Exploratory Essay." In J. L. Perry and K. L. Kraemer (eds.), *Public Management: Public and Private Perspectives.* Palo Alto, Calif.: Mayfield, 1983.

Musolf, L., and Seidman, H. "The Blurred Boundaries of Public Administration." *Public Administration Review,* 1980, *40,* 124–130.

Nachmias, D., and Nachmias, C. *Research Methods in the Social Sciences.* (3rd ed.) New York: St. Martin's Press, 1987.

Nagel, T. *Mortal Questions.* Cambridge, England: Cambridge University Press, 1979.

Naisbitt, J., and Aburdene, P. *Megatrends 2000: Ten New Directions for the 1990s.* New York: Morrow, 1990.

Nathan, R. P. *The Plot That Failed: Nixon and the Administrative Presidency.* New York: Wiley, 1975.

Nathan, R. P. *Social Science in Government: Uses and Misuses.* New York: Basic Books, 1988.

National Security Strategy of the United States. Washington, D.C.: The White House, 1990.

Needleman, C. "Discrepant Assumptions in Empirical Research: The Case of Juvenile Court Screening." *Social Problems,* 1981, *28*(3), 257–260.

Nelkin, D. *Methadone Maintenance: A Technological Fix.* New York: G. Braziller, 1973.

Nelson, R. *The Moon and the Ghetto.* New York: W. W. Norton, 1977.

Nelson, R. R., and Winter, S. G. "In Search of Useful Theory of Innovation." *Research Policy,* 1977, *6,* 36–76.

Nelson, R. R., and Winter, S. G. *An Evolutionary Theory of Economic Change.* Cambridge, Mass.: Belknap Press, 1982.

Neter, J., Wasserman, W., and Kutner, M. H. *Applied Linear Regression Models.* Homewood, Ill.: Irwin, 1989.

Neustadt, R. *Lead Poisoning.* Teaching case. Kennedy School of Government, Harvard University, 1975.

Neustadt, R. E. *Presidential Power: The Politics of Leadership.* New York: Wiley, 1960.

Nicholas, J. M. "The Comparative Impact of Organization Development Interventions on Hard-Criteria Measures." *Academy of Management Review,* 1982, *7,* 531–542.

Niskanen, W. A., Jr. *Bureaucracy and Representative Government.* Chicago: Aldine, 1971.

Northrop, A., Dutton, W. H., and Kraemer, K. L. "The Management of Computer Applications in Local Government." *Public Administration Review,* 1982, *42,* 234–243.

Northrop, A., Kraemer, K. L., Dunkle, D., and King, J. L. "Payoffs from Computerization: Lessons Over Time." *Public Administration Review,* 1990, *50,* 505–514.

Nutt, P. C. "Calling Out and Calling Off the Dogs: Managerial Diagnosis in Public Service Organizations." *Academy of Management Review,* 1979, *4,* 203–214.

Nutt, P. C., and Backoff, R. W. "A Strategic Management Process for Public and Third-Sector Organizations." *Journal of the American Planning Association,* 1987, *53,* 44–57.

Nutt, P. C., and Backoff, R. W. *The Strategic Management of Public and Third-Sector Organizations.* San Francisco: Jossey-Bass, 1992.

Office of the Secretary of Defense, Study Team. *Management Study of the Office of the Secretary of Defense.* Washington, D.C.: The Pentagon, 1987.

Ogilvy, J. A. "Scenarios for the Future of Governance." *The Bureaucrat,* 1987, 13–16.

O'Leary, R. "The Impact of Federal Court Decisions on the Policies and Administration of the U.S. Environmental Protection Agency." *Administrative Law Review,* 1989, *41*(4), 549–574.

O'Leary, R., and Wise, C. "Public Managers, Judges, and Legislators: Redefining the 'New Partnership.'" *Public Administration Review,* 1991, *52*(4), 316–327.

Olson, M. *The Logic of Collective Action*. Cambridge, Mass.: Harvard University Press, 1965.

O'Neill, T. *Man of the House: The Life and Political Memoirs of Speaker Tip O'Neill*. New York: Random House, 1987.

Osborne, D., and Gaebler, T. *Reinventing Government: How the Entrepreneurial Spirit Is Transforming the Public Sector*. Reading, Mass.: Addison-Wesley, 1992.

Ostrom, E. *Governing the Commons*. Cambridge, England: Cambridge University Press, 1990.

Ostrom, E., and Ostrom, V. "Public Choice: A Different Approach to the Study of Public Administration." *Public Administration Review*, 1971, *31*, 302–316.

Ostrom, V. *The Intellectual Crisis in American Public Administration*. University: University of Alabama Press, 1973.

O'Toole, L. J. "Policy Recommendations for Multi-Actor Implementation: An Assessment of the Field." *Journal of Public Policy*, 1986, *6*(2), 181–210.

O'Toole, L. J. "Multiorganizational Policy Implementation: Some Limitations and Possibilities for Rational Choice Contributions." Paper presented at the Workshop on Games in Hierarchies and Networks, Max-Planck-Institut fur Gesellschaftsforschung, Koln, Germany, Sept. 1991.

Ott, J. F. *The Organizational Culture Perspective*. Belmont, Calif.: Dorsey Press, 1989.

Ouchi, W. G. "A Conceptual Framework for the Design of Organizational Control Mechanisms." *Management Science*, 1979, *25*(9), 835–836.

Oye, K. (ed.). *Cooperation Under Anarchy*. Princeton, N.J.: Princeton University Press, 1986.

Packard Commission (President's Blue Ribbon Task Force on Defense Management). *A Quest for Excellence: Final Report to the President*. Washington, D.C.: U.S. Government Printing Office, 1986.

Palumbo, D., and Maynard-Moody, S. *Contemporary Public Administration*. New York: Longman, 1991.

Parmerdee, M. A., Near, J. P., and Jessen, T. C. "Correlates of Whistleblowers' Perceptions of Organizational Retaliation." *Administrative Science Quarterly*, 1982, *27*, 17–34.

Parsons, T. *Structure and Process in Modern Societies*. New York: Free Press, 1960.

Peltzman, S. "Toward a More General Theory of Regulation." *Journal of Law and Economics*, 1976, *19*, 211–240.

Perkins, D.N.T., Nieva, V. F., and Flawler, E. E. *Managing Creation: The Challenge of Building a New Organization*. New York: Wiley, 1983.

Perrow, C. *Complex Organizations: A Critical Essay*. (3rd ed.) New York: Random House, 1986.

Perry, J. L. "The Effective Public Administrator." In J. L. Perry (ed.), *Handbook of Public Administration*. San Francisco: Jossey-Bass, 1989.

Perry, J. L., and Danziger, J. N. "The Adoptability of Innovations: An Empirical Assessment of Computer Applications in Local Government." *Administration and Society*, 1980, *11*, 461–492.

Perry, J. L., and Kraemer, K. L. "Innovation Attributes, Policy Intervention, and the Diffusion of Computer Applications Among Local Governments." *Policy Sciences,* 1978, *9,* 179–205.

Perry, J. L., and Kraemer, K. L. *Public Management: Public and Private Perspectives.* Palo Alto, Calif.: Mayfield, 1983.

Perry, J. L., and Kraemer, K. L. "Research Methodology in the *Public Administration Review,* 1975–1984." *Public Administration Review,* 1986, *46,* 215–234.

Perry, J. L., and Porter, L. "Factors Affecting the Context for Motivation in Public Organizations." *Academy of Management Review,* 1982, *7,* 89–98.

Perry, J. L., and Rainey, H. G. "The Public-Private Distinction in Organization Theory: A Critique and Research Strategy." *Academy of Management Review,* 1988, *13*(2), 182–201.

Perry, J. L., and Wise, L. "The Motivational Bases of Public Service." *Public Administration Review,* 1990, *50,* 367–373.

Pesso, T. "Local Welfare Offices: Managing the Intake Process." *Public Policy,* 1978, *28*(2), 305–330.

Peters, T. J. *Thriving on Chaos: Handbook for a Management Revolution.* New York: Knopf, 1987.

Peters, T. J. *Thriving on Chaos: Handbook for a Management Revolution.* (Rev. ed.) New York: HarperCollins, 1988.

Peters, T. J. "Part One: Get Innovative or Get Dead." *California Management Review,* 1990, *33*(1), 9–26.

Peters, T. J., and Austin, N. *A Passion for Excellence.* New York: Random House, 1985.

Peters, T. J., and Waterman, R. H., Jr. *In Search of Excellence.* New York: HarperCollins, 1982.

Pfeffer, J., and Salancik, G. R. *The External Control of Organizations: A Resource-Dependence Perspective.* New York: HarperCollins, 1978.

Poister, T. H. "Crosscutting Themes in Public Sector Revitalization." *Public Productivity Review,* 1988, *11,* 29–36.

Poister, T. H., and Streib, G. "Management Tools in Municipal Government: Trends Over the Past Decade." *Public Administration Review,* 1989, *49,* 240–248.

Polanyi, M. *Personal Knowledge.* New York: Routledge & Kegan Paul, 1958.

Polanyi, M. *The Tacit Dimension.* Garden City, N.Y.: Anchor Books, 1967.

Porter, E. A. "Focus on the Future." *The Bureaucrat,* 1987, 9–12.

Porter, M. E. *Competitive Strategy: Techniques for Analyzing Industries and Competitors.* New York: Free Press, 1980.

Porter, M. E. *Competitive Advantage: Creating and Sustaining Superior Performance.* New York: Free Press, 1985.

Porter, M. E. *The Competitive Advantage of Nations.* New York: Free Press, 1989.

Potts, S. D. *Revised Postemployment Restrictions of 18 U.S.C. Section 207.* Washington, D.C.: Office of Government Ethics, 1990.

Pressman, J. L., and Wildavsky, A. *Implementation.* Berkeley: University of California Press, 1974.

Prottas, J. M. *People-Processing: The Street-Level Bureaucrat in Public Service Bureaucracies*. Lexington, Mass.: Lexington Books, 1979.

Provan, K. G., and Milward, H. B. "Institutional-Level Norms and Organizational Involvement in a Service Implementation Network." *Journal of Public Administration Research and Theory*, 1991, *1*(4), 391–417.

Quinn, J. B. *Strategies for Change: Logical Incrementalism*. Homewood, Ill.: Irwin, 1980.

Quirk, P. J. *Industry Influence in Federal Regulatory Agencies*. Princeton, N.J.: Princeton University Press, 1981.

Rainey, H. G. "Public Agencies and Private Firms: Incentives, Goals, and Individual Roles." *Administration and Society*, 1983, *15*, 207–242.

Rainey, H. G. "Public Management: Recent Research on the Political Context and Managerial Roles, Structures, and Behaviors." *Journal of Management*, 1989, *15*(2), 229–250.

Rainey, H. G. "Public Management: Recent Developments and Current Prospects." In N. Lynn and A. Wildavsky (eds.), *Public Administration: State of the Discipline*. Chatham, N.J.: Chatham House, 1990.

Rainey, H. G. *Understanding and Managing Public Organizations*. San Francisco: Jossey-Bass, 1991.

Rainey, H. G., Backoff, R. W., and Levine, C. "Comparing Public and Private Organizations." *Public Administration Review*, 1976, *36*, 233–246.

Rainey, H. G., and Perry, J. L. "Building Public Management Research and Practice." In P. Ingraham and D. Kettl (eds.), *Issues for the American Public Service: A Volume in Memory of Charles H. Levine*, forthcoming.

Randall, R. "Presidential Power Versus Bureaucratic Intransigence: The Influence of the Nixon Administration on Welfare Policy." *American Political Science Review*, 1979, *73*, 795–810.

Ravetz, J. *Scientific Knowledge and Its Social Problems*. Oxford, England: Clarendon Press, 1966.

Rhinehard, J. B., and others. "Comparative Study of Need Satisfaction in Governmental and Business Hierarchies." *Journal of Applied Psychology*, 1969, *53*, 230–235.

Rhodes, R. *The Making of the Atomic Bomb*. New York: Simon & Schuster, 1988.

Riker, W. H. *The Art of Political Manipulation*. New Haven, Conn.: Yale University Press, 1986.

Ring, P. S., and Perry, J. L. "Strategic Management in Public and Private Organizations: Implications of Distinctive Contexts and Constraints." *Academy of Management Review*, 1985, *10*(2), 276–286.

Ripley, R. B., and Franklin, G. A. *Policy Implementation and Bureaucracy*. (2nd ed.) Belmont, Calif.: Dorsey Press, 1986.

Roberts, N. C., and King, P. L. "Policy Entrepreneurs: Their Activity Structure and Function in the Policy Process." *Journal of Public Administration Research and Theory*, 1991, *1*(1), 147–175.

Robinson, G. K. *Journal to Passage: The Ohio Mental Health Act*. Washington,

D.C.: Office of Treatment Improvement, Public Health Service, U.S. Department of Health and Human Services, 1991.

Roethlisberger, F. J., and Dickson, W. J. *Management and the Worker.* Cambridge, Mass.: Harvard University Press, 1939.

Rogers Commission (U.S. Presidential Commission on the Space Shuttle *Challenger* Accident). *Report to the President.* Washington, D.C.: U.S. Government Printing Office, 1986.

Rogers, E. *Diffusion of Innovations.* (3rd ed.) New York: Free Press, 1983.

Romzek, B. S., and Dubnick, M. J. "Accountability in the Public Sector: Lessons from the *Challenger* Tragedy." *Public Administration Review,* 1987, *47*(3), 227–238.

Roosevelt, F. D. Address delivered at the dedication of the George Washington Bridge, Oct. 24, 1931.

Rose-Ackerman, S. "Reforming Public Bureaucracy Through Economic Incentives." *Journal of Law, Economics, and Organization,* 1981, *2*(1), 131–161.

Rosenberg, A. *Philosophy of Social Science.* Boulder, Colo.: Westview Press, 1988.

Rosenbloom, D. *Public Administration and Law.* New York: Marcel Dekker, 1983.

Rosenthal, S. R. *Managing Government Operations.* Glenview, Ill.: Scott, Foresman, 1982.

Rosenthal, S. R. *Assignment Collections.* Teaching case. School of Management, Boston University, 1984.

Rosenthal, U., Charles, M. T., and t'Hart, P. (eds.). *Coping with Crisis.* Springfield, Ill.: Thomas, 1989.

Rothman, D. J., and Rothman, S. M. *The Willowbrook Wars.* New York: HarperCollins, 1984.

Rumsfeld, D. "A Politician-Turned-Executive Surveys Both Worlds." In J. L. Perry and K. L. Kraemer (eds.), *Public Management: Public and Private Perspectives.* Palo Alto, Calif.: Mayfield, 1983.

Sabatier, P., and Mazmanian, D. "The Conditions of Effective Implementation: A Guide to Accomplishing Policy Objectives." *Policy Analysis,* 1979, *5*(4), 481–425.

Sabatier, P., and Pelkey, N. "Incorporating Multiple Actors and Guidance Instruments into Models of Regulatory Policymaking: An Advocacy Coalition Framework." *Administration & Society,* 1987, *19*, 236–263.

Sabrosky, A. N., Thompson, J. C., and McPherson, K. A. "Organized Anarchies: Military Bureaucracy in the Future." In W. B. Littrell, G. Sjober, and L. A. Zurcher (eds.), *Bureaucracy as a Social Problem.* Greenwich, Conn.: JAI Press, 1983.

Safayeni, F. R., Purdy, R. L., and Higgins, C. A. "Social Meaning of Personal Computers for Managers and Professionals: Methodology and Results." *Behavior and Information Technology,* 1989, *8,* 99–107.

Salamon, L. M. "Rethinking Public Management: Third-Party Government and the Changing Forms of Government Action." *Public Policy,* 1981, *29*(3), 255–275.

Salamon, L. M. (ed.) *Beyond Privatization: The Tools of Government Action.* Washington, D.C.: Urban Institute Press, 1989.

Sanders, E. "Industrial Concentration, Sectional Competition, and Antitrust Politics in America, 1880–1980." In K. Orren and S. Skowronek (eds.), *Studies in American Political Development.* New Haven, Conn.: Yale University Press, 1986.

Sanger, M. B., and Levin, M. A. "Move Over, Policy Analysis: It's Management That Counts." *Governing,* 1991, *9,* 9.

Sanger, M. B., and Levin, M. A. "Using Old Stuff in New Ways: Innovation as a Case of Evolutionary Tinkering." *Journal of Policy Analysis and Management,* 1992, *11*(1), 88–115.

Sarason, S. *The Creation of Settings and the Future Societies.* San Francisco: Jossey-Bass, 1972.

Savas, E. *Privatization: The Key to Better Government.* Chatham, N.J.: Chatham House, 1987.

Schaff, R. L., and Goodrick, D. *From an In-Patient to Community-Based Service Foundation: The Transformation of Ohio's Mental Health System.* Washington, D.C.: National Technical Assistance Center for Mental Health Planning, National Institute for Mental Health, 1988.

Schank, R. C. *Tell Me a Story: A New Look at Real and Artificial Memory.* New York: Charles Scribner's Sons, 1990.

Schank, R., and Abelson, R. *Scripts, Plans, and Knowledge.* Hillsdale, N.J.: Erlbaum, 1977.

Schattschneider, E. E. *The Semi-Sovereign People: A Realists's View of Democracy in America.* Troy, Mo.: Holt, Rinehart & Winston, 1960.

Schauer, F. *Playing by the Rules: A Philosophical Examination of Rule-Based Decision Making in Law and in Life.* Oxford, England: Clarendon Press, 1991.

Schön, D. *The Reflective Practitioner.* New York: Basic Books, 1983.

Schorr, A. *Common Decency: Domestic Policies After Reagan.* New Haven, Conn.: Yale University Press, 1986.

Schuerman, J. R., Stagner, M., Johnson, P., and Mullen, E. *Child Abuse and Neglect Decision Making in Cook County: Final Report to the Illinois Department of Children and Family Services.* Chicago: Chapin Hall Center for Children, University of Chicago, 1988.

Schutz, A. *The Phenomenology of the Social World.* Evanston, Ill.: Northwestern University Press, 1967.

Schwartz, B. *Swann's Way: The School Busing Case and the Supreme Court.* New York: Oxford University Press, 1986.

Seidman, H., and Gilmour, R. *Politics, Position, and Power: From the Positive to the Regulatory State.* (4th ed.) New York: Oxford University Press, 1986.

Selznick, P. *TVA and the Grass Roots: A Study in the Sociology of Formal Organization.* New York: HarperCollins, 1949.

Sen, A. K. "Goals, Commitment, and Identity." *Journal of Law, Economics, and Organization,* 1985, *1,* 341–355.

Senate Armed Services Committee. *Defense Organization and the Need for Change.* Staff report. Washington, D.C.: U.S. Government Printing Office, 1985.

Senate Committee on Governmental Affairs. *Ethics in Government Act.* Report to the 95th Congress, 1st session. Washington, D.C.: U.S. Government Printing Office, 1977.

Sensenbrenner, J. "Quality Comes to City Hall." *Harvard Business Review,* 1991, *69*(2), 64–75.

Shafritz, J. M., Hyde, A., and Rosenbloom, D. H. *Personnel Management in Government: Politics and Process.* (3rd ed.) New York: Marcel Dekker, 1986.

Shangraw, R. F., and Crow, M. M. "Public Administration as a Design Science." *Public Administration Review,* 1989.

Shanor, R. R. *The City That Never Was.* New York: Viking Penguin, 1988.

Shapiro, M. "Courts." In F. I. Greenstein and N. Polsby (eds.), *Handbook of Political Science.* Vol. 5: *Governmental Institutions and Processes.* Reading, Mass.: Addison-Wesley, 1975.

Shapiro, M. *Courts: A Comparative and Political Analysis.* Chicago: University of Chicago Press, 1981.

Sharpe, L. J. "Central Coordination and the Policy Network." *Political Studies,* 1985, *33,* 361–381.

Sher, G. *Desert.* Princeton, N.J.: Princeton University Press, 1987.

Simon, H. A. *Administrative Behavior.* New York: Free Press, 1946a.

Simon, H. A. "The Proverbs of Administration." *Public Administration Review,* 1946b, *6,* 53–67.

Simon, H. A. *Administrative Behavior.* New York: Macmillan, 1957.

Simon, H. A. *The Sciences of the Artificial.* Cambridge, Mass.: MIT Press, 1969.

Simon, H. A., and Thompson, V. A. "Public Administration Revisited." *Society,* 1991, *28,* 41–45.

Skinner, W. *Elizabeth Best.* Teaching case. Harvard Business School, 1975.

Skocpol, T. "Bringing the State Back In: Strategies of Analysis in Current Research." In P. Evans, D. Rueschemeyr, and T. Skocpol (eds.), *Bringing the State Back In.* Cambridge, England: Cambridge University Press, 1985.

Smith, R. G. *Ad Hoc Governments: Special-Purpose Transportation Authorities in Britain and the United States.* Newbury Park, Calif.: Sage, 1974.

Smith, S. R. "Managing the Community: Privatization, Government, and the Nonprofit Sector." Paper presented at the annual meeting of the American Political Science Association, San Francisco, 1990.

Solomon, E. "Private and Public Sector Managers: An Empirical Investigation of Job Characteristics and Organizational Climate." *Journal of Applied Psychology,* 1986, *71,* 247–259.

Sosin, M. "Social Problems Covered by Private Agencies: An Application of Niche Theory." *Social Service Review,* 1985, *59*(1), 75–94.

"Special Report: The Hollow Corporation." *Business Week,* Mar. 3, 1986.

Spielberg, N., and Anderson, B. D. *Seven Ideas That Shook the Universe.* New York: Wiley, 1987.

Stallings, R., and Ferris, J. "Public Administration Research: Work in PAR, 1940–1984." *Public Administration Review,* 1988, *48,* 580–587.

Steinwald, B. "Changes in Medical Case Mix: DRG Creep or Sicker Patients?" Paper presented at workshop in health administration studies, University of Chicago, Nov. 1987.

Stephens, O. *The Supreme Court and Confessions of Guilt.* Knoxville: University of Tennessee Press, 1973.

Stern, R. S., and Epstein, A. M. "Institutional Responses to Prospective Payment Based on Diagnosis-Related Groups." *New England Journal of Medicine,* 1985, *312*(10), 621–627.

Stone, D. A. *Policy Paradox and Political Reason.* Glenview, Ill.: Scott, Foresman, 1988.

Straussman, J. "Courts and Public Purse Strings: Have Portraits of Budgeting Missed Something?" *Public Administration Review,* 1986, *46*(4), 345–351.

Susskind, L., and Cruikshank, J. *Breaking the Impasse: Consensual Approaches to Resolving Public Disputes.* New York: Basic Books, 1987.

Swiss, J. E. *Public Management Systems: Monitoring and Managing Government Performance.* Englewood Cliffs, N.J.: Prentice-Hall, 1991.

Taggert, W. A. "Redefining the Power of the Federal Judiciary: The Impact of Court-Ordered Prison Reform on State Expenditures for Corrections." *Law and Society Review,* 1989, *23*(2), 241–271.

Tarschys, D. "Rational Decremental Budgeting: Elements of an Expenditure Policy for the 1980s." *Policy Sciences,* 1981, *14,* 49–58.

Taylor, F. W. *The Principles of Scientific Management.* New York: HarperCollins, 1914.

Taylor, M. *Community, Anarchy, and Liberty.* Cambridge, England: Cambridge University Press, 1982.

Testa, M. F., and Goerge, R. M. *Final Report to the Administration for Children, Youth, and Families.* Springfield: Illinois Department of Health and Human Services, 1988.

Thompson, D. F. *Political Ethics and Public Office.* Cambridge, Mass.: Harvard University Press, 1987.

Thompson, J. D. *Organizations in Action.* New York: McGraw-Hill, 1967.

Tobin, A. J. "Authorities as a Governmental Technique." Paper presented at the Third Annual Institute, Rutgers University, Mar. 1953.

Toffler, A. *Future Shock.* New York: Bantam Books, 1971.

Tornatzky, L. G., and Fleischer, M. *The Process of Technological Innovation.* Lexington, Mass.: Lexington Books, 1990.

Torrey, E. F., Wolfe, S. M., and Flynn, L. M. *Care of the Seriously Mentally Ill.* Washington, D.C.: Public Citizen Research Group and National Alliance for the Mentally Ill, 1988.

Toulmin, S. E. *The Uses of Argument.* Cambridge, England: Cambridge University Press, 1958.

Trento, J. J. *Prescription for Disaster: From the Glory of Apollo to the Betrayal of the Shuttle.* New York: Crown, 1987.

Trigg, R. *Reality at Risk: A Defense of Realism in Philosophy and the Sciences.* Savage, Md.: Barnes & Noble, 1980.

Tsebelis, G. *Nested Games: Rational Choice in Comparative Politics*. Berkeley: University of California Press, 1990.

Turner, B. A. "The Organizational and Interorganizational Development of Disasters." *Administrative Science Quarterly*, 1976, *21*, 378–397.

Tweedie, J. "Discretion to Use Rules: Individual Interests and Collective Welfare in School Admissions." *Law and Policy*, 1989, *11*(2), 189–213.

Tyack, D., and Benavot, A. "Courts and Public Schools: Educational Litigation in Historical Perspective." *Law and Society Review*, 1985, *19*(3), 339–380.

Tyler, T. R. *Why People Obey the Law*. New Haven, Conn.: Yale University Press, 1990.

Tyler, T. R., and others. "Maintaining Allegiance Toward Political Authorities: The Role of Prior Attitudes and the Use of Fair Procedures." *American Journal of Political Science*, 1989, *33*, 629–652.

Ukeles, J. B. *Doing More with Less: Turning Public Management Around*. New York: AMACOM, 1982.

U.S. Bureau of the Census. *Government Finances in 1987–88*. Washington, D.C.: U.S. Government Printing Office, 1989.

U.S. Department of Education, Office of Educational Research and Improvement. *Blue Ribbon Schools Program: Schools Recognized, 1982–83 Through 1989–90*. Washington, D.C.: U.S. Government Printing Office, 1990.

U.S. General Accounting Office. *PPBS in DoD*. Washington, D.C.: U.S. General Accounting Office, 1985.

U.S. General Accounting Office. *Defense Management: Status of Recommendations by Blue Ribbon Commission on Defense Management*. Washington, D.C.: U.S. General Accounting Office, 1988.

U.S. General Accounting Office. *Department of Defense: Improving Management to Meet the Challenges of the 1990s*. Washington, D.C.: U.S. General Accounting Office, 1990.

Ure, A. *The Philosophy of Manufactures: On an Exposition of the Scientific, Moral, and Commercial Economy of the Factory System in Great Britain*. London: Cass, 1967. (Originally published 1835.)

Van Maanen, J. "Observations on the Making of Policemen." In P. K. Manning and J. Van Maanen (eds.), *Policing: A View from the Street*. Santa Monica, Calif.: Goodyear, 1978.

Van Maanen, J. *Tales of the Field: On Writing Ethnography*. Chicago: University of Chicago Press, 1988.

Vaughan, D. "Autonomy, Interdependence, and Social Control: NASA and the Space Shuttle Disaster." *Administrative Science Quarterly*, 1990, *35*, 225–257.

Volcker Commission (National Commission on the Public Service). *Rebuilding the Public Service: The Report*. Washington, D.C.: U.S. Government Printing Office, 1989.

Waldman, S. "Lead and Your Kids." *Newsweek*, July 15, 1991, pp. 42–48.

Waldo, D. "Organization Theory: An Elephantine Problem." *Public Administration Review*, 1961, *21*, 210–225.

Waldo, D. "Scope of the Theory of Public Administration." In J. C. Charlesworth (ed.), *Theory and Practice of Public Administration: Scope, Objectives, and Methods.* Philadelphia: American Academy of Political and Social Science, 1968.

Waldo, D. "Organization Theory: Revisiting the Elephant." *Public Administration Review,* 1978, *38,* 589–597.

Waldo, D. *The Enterprise of Administration.* Novato, Calif.: Chandler & Sharp, 1980.

Walsh, A. H. *The Public's Business: The Politics and Practices of Government Corporations.* Cambridge, Mass.: MIT Press, 1978.

Wamsley, G. L., and Zald, M. N. *The Political Economy of Public Organizations.* Lexington, Mass.: Heath, 1973.

Wamsley, G. L., and Zald, M. N. "The Political Economy of Public Organizations." In J. L. Perry and K. L. Kraemer (eds.), *Public Management: Public and Private Perspectives.* Palo Alto, Calif.: Mayfield, 1983.

Wamsley, G. L., and others. *Refounding Public Administration.* Newbury Park, Calif.: Sage, 1990.

Warren, R. L., Rose, S. M., and Bergunder, A. F. *The Structure of Urban Reform.* Lexington, Mass.: Lexington Books, 1974.

Warwick, D. P. *A Theory of Public Bureaucracy.* Cambridge, Mass.: Harvard University Press, 1975.

Wasby, S. *The Impact of the United States Supreme Court: Some Perspectives.* Belmont, Calif.: Dorsey Press, 1970a.

Wasby, S. "The Supreme Court's Impact: Some Problems of Conceptualization and Measurement." *Law and Society Review,* 1970b, *5*(1), 41–60.

Wasby, S. *Small-Town Police and the Supreme Court.* Lexington, Mass.: Lexington Books, 1973.

Weaver, S. *Decision to Prosecute.* Cambridge, Mass.: MIT Press, 1977.

Webb, J. E. *Space-Age Management: The Large-Scale Approach.* New York: McGraw-Hill, 1969.

Wechsler, B. "The Uses of Strategic Management in State Governments." In J. Rabin, G. Miller, and B. Hildreth (eds.), *Handbook of Strategic Management.* New York: Marcel Dekker, 1989.

Wechsler, B., and Backoff, R. W. "Policy-Making and Administration in Stage Agencies: Strategic Management Approaches." *Public Administration Review,* 1986, *46,* 321–327.

Wechsler, B., and Backoff, R. W. "The Dynamics of Strategy in Public Organizations." *Journal of the American Planning Association,* 1987, *53,* 34–43.

Weick, K. E. *The Social Psychology of Organizing.* (2nd ed.) Reading, Mass.: Addison-Wesley, 1979.

Weick, K. E. "Organizational Culture as a Source of Reliability." *California Management Review,* 1987, *209,* 112–127.

Weick, K. E., and Browning, L. D. "Argument and Narration in Organizational Communication." *Journal of Management,* 1986, *12,* 243–259.

Weinberg, M. *Managing the State.* Cambridge, Mass.: MIT Press, 1977.

Weinberg, M. "Public Management and Private Management: A Diminishing Gap?" *Journal of Policy Analysis and Management,* 1983, *3,* 107–125.

Weisner, C., and Room, R. "Financing and Ideology in Alcohol Treatment." *Social Problems,* 1984, *32*(2), 167–184.

Weiss, H. "Why Business and Government Exchange Executives." *Harvard Business Review,* 1974, *52,* 129–14.

Weiss, J. A. "Ideas and Inducements in Mental Health Policy," *Journal of Policy Analysis and Management,* 1990, *9*(2), 178–200.

Weiss, J. A., and Gruber, J. E. "Using Knowledge for Control in Fragmented Policy Arenas." *Journal of Policy Analysis and Management,* 1984, *3*(2), 225–247.

Weitzel, W., and Jonsson, E. "Decline in Organizations: A Literature Integration and Extension." *Administration Science Quarterly,* 1989, *34,* 91–109.

Wertheimeer, A. "Jobs, Qualifications, and Preferences." *Ethics,* 1983, *94,* 99–112.

Wheelen, T. L., and Hunger, J. D. *Strategic Management and Business Policy.* (2nd ed.) Reading, Mass.: Addison-Wesley, 1986.

White, J. "On the Growth of Knowledge in Public Administration." *Public Administration Review,* 1986, *46,* 15–24.

White, L. *Introduction to the Study of Public Administration.* New York: Macmillan, 1926.

Wholey, J. S. "The Job Corps: Congressional Uses of Evaluation Findings." In J. S. Wholey, M. A. Abramson, and C. Bellavita (eds.), *Performance and Credibility: Developing Excellence in Public and Nonprofit Organizations.* Lexington, Mass.: Lexington, 1986.

Whorton, J. W., Jr., Feldt, J. A., and Dunn, D. D. "Exploring the Values Underlying Evaluation in Research: A Social Judgment Analysis." *Knowledge in Society,* 1988–89, *1,* 40–56.

Wiebe, R. H. *The Search for Order, 1877–1920.* New York: Hill and Wang, 1967.

Wildavsky, A. *The Politics of the Budgetary Process.* Boston: Little, Brown, 1964.

Wildavsky, A. *Speaking Truth to Power: The Art and Craft of Policy Analysis.* Boston: Little, Brown, 1979.

Wildavsky, A. "Choosing Preferences by Constructing Institutions: A Cultural Theory of Preference Formation." *American Political Science Review,* 1987, *81,* 3–21.

Wildavsky, A. *The New Politics of the Budgetary Process.* Glenview, Ill.: Scott, Foresman, 1988.

Wilkins, A. L., and Ouchi, W. G. "Efficient Cultures: Exploring the Relationship Between Culture and Organizational Performance." *Administrative Science Quarterly,* 1983, *28,* 468–481.

Williams, B. *Moral Luck.* Cambridge, England: Cambridge University Press, 1981.

Williams, W. *Government by Agency: Lessons from the Social Program Grants-in-Aid Experience.* Orlando, Fla.: Academic Press, 1980.

Williamson, O. *The Economic Institutions of Capitalism.* New York: Free Press, 1985.

Wills, R. L., Caswell, J. A., and Culbertson, J. D. *Issues After a Century of Federal Competition Policy.* Lexington, Mass.: Lexington Books, 1987.

Wilson, J. Q. *Bureaucracy: What Government Agencies Do and How They Do It.* New York: Basic Books, 1989.

Wilson, W. "The Study of Administration." *Political Science Quarterly,* 1887, *2*(1), 197–222.

Wise, C. R. *The Dynamics of Legislation.* San Francisco: Jossey-Bass, 1991.

Wise, C. R. "Public Service Configurations and Public Organizations: Public Organization Design in the Post-Privatization Era." *Public Administration Review,* 1990, *50*(2), 141–155.

Wolch, J. R. *The Shadow State: Government and Voluntary Sector in Transition.* New York: Foundation Center, 1990.

Woll, P. *American Bureaucracy.* New York: W. W. Norton, 1977.

Wood, D. "Principals, Bureaucrats, and Responsiveness in Clean Air Enforcement." *American Political Science Review,* 1988, *82*, 213–234.

Wood, R. C. *1,400 Government: The Political Economy of the New York Metropolitan Region.* Cambridge, Mass.: Harvard University Press, 1961.

Wood, R. C. "Professionals at Bay: Managing Boston's Public Schools." *Journal of Policy Analysis and Management,* 1982, *1*(4), 454–468.

Wood, R. C. *Remedial Law: When Courts Become Administrators.* Amherst: University of Massachusetts Press, 1990.

Woodward, J. *Industrial Organization: Theory and Practice.* London: Oxford University Press, 1965.

Worden, B. "Revising the Revolution." *New York Review of Books,* Jan. 17, 1991, pp. 38–40.

Wright, P. "The Harassed Decision Maker: Time Pressures, Distractions, and the Use of Evidence." *Journal of Applied Psychology,* 1974, *59*, 551–561.

Yarbrough, T. E. "The Judge as Manager: The Case of Judge Frank Johnson." *Journal of Policy Analysis and Management,* 1982, *1*(3), 386–400.

Yarbrough, T. E. "The Political Work of Federal Judges as Managers." *Public Administration Review,* 1985, *45*, 660–666.

Yin, R. K. "Production Efficiency Versus Bureaucratic Self-Interest: Two Innovative Processes?" *Policy Science,* 1977, *8*, 381–399.

Yin, R. K. "Studying the Implementation of Public Programs." In W. W. Williams (ed.), *Studying Implementation: Methodological and Administrative Issues.* Chatham, N.J.: Chatham House, 1982a.

Yin, R. K. "Studying Phenomenon and Context Across Sites." *American Behavioral Scientist,* 1982b, *26*, 84–100.

Yin, R. K. *Case-Study Research.* Newbury Park, Calif.: Sage, 1989.

Yin, R. K., and others. *A Review of Case Studies of Technological Innovations in State and Local Services.* Washington, D.C.: Rand Corporations, 1976.

Zimmerman, M. J. "Luck and Moral Responsibility," *Ethics,* 1987, *97,* 374–386.

Zmud, R. W. "Diffusion of Modern Software Practices: Influence of Centralization and Formalization." *Management Science,* 1982, *28,* 1421–1431.

Zuckerman, H., and Merton, R. "Patterns of Evaluation in Science." *Minerva,* 1971, *9,* 66–10.

NAME INDEX

SUBJECT INDEX